THE NEW YORK
OLD-TIME RADIO
SCHEDULE BOOK

VOLUME 2
1938-1945

KEITH D. LEE

The New York Old-Time Radio Schedule Book — Volume 2, 1938-1945
© 2011 Keith D. Lee. All Rights Reserved.

No part of this book may be reproduced in any form or by any means, electronic, mechanical, digital, photocopying or recording, except for the inclusion in a review, without permission in writing from the publisher.

Published in the USA by:
BearManor Media
PO Box 1129
Duncan, Oklahoma 73534-1129
www.bearmanormedia.com

ISBN 978-1-59393-669-3

Printed in the United States of America.
Book design by Brian Pearce | Red Jacket Press.

TABLE OF CONTENTS

Introduction 5

Listings for 1938 9

Listings for 1939 67

Listings for 1940 125

Listings for 1941 183

Listings for 1942 241

Listings for 1943 299

Listings for 1944 357

Listings for 1945 415

INTRODUCTION

The purpose of this series of books is not to be the ultimate source of OTR information; rather, it is to be used alongside the sources listed below. This book is meant to be used not only by OTR fans who want to research the history of OTR; but, to also remind the older generation of the superior quality of entertainment they once had and to introduce to future generations the wonderful imagination and creativity that was once OTR.

These books are a list of national and local New York-based OTR shows from Fall, 1929 through Summer, 1954, in an easy-to-read grid format. Each section lists the OTR shows that were playing during that particular calendar season in that particular OTR year. The shows that are listed were on the four major OTR networks (Blue/ABC, CBS, MBS, and NBC) and their local New York affiliates from 9am to 11pm, Monday through Sunday.

In reading any of the sample chapters, please note the following:

Each cell in the grid represents a fifteen minute block of time.

Each blank cell means that the preceding show is still on. I deferred from using quotation marks because it looked too unreadable.

A slash between the names of two or more daily shows either in the same cell or adjoining cells signifies that those shows shared that timeslot on intermittant days for each week during that particular calendar season. In the case of weekly shows, a slash signifies that the shows shared the same timeslot for part of that particular calendar season.

Such generic show titles as "Concert Orchestra," "Dance Orchestra," "Health Talk," "Music," "News," "Public Affairs," "Sports," "Symphony Orchestra," and "Talk," and any combination thereof, are used. In the case of a daily show, such a generic title signifies the type of show on during the week. In the case of a weekly show, the networks or their affiliated stations couldn't find a sponsor for that timeslot and filled it with a generic show of music, talk, etc.

The information has been thoroughly checked for absolute correctness based on the OTR sources that still exist, contradictions and errors in them notwithstanding. Every effort has been made to correct errors introduced in the process of typesetting these books, but corrections are welcome and can be sent to the publisher.

This series of books are the summation of two and one half years of research using the following sources:

New York Times (1929-1954).

Summers, Harrison B. *A Thirty Year History of Radio Programs 1926-1956.* Ayer Company, NH, 1958.

Dunning, John. *The Encyclopedia of Old-Time Radio.* Oxford University Press, NY, 1998.

Hickerson, Jay. *The New, Revised Ultimate History of Network Radio Programming and Guide to All Circulating Shows.* Self Published, CT, 1996.

Since there aren't too many OTR sources left anymore and many of them contradict one another, many thanks are necessary to the fellow OTR fans who helped me gather the correct schedule information for this book. Thanks to Elizabeth McLeod and Jay Hickerson for allowing me access to their voluminous expertise. Thanks to Tom Van Der Voort for sending me copies of his many OTR magazines. Thanks to Charlie Summers for allowing me to advertise on his OTR list and digest. Thanks to Lou Genco for advertising my book on his OTR website. A final thank you to the many OTR fans who sent me their information and remembrances. All have been very helpful in figuring out what shows went where and when. Hopefully, this will inspire the next generations to research even more into the history of OTR.

LISTINGS FOR 1938

EVENING — WINTER, 1938

Sunday

	BLUE	CBS	MBS	NBC
6pm	Green Brothers Orchestra	The Park Avenue Penners	Thirty Minutes in Hollywood, George Jessel	The Catholic Hour
6:15				
6:30	The Original Microphone Play	Double Everything	Don Betzner Orchestra	A Tale of Today
6:45				
7pm	Paths to Prosperity	Vick's Open House	The American Forum of the Air	The Jello Program, Jack Benny
7:15				
7:30	The Baker's Broadcast	The Gulf Headliners, Phil Baker	Comedy Stars of Broadway	Interesting Neighbors
7:45			Dance Orchestra	
8pm	Detective Stories	The People's Choice	Epic of America	The Chase and Sanborn Hour
8:15				
8:30	Ernest Gill's California Concert	Earaches of 1938	Sammy Kaye Orchestra	
8:45		Elmer Davis, news (8:55pm)		
9pm	The Hollywood Playhouse	The Ford Sunday Evening Hour	The Madrigal Singers	The Manhattan Merry-Go-Round
9:15				
9:30	Walter Winchell's Jergens Journal		The News Testers	The American Album of Familiar Music
9:45	Irene Rich Dramas		The Charioteers Quartet	
10pm	Freddy Martin Orchestra	The Zenith Foundation	The Bach Cantata Series	Rising Musical Stars
10:15				
10:30	Cheerio's Musical Mosaics	Headlines and Bylines	Johnny Messner Orchestra	Do You Want to Be an Actor
10:45				

EVENING — WINTER, 1938

Monday

BLUE	CBS	MBS	NBC	
The US Army Band	Howard Phillips, songs	Uncle Don	Creagh Matthews, songs	*6pm*
	History Behind the Headlines		Top Hatters Orchestra	*6:15*
The Revelers Quartet	George Hall Orchestra	Vincent Connolly, news	Joan Edwards, songs	*6:30*
Lowell Thomas, news	Doris Rhodes, songs	Ray Keating Orchestra	Emery Deutsch Orchestra	*6:45*
Music is My Hobby	Poetic Melodies	Stan Lomax, sports	Amos 'n' Andy	*7pm*
The Three Cheers	American Viewpoints	The Answer Man	Uncle Ezra's Radio Station	*7:15*
Lum and Abner	Howard Shaw, songs	The Lone Ranger	New York on Parade	*7:30*
Tino Rossi, songs	Boake Carter, news			*7:45*
Harry Salter Orchestra	Tish	Morton Gould Orchestra	Burns and Allen	*8pm*
				8:15
Grand Hotel	Pick and Pat	The Charioteers Quartet	The Voice of Firestone	*8:30*
	Elmer Davis, news (8:55pm)	Vocal Varieties		*8:45*
Philadelphia Symphony Orchestra	The Lux Radio Theater	Gabriel Heatter, news	Fibber Magee and Molly	*9pm*
		Vic Arden Orchestra		*9:15*
		Benay Venuta's Variety Program	The Hour of Charm	*9:30*
				9:45
Twenty Thousand Years in Sing Sing	Lady Esther Serenade	True or False	The Carnation Contented Hour	*10pm*
				10:15
The National Radio Forum	Brave New World	Pageant of Melody	For Men Only, Fred Uttal	*10:30*
				10:45

EVENING — WINTER, 1938

Tuesday

	BLUE	CBS	MBS	NBC
6pm	Rakov Orchestra	Let's Pretend	Uncle Don	Science in the News
6:15				Joan Edwards, songs
6:30	The Serenaders	Selected Stories	Vincent Connolly, news	Hal McIntyre Orchestra
6:45	Lowell Thomas, news	Barry Wood Orchestra	Don Betzner Orchestra	
7pm	Easy Aces	Poetic Melodies	Stan Lomax, sports	Amos 'n' Andy
7:15	Mr. Keen, Tracer of Lost Persons	Hollywood Screen Scoops	The Charioteers Quartet	Vocal Varieties
7:30	Dorothy Thompson, news	Second Husband	Headlines	Dick Gasperre Orchestra
7:45	Vivian Della Chiesa, songs		Livingston Orchestra	Doctor Dollar
8pm	Those We Love	Big Town	Richard Himber Orchestra	Johnny Presents
8:15				
8:30	It Can Be Done	The Lifebuoy Program, Al Jolson	World Neighbors	Lady Esther Serenade
8:45		Elmer Davis, news (8:55pm)		
9pm	The Alemite Half-Hour	Watch the Fun Go By, Al Pearce	Gabriel Heatter, news	Vox Pop
9:15			Comedy Stars of Broadway	
9:30	Alias Jimmy Valentine	Jack Oakie's College	Jazz Nocturne	Mardi Gras
9:45				
10pm	Hugh S. Johnson, comment	Benny Goodman's Swing School	The Hour of Romance	
10:15	The Kidoodlers Novelty Quartet			
10:30	Cella Gamba, violin	Howard Phillips, songs	Symphonic Strings	Jimmy Fidler, gossip
10:45		The Four Clubmen		Dale Carnegie, inspirational

EVENING — WINTER, 1938

Wednesday

BLUE	CBS	MBS	NBC	
Rex Maupin Orchestra	Dear Teacher	Uncle Don	Our American Schools	6pm
	George Hall Orchestra		Top Hatters Orchestra	6:15
The Revelers Quartet		Vincent Connolly, news	The Rhythmnaires	6:30
Lowell Thomas, news	Barry Wood Orchestra	Public Affairs	Blue Barron Orchestra	6:45
Easy Aces	Poetic Melodies	Stan Lomax, sports	Amos 'n' Andy	7pm
Mr. Keen, Tracer of Lost Persons	Hobby Lobby	The Answer Man	Uncle Ezra's Radio Station	7:15
Lum and Abner		The Lone Ranger	Hendrik Willem Van Loon, news	7:30
Science on the March	Boake Carter, news		Cheer Up, America	7:45
The Roy Shield Revue	The Cavalcade of America	The Broadway Melody Hour	One Man's Family	8pm
				8:15
Harriet Parsons, gossip	Texaco Town, Eddie Cantor	The Pickard Family, songs	Lady Esther Serenade	8:30
Jimmy Kemper, songs	Elmer Davis, news (8:55pm)			8:45
Cleveland Symphony Orchestra	Chesterfield Presents	Gabriel Heatter, news	Town Hall Tonight, Fred Allen	9pm
		Pauline Alpert, piano		9:15
	Ben Bernie, the Old Maestro	Let's Visit		9:30
				9:45
Hugh S. Johnson, comment	Gangbusters	Horace Heidt Orchestra	Your Hollywood Parade	10pm
Nola Day, songs				10:15
The NBC Minstrels	Del Casino, songs	Hobby Lobby		10:30
	American Viewpoints			10:45

EVENING — WINTER, 1938

Thursday

	BLUE	CBS	MBS	NBC
6pm	Rex Maupin Orchestra	Let's Pretend	Uncle Don	George R. Holmes, news
6:15				Chick Webb Orchestra
6:30	The Serenaders	George Hall Orchestra	Vincent Connolly, news	Joan Edwards, songs
6:45	Lowell Thomas, news	Doris Rhodes, songs	Radie Harris, gossip	Happy Felton Orchestra
7pm	Easy Aces	Poetic Melodies	Stan Lomax, sports	Amos 'n' Andy
7:15	Mr. Keen, Tracer of Lost Persons	Hollywood Screen Scoops	Don Betzner Orchestra	Vocal Varieties
7:30	Freddy Martin Orchestra	We, the People	Headlines	The Sheaffer Revue
7:45			The WOR Follies	
8pm	The March of Time	The Kate Smith Hour	Ray Sinatra Orchestra	The Royal Gelatin Hour, Rudy Vallee
8:15				
8:30	Barry McKinley, songs		George Olsen Orchestra	
8:45	The Eastman School of Music	Elmer Davis, news (8:55pm)		
9pm		Major Bowes' Original Amateur Hour	Gabriel Heatter, news	Good News of 1938
9:15			Comedy Stars of Broadway	
9:30	America's Town Meeting of the Air		Sinfonietta	
9:45				
10pm		Essays in Music	The Witch's Tale	The Kraft Music Hall, Bing Crosby
10:15				
10:30	Jamboree	Hollywood Showcase	Henry Weber's Musical Revue	
10:45				

EVENING — WINTER, 1938

Friday

BLUE	CBS	MBS	NBC	
Roy Shield Orchestra	The Children's Concert	Uncle Don	Education in the News	6pm
Views and News of South America			The Rhythmnaires	6:15
The Revelers Quartet	The Eton Boys Quartet	Vincent Connolly, news	Howard Smith, piano	6:30
Lowell Thomas, news	Song Time	Raymond Gram Swing, news	Blue Barron Orchestra	6:45
Mary Small, songs	Poetic Melodies	Stan Lomax, sports	Amos 'n' Andy	7pm
How to Live	Arthur Godfrey, songs	The Answer Man	Uncle Ezra's Radio Station	7:15
Lum and Abner	Margaret Daum, songs	The Lone Ranger	Hendrik Willem Van Loon, news	7:30
Tino Rossi, songs	Boake Carter, news		Bughouse Rhythm	7:45
Grand Central Station	The Hammerstein Music Hall	Ernie Fio Rito Orchestra	The Cities Service Concerts	8pm
		The Charioteers Quartet		8:15
Death Valley Days	Chesterfield Presents	Dale Carnegie, inspirational		8:30
	Elmer Davis, news (8:55pm)	Let's Play Games		8:45
Nola Day, songs	Hollywood Hotel	Gabriel Heatter, news	Waltz Time	9pm
Howard Marshall, news		Vic Arden Orchestra		9:15
Tommy Dorsey Orchestra		Bamberger Little Orchestra	The Court of Human Relations	9:30
				9:45
Madison Square Garden Boxing	The Song Shop	Twenty Years Ago and Today	The First Nighter Program	10pm
				10:15
		Johnny Messner Orchestra	Jimmy Fidler, gossip	10:30
	American Viewpoints		Dorothy Thompson, news	10:45

EVENING — WINTER, 1938

Saturday

	BLUE	CBS	MBS	NBC
6pm	Music By Meakin	Columbia's Chorus Quest	Uncle Don	El Chico
6:15				
6:30	Harold Nagel Orchestra	Syncopation Piece	Vincent Connolly, news	The Sports Question Box
6:45			Dance Orchestra	Religion in the News
7pm	Message of Israel	The Saturday Night Swing Club	Stan Lomax, sports	Kaltenmeyer's Kindergarten
7:15			Dance Orchestra	
7:30	Uncle Jim's Question Bee	The Voice of Niagara	Don Betzner Orchestra	Alistair Cooke, comment
7:45				The Jean Sablon Show
8pm	Allen Roth Orchestra	The Columbia Workshop	Pat Barne's Barnstormers	Believe It or Not
8:15				
8:30	Spelling Bee	Johnny Presents	Olga Baclanova's Continental Revue	The Log Cabin Jamboree, Jack Haley
8:45		Elmer Davis, news (8:55pm)		
9pm	The National Barn Dance	Professor Quiz	John Steele, news	Special Delivery
9:15			Chicago Symphony Orchestra	
9:30		By Popular Demand		American Portraits
9:45				
10pm	NBC Symphony Orchestra	Your Hit Parade		NBC Symphony Orchestra
10:15				
10:30				
10:45		Songs		

DAYTIME — WINTER, 1938

Sunday

	BLUE	CBS	MBS	NBC
9am	The Children's Hour	Wings Over Jordan	Rainbow House	Turn Back the Clock
9:15				Vagabond Adventures
9:30		Ambade for Strings		J. Alden Edkins, songs
9:45				
10am	Russian Melodies	The CBS Church of the Air	News	The National Radio Pulpit
10:15			Frank Dailey Orchestra	
10:30	Dreams of Long Ago	The Horn and Hardart Children's Hour	Victor Lindlahr, health	The Madrigal Singers
10:45				
11am	The Musical Story Lady		The Northwestern Reviewing Stand	The Silver Flute
11:15	Neighbor Nell		Martha and Hal, songs	
11:30	Felix Knight, songs	Major Bowes' Capitol Family	The Embassy Trio	Angler and Hunter
11:45	The Bill Stern Sports Review		Don Redman Orchestra	The Norsemen Quartet
12pm	The Southernaires Quartet		Dr. Charles Courboin, organ	Home Symphony Orchestra
12:15				
12:30	The Radio City Music Hall	The Salt Lake Tabernacle Choir	Uncle Don Reads The Comics	The University of Chicago Round Table
12:45				
1pm		The CBS Church of the Air	The Garden of Memories	Al and Lee Reiser, piano
1:15				Henry Busse Orchestra
1:30	There Was a Woman	Public Affairs	The Gotham String Quartet	The Tuskagee Institute Choir
1:45		Poet's Gold		

DAYTIME — WINTER, 1938

Monday-Friday

BLUE	CBS	MBS	NBC	
The Breakfast Club	Dear Columbia / Arthur Godfrey, songs	Ed Fitzgerald and Company	Women and the News	9am
	Songs	Music / Modern Living	Frank Luther, songs	9:15
	The Road of Life	Music	Music / Alice Joy, the Dream Singer	9:30
	Bachelor's Children	Music / Martha and Hal, songs	Dan Harding's Wife	9:45
Margo of Crestwood	Pretty Kitty Kelly	The Pure Food Hour /	Mrs. Wiggs of the Cabbage Patch	10am
Cabin at the Crossroads	The Story of Myrt and Marge	Talk	John's Other Wife	10:15
Attorney at Law	Tony Wons' Scrapbook / Emily Post, etiquette		Just Plain Bill	10:30
Kitchen Cavalcade	Ma Perkins		The Woman in White	10:45
The Story of Mary Marlin	Music / Heinz Magazine of the Air	Talk / Nell Vinick, beauty	David Harum	11am
Pepper Young's Family	Carol Kennedy's Romance	The Story of Myrt and Marge	Mary Noble, Backstage Wife	11:15
Vic and Sade	Big Sister	Hilltop House	Talk / How to Be Charming	11:30
The Gospel Singer	Aunt Jenny's True Life Stories	Myra Kingsley, astrology	Hello, Peggy / The Mystery Chef	11:45
Religious Talk	Mary Margaret McBride, talk	Music / Victor Lindlahr, health	Girl Alone	12pm
Bailey Axton, songs	Edwin C. Hill, news	Songs / The Theater Club	The O'Neills	12:15
The National Farm and Home Hour	The Romance of Helen Trent	Vincent Connolly, news	Stella Dallas	12:30
	Our Gal Sunday	We Are Four	Music	12:45
	Betty and Bob	Dramatized Health Talk	Stock Market Reports	1pm
	Betty Crocker, cooking / Hymns of All Churches	Talk / Carson Robison's Buckeroos	The Escorts and Betty	1:15
Sue Blake	Arnold Grimm's Daughter	Pepper Young's Family	Words and Music	1:30
Songs	Hollywood in Person	The Voice of Experience		1:45

DAYTIME — WINTER, 1938

Sunday

	BLUE	CBS	MBS	NBC
2pm	The Magic Key of RCA	Boris Morros Orchestra		Bob Becker's Dog Talks
2:15				Cook's Travelogue
2:30		Dr. Christian	The New Poetry Hour	Thatcher Colt Mysteries
2:45				
3pm	On Broadway	New York Philharmonic Orchestra	On a Sunday Afternoon	The Radio Newsreel
3:15				
3:30	The Armco Iron Master			Sunday Drivers
3:45			The Trail Blazers	
4pm	National Vespers		The Court of Human Relations	Romance Melodies
4:15				
4:30	Jean Ellington, songs		Livingston Orchestra	The World is Yours
4:45	Dog Heroes			
5pm	The Metropolitan Opera Auditions	Heinz Magazine of the Air	Singing Lady Musical Plays	Ry-Krisp Presents Marion Talley
5:15				
5:30	Smilin' Ed McConnell, songs	Guy Lombardo Orchestra	The Shadow	The Mickey Mouse Theater of the Air
5:45	Edward Davies, songs			

DAYTIME — WINTER, 1938

Monday-Friday

BLUE	CBS	MBS	NBC	
Music	News Through a Woman's Eyes	Kitty Keane, Inc.	Music / Your Health	*2pm*
Music / Let's Talk It Over	The O'Neills	Talk and Music		*2:15*
Music	The American School of the Air	Houseboat Hannah	Talk and Music	*2:30*
		Songs / Beatrice Fairfax, advice		*2:45*
Music / The Radio Guild	Music	Martha Deane, talk	Pepper Young's Family	*3pm*
			Ma Perkins	*3:15*
			Vic and Sade	*3:30*
		David Harum	The Guiding Light	*3:45*
Club Matinee, Ransom Sherman	Music / Informational Talk	News	Lorenzo Jones	*4pm*
	Music / Between the Bookends	Young Widder Brown	The Story of Mary Marlin	*4:15*
	The Goldbergs	The Johnson Family	Hughesreel	*4:30*
	Dr. Allan Dafoe, health	Talk and Music	The Road of Life	*4:45*
Music / Neighbor Nell	Follow the Moon	Women in the News	Dick Tracy	*5pm*
Don Winslow of the Navy	The Life of Mary Southern	Charlie Chan	Terry and the Pirates	*5:15*
Music / The Singing Story Lady	Music / Informational Talk	Little Orphan Annie	Jack Armstrong, the All-American Boy	*5:30*
The Tom Mix Ralston Straight Shooters	Hilltop House	Songs / Junior G-Men	Little Orphan Annie	*5:45*

DAYTIME — WINTER, 1938

Saturday

	BLUE	CBS	MBS	NBC
9am	The Breakfast Club	Ray Bloch Orchestra	Ed Fitzgerald and Company	The Wise Man
9:15		The Eton Boys Quartet	Organ Recital	The Sunshine Express
9:30		Fiddler's Fancy	Tex Fletcher, songs	
9:45			Natural History Talk	The Landt Trio and White
10am	The Woman of Tomorrow	Fred Feibel, organ	The Marriage Clinic	Amanda's Party
10:15				The Charioteers Quartet
10:30	Child Grows Up	The Jewel Cowboys	Get Thin to Music	Manhatters Orchestra
10:45	Swing Serenade		Music	
11am	Madia Severn, songs	The New York Philharmonic Children's Concert	The Sleepy Hollow Gang	The Florence Hale Radio Forum
11:15	The Minute Men Quartet			Musical Tete-A-Tete
11:30	Our Barn		The US Army Band	Ford Rush, the Happy Minstrel
11:45				Joan Brooks, songs
12pm	Call to Youth	Captivators Orchestra	The Parents Club of the Air	Abram Chasin's Music Series
12:15	Bailey Axton, songs		This Wonderful World	
12:30	The National Farm and Home Hour	George Hall Orchestra	Vincent Connolly, news	Rex Battle Orchestra
12:45			Steve Severn's Pet Club	
1pm		Orientale	Joan Merritt, songs	Dance Orchestra
1:15		John Sturgess, songs	Microphone in the Sky	
1:30	The Cadet's Quartet	Buffalo Presents	Carnegie Tech Symphony Orchestra	Campus Capers
1:45	The Metropolitan Opera			

DAYTIME — WINTER, 1938

Saturday

	BLUE	CBS	MBS	NBC
2pm		Madison Ensemble	Benay Venuta's Variety Program	Dance Orchestra
2:15		Ann Leaf at the Organ		
2:30		Motor City Melody		Your Host is Buffalo
2:45				
3pm		Merrymakers Orchestra	The Norman Brokenshire Show	Golden Memories
3:15				
3:30		Waltzes of the World		Bill Krenz Orchestra
3:45		Between the Bookends		
4pm			The International Salon	Great Plays
4:15		Dictators Orchestra		
4:30			Organ Recital	
4:45		The Four Clubmen	Bookshelf Spotlight	
5pm	Rakov Orchestra	The Story of Industry	Sammy Kaye Orchestra	Top Hatters Orchestra
5:15				
5:30	Hal Grayson Orchestra	Al Goldman Orchestra		The Stamp Club
5:45				Dance Orchestra

EVENING — SPRING, 1938

Sunday

	BLUE	CBS	MBS	NBC
6pm	Josef Cherniavsky Orchestra	The Park Avenue Penners	Thirty Minutes in Hollywood, George Jessel	The Catholic Hour
6:15				
6:30	The Original Microphone Play	Phil Cook's Almanac	Stan Lomax, sports	A Tale of Today
6:45			Colonel Stoopnagle	
7pm	Paths to Prosperity	The Story of Joan and Kermit	The American Forum of the Air	The Jello Program, Jack Benny
7:15				
7:30	The Baker's Broadcast	The Gulf Headliners, Phil Baker	Comedy Stars of Broadway	Interesting Neighbors
7:45			News	
8pm	Spy at Large	St. Louis Blues	Their Greatest Stories	The Chase and Sanborn Hour
8:15				
8:30	Songs We Remember	Musical Gazette	The Charioteers Quartet	
8:45		Elmer Davis, news (8:55pm)	The News Testers	
9pm	The Hollywood Playhouse	The Ford Sunday Evening Hour	The Court of Human Relations	The Manhattan Merry-Go-Round
9:15				
9:30	Walter Winchell's Jergens Journal		Harry Funk Orchestra	The American Album of Familiar Music
9:45	Irene Rich Dramas			
10pm	Paul Martin Orchestra	Grand Central Station	The Goodwill Hour	The Hour of Charm
10:15				
10:30	Cheerio's Musical Mosaics	Headlines and Bylines	Your Sunday Date	Norman Cloutier Orchestra
10:45				

EVENING — SPRING, 1938

Monday

BLUE	CBS	MBS	NBC	
Eichler Orchestra	Ed Thogersen, sports	Uncle Don	Creagh Matthews, songs	6pm
The Revelers Quartet	Among Your Souvenirs		Top Hatters Orchestra	6:15
Rakov Orchestra	Boake Carter, news	Vincent Connolly, news	Paul Douglas, sports	6:30
Lowell Thomas, news	Lum and Abner	Design for Happiness	The Adrian Rollini Trio	6:45
Clem McCarthy, sports	Just Entertainment	Stan Lomax, sports	Amos 'n' Andy	7pm
The Three Cheers	Jack Shannon, songs	The Answer Man	Uncle Ezra's Radio Station	7:15
Rose Marie, songs	The Camel Caravan, Eddie Cantor	The Lone Ranger	Melody in Rhythm	7:30
The Steinie Bottle Boys			Angler and Hunter	7:45
Ruby Newman Orchestra	The Monday Night Show, Lou Holtz	Isham Jones Orchestra	Burns and Allen	8pm
				8:15
Those We Love	Pick and Pat	Raymond Gram Swing, news	The Voice of Firestone	8:30
	Elmer Davis, news (8:55pm)	Vic Arden Orchestra		8:45
Philadelphia Symphony Orchestra	The Lux Radio Theater	Gabriel Heatter, news	Victor Herbert Musical Dramas	9pm
		The Johnson Family		9:15
		The Witch's Tale		9:30
				9:45
The Eastman School of Music	Lady Esther Serenade	True or False	The Carnation Contented Hour	10pm
				10:15
The National Radio Forum	Brave New World	Pageant of Melody	For Men Only, Fred Uttal	10:30
				10:45

EVENING — SPRING, 1938

Tuesday

	BLUE	CBS	MBS	NBC
6pm	Johnny Richards Orchestra	Ed Thogersen, sports	Uncle Don	Science in the News
6:15		George Hall Orchestra		Nina Dean, songs
6:30	Johnny Johnson, songs	Boake Carter, news	Vincent Connolly, news	Paul Douglas, sports
6:45	Lowell Thomas, news	Recital in Swingtime	The Rodeo Ramblers	Hal McIntyre Orchestra
7pm	Easy Aces	Just Entertainment	Stan Lomax, sports	Amos 'n' Andy
7:15	Mr. Keen, Tracer of Lost Persons	Hollywood Screen Scoops	The Charioteers Quartet	Vocal Varieties
7:30	Dorothy Thompson, news	Second Husband	Headlines	You, the Unseen Jury
7:45	Magic Melodies		Famous Fortunes	
8pm	Madriguera Love	Big Town	Morton Gould Orchestra	Johnny Presents
8:15				
8:30	It May Have Happened	The Lifebuoy Program, Al Jolson	The Green Hornet	Lady Esther Serenade
8:45		Elmer Davis, news (8:55pm)		
9pm	The Alemite Half-Hour	Watch the Fun Go By, Al Pearce	Gabriel Heatter, news	Vox Pop
9:15			The Johnson Family	
9:30	Alias Jimmy Valentine	Benny Goodman's Swing School	Benay Venuta's Variety Program	Fibber Magee and Molly
9:45				
10pm	Jamboree	Time to Shine	True Detective Mysteries	Believe It or Not
10:15			The Charioteers Quartet	
10:30	The Eastman School of Music	Ray Heatherton Orchestra	Johnny Messner Orchestra	Jimmy Fidler, gossip
10:45		The Four Clubmen		Dale Carnegie, inspirational

EVENING — SPRING, 1938

Wednesday

BLUE	CBS	MBS	NBC	
Eichler Orchestra	Ed Thogersen, sports	Uncle Don	Our American Schools	6pm
The Revelers Quartet	Doris Rhodes, songs		Top Hatters Orchestra	6:15
Alma Kitchell, talk	Boake Carter, news	Vincent Connolly, news	Paul Douglas, sports	6:30
Lowell Thomas, news	Lum and Abner	Design for Happiness	Nola Day, songs	6:45
Easy Aces	Just Entertainment	Stan Lomax, sports	Amos 'n' Andy	7pm
Mr. Keen, Tracer of Lost Persons	American Viewpoints	The Answer Man	Uncle Ezra's Radio Station	7:15
Rose Marie, songs		The Lone Ranger	Hendrik Willem Van Loon, news	7:30
Science on the March	Barry Wood Orchestra		Happy Jack Turner, songs	7:45
The Roy Shield Revue	The Cavalcade of America	The Broadway Melody Hour	One Man's Family	8pm
				8:15
Harriet Parsons, gossip	Ben Bernie, the Old Maestro	Let's Visit	The Raleigh and Kool Show	8:30
Barry McKinley, songs	Elmer Davis, news (8:55pm)			8:45
String Symphony	Chesterfield Presents	Gabriel Heatter, news	Town Hall Tonight, Fred Allen	9pm
		The Johnson Family		9:15
Under Western Skies	The Word Game	Jazz Nocturne		9:30
				9:45
Choir Symphonette	Gangbusters	Symphonic Strings	Kay Kyser's College of Musical Knowledge	10pm
Nola Day, songs				10:15
The NBC Minstrels	It Can Be Done	Jimmy Dorsey Orchestra		
				10:45

EVENING — SPRING, 1938

Thursday

	BLUE	CBS	MBS	NBC
6pm	Rakov Orchestra	Ed Thogersen, sports	Uncle Don	George R. Holmes, news
6:15		Doris Rhodes, songs		Chick Webb Orchestra
6:30	The Tune Twisters	Boake Carter, news	Vincent Connolly, news	Paul Douglas, sports
6:45	Lowell Thomas, news	Barry Wood Orchestra	Radie Harris, gossip	Blue Barron Orchestra
7pm	Easy Aces	Just Entertainment	Stan Lomax, sports	Amos 'n' Andy
7:15	Mr. Keen, Tracer of Lost Persons	Hollywood Screen Scoops	Bob Edge's Outdoor Talks	Vocal Varieties
7:30	Sylvia Froos, songs	We, the People	Headlines	The Sheaffer Revue
7:45	The Steinie Bottle Boys		Vocal Varieties	
8pm	The March of Time	The Kate Smith Hour	Sinfonietta	The Royal Gelatin Hour, Rudy Vallee
8:15				
8:30	Jim Kemper and Company		The Green Hornet	
8:45	Shefter and Brenner, piano	Elmer Davis, news (8:55pm)		
9pm	The Eastman School of Music	Major Bowes' Original Amateur Hour	Gabriel Heatter, news	Good News of 1938
9:15			The Johnson Family	
9:30	America's Town Meeting of the Air		Ray Sinatra Orchestra	
9:45				
10pm		Essays in Music	The Coolidge Quartet	The Kraft Music Hall, Bing Crosby
10:15				
10:30	The Eastman School of Music	Americans at Work	Henry Weber's Musical Revue	
10:45				

EVENING — SPRING, 1938

Friday

BLUE	CBS	MBS	NBC	
Roy Shield Orchestra	Ed Thogersen, sports	Uncle Don	Education in the News	*6pm*
The Revelers Quartet	Maxine Sullivan, songs		Piano Time	*6:15*
Johnny Johnston, songs	Boake Carter, news	Vincent Connolly, news	Paul Douglas, sports	*6:30*
Lowell Thomas, news	Lum and Abner	Design for Happiness	Blue Barron Orchestra	*6:45*
Clem McCarthy, sports	Just Entertainment	Stan Lomax, sports	Amos 'n' Andy	*7pm*
Cesar Saerchinger, news	Arthur Godfrey, songs	The Answer Man	Uncle Ezra's Radio Station	*7:15*
Nola Day, songs	Hollace Shaw, songs	The Lone Ranger	New York on Parade	*7:30*
Craig Matthews, songs				*7:45*
Maurice Spitalny Orchestra	The Ghost of Benjamin Sweet	What's My Name	The Cities Service Concerts	*8pm*
				8:15
Death Valley Days	Chesterfield Presents	Andrew Kelly: Philosopher		*8:30*
	Elmer Davis, news (8:55pm)	Vic Arden Orchestra		*8:45*
The Royal Crown Revue, Tim and Irene	Hollywood Hotel	Gabriel Heatter, news	Waltz Time	*9pm*
		The Johnson Family		*9:15*
Spelling Bee		Bamberger Little Orchestra	The Court of Human Relations	*9:30*
				9:45
Madison Square Garden Boxing	The Song Shop	Twenty Years Ago and Today	The First Nighter Program	*10pm*
				10:15
		Invitation to Waltz	Jimmy Fidler, gossip	*10:30*
	American Viewpoints		Dorothy Thompson, news	*10:45*

EVENING — SPRING, 1938

Saturday

	BLUE	CBS	MBS	NBC
6pm	The Tune Twisters	The Hollywood Children's Hour	Uncle Don	El Chico
6:15	The Master Builder			
6:30	Chick Webb Orchestra	Artie Shaw Orchestra	Vincent Connolly, news	Paul Douglas, sports
6:45			Music	Religion in the News
7pm	Message of Israel	Syncopation Piece	Stan Lomax, sports	Kaltenmeyer's Kindergarten
7:15			The Charioteers Quartet	
7:30	Uncle Jim's Question Bee	The Columbia Workshop	Xavier Cugat Orchestra	Alistair Cooke, comment
7:45				Barry McKinley, songs
8pm	Clem McCarthy, sports	The Saturday Night Swing Club	Ted Fio Rito Orchestra	Believe It or Not
8:15	RCA Victor Orchestra			
8:30		Johnny Presents	Pat Barnes' Barnstormers	Enric Madriguera Orchestra
8:45	Songs	Elmer Davis, news (8:55pm)		
9pm	The National Barn Dance	Professor Quiz	John Steele, news	Allen Roth Orchestra
9:15			Chicago Symphony Orchestra	
9:30		Saturday Night Serenade		American Portraits
9:45				
10pm	NBC Symphony Orchestra	Your Hit Parade		NBC Symphony Orchestra
10:15				
10:30				
10:45		American Viewpoints		

DAYTIME — SPRING, 1938

Sunday

	BLUE	CBS	MBS	NBC
9am	The Children's Hour	Julius Mattfeld, organ	Rainbow House	Turn Back the Clock
9:15				Vagabond Adventures
9:30		Ambade for Strings		Melody Moments
9:45				
10am	Russian Melodies	The CBS Church of the Air	News	The National Radio Pulpit
10:15			Mildred Bailey Orchestra	
10:30	Dreams of Long Ago	The Horn and Hardart Children's Hour	Victor Lindlahr, health	Music and American Youth
10:45				
11am	The Musical Story Lady		Old-Time Tunes	The Silver Flute
11:15	Neighbor Nell		The Northwestern Reviewing Stand	
11:30	Louise Florea, songs	Major Bowes' Capitol Family	The Storyteller	America Abroad
11:45	The Bill Stern Sports Review		Thomas Conrad Sawyer, comment	The Norsemen Quartet
12pm	The Southernaires Quartet		Dr. Charles Courboin, organ	Home Symphony Orchestra
12:15				
12:30	The Radio City Music Hall	The Salt Lake Tabernacle Choir	Uncle Don Reads the Comics	The University of Chicago Round Table
12:45				
1pm		The CBS Church of the Air	The Garden of Memories	The Madrigal Singers
1:15				
1:30	Empires of the Moon	Europe Calling	Rhumba Rhythms and Tangos	The Silver Strings
1:45		Poet's Gold	Charlie and Jane, songs	

DAYTIME — SPRING, 1938

Monday-Friday

BLUE	CBS	MBS	NBC	
The Breakfast Club	Dear Columbia / Arthur Godfrey, songs	Ed Fitzgerald and Company	Talk and Music	9am
	Songs	Music / Modern Living	Frank Luther, songs	9:15
	The Road of Life	Music	The Landt Trio and White	9:30
	Bachelor's Children		Amanda's Party	9:45
Cabin at the Crossroads	Pretty Kitty Kelly	The Pure Food Hour /	Mrs. Wiggs of the Cabbage Patch	10am
Margo of Castlewood	The Story of Myrt and Marge	Talk	John's Other Wife	10:15
Attorney at Law	Hilltop House		Just Plain Bill	10:30
Kitchen Cavalcade	Stephouse		The Woman in White	10:45
The Story of Mary Marlin	Music / Ruth Carhart, songs	Talk / Nell Vinick, beauty | Harum	David	11am
Pepper Young's Family	Richard Maxwell, songs	The Story of Myrt and Marge	Mary Noble, Backstage Wife	11:15
Vic and Sade	Big Sister	Hilltop House	Talk / How to Be Charming	11:30
The Gospel Singer	Aunt Jenny's True Life Stories	Music	Hello, Peggy / The Mystery Chef	11:45
Religious Talk	Mary Margaret McBride, talk	Songs / Victor Lindlahr, health	Dan Harding's Wife	12pm
Bailey Axton, songs	The Goldbergs	Talk / The Radio Garden Club	The O'Neills	12:15
The National Farm and Home Hour	The Romance of Helen Trent	Vincent Connolly, news	Stella Dallas	12:30
	Our Gal Sunday	The Consumers' Club	Music	12:45
	Betty and Bob	Dramatized Health Talk	Stock Market Reports	1pm
	Betty Crocker, cooking / Hymns of All Churches	Music	The Escorts and Betty	1:15
Mother In Law	Arnold Grimm's Daughter	Pepper Young's Family	Words and Music	1:30
Songs	Valiant Lady	The Voice of Experience		1:45

DAYTIME — SPRING, 1938

Sunday

	BLUE	CBS	MBS	NBC
2pm	The Magic Key of RCA	Walberg Brown Strings	The Lamplighter	The Kidoodlers Novelty Quartet
2:15			Tex Fletcher, songs	Vincente Gomez, guitar
2:30		Dr. Christian	The New Poetry Hour	Sunday Dinner at Aunt Fanny's
2:45				
3pm	On Broadway	New York Philharmonic Orchestra	On a Sunday Afternoon	The Radio Newsreel
3:15				
3:30	Smilin' Ed McConnell, songs			Sunday Drivers
3:45	William Primrose, violin		The Butler Rodeo Ramblers	
4pm	National Vespers		The Coolidge Quartet	Romance Melodies
4:15				
4:30	Jean Ellington, songs		Benay Venuta's Variety Program	The World is Yours
4:45	The Vagabond Quartet			
5pm	There Was a Woman	The Texas Rangers Quartet	The Musical Steelmakers	Ry-Krisp Presents Marion Talley
5:15				
5:30	The Serbian Choral Society	Guy Lombardo Orchestra	A Good Place to Eat	The Mickey Mouse Theater of the Air
5:45	Howard Marshall, news			

DAYTIME — SPRING, 1938

Monday-Friday

BLUE	CBS	MBS	NBC	
Music	Ma Perkins	Kitty Keane, Inc.	Music / Your Health	2pm
Music / Let's Talk It Over	The O'Neills	Way Down East		2:15
Music	The American School of the Air	Houseboat Hannah	Talk and Music	2:30
		Music / The Heart of Julia Blake		2:45
Music / The Radio Guild	Music	Martha Deane, talk	Pepper Young's Family	3pm
			Ma Perkins	3:15
	Music / Kate Smith's Column		Vic and Sade	3:30
	Music	David Harum	The Guiding Light	3:45
Club Matinee, Ransom Sherman	Music / Informational Talk	News	Lorenzo Jones	4pm
	Songs	Young Widder Brown	The Story of Mary Marlin	4:15
	Music / Informational Talk	Songs / Between the Bookends	Hughesreel	4:30
	Music	Music	The Road of Life	4:45
Music / Neighbor Nell		Women in the News	Dick Tracy	5pm
Don Winslow of the Navy		The Butler Rodeo Ramblers	Terry and the Pirates	5:15
Music / The Singing Story Lady	Music / March of Games	Little Orphan Annie	Your Family and Mine	5:30
Music / The Stamp Club	Music / Informational Talk	Songs / Junior G-Men	Little Orphan Annie	5:45

DAYTIME — SPRING, 1938

Saturday

	BLUE	CBS	MBS	NBC
9am	The Breakfast Club	The Eton Boys Quartet	Ed Fitzgerald and Company	The Wise Man
9:15		Richard Maxwell, songs	The Hymn Singer	The Sunshine Express
9:30		Fiddler's Fancy	The Storyteller	
9:45			Natural History Talk	The Landt Trio and White
10am	The Woman of Tomorrow	Lew White, organ	The Marriage Clinic	Amanda's Party
10:15				The Charioteers Quartet
10:30	Child Grows Up	The Jewel Cowboys	The Newark Drama School	Manhatters Orchestra
10:45	Swing Serenade			
11am	Vaughn de Leath, songs	Cincinnati Conservatory Symphony	The Sleepy Hollow Gang	The Florence Hale Radio Forum
11:15	The Minute Men Quartet			Musical Tete-A-Tete
11:30	Our Barn		The US Army Band	Anne Steese Richardson, talk
11:45				
12pm	Call to Youth	Melody Ramblings	The Parents Club of the Air	Abram Chasin's Music Series
12:15	Carol Weymann, songs	Romany Trails	This Wonderful World	
12:30	The National Farm and Home Hour	George Hall Orchestra	Vincent Connolly, news	Rex Battle Orchestra
12:45			Steve Severn's Pet Club	
1pm			Elinor Sherry, songs	Olman Orchestra
1:15			Microphone in the Sky	
1:30	Hal McIntyre Orchestra	Buffalo Presents	Carnegie Tech Symphony Orchestra	Your Host is Buffalo
1:45				

DAYTIME — SPRING, 1938

Saturday

	BLUE	CBS	MBS	NBC
2pm	Jean Ellington, songs	Madison Ensemble	Spotlight Revue	Campus Capers
2:15				
2:30	Bill Krenz Orchestra	Motor City Melody	Afternoon Varieties	The People's Lobby
2:45				
3pm	Public Affairs	Merrymakers Orchestra	Benay Venuta's Variety Program	Golden Melodies
3:15				
3:30		Waltzes of the World		Swingology
3:45				
4pm	Club Matinee, Ransom Sherman	Charles Paul, organ	Horse Racing	The Stamp Club
4:15		Horse Racing		The Men of the West
4:30			The Butler Rodeo Ramblers	Top Hatters Orchestra
4:45		The Pictures Speak	Melody Moments	
5pm	Rakov Orchestra		Pancho Orchestra	Great Plays
5:15				
5:30	Dance Orchestra	Bill McCune Orchestra	Art Kassel Orchestra	
5:45			Questionnaire	

EVENING — SUMMER, 1938

Sunday

	BLUE	CBS	MBS	NBC
6pm	Josef Cherniavsky Orchestra	Howard Barlow Orchestra	Dick Barrie Orchestra	The Catholic Hour
6:15				
6:30	The Canadian Grenadiers	The Laugh Liner	Stan Lomax, sports	A Tale of Today
6:45			Public Affairs	
7pm	H. L. Spitalny Orchestra	Phil Cook's Almanac	Hawaii Calls	Hobby Lobby
7:15				
7:30	Norman Cloutier Orchestra	The Passing Parade	News	Interesting Neighbors
7:45			Invitation to Waltz	
8pm	Spy at Large	Lud Gluskin Orchestra	Dance Orchestra	The Chase and Sanborn Hour
8:15				
8:30	Songs We Remember	The Lewisohn Stadium Concerts	Impressions, Raoul Nadeau	
8:45		Elmer Davis, news (8:55pm)		
9pm	Win Your Lady		Dance Orchestra	The Manhattan Merry-Go-Round
9:15				
9:30	Ben Grauer's Column Quiz		The Jack Arthur Revue	The American Album of Familiar Music
9:45	Irene Rich Dramas			
10pm	Dance Orchestra		The Goodwill Hour	Horace Heidt Orchestra
10:15				
10:30	Cheerio's Musical Mosaics	Headlines and Bylines	Your Sunday Date	The University of Chicago Round Table
10:45				

LISTINGS FOR 1938

EVENING — SUMMER, 1938

Monday

BLUE	CBS	MBS	NBC	
Barry McKinley, songs	Ed Thogersen, sports	Uncle Don	Creagh Matthews, songs	6pm
The Revelers Quartet	Shirley Sadler, songs		Beano Rabinoff, violin	6:15
Rakov Orchestra	St. Louis Orchestra	Vincent Connolly, news	Paul Douglas, sports	6:30
Lowell Thomas, news		Livingston Orchestra	The Adrian Rollini Trio	6:45
Alias Jimmy Valentine	Ray Heatherton Orchestra	Stan Lomax, sports	Amos 'n' Andy	7pm
	American Viewpoints	The Answer Man	Rose Marie, songs	7:15
Music is My Hobby	Dance Orchestra	The Lone Ranger	Angler and Hunter	7:30
It's News to Me	Boake Carter, news		The Jack Berch Show	7:45
Ruby Newman Orchestra	The Monday Night Show, Henny Youngman	Ernie Fio Rito's Studies in Contrast	Believe It or Not	8pm
				8:15
Those We Love	Pick and Pat	Let's Visit	The Voice of Firestone	8:30
	Elmer Davis, news (8:55pm)			8:45
Edwin Franko Goldman Band	The Mercury Theater on the Air	Harlan E. Read, news	Josef Cherniavsky Orchestra	9pm
		The Camera Speaks		9:15
		Pat Barnes Barnstormers		9:30
				9:45
True or False	Lady Esther Serenade	Mr. Mergenthwickers Lobbies	The Carnation Contented Hour	10pm
				10:15
The National Radio Forum	Music	Pageant of Melody	Dance Orchestra	10:30
	American Viewpoints			10:45

EVENING — SUMMER, 1938

Tuesday

	BLUE	CBS	MBS	NBC
6pm	Sabin Orchestra	Ed Thogersen, sports	Uncle Don	Science in the News
6:15		Barry Wood Orchestra		Tito and His Swingtet
6:30	Marlowe and Lyon, piano	The Story of a Song	Vincent Connolly, news	Paul Douglas, sports
6:45	Lowell Thomas, news		The Smarties Quartet	Hal McIntyre Orchestra
7pm	Easy Aces	Ray Heatherton Orchestra	Stan Lomax, sports	Amos 'n' Andy
7:15	Mr. Keen, Tracer of Lost Persons	Hollywood Screen Scoops	Vinceny Pirro Orchestra	Vocal Varieties
7:30	The Ink Spots	Second Husband	Sam Balter, sports	The Adrian Rollini Trio
7:45	The Jack Berch Show		Don't You Believe It	Public Affairs
8pm	The Marglis Brass Choir	Four Corners Theater	Morton Gould Orchestra	Johnny Presents
8:15				
8:30	Information, Please	The Get Together Program, Jack Berch	The Green Hornet	Lady Esther Serenade
8:45		Elmer Davis, news (8:55pm)		
9pm	Now and Then with Frank	Grand Central Station	Harlan E. Read news	Vox Pop
9:15			Vocal Varieties	
9:30	Jamboree	Benny Goodman's Swing School	Say It With Words	Attorney at Law
9:45				
10pm		Time to Shine	True Detective Mysteries	Kelsey Orchestra
10:15			Raymond Gram Swing, news	
10:30	Felix Knight, songs	The Chicago Band Concert	Enric Madriguera Orchestra	Jimmy Fidler, gossip
10:45	Jay Franklin, news			Jesse Crawford, organ

EVENING — SUMMER, 1938

Wednesday

BLUE	CBS	MBS	NBC	
Edgar Hayes Orchestra	Ed Thogersen, sports	Uncle Don	Our American Schools	6pm
The Revelers Quartet	Lew White, organ		Top Hatters Orchestra	6:15
Alma Kitchell's Brief Case	Enoch Light Orchestra	Vincent Connolly, news	Paul Douglas, sports	6:30
Lowell Thomas, news	Doris Rhodes, songs	Mal Hallett Orchestra	Nola Day, songs	6:45
Easy Aces	Ray Heatherton Orchestra	Stan Lomax, sports	Amos 'n' Andy	7pm
Mr. Keen, Tracer of Lost Persons		The Answer Man	The Adrian Rollini Trio	7:15
Ralph Blaine, songs	History Behind the Headlines	The Lone Ranger	The Revelers Quartet	7:30
Science on the March	Boake Carter, news		The Jack Berch Show	7:45
The Roy Shield Revue	The People's Platform	Josef Cherniavsky Orchestra	One Man's Family	8pm
				8:15
Choral Recital	Chesterfield Presents	Drums	The Raleigh and Kool Show	8:30
	Elmer Davis, news (8:55pm)			8:45
It May Have Happened	Meet the Champ	Harlan E. Read, news	Town Hall Varieties, Colonel Stoopnagle	9pm
		The Novelty Choir		9:15
Under Western Skies	Mark Warnow Orchestra	Guy Lombardo Orchestra	George Jessel Jamboree	9:30
				9:45
Madison Square Garden Boxing	The Word Game	The WPA Theater	Kay Kyser's College of Musical Knowledge	10pm
				10:15
	It Can Be Done	Melodies from the Sky		10:30
				10:45

EVENING — SUMMER, 1938

Thursday

	BLUE	CBS	MBS	NBC
6pm	Edgar Hayes Orchestra	Ed Thogersen, sports	Uncle Don	Jesse Crawford, organ
6:15		Doris Rhodes, songs		Laura Suarez, songs
6:30	The Tune Twisters	Music	Vincent Connolly, news	Paul Douglas, sports
6:45	Lowell Thomas, news		Glenn Miller Orchestra	Blue Barron Orchestra
7pm	Easy Aces	Ray Heatherton Orchestra	Stan Lomax, sports	Amos 'n' Andy
7:15	Mr. Keen, Tracer of Lost Persons	Hollywood Screen Scoops	Bob Edge's Outdoor Talks	Vocal Varieties
7:30	Elvira Rios, songs	Del Casino, songs	Sam Balter, sports	The Schaefer All-Star Parade
7:45	The Jack Berch Show	Boake Carter, news	Don't You Believe It	
8pm	Stepping Ahead with America	Men Against Death	Sinfonietta	The Royal Gelatin Hour, Rudy Vallee
8:15				
8:30	Robert Dolan Orchestra	Edwin Franko Goldman Band	The Green Hornet	
8:45		Elmer Davis, news (8:55pm)		
9pm	Pulitzer Prize Plays	Major Bowes' Original Amateur Hour	Harlan E. Read, news	Promenade Symphony of Toronto
9:15			The Charioteers Quartet	
9:30			Guy Lombardo Orchestra	
9:45				
10pm	Music	Essays in Music	Press Time	The Kraft Music Hall, Bob Burns
10:15				
10:30	People I Have Known	Americans at Work	Henry Weber's Musical Revue	
10:45				

EVENING — SUMMER, 1938

Friday

BLUE	CBS	MBS	NBC	
Josef Hontis Orchestra	Ed Thogersen, sports	Uncle Don	Education in the News	6pm
The Revelers Quartet	Enoch Light Orchestra		Piano Time	6:15
Instrumental Ensemble		Vincent Connolly, news	Paul Douglas, sports	6:30
Lowell Thomas, news	Byran Field, sports	Livingston Orchestra	Jimmy Kemper, songs	6:45
Dick Todd, songs	Ray Heatherton Orchestra	Stan Lomax, sports	Amos 'n' Andy	7pm
Music is My Hobby	Hollace Shaw, songs	The Answer Man	Rose Marie, songs	7:15
Carol Weymann, songs	Adventures in Science	The Lone Ranger	The Revelers Quartet	7:30
The Three Cheers	Boake Carter, news		The Jack Berch Show	7:45
Maurice Spitalny Orchestra	The Ghost of Benjamin Sweet	What's My Name	The Cities Service Concerts	8pm
				8:15
Norman Cloutier Orchestra	St. Louis Blues	Richard Maxwell, songs		8:30
	Elmer Davis, news (8:55pm)	James Melton, songs		8:45
The Royal Crown Revue, Tim and Irene	Design for Dancing	Harlan E. Read, news	Waltz Time	9pm
		Jimmie Grier Orchestra		9:15
The March of Time		Ted Fio Rito Orchestra	Death Valley Days	9:30
				9:45
Julian Fuhs Orchestra	Edwin Franko Goldman Band	Famous First Facts	The First Nighter Program	10pm
				10:15
The Ink Spots	Barry Wood Orchestra	Curtain Time	Jimmy Fidler, gossip	10:30
Jay Franklin, news	American Viewpoints		Jesse Crawford, organ	10:45

EVENING — SUMMER, 1938

Saturday

	BLUE	CBS	MBS	NBC
6pm	Paul Martin Orchestra	Ed Thorgersen, sports	Uncle Don	El Chico
6:15		Songs		
6:30	Blue Barron Orchestra	Mal Hallett Orchestra	Vincent Connolly, news	Paul Douglas, sports
6:45			Dance Orchestra	The Art of Living
7pm	Message of Israel	The Columbia Workshop	Stan Lomax, sports	Richard Himber Orchestra
7:15			The Charioteers Quartet	
7:30	Uncle Jim's Question Bee	Syncopation Piece	Sam Balter, sports	The RCA Victor Campus Club
7:45			Glenn Miller Orchestra	
8pm	Antal Kooze, violin	The Saturday Night Swing Club	Percy Faith Orchestra	Kaltenmeyer's Kindergarten
8:15				
8:30	Original Dramas	Johnny Presents	The Robin Hood Dell Concerts	Fats Waller's Rhythm Club
8:45		Elmer Davis, news (8:55pm)		Barry McKinley, songs
9pm	The National Barn Dance	Professor Quiz		America Dances
9:15				
9:30		Saturday Night Serenade		
9:45				
10pm	Jacques Renard Orchestra	Your Hit Parade		Crickets
10:15				
10:30	Allen Roth Orchestra		Dance Orchestra	Dance Orchestra
10:45		American Viewpoints		

DAYTIME — SUMMER, 1938

Sunday

	BLUE	CBS	MBS	NBC
9am	The Children's Hour	Julius Mattfeld, organ	Rainbow House	Turn Back the Clock
9:15				Vagabond Adventures
9:30		Aubade for Strings		Melody Moments
9:45				
10am	Russian Melodies	The CBS Church of the Air	News	Highlights of the Bible
10:15			Mildred Bailey Orchestra	
10:30	Dreams of Long Ago	The Horn and Hardart Children's Hour	Uncle Don Reads the Comics	The Blaisdell Woodwinds
10:45				
11am	The Musical Story Lady		Old-Time Tunes	The Pine Tavern
11:15	Neighbor Nell		The Northwestern Reviewing Stand	
11:30	The Adrian Rollini Trio	Major Bowes' Capitol Family	Tex Fletcher, songs	The Madrigal Singers
11:45	The Bill Stern Sports Review		Walter Flangdorff, organ	
12pm	The Southernaires Quartet		Dick Barrie Orchestra	The Silver Strings
12:15				
12:30	The Radio City Music Hall	The Salt Lake Tabernacle Choir	Uncle Don Reads the Comics	Walter Logan's Musicale
12:45				
1pm		The CBS Church of the Air	The American Wildlife	Shakespeare's England
1:15			The Charioteers Quartet	
1:30	Way Down Home	Europe Calling	Men With Wings	Glenn Darwin, songs
1:45		Poet's Gold		

DAYTIME — SUMMER, 1938

Monday-Friday

BLUE	CBS	MBS	NBC	
The Breakfast Club	Music / Arthur Godfrey, songs	Music	The Landt Trio and White	9am
	Montana Slim, songs	Music / Modern Living	Frank Luther, songs	9:15
	Joyce Jordan, Girl Intern	Get Thin to Music	Music	9:30
Jane Arden	Bachelor's Children	Music	Amanda Snow, songs / The Mystery Chef	9:45
Just Neighbors	Pretty Kitty Kelly	The Singing Strings	Mrs. Wiggs of the Cabbage Patch	10am
Margo of Castlewood	The Story of Myrt and Marge	Talk and Music	John's Other Wife	10:15
Josh Higgins of Finchville	Hilltop House		Just Plain Bill	10:30
Ma Perkins	Stephouse		The Woman in White	10:45
The Story of Mary Marlin	Music / Richard Maxwell, songs	Talk / Nell Vinick, beauty| Harum	David	11am
Vic and Sade	Music / Ruth Carhart, songs	The Buckeye Four	Lorenzo Jones	11:15
Pepper Young's Family	Big Sister	Music / Your Blessings	Music	11:30
Getting the Most Out of Life	Aunt Jenny's True Life Stories	Music	The Road of Life	11:45
Music	Mary Margaret McBride, talk	Music	Dan Harding's Wife	12pm
Bailey Axton, songs	RFD #1, Irene Beasley	Talk	The O'Neills	12:15
The National Farm and Home Hour	The Romance of Helen Trent	Vincent Connolly, news	Time for Thought	12:30
	Our Gal Sunday	The Consumers' Club	Music	12:45
	The Goldbergs	Dramatized Health Talk	Stock Market Reports	1pm
	Vic and Sade	Songs / Between the Bookends	Hi Boys	1:15
Mother In Law	The Road of Life	Music / The Radio Garden Club	Words and Music	1:30
Songs	The Gospel Singer	Sheilah Taylor, gossip / The Marriage License Bureau		1:45

DAYTIME — SUMMER, 1938

Sunday

	BLUE	CBS	MBS	NBC
2pm	The Magic Key of RCA	Walberg Brown Strings	The Lamplighter	Sunday Dinner at Aunt Fanny's
2:15			Songs	
2:30		Don Murray Orchestra		Sunday Drivers
2:45			Charlie and Jane, songs	
3pm	On Broadway	Everybody's Music	On a Sunday Afternoon	Chautauqua Symphony Orchestra
3:15				
3:30	Music of the '90's			
3:45			Livingston Orchestra	
4pm	National Vespers	The Farmer Takes the Mike	Benay Venuta's Variety Program	Variety Show from Denver
4:15				
4:30	Nola Day and Barry McKinley, songs	The Toronto Glee Concerts		The World is Yours
4:45				
5pm	There Was a Woman	The Texas Rangers Quartet	The Musical Steelmakers	Ry-Krisp Presents Marion Talley
5:15				
5:30	The Jean Sablon Show	Guy Lombardo Orchestra	Dick Barrie Orchestra	Spy Secrets
5:45	What's New in South America			

DAYTIME — SUMMER, 1938

Monday-Friday

BLUE	CBS	MBS	NBC	
Music / Adventures in Reading	Music	Music	Betty and Bob	2pm
Music / Let's Talk It Over			Arnold Grimm's Daughter	2:15
Music			Valiant Lady	2:30
		Music / The Heart of Julia Blake	Betty Crocker, cooking / Hymns of All Churches	2:45
Music	Music / Dear Columbia	Martha Deane, talk	The Story of Mary Marlin	3pm
			Ma Perkins	3:15
	Music		Pepper Young's Family	3:30
		David Harum	The Guiding Light	3:45
Club Matinee, Ransom Sherman	Music / Informational Talk	News	Mary Noble, Backstage Wife	4pm
	Songs	The Story of Myrt and Marge	Stella Dallas	4:15
	Music / Informational Talk	Hilltop House	Happy Jack Turner, songs	4:30
		Talk and Music	Girl Alone	4:45
Music / Neighbor Nell	Music	Women in the News	Music / Nature Study	5pm
Don Winslow of the Navy		Music	Music	5:15
Music / The Singing Story Lady	Music / March of Games		Your Family and Mine	5:30
Music / The Stamp Club	Music / Informational Talk	The Johnson Family	Little Orphan Annie	5:45

DAYTIME — SUMMER, 1938

Saturday

	BLUE	CBS	MBS	NBC
9am	The Breakfast Club	Richard Maxwell, songs	Music	The Wise Man
9:15		Montana Slim, songs	Leo Freudberg Orchestra	The Saturday Morning Club
9:30		Fiddler's Fancy	Get Thin to Music	
9:45			Natural History Talk	The Landt Trio and White
10am	The Woman of Tomorrow	Lew White, organ	The Marriage Clinic	Amanda's Party
10:15				The Charioteers Quartet
10:30	Child Grows Up	The Jewel Cowboys	Organ Recital	Chautauqua Concert for Young People
10:45	Swing Serenade		The Day You Were Born	
11am	Vaughn de Leath, songs	Music	Manhatters Orchestra	Bailey Axton, songs
11:15	The Radio City Four	Marty Dale, piano		Ford Rush, the Happy Minstrel
11:30	Our Barn	Junior Musicomedy	The US Army Band	Musical Tete-A-Tete
11:45				Anna Steese Richardson, talk
12pm	Call to Youth	Music	This Wonderful World	Music
12:15	Carol Weymann, songs		The Sleepy Hollow Gang	
12:30	The National Farm and Home Hour		Vincent Connolly, news	Along Gypsy Trails
12:45		Enoch Light Orchestra	Songs	
1pm			Music	Gray Gordon Orchestra
1:15		The Rhythmnaires	Elinor Sherry, songs	
1:30	Ray Kinney Orchestra	Buffalo Presents	Organ Recital	Your Host is Buffalo
1:45				

DAYTIME — SUMMER, 1938

Saturday

	BLUE	CBS	MBS	NBC
2pm	Rex Maupin Orchestra	Madison Ensemble	Spotlight Revue	Campus Capers
2:15				
2:30	Larry Clinton Orchestra	Motor City Melodies		Golden Melodies
2:45	Willie Farmer Orchestra			
3pm	Rakov Orchestra	Merrymakers Orchestra	Benay Venuta's Variety Program	Rhythm and Rhyme
3:15				
3:30	Ricardo and His Caballeros	John Stergess, songs	Horse Racing	Joseph Gallichio Orchestra
3:45				
4pm	Club Matinee, Ransom Sherman	Charles Paul, organ	Dance Orchestra	The Stamp Club
4:15		Dancepators Orchestra		The Men of the West
4:30			Horse Racing	The Adrian Rollini Trio
4:45		The Four Clubmen		Judy and Lanny, songs
5pm	The Tune Twisters	Leon Goldman Orchestra	Pancho Orchestra	Green Brothers Orchestra
5:15				
5:30	Sabin Orchestra	Dance Orchestra	Mitchell Ayres Orchestra	The Kidoodlers Novelty Quartet
5:45				Frank Hawkes, aviation

EVENING — FALL, 1938

Sunday

	BLUE	CBS	MBS	NBC
6pm	New Friends of Music	The Silver Theater	Will Osborne Orchestra	The Catholic Hour
6:15				
6:30		The Laugh Liner	The Show of the Week	A Tale of Today
6:45				
7pm	Inter-American Conference	The People's Platform	Stan Lomax, sports	The Jello Program, Jack Benny
7:15			Dick Jurgens Orchestra	
7:30	Sunday Evenings at Seth Parkers	The Passing Parade	Frank Singiser, news	The Fitch Bandwagon
7:45			Hawaii Calls	
8pm	Out of the West	The Mercury Theater on the Air	The Bach Cantata Series	The Chase and Sanborn Hour
8:15				
8:30			Say It With Words	
8:45		Elmer Davis, news (8:55pm)		
9pm	The Hollywood Playhouse	The Ford Sunday Evening Hour	Sunday in Manhattan	The Manhattan Merry-Go-Round
9:15				
9:30	Walter Winchell's Jergens Journal		The Charioteers Quartet	The American Album of Familiar Music
9:45	Irene Rich Dramas		Gabriel Heater, news	
10pm	Russ Morgan Orchestra	Accent on Music	The Goodwill Hour	Horace Heidt Orchestra
10:15				
10:30	Cheerio's Musical Mosaics	Headlines and Bylines		Prospects of World Peace
10:45				

EVENING — FALL, 1938

Monday

BLUE	CBS	MBS	NBC	
Glucksman Orchestra	News and Sports	Uncle Don	Science in the News	6pm
	Howie Wing		Malcolm Claire, stories	6:15
Thomas Dewey's Campaign Speech	Bob Trout, news	Vincent Connolly, news	The Adrian Rollini Trio	6:30
Lowell Thomas, news	St. Louis Blues	The Stamp Club	Father and Son	6:45
Alias Jimmy Valentine	Ray Heatherton Orchestra	Stan Lomax, sports	Amos 'n' Andy	7pm
	Lum and Abner	The Answer Man	Edwin C. Hill, news	7:15
No Talent Wanted	The Camel Caravan, Eddie Cantor	The Lone Ranger	The Right Thing to Do	7:30
Science on the March				7:45
Carson Robison's Buckeroos	The Monday Night Show, Henny Youngman	Ernie Fio Rito's Studies in Contrast	Al Pearce and His Gang	8pm
				8:15
Those We Love	Pick and Pat	Famous First Facts	The Voice of Firestone	8:30
	Elmer Davis, news (8:55pm)			8:45
Public Affairs /	The Lux Radio Theater	Gabriel Heatter, news	The Hour of Charm	9pm
Music		James Melton, songs		9:15
		WOR Symphony Orchestra	Eddy Duchin Orchestra	9:30
				9:45
True or False	Guy Lombardo Orchestra	Mysteries of the Mind	The Carnation Contented Hour	10pm
				10:15
The National Radio Forum	The Story of a Song	Pageant of Melody	Larry Clinton Orchestra	10:30
				10:45

EVENING — FALL, 1938

Tuesday

	BLUE	CBS	MBS	NBC
6pm	Eucharistic Orchestra	News and Sports	Uncle Don	Relaxation Time
6:15		Howie Wing		
6:30	The Adrian Rollini Trio	Bob Trout, news	Vincent Connolly, news	Angler and Hunter
6:45	Lowell Thomas, news	Barry Wood Orchestra	The World We Live In	Jesse Crawford, organ
7pm	Easy Aces	Ray Heatherton Orchestra	Stan Lomax, sports	Amos 'n' Andy
7:15	Mr. Keen, Tracer of Lost Persons	Hollywood Screen Scoops	C. J. Ingram, comment	Vocal Varieties
7:30	Around New York	Second Husband	Don't You Believe It	Quite by Accident
7:45			Sam Balter, sports	
8pm	Usifer Orchestra	Big Town	The Green Hornet	Johnny Presents
8:15				
8:30	Information, Please	The Lifebuoy Program, Al Jolson	Morton Gould Orchestra	For Men Only, Fred Uttal
8:45		Elmer Davis, news (8:55pm)		
9pm	Mary and Bob's True Story Hour	We, the People	Harold Hoffman, news	Battle of the Sexes
9:15			WOR Symphony Orchestra	
9:30	Jamboree	Benny Goodman's Swing School		Fibber Magee and Molly
9:45			Gabriel Heatter, news	
10pm		Dr. Christian	True Detective Mysteries	The Pepsodent Show, Bob Hope
10:15			The Three Marshalls	
10:30	Ralph Blaine, songs	Maxine Sullivan, songs	Sammy Kaye Orchestra	Jimmy Fidler, gossip
10:45	Jay Franklin, news	American Viewpoints		Jesse Crawford, organ

EVENING — FALL, 1938

Wednesday

BLUE	CBS	MBS	NBC	
The Adrian Rollini Trio	News and Sports	Uncle Don	Our American Schools	6pm
Jesse Crawford, organ	Howie Wing		Malcolm Claire, stories	6:15
The Jester's Trio	Bob Trout, news	Vincent Connolly, news	Lester and Marion Baum, songs	6:30
Lowell Thomas, news	Nan Wynn, songs	The Stamp Club	Father and Son	6:45
Easy Aces	Ray Heatherton Orchestra	Stan Lomax, sports	Amos 'n' Andy	7pm
Mr. Keen, Tracer of Lost Persons	Lum and Abner	The Answer Man	Edwin C. Hill, news	7:15
Ralph Blaine, songs	The Ask-It Basket	The Lone Ranger	The Revelers Quartet	7:30
The Golden Theater Group			Sweetheart Theater	7:45
The Gypsy Theater	Gangbusters	Alfredo Antonini Orchestra	One Man's Family	8pm
				8:15
Hobby Lobby	Chesterfield Presents	Press Time	The Raleigh and Kool Show	8:30
	Elmer Davis, news (8:55pm)			8:45
Frank Hodiak Orchestra	The Texaco Star Theater	Gabriel Heatter, news	Town Hall Tonight, Fred Allen	9pm
		John Steele, news		9:15
Maurice Spitalny Orchestra		Percy Faith Orchestra		9:30
				9:45
The Fisk Jubilee Choir	Everybody's Music	Famous Jury Trials	Kay Kyser's College of Musical Knowledge	10pm
				10:15
The NBC Minstrels	It Can Be Done	Melodies from the Skies		10:30
				10:45

EVENING — FALL, 1938

Thursday

	BLUE	CBS	MBS	NBC
6pm	Norman Cloutier Orchestra	Red Grange, sports	Uncle Don	Public Affairs
6:15	Beverly Lane, songs	Howie Wing		Malcolm Claire, stories
6:30	First Time Prize	Bob Trout, news	Vincent Connolly, news	Ed Dooley, sports
6:45	Lowell Thomas, news	The Adrian Rollini Trio	The Charioteers Quartet	Nola Day, songs
7pm	Easy Aces	Ray Heatherton Orchestra	Stan Lomax, sports	Amos 'n' Andy
7:15	Mr. Keen, Tracer of Lost Persons	Hollywood Screen Scoops	Radie Harris, gossip	Vocal Varieties
7:30	The Bill Stern Sports Review	The Joe Penner Show	Don't You Believe It	The Schaefer All-Star Parade
7:45	Song Varieties		Sam Balter, sports	
8pm	Interesting Neighbors	The Kate Smith Hour	The Green Hornet	The Royal Gelatin Hour, Rudy Vallee
8:15				
8:30	The Eastman School of Music		Sinfonietta	
8:45		Elmer Davis, news (8:55pm)		
9pm		Major Bowes' Original Amateur Hour	Gabriel Heatter, news	Good News of 1939
9:15	Dr. Harlan Barrows, talk		Will Osborne Orchestra	
9:30	America's Town Meeting of the Air		We Want a Touchdown	
9:45				
10pm		The Columbia Workshop	Eddy Duchin Orchestra	The Kraft Music Hall, Bing Crosby
10:15				
10:30	People I Have Known	Americans at Work	Henry Weber's Musical Revue	
10:45				

EVENING — FALL, 1938

Friday

BLUE	CBS	MBS	NBC	
Alma Kitchell's Briefcase	News and Sports	Uncle Don	Relaxation Time	*6pm*
Dance Orchestra	Howie Wing			*6:15*
The Jester's Trio	Bob Trout, news	Vincent Connolly, news	George R. Holmes, news	*6:30*
Lowell Thomas, news	Public Affairs	The Stamp Club	Father and Son	*6:45*
Dick Todd, songs	Ray Heatherton Orchestra	Stan Lomax, sports	Amos 'n' Andy	*7pm*
Oscar Shumsky, violin	Lum and Abner	The Answer Man	Jimmy Fidler, gossip	*7:15*
Carol Weyman, songs	The Wonder Show, Jack Haley	The Lone Ranger	The Revelers Quartet	*7:30*
The Golden Theater Group			Sweetheart Theater	*7:45*
Criminal Case Histories with Warden Lawes	The First Nighter Program	What's My Name	The Cities Service Concerts	*8pm*
				8:15
If I Had the Chance	Burns and Allen	Symphonic Strings		*8:30*
	Elmer Davis, news (8:55pm)			*8:45*
Paul Martin Orchestra	Hollywood Hotel	Gabriel Heatter, news	Waltz Time	*9pm*
		Richard Maxwell, songs		*9:15*
The March of Time		Moonbeams	Death Valley Days	*9:30*
				9:45
Madison Square Garden Boxing	Grand Central Station	Curtain Time	Guy Lombardo Orchestra	*10pm*
				10:15
	The Jack Berch Show	Helene Daniels, songs	Cesar Saerchinger, news	*10:30*
	American Viewpoints	Jimmy Dorsey Orchestra	Jesse Crawford, organ	*10:45*

EVENING — FALL, 1938

Saturday

	BLUE	CBS	MBS	NBC
6pm	El Chico	Ed Thorgersen, sports	Uncle Don	Kaltenmeyer's Kindergarten
6:15		Bill McCune Orchestra		
6:30	Gene Brown Orchestra	Bob Trout, news	Vincent Connolly, news	Ed Dooley, sports
6:45		Shirley Sadler, songs	Uncommon Knowledge	Religion in the News
7pm	Message of Israel	The Saturday Night Swing Club	Stan Lomax, sports	Avalon Variety Time, Red Foley
7:15			Dance Orchestra	
7:30	Uncle Jim's Question Bee	The Joe E. Brown Show		Richard Himber Orchestra
7:45			Sam Balter, sports	The Lives of Great Men
8pm	Al Donahue Orchestra	Johnny Presents	The Sousa Memorial	Tommy Riggs and Betty Lou
8:15				
8:30	Original Dramas	Professor Quiz	George Olsen Orchestra	Fred Waring Orchestra
8:45		Elmer Davis, news (8:55pm)		
9pm	The National Barn Dance	Men Against Death	Hawaii Calls	Vox Pop
9:15				
9:30		Among Our Souvenirs	George Fisher, gossip	The Cross Country Swing Concert
9:45			The Charioteers Quartet	
10pm	NBC Symphony Orchestra	Your Hit Parade	Paducah Plantation, Whitey Ford	
10:15				
10:30			Meriwether's Minstrels	Fats Waller's Rhythm Club
10:45		Capitol Opinions		

DAYTIME — FALL, 1938

Sunday

	BLUE	CBS	MBS	NBC
9am	The Children's Hour	From the Organ Loft	Rainbow House	Turn Back the Clock
9:15		News		Vagabond Adventures
9:30		Wings Over Jordan		Melody Moments
9:45			The Sing a Song of Safety Club	
10am	Tone Pictures	The CBS Church of the Air	News	The National Radio Pulpit
10:15			Frank Dailey Orchestra	
10:30	Dreams of Long Ago	The Horn and Hardart Children's Hour	Uncle Don Reads the Comics	The Ancient Instruments Concert
10:45				
11am	The Musical Story Lady		Leo Freudberg Orchestra	The Pine Tavern
11:15	Neighbor Nell		Meeting Today's Problems	
11:30	The Southernaires Quartet	Major Bowes' Capitol Family	Van Alexander Orchestra	The Madrigal Singers
11:45			Miracles Do Happen	The House That Went Away
12pm	The Radio City Music Hall		Dr. Charles Courboin, organ	Shakespeare's England
12:15				
12:30		The Salt Lake Tabernacle Choir	The Lamplighter	The University of Chicago Round Table
12:45			News	
1pm	Great Plays	The CBS Church of the Air	The Wild Life Program	Walter Logan's Musicale
1:15			Edward Hopple, songs	
1:30		Europe Calling	Men With Wings	Charlotte Lansing, songs
1:45		Aubade for Strings		Bob Becker's Dog Talks

DAYTIME — FALL, 1938

Monday-Friday

BLUE	CBS	MBS	NBC	
The Breakfast Club	Richard Maxwell, songs	Music / The Hymn Singer	The Band Goes to Town	9am
The Woman of Tomorrow	Montana Slim, songs	Modern Living / The Lamplighter	The Family Man	9:15
The Breakfast Club	Joyce Jordan, Girl Intern	Get Thin to Music	Happy Jack Turner, songs	9:30
	Bachelor's Children	Music	Amanda's Party / The Mystery Chef	9:45
Paul Page, songs	Pretty Kitty Kelly	The Pure Food Hour /	Mrs. Wiggs of the Cabbage Patch	10am
Jane Arden	The Story of Myrt and Marge	Talk	John's Other Wife	10:15
Music / Smilin' Ed McConnell, songs	Hilltop House		Just Plain Bill	10:30
Ma Perkins	Stepmother		The Woman In White	10:45
The Story of Mary Marlin	Music	Talk / Nell Vinick, beauty	David Harum	11am
Vic and Sade		Songs / The Heart of Julia Blake	Lorenzo Jones	11:15
Pepper Young's Family	Big Sister	The Gloomchasers / The Theater Club	Young Widder Brown	11:30
Getting the Most Out of Life	Aunt Jenny's True Life Stories	Songs	The Road of Life	11:45
Music	Mary Margaret McBride, talk / Kate Smith Speaks	Music / Victor Lindlahr, health	Songs / Dan Harding's Wife	12pm
Songs / Neighbor Nell	Her Honor, Nancy James	Music / The Voice of the Farm	The O'Neills	12:15
The National Farm and Home Hour	The Romance of Helen Trent	Vincent Connolly, news	Time for Thought	12:30
	Our Gal Sunday	The Consumers' Quiz	Music	12:45
	The Goldbergs	Dramatized Health Talk	Stock Market Reports	1pm
Your Farm Reporter	Vic and Sade	Music / The Radio Garden Club	Music / Let's Talk It Over	1:15
Music / Peables Takes Charge	The Road of Life	Music	Words and Music	1:30
Songs	The Gospel Singer	The Marriage License Bureau / The Voice of Experience	Those Happy Gilmans	1:45

DAYTIME — FALL, 1938

Sunday

	BLUE	CBS	MBS	NBC
2pm	The Magic Key of RCA	Walberg Brown Strings	The Marties Vocal Group	Sunday Dinner at Aunt Fanny's
2:15			Music	
2:30		Carl Kimbell, shopping		The Kidoodlers Novelty Quartet
2:45			Salvatore de Stefano, songs	Olympic Talk
3pm	Dog Heroes	Everybody's Music	On a Sunday Afternoon	Sunday Drivers
3:15	The Three Cheers			
3:30	Sports Comments		The People's Rally	Richard Himber Orchestra
3:45				
4pm	National Vespers		Benay Venuta's Variety Program	Dance Orchestra
4:15				
4:30	Music from the Straw Hat Revue	The Texas Rangers Quartet	The Court of Human Relations	The World is Yours
4:45				
5pm	The Metropolitan Opera Auditions	Buddy Clark's Musical Weekly	The Musical Steelmakers	Sunday Afternoon in Rosedale
5:15				
5:30	Vincent Gomez, guitar	Ben Bernie, the Old Maestro	The Shadow	Spelling Bee
5:45	What's New in South America			

DAYTIME — FALL, 1938

Monday-Friday

BLUE	CBS	MBS	NBC	
Informational Talk	RFD #1, Irene Beasley	Two on a Shoestring	Betty and Bob	2pm
	Music	Music / The Girl from Maine	Arnold Grimm's Daughter	2:15
The Little Variety Show / Music	The American School of the Air	Songs	Valiant Lady	2:30
		Music / Ed Fitzgerald, talk	Betty Crocker, cooking / Hymns of All Churches	2:45
Music	Music	Martha Deane, talk	The Story of Mary Marlin	3pm
			Ma Perkins	3:15
			Pepper Young's Family	3:30
Between the Bookends		David Harum	The Guiding Light	3:45
Club Matinee, Ransom Sherman		News	Mary Noble, Backstage Wife	4pm
		The Story of Myrt and Marge	Stella Dallas	4:15
	Informational Talk /	Hilltop House	Life Can Be Beautiful	4:30
	Music	Music	Girl Alone	4:45
The Affairs of Anthony	Let's Pretend /	Women Make the News	Dick Tracy	5pm
Terry and the Pirates	March of Games	The Johnson Family	Your Family and Mine	5:15
Don Winslow of the Navy	Doris Rhodes, songs	Little Orphan Annie	Jack Armstrong, the All-American Boy	5:30
The Tom Mix Ralston Straight Shooters	The Mighty Show	Songs / Dad and Junior	Little Orphan Annie	5:45

DAYTIME — FALL, 1938

Saturday

	BLUE	CBS	MBS	NBC
9am	The Breakfast Club	Richard Maxwell, songs	Syncopators Orchestra	The Wise Man
9:15		Montana Slim, songs		Music Internationale
9:30		Fiddler's Fancy	Get Thin to Music	
9:45			Natural History Talk	Amanda's Party
10am	The Three Romeos	National Hillbilly Champions	The Marriage Clinic	The Saturday Morning Club
10:15	Viennese Ensemble			
10:30	Child Grows Up	Four Corners Theater	Steve Severn's Pet Club	The Charioteers Quartet
10:45	Swing Serenade		Raoul Nardeau, songs	The NEA Program
11am	Vaughn de Leath, songs	Cincinnati Conservatory Symphony	The Model Airplane Club	No School Today
11:15	The Radio City Four		Marriage License Romances	
11:30	Our Barn		The US Army Band	Music for You
11:45				
12pm	Choir Symphonette	Kate Smith Speaks	This Wonderful World	Bailey Axton, songs
12:15	Carol Wellmann, songs	Melody Ramblings	Collegiate Revue	Al and Lee Reiser, piano
12:30	The National Farm and Home Hour	Enoch Light Orchestra	Vincent Connolly, news	Call to Youth
12:45			The Gloomchasers	Along Gypsy Trails
1pm		St. Louis Blues		Robert Dolan Orchestra
1:15				
1:30	Ray Kinney Orchestra	Buffalo Presents	Healey Orchestra	Campus Capers
1:45	Sports		Sports	Sports

DAYTIME — FALL, 1938

Saturday

	BLUE	CBS	MBS	NBC
2pm		Sports		
2:15				
2:30				
2:45				
3pm				
3:15				
3:30				
3:45				
4pm		Charles Paul, organ		
4:15			Sports Scores	
4:30		Dancepators Orchestra	Sports	Top Hatters Orchestra
4:45				
5pm	Allen Roth Orchestra	Leon Goldman Orchestra		Cosmopolitan Rhythms
5:15				The Stamp Club
5:30	Gray Gordon Orchestra	Eddy Duchin Orchestra		Swingology
5:45				

LISTINGS FOR 1939

EVENING — WINTER, 1939

Sunday

	BLUE	CBS	MBS	NBC
6pm	New Friends of Music	The Silver Theater	My Lucky Break	The Catholic Hour
6:15				
6:30		Gateway to Hollywood	The Show of the Week	A Tale of Today
6:45				
7pm	Eugene Conley, songs	The People's Platform	The Bach Cantata Series	The Jello Program, Jack Benny
7:15				
7:30	Sunday Evenings at Seth Parkers	The Gulf Screen Guild Show	Frank Singiser, news	The Fitch Bandwagon
7:45			The Norman Brokenshire Show	
8pm	Cleveland Symphony Orchestra	This is New York	The American Forum of the Air	The Chase and Sanborn Hour
8:15				
8:30				
8:45		Elmer Davis, news (8:55pm)		
9pm	The Hollywood Playhouse	The Ford Sunday Evening Hour	Sunday in Manhattan	The Manhattan Merry-Go-Round
9:15				
9:30	Walter Winchell's Jergens Journal		Larry Clinton Orchestra	The American Album of Familiar Music
9:45	Irene Rich Dramas			
10pm	Maurice Spitalny Orchestra	The Old Gold Program, Robert Benchley	The Goodwill Hour	The Circle
10:15				
10:30	Cheerio's Musical Mosaics	Headlines and Bylines		
10:45		Capitol Opinions		

EVENING — WINTER, 1939

Monday

BLUE	CBS	MBS	NBC	
Bob Armstrong Orchestra	News and Sports	Uncle Don	Science in the News	6pm
Patricia Gilmore, songs	Howie Wing		Malcolm Claire, stories	6:15
Ray Perkins, piano	Bob Trout, news	Frank Singiser, news	Rose Marie, songs	6:30
Lowell Thomas, news	Enoch Light Orchestra	The Johnson Family	Del Courtney Orchestra	6:45
Alias Jimmy Valentine	County Seat	Stan Lomax, sports	Amos 'n' Andy	7pm
	Lum and Abner	The Answer Man	Edwin C. Hill, news	7:15
No Talent Wanted	The Camel Caravan, Eddie Cantor	The Lone Ranger	Red Norvo Orchestra	7:30
Science on the March				7:45
Carson Robison's Buckeroos	The Cavalcade of America	Ernie Fio Rito's Studies in Contrast	Al Pearce and His Gang	8pm
				8:15
Those We Love	Pick and Pat	Jacques Reynard Orchestra	The Voice of Firestone	8:30
	Elmer Davis, news (8:55pm)			8:45
The Budd Hulick Show	The Lux Radio Theater	Gabriel Heatter, news	The Hour of Charm	9pm
		The Changing World		9:15
The Two Westminster College Choirs		WOR Symphony Orchestra	Eddy Duchin Orchestra	9:30
				9:45
True or False	Guy Lombardo Orchestra	Mysteries of the Mind	The Carnation Contented Hour	10pm
				10:15
The National Radio Forum	The Columbia Workshop	Pageant of Melody	Horace Heidt Orchestra	10:30
				10:45

EVENING — WINTER, 1939

Tuesday

	BLUE	CBS	MBS	NBC
6pm	Eddie Rogers Orchestra	News and Sports	Uncle Don	Relaxation Time
6:15		Howie Wing		
6:30	The Adrian Rollini Trio	Bob Trout, news	Frank Singiser, news	Angler and Hunter
6:45	Lowell Thomas, news	Barry Wood Orchestra	The Johnson Family	Ralph Blaine, songs
7pm	Easy Aces	County Seat	Stan Lomax, sports	Amos 'n' Andy
7:15	Mr. Keen, Tracer of Lost Persons	Jimmy Fidler, gossip	Raymond Gram Swing, news	Vocal Varieties
7:30	Around New York	Second Husband	Don't You Believe It	Xavier Cugat Orchestra
7:45			Sam Balter, sports	The Right Thing to Do
8pm	Operettas	Big Town	The Green Hornet	Johnny Presents
8:15				
8:30	Information, Please	The Lifebuoy Program, Al Jolson	Morton Gould Orchestra	For Men Only, Fred Uttal
8:45		Elmer Davis, news (8:55pm)		
9pm	Mary and Bob's True Story Hour	We, the People	Harold Hoffman, news	Battle of the Sexes
9:15			The Gloomchasers	
9:30	Paul Martin Orchestra	Benny Goodman's Swing School		Fibber Magee and Molly
9:45				
10pm	If I Had the Chance	Dr. Christian	True Detective Mysteries	The Pepsodent Show, Bob Hope
10:15			Sammy Kaye Orchestra	
10:30	Lanny Corey's Rhythm	The Jack Berch Show		Uncle Ezra's Radio Station
10:45		American Viewpoints		Jimmy Kemper, songs

EVENING — WINTER, 1939

Wednesday

BLUE	CBS	MBS	NBC	
Jesse Crawford, organ	News and Sports	Uncle Don	Our American Schools	6pm
The Adrian Rollini Trio	Howie Wing		Malcolm Claire, stories	6:15
The Jesters Trio	Bob Trout, news	Frank Singiser, news	Rose Marie, songs	6:30
Lowell Thomas, news	Enoch Light Orchestra	The Johnson Family	Orchestra and Vocalists	6:45
Easy Aces	County Seat	Stan Lomax, sports	Amos 'n' Andy	7pm
Mr. Keen, Tracer of Lost Persons	Lum and Abner	The Answer Man	Edwin C. Hill, news	7:15
Horace Heidt Orchestra	The Ask-It Basket	The Lone Ranger	The Revelers Quartet	7:30
			Sweetheart Theater	7:45
The Roy Shield Revue	Gangbusters	Alfredo Antonini Orchestra	One Man's Family	8pm
				8:15
Hobby Lobby	Chesterfield Presents	A Tune and a Tale	The Raleigh and Kool Show	8:30
	Elmer Davis, news (8:55pm)			8:45
The Fisk Jubilee Choir	The Texaco Star Theater	Gabriel Heatter, news	Town Hall Tonight, Fred Allen	9pm
		John Steele, news		9:15
Wings for the Martins		Percy Faith Orchestra		9:30
				9:45
Ransom Sherman Variety	It Can Be Done	Famous Jury Trials	Kay Kyser's College of Musical Knowledge	10pm
				10:15
Public Interest in Democracy	Buddy Clark's Musical Weekly	Melodies from the Skies		10:30
				10:45

EVENING — WINTER, 1939

Thursday

	BLUE	CBS	MBS	NBC
6pm	Johnny Richards Orchestra	News and Sports	Uncle Don	Operalogue
6:15	Patricia Gilmore, songs	Howie Wing		Malcolm Claire, stories
6:30	Tito and His Swingtet	Bob Trout, news	Frank Singiser, news	The Bill Stern Sports Review
6:45	Lowell Thomas, news	Doris Rhodes, songs	The Johnson Family	Rose Marie, songs
7pm	Easy Aces	Nan Wynn, songs	Stan Lomax, sports	Amos 'n' Andy
7:15	Mr. Keen, Tracer of Lost Persons	Adventures in Science	Radie Harris, gossip	Vocal Varieties
7:30	Swing to Chiclets	The Joe Penner Show	Don't You Believe It	The Schaefer All-Star Parade
7:45			Sam Balter, sports	
8pm	The Parade of Progress in Foods	The Kate Smith Hour	The Green Hornet	The Royal Gelatin Hour, Rudy Vallee
8:15				
8:30	The Eastman School of Music		Sinfonietta	
8:45		Elmer Davis, news (8:55pm)		
9pm		Major Bowes' Original Amateur Hour	Gabriel Heatter, news	Good News of 1939
9:15	Dr. Harlan Barrows, talk		Public Affairs	
9:30	America's Town Meeting of the Air		Famous First Facts	
9:45				
10pm		Tune-Up Time	Henry Weber's Musical Revue	The Kraft Music Hall, Bing Crosby
10:15				
10:30	The NBC Minstrels		Dance Orchestra	
10:45		American Viewpoints		

EVENING — WINTER, 1939

Friday

BLUE	CBS	MBS	NBC	
Alma Kitchell's Briefcase	News and Sports	Uncle Don	Relaxation Time	6pm
Dorothy Rochelle, songs	Howie Wing			6:15
The Jesters Trio	Bob Trout, news	Frank Singiser, news	George R. Holmes, news	6:30
Lowell Thomas, news	Doris Rhodes, songs	The Johnson Family	The Adrian Rollini Trio	6:45
Artie Shaw Orchestra	County Seat	Stan Lomax, sports	Amos 'n' Andy	7pm
	Lum and Abner	The Answer Man	Jimmy Fidler, gossip	7:15
Bert Lytell's Adventures	The Wonder Show, Jack Haley	The Lone Ranger	The Revelers Quartet	7:30
Public Affairs			Sweetheart Theater	7:45
Criminal Case Histories with Warden Lawes	The First Nighter Program	What's My Name	The Cities Service Concerts	8pm
				8:15
Jamboree	Burns and Allen	Jimmy Dorsey Orchestra		8:30
	Elmer Davis, news (8:55pm)			8:45
Paducah Plantation, Red Foley	The Campbell Playhouse	Gabriel Heatter, news	Waltz Time	9pm
		Larry Clinton Orchestra		9:15
Horse and Buggy Days		There's a Law Against It	Death Valley Days	9:30
				9:45
Madison Square Garden Boxing	Grand Central Station	Curtain Time	Guy Lombardo Orchestra	10pm
				10:15
	Kansas City Symphony Orchestra	Jacques Reynard Orchestra	Uncle Ezra's Radio Station	10:30
			Cesar Saerchinger, news	10:45

EVENING — WINTER, 1939

Saturday

	BLUE	CBS	MBS	NBC
6pm	El Chico	News and Sports	Uncle Don	Kaltenmeyer's Kindergarten
6:15		Leighton Noble Orchestra		
6:30	Renfrew of the Mounted	The Saturday Night Swing Club	Frank Singiser, news	Gray Gordon Orchestra
6:45			Of Mutual Interest	Religion in the News
7pm	Message of Israel	Americans at Work	Stan Lomax, sports	Avalon Variety Time, Red Skelton
7:15			Jacques Reynard Orchestra	
7:30	Uncle Jim's Question Bee	The Joe E. Brown Show		The Lives of Great Men
7:45			Sam Balter, sports	The Castilla Twins
8pm	Ben Cutler Orchestra	Johnny Presents	Jazz Nocturne	Tommy Riggs and Betty Lou
8:15				
8:30	Brent House	Professor Quiz	Symphonic Strings	Fred Waring Orchestra
8:45		Elmer Davis, news (8:55pm)		
9pm	The National Barn Dance	Honolulu Bound, Phil Baker	Hawaii Calls	Vox Pop
9:15				
9:30		Among Our Souvenirs	George Fisher, gossip	The Hall of Fun
9:45		The Deep River Boys	The Sons of the Pioneers	
10pm	NBC Symphony Orchestra	Your Hit Parade	Impressions	Public Affairs
10:15				
10:30			Larry Clinton Orchestra	Red Norvo Orchestra
10:45		Capitol Opinions		

DAYTIME — WINTER, 1939

Sunday

	BLUE	CBS	MBS	NBC
9am	The Children's Hour	From the Organ Loft	Rainbow House	Turn Back the Clock
9:15				Vagabond Adventures
9:30		Wings Over Jordan		Melody Moments
9:45				
10am	Russian Melodies	The CBS Church of the Air	News	The National Radio Pulpit
10:15			Mildred Bailey Orchestra	
10:30	The Blaisdell Woodwinds	The Horn and Hardart Children's Hour	Uncle Don Reads the Comics	The Ancient Instruments Concert
10:45				
11am	The Musical Story Lady		Sunday Morning Symphony Orchestra	Julio Oyanguren, guitar
11:15	Neighbor Nell			Chimney House
11:30	The Southernaires Quartet	Major Bowes' Capitol Family		Walter Logan's Musicale
11:45				
12pm	The Radio City Music Hall		Dr. Charles Courboin, organ	The Madrigal Singers
12:15				
12:30		The Salt Lake Tabernacle Choir	The Lamplighter	The University of Chicago Round Table
12:45			News	
1pm	Great Plays	The CBS Church of the Air	Milton Katims Orchestra	The Singing Story Lady
1:15				
1:30		Salute to the New York World's Fair	Salute to the New York World's Fair	Salute to the New York World's Fair
1:45				

DAYTIME — WINTER, 1939

Monday-Friday

BLUE	CBS	MBS	NBC	
The Breakfast Club	Richard Maxwell, songs	Talk and Music	Happy Jack Turner, songs	*9am*
The Woman of Tomorrow	Montana Slim, songs	Music / Modern Living	The Family Man	*9:15*
The Breakfast Club	Joyce Jordan, Girl Intern	The Gloomchasers /	The Band Goes to Town	*9:30*
	Bachelor's Children	Steve Severn's Pet Club	The Wife Saver / The Gospel Singer	*9:45*
The Story of the Month	Pretty Kitty Kelly	The Pure Food Hour /	Central City	*10am*
Jane Arden	The Story of Myrt and Marge	Talk	John's Other Wife	*10:15*
Music / Smilin' Ed McConnell, songs	Hilltop House		Just Plain Bill	*10:30*
Breen and DeRose, songs	Stepmother		The Woman in White	*10:45*
The Story of Mary Marlin	Music / The Fact Finder	Talk and Music	David Harum	*11am*
Vic and Sade	Scattergood Baines	Songs / The Heart of Julia Blake	Lorenzo Jones	*11:15*
Pepper Young's Family	Big Sister	Get Thin to Music	Young Widder Brown	*11:30*
Getting the Most Out of Life	Aunt Jenny's True Life Stories	Music / The Theater Club	The Road of Life	*11:45*
Music	Mary Margaret McBride, talk / Kate Smith Speaks	Music / Victor Lindlahr, health	Dan Harding's Wife	*12pm*
Songs / Neighbor Nell	Her Honor, Nancy James	Music / The Voice of the Farm	The O'Neills	*12:15*
The National Farm and Home Hour	The Romance of Helen Trent	Vincent Connolly, news	Time for Thought	*12:30*
	Our Gal Sunday	The Consumers' Quiz	Stock Market Reports	*12:45*
	The Goldbergs	Dramatized Health Talk	Music	*1pm*
Your Farm Reporter	Life Can Be Beautiful	Music / The Radio Garden Club	Music / Let's Talk It Over	*1:15*
Music / Peables Takes Charge	The Road of Life	Music	Talk / Words and Music	*1:30*
Songs	This Day is Ours	The Marriage License Bureau / The Voice of Experience	Those Happy Gilmans	*1:45*

DAYTIME — WINTER, 1939

Sunday

	BLUE	CBS	MBS	NBC
2pm	The Magic Key of RCA	Americans All, Immigrants All	Alan Gerard, songs	Sunday Dinner at Aunt Fanny's
2:15			Meeting Today's Problems	
2:30		The Problem Clinic	Salvatore Mario de Stefano, harp	Barry McKinley, songs
2:45			The New Poetry Hour	Fables in Verse
3pm	Frank Simon Orchestra	New York Philharmonic Orchestra	On a Sunday Afternoon	Sunday Drivers
3:15				
3:30	Festival of Music		The People's Rally	Vivian Della Chiesa, songs
3:45				Bob Becker's Dog Talks
4pm	National Vespers		Benay Venuta's Variety Program	Ranger's Serenade
4:15				
4:30	Amanda's Party			The Crawford Caravan
4:45				
5pm	The Metropolitan Opera Auditions	Words Without Music	The Musical Steelmakers	Sunday Afternoon in Rosedale
5:15				
5:30	Cook's Travelogue	Ben Bernie, the Old Maestro	The Shadow	Spelling Bee
5:45	Dog Heroes			

DAYTIME — WINTER, 1939

Monday-Friday

BLUE	CBS	MBS	NBC	
Informational Talk	Doc Barclay's Daughters	Songs	Betty and Bob	2pm
	RFD #1, Irene Beasley	Lynn Cole Orchestra /	Arnold Grimm's Daughter	2:15
The Little Variety Show /	The American School of the Air	Ed Fitzgerald, talk	Valiant Lady	2:30
Music		Music / Ed Fitzgerald, talk (Mon, Weds, Fri)	Betty Crocker, cooking / Hymns of All Churches	2:45
Music	Music	Martha Deane, talk	The Story of Mary Marlin	3pm
			Ma Perkins	3:15
			Pepper Young's Family	3:30
Between the Bookends		David Harum	The Guiding Light	3:45
Club Matinee, Ransom Sherman	Informational Talk	News	Mary Noble, Backstage Wife	4pm
	Music	The Story of Myrt and Marge	Stella Dallas	4:15
		Hilltop House	Vic and Sade	4:30
		Music	Girl Alone	4:45
Music	Music / Current Questions Before the Senate	Women Make the News	Dick Tracy	5pm
Terry and the Pirates	Let's Pretend /	Music	Your Family and Mine	5:15
Don Winslow of the Navy	March of Games / Drama of the Sky	Little Orphan Annie	Jack Armstrong, the All-American Boy	5:30
The Tom Mix Ralston Straight Shooters	The Mighty Show	Music / The Children's Corner	Little Orphan Annie	5:45

DAYTIME — WINTER, 1939

Saturday

	BLUE	CBS	MBS	NBC
9am	The Breakfast Club	Richard Maxwell, songs	The Marriage License Bureau	The Wise Man
9:15		Montana Slim, songs	Syncopators Orchestra	The Saturday Morning Club
9:30		Fiddler's Fancy		
9:45			Manhatters Orchestra	The Gospel Singer
10am	The Three Romeos	National Hillbilly Champions	The Marriage Clinic	No School Today
10:15	Amanda's Party			
10:30	Swing Serenade	Four Corners Theater	Once Upon a Time	The Florence Hale Radio Column
10:45	Child Grows Up			The Charioteers Quartet
11am	Music Internationale	The New York Philharmonic Children's Concert	Raoul Nadeau, songs	Betty Moore, talk
11:15			Hayden Planetarium Talks	Dol Brissett Orchestra
11:30	Our Barn		The US Army Band	The Eastman School of Music
11:45				
12pm	The American Education Forum	Kate Smith Speaks	The Man on the Farm	Manhattan Melodies
12:15		Melody Ramblings		
12:30	The National Farm and Home Hour	Enoch Light Orchestra	Vincent Connolly, news	Call to Youth
12:45			Miracles Do Happen	Along Gypsy Trails
1pm		St. Louis Blues	The Columbia University Public Discussion	Robert Dolan Orchestra
1:15				
1:30	Ray Kinney Orchestra	Music for Moderns	Shirley Howard, songs	Campus Capers
1:45			Hitmakers Orchestra	

DAYTIME — WINTER, 1939

Saturday

	BLUE	CBS	MBS	NBC
2pm	Joe Reichman Orchestra	Men Against Death	Intercollegiate Debates	The Metropolitan Opera
2:15				
2:30	Del Courtney Orchestra	Buffalo Presents	Tony Candolari Orchestra	
2:45		Fran Hines, songs		
3pm	Rakov Orchestra	Merrymakers Orchestra	The London Music Hall	
3:15				
3:30	Allen Roth Orchestra	Poetic Strings		
3:45				
4pm	Club Matinee, Ransom Sherman	Public Affairs	Horse Racing	
4:15				
4:30		Dancepators Orchestra	The Gloomchasers	
4:45				
5pm	Sammy Watkins Orchestra	What Price America	Sammy Kaye Orchestra	Cosmopolitan Rhythms
5:15				The Stamp Club
5:30	Southwestern Stars	Eddy Duchin Orchestra		Swingology
5:45			Talk About Books	

EVENING — SPRING, 1939

Sunday

	BLUE	CBS	MBS	NBC
6pm	Watson, Flotsom and Jetsam	The Silver Theater	My Lucky Break	The Catholic Hour
6:15				
6:30	Jan Savitt Orchestra	Gateway to Hollywood	The Show of the Week	The Grouch Club
6:45				
7pm	Public Affairs	The People's Platform	The Bach Cantata Series	The Jello Program, Jack Benny
7:15	Eugene Conley, songs			
7:30	The Radio Guild	The Gulf Screen Guild Show	Frank Singiser, news	The Fitch Bandwagon
7:45			Stan Lomax, sports	
8pm	Cleveland Symphony Orchestra	The Dance Hour	The American Forum of the Air	The Chase and Sanborn Hour
8:15				
8:30				
8:45		Elmer Davis, news (8:55pm)		
9pm	The Hollywood Playhouse	The Ford Sunday Evening Hour	The People's Rally	The Manhattan Merry-Go-Round
9:15				
9:30	Walter Winchell's Jergens Journal		Richard Himber Orchestra	The American Album of Familiar Music
9:45	Irene Rich Dramas		The Three Marshalls	
10pm	Jan Savitt Orchestra	The Old Gold Program, Robert Benchley	The Goodwill Hour	The Circle
10:15				
10:30	Cheerio's Musical Mosaics	H. V. Kaltenborn, news		
10:45		Barry Wood Orchestra		

EVENING — SPRING, 1939

Monday

BLUE	CBS	MBS	NBC	
Bob Armstrong Orchestra	News and Sports	Uncle Don	Science in the News	6pm
Patricia Gilmore, songs	Howie Wing		Malcolm Claire, stories	6:15
Ray Perkins, piano	Bob Trout, news	Frank Singiser, news	George Hicks, news	6:30
Lowell Thomas, news	Enoch Light Orchestra	The Johnson Family	Bill Stern, sports	6:45
Orphans of Divorce	Amos 'n' Andy	Stan Lomax, sports	Mr. District Attorney	7pm
	Lum and Abner	The Answer Man	Public Affairs	7:15
Jimmy Kemper, songs	The Camel Caravan, Eddie Cantor	The Lone Ranger	Red Norvo Orchestra	7:30
Science on the March				7:45
Paul Martin Orchestra	The Cavalcade of America	Name Three	Al Pearce and His Gang	8pm
James J. Walker, comment				8:15
Tune Types	The Model Minstrels	Take a Note	The Voice of Firestone	8:30
	Elmer Davis, news (8:55pm)			8:45
The Eastman School of Music	The Lux Radio Theater	Gabriel Heatter, news	The Hour of Charm	9pm
		The Changing World		9:15
The National Radio Forum		WOR Symphony Orchestra	Eddy Duchin Orchestra	9:30
				9:45
True or False	Guy Lombardo Orchestra	Sammy Kaye Orchestra	The Carnation Contented Hour	10pm
		Bob Crosby Orchestra		10:15
Dr. I. Q., the Mental Banker	The Columbia Workshop	Pageant of Melody	Ruby Newman Orchestra	10:30
				10:45

EVENING — SPRING, 1939

Tuesday

	BLUE	CBS	MBS	NBC
6pm	Rita Rio Orchestra	News and Sports	Uncle Don	Eugene Conley, songs
6:15		Howie Wing		Malcolm Claire, stories
6:30	The Adrian Rollini Trio	Bob Trout, news	Frank Singiser, news	Angler and Hunter
6:45	Lowell Thomas, news	The Foundation of Democracy	The Johnson Family	Bill Stern, sports
7pm	Easy Aces	Amos 'n' Andy	Stan Lomax, sports	Mr. District Attorney
7:15	Mr. Keen, Tracer of Lost Persons	Jimmy Fidler, gossip	John Chapman, news	Vocal Varieties
7:30	Around New York	Second Husband	Woody Herman Orchestra	John T. Flynn, news
7:45			Sam Balter, sports	The Right Thing to Do
8pm	The Inside Story	Big Town	The Green Hornet	Johnny Presents
8:15				
8:30	Information, Please	The Tuesday Night Party, Dick Powell	Morton Gould Orchestra	For Men Only, George Jessel
8:45		Elmer Davis, news (8:55pm)		
9pm	Mary and Bob's True Story Hour	We, the People	Harold Hoffman, news	Battle of the Sexes
9:15			Dance Orchestra	
9:30	Dr. Rockwell's Brain Trust	Benny Goodman's Swing School	How to Make a Living	Fibber Magee and Molly
9:45				
10pm	If I Had the Chance	Cincinnati Conservatory Symphony	Benno Rabinoff, violin	The Pepsodent Show, Bob Hope
10:15				
10:30	Al Roth and Company	Barry Wood Orchestra	Ray Nelson Orchestra	Uncle Ezra's Radio Station
10:45		American Viewpoints		Name the Place

EVENING — SPRING, 1939

Wednesday

BLUE	CBS	MBS	NBC	
Jesse Crawford, organ	News and Sports	Uncle Don	Our American Schools	6pm
The Adrian Rollini Trio	Howie Wing		Malcolm Claire, stories	6:15
The Jester's Trio	Bob Trout, news	Frank Singiser, news	George Hicks, news	6:30
Lowell Thomas, news	Barry Wood Orchestra	The Johnson Family	Bill Stern, sports	6:45
Easy Aces	Amos 'n' Andy	Stan Lomax, sports	Mr. District Attorney	7pm
Mr. Keen, Tracer of Lost Persons	Lum and Abner	The Answer Man	Science in the News	7:15
George Jessel Jamboree	The Ask-It Basket	The Lone Ranger	The Revelers Quartet	7:30
			Sweetheart Theater	7:45
The Roy Shield Revue	Gangbusters	Alfredo Antonini Orchestra	One Man's Family	8pm
				8:15
Hobby Lobby	Chesterfield Presents	Welcome Neighbor	The Raleigh and Kool Show	8:30
	Elmer Davis, news (8:55pm)			8:45
Horse and Buggy Days	The Texaco Star Theater	Gabriel Heatter, news	Town Hall Tonight, Fred Allen	9pm
		Dance Orchestra		9:15
Wings for the Martins		Percy Faith Orchestra		9:30
				9:45
Ransom Sherman Variety	Ninety-Nine Men and a Girl, Hildegarde	There's a Law Against It	Kay Kyser's College of Musical Knowledge	10pm
				10:15
Public Interest in Democracy	It Can Be Done	Melodies from the Skies		10:30
				10:45

EVENING — SPRING, 1939

Thursday

	BLUE	CBS	MBS	NBC
6pm	George Duffy Orchestra	News and Sports	Uncle Don	Operalogue
6:15	Patricia Gilmore, songs	Howie Wing		Malcolm Claire, stories
6:30	The Milt Hearth Trio	Bob Trout, news	Frank Singiser, news	Harold Sears Orchestra
6:45	Lowell Thomas, news	Nan Wynn, songs	The Johnson Family	Bill Stern, sports
7pm	Easy Aces	Amos 'n' Andy	Stan Lomax, sports	Mr. District Attorney
7:15	Mr. Keen, Tracer of Lost Persons	Bob Edge's Outdoor Talks	The Inquiring Reporter	Vocal Varieties
7:30	Swing to Chiclets	The Joe E. Brown Show	Radie Harris, gossip	The Schaefer All-Star Parade
7:45			Sam Balter, sports	
8pm	The Parade of Progress in Foods	The Kate Smith Hour	The Green Hornet	The Royal Gelatin Hour, Rudy Vallee
8:15				
8:30	The Eastman School of Music		Sinfonietta	
8:45		Elmer Davis, news (8:55pm)		
9pm		Major Bowes' Original Amateur Hour	Gabriel Heatter, news	Good News of 1939
9:15	The Radio City Four		John Steele, news	
9:30	America's Town Meeting of the Air		Famous First Facts	
9:45				
10pm		Tune-Up Time	Eddy Duchin Orchestra	The Kraft Music Hall, Bing Crosby
10:15				
10:30	The NBC Minstrels		Henry Weber's Musical Revue	
10:45		American Viewpoints		

EVENING — SPRING, 1939

Friday

BLUE	CBS	MBS	NBC	
Alma Kitchell's Briefcase	News and Sports	Uncle Don	Get Ready for Tomorrow	6pm
The Milt Hearth Trio	Howie Wing		Malcolm Claire, stories	6:15
The Jester's Trio	Bob Trout, news	Frank Singiser, news	George Hicks, news	6:30
Lowell Thomas, news	Enoch Light Orchestra	The Johnson Family	Bill Stern, sports	6:45
Vocal Varieties	Amos 'n' Andy	Stan Lomax, sports	Mr. District Attorney	7pm
Jan Savitt Orchestra	Lum and Abner	The Answer Man	Jimmy Fidler, gossip	7:15
ABC of Radio Broadcasting	Buddy Clark's Musical Weekly	The Lone Ranger	The Revelers Quartet	7:30
The Adrian Rollini Trio			Sweetheart Theater	7:45
Don't Forget	The First Nighter Program	Guess Where	The Cities Service Concerts	8pm
				8:15
Jamboree	Burns and Allen	Author, Author		8:30
	Elmer Davis, news (8:55pm)			8:45
Paducah Plantation, Red Foley	The Campbell Playhouse	Gabriel Heatter, news	Waltz Time	9pm
		Dance Orchestra		9:15
The March of Time		Will Osborne Orchestra	Death Valley Days	9:30
				9:45
Madison Square Garden Boxing	Grand Central Station	The Boone County Jamboree	Guy Lombardo Orchestra	10pm
				10:15
	Believe It or Not	Jack Teagarden Orchestra	Uncle Ezra's Radio Station	10:30
			Cesar Saerchinger, news	10:45

EVENING — SPRING, 1939

Saturday

	BLUE	CBS	MBS	NBC
6pm	El Chico	News and Sports	Uncle Don	Kaltenmeyer's Kindergarten
6:15		Adventures in Science		
6:30	Renfrew of the Mounted	St. Louis Blues	Frank Singiser, news	Bill Stern, sports
6:45			Of Mutual Interest	Religion in the News
7pm	Message of Israel	Americans at Work	Stan Lomax, sports	Orchestra and Vocalists
7:15			Woody Herman Orchestra	
7:30	Uncle Jim's Question Bee	County Seat	The Charioteers Quartet	The Lives of Great Men
7:45			Sam Balter, sports	The Castilla Twins
8pm	Dance Orchestra	Johnny Presents	Tropical Serenade, Sagi Vela	Tommy Riggs and Betty Lou
8:15				
8:30	Brent House	Professor Quiz	San Francisco Symphony Orchestra	Avalon Variety Time, Red Skelton
8:45		Elmer Davis, news (8:55pm)		
9pm	The National Barn Dance	Honolulu Bound, Phil Baker	George Fisher, gossip	Vox Pop
9:15			The Sons of the Pioneers	
9:30		Stepping Along, Lew Parker	Symphonic Strings	The Hall of Fun
9:45				
10pm	NBC Symphony Orchestra	Your Hit Parade	Ted Osborne Orchestra	Arch Oboler's Plays
10:15				
10:30			The Gloomchasers	The Cross Country Swing Concert
10:45		Capitol Opinions		

DAYTIME — SPRING, 1939

Sunday

	BLUE	CBS	MBS	NBC
9am	The Children's Hour	From the Organ Loft	Rainbow House	Turn Back the Clock
9:15				Vagabond Adventures
9:30		Wings Over Jordan		Melody Moments
9:45				
10am	The American Art Quartet	The CBS Church of the Air	News	The National Radio Pulpit
10:15			Mildred Bailey Orchestra	
10:30	Russian Melodies	The Horn and Hardart Children's Hour	Uncle Don Reads the Comics	The Ancient Instruments Concert
10:45				
11am	The Musical Story Lady		Sunday Morning Symphony Orchestra	Julio Oyanguren, guitar
11:15	Neighbor Nell			Chimney House
11:30	The Southernaires Quartet	Major Bowes' Capitol Family		Tapestry Musicale
11:45				
12pm	The Radio City Music Hall		Dr. Charles Courboin, organ	Music for Moderns
12:15				
12:30		The Salt Lake Tabernacle Choir	The Lamplighter	The University of Chicago Round Table
12:45			Don Arres, songs	
1pm	Great Plays	The CBS Church of the Air	Milton Katims Orchestra	The Singing Story Lady
1:15				
1:30		Salute to the New York World's Fair	Salute to the New York World's Fair	Salute to the New York World's Fair
1:45				

DAYTIME — SPRING, 1939

Monday-Friday

BLUE	CBS	MBS	NBC	
The Breakfast Club	Richard Maxwell, songs	Music / Arthur Godfrey, songs	Happy Jack Turner, songs	*9am*
The Woman of Tomorrow	Manhattan Mother	Music / Modern Living	The Band Goes to Town	*9:15*
The Breakfast Club	Joyce Jordan, Girl Intern	Women Make the News	The Family Man	*9:30*
	Bachelor's Children	Talk and Music	The Gospel Singer	*9:45*
The Story of the Month	Pretty Kitty Kelly	The Pure Food Hour /	Central City	*10am*
Jane Arden	The Story of Myrt and Marge	Talk	John's Other Wife	*10:15*
Music / Smilin' Ed McConnell, songs	Hilltop House		Just Plain Bill	*10:30*
Breen and DeRose, songs	Stepmother		The Woman in White	*10:45*
The Story of Mary Marlin	Music / Music from Hollywood	Talk and Music	David Harum	*11am*
Vic and Sade	Scattergood Baines	Songs / The Heart of Julia Blake	Lorenzo Jones	*11:15*
Pepper Young's Family	Big Sister	Get Thin to Music	Young Widder Brown	*11:30*
Getting the Most Out of Life	Aunt Jenny's True Life Stories	Talk / The Theater Club	The Road of Life	*11:45*
Songs / Nellie Revell, talk	Mary Margaret McBride, talk / Kate Smith Speaks	Music / Victor Lindlahr, health	The Carters of Elm Street	*12pm*
Music	Her Honor, Nancy James	Music / The Voice of the Farm	The O'Neills	*12:15*
The National Farm and Home Hour	The Romance of Helen Trent	Vincent Connolly, news	Time for Thought	*12:30*
	Our Gal Sunday	The Consumers' Quiz	Stock Market Reports	*12:45*
	The Goldbergs	Dramatized Health Talk	Music	*1pm*
Your Farm Reporter	Life Can Be Beautiful	The Story of Myrt and Marge	Music / Let's Talk It Over	*1:15*
Peables Takes Charge	The Road of Life	Hilltop House	Talk / Words and Music	*1:30*
Songs	This Day is Ours	The Radio Garden Club / The Voice of Experience	Those Happy Gilmans	*1:45*

DAYTIME — SPRING, 1939

Sunday

	BLUE	CBS	MBS	NBC
2pm	The Magic Key of RCA	Americans All, Immigrants All	Live and Learn	Sunday Dinner at Aunt Fanny's
2:15			Meeting Today's Problems	
2:30		Words Without Music	The New Poetry Hour	Barry McKinley, songs
2:45				The Kidoodlers Novelty Quartet
3pm	The Crawford Caravan	New York Philharmonic Orchestra	Sports	Sunday Drivers
3:15				
3:30	Festival of Music			Name the Place
3:45				Bob Becker's Dog Talks
4pm	National Vespers			Oscar Shumsky, violin
4:15				Deliberate Reflections
4:30	Vivian Della Chiesa, songs			The World is Yours
4:45				
5pm	The Metropolitan Opera Auditions	World News Roundup	The Musical Steelmakers	Ranger's Serenade
5:15				
5:30	The Reader's Guide	Ben Bernie, the Old Maestro	Benay Venuta's Variety Program	Spelling Bee
5:45	Dog Heroes			

DAYTIME — SPRING, 1939

Monday-Friday

BLUE	CBS	MBS	NBC	
Informational Talk	Doc Barclay's Daughters	Martha Deane, talk	Betty and Bob	*2pm*
	The Life and Love of Dr. Susan		Arnold Grimm's Daughter	*2:15*
The Little Variety Show /	The American School of the Air		Valiant Lady	*2:30*
Music		David Harum	Betty Crocker, cooking / Hymns of All Churches	*2:45*
Music	Music	Sports	The Story of Mary Marlin	*3pm*
			Ma Perkins	*3:15*
			Pepper Young's Family	*3:30*
Songs / Amanda's Party			The Guiding Light	*3:45*
Club Matinee, Ransom Sherman	Informational Talk		Mary Noble, Backstage Wife	*4pm*
	Music		Stella Dallas	*4:15*
			Vic and Sade	*4:30*
			Girl Alone	*4:45*
Music	Music / Current Questions Before the Senate		Dick Tracy	*5pm*
Sheriff Bob	Music		Your Family and Mine	*5:15*
Don Winslow of the Navy	March of Games / Informational Talk	Smilin' Jack	Jack Armstrong, the All-American Boy	*5:30*
Street Interviews	The Mighty Show	Music	Little Orphan Annie	*5:45*

DAYTIME — SPRING, 1939

Saturday

	BLUE	CBS	MBS	NBC
9am	The Breakfast Club	Richard Maxwell, songs	Steve Severn's Pet Club	Texas Jim Robertson, songs
9:15		Montana Slim, songs	Syncopators Orchestra	Norman Cloutier Orchestra
9:30		Melody Ramblings	Women Make the News	
9:45		Fiddler's Fancy	Natural History Talk	The Crackerjack Quartet
10am	The Ranch Boys Trio	National Hillbilly Champions	The Marriage Clinic	The Wise Man
10:15	Amanda's Party			No School Today
10:30	Barry McKinley, songs	Saturday Morning Serenade	Once Upon a Time	The Florence Hale Radio Column
10:45	Child Grows Up			The Armchair Quartet
11am	Music Internationale	Cincinnati Conservatory Symphony	Organ Recital	Music Styled for You
11:15			Hayden Planetarium Talks	
11:30	Our Barn		The US Army Band	The National Federation of Music Clubs
11:45				
12pm	The American Education Forum	Kate Smith Speaks	The Man on the Farm	Manhattan Melodies
12:15		When We Were Young		
12:30	The National Farm and Home Hour	Let's Pretend	Vincent Connolly, news	Call to Youth
12:45			Leo Freudberg Orchestra	Along Gypsy Trails
1pm		Enoch Light Orchestra	The Columbia University Public Discussion	Jean Ellington, songs
1:15				The Stamp Club
1:30	The Little Variety Show	Moods for Moderns	Bernie Cummins Orchestra	Campus Capers
1:45			Radio Garden Club	

DAYTIME — SPRING, 1939

Saturday

	BLUE	CBS	MBS	NBC
2pm	The Metropolitan Opera	Men Against Death	Manhatters Orchestra	
2:15			Hitmakers Orchestra	Ray Kinney Orchestra
2:30		Kansas City Symphony Orchestra	Sports	
2:45		Fran Hines, songs		Matinee in Rhythm
3pm		Sports		Golden Memories
3:15				
3:30				Al Roth and Company
3:45				
4pm				Dol Brissett Orchestra
4:15				
4:30				Southwestern Stars
4:45				
5pm				The Three Cheers
5:15				Youth Meets the Government
5:30	Benny Carter Orchestra	Jack Marshard Orchestra	Sammy Kaye Orchestra	
5:45				

EVENING — SUMMER, 1939

Sunday

	BLUE	CBS	MBS	NBC
6pm	The Canadian Grenadiers	The Gay Nineties Revue	My Lucky Break	The Catholic Hour
6:15				
6:30	The Dinah Shore Show	The Gateway to Hollywood Summer Theater	The Show of the Week	The Grouch Club
6:45	European News			
7pm	Vicki Chase, songs	The Alibi Club	The Green Hornet	The Aldrich Family
7:15				
7:30	The Radio Guild	The Gulf Musical Playhouse	Frank Singiser, news	The Fitch Bandwagon
7:45			Stan Lomax, sports	
8pm	NBC Symphony Orchestra	The Adventures of Ellery Queen	The American Forum of the Air	The Chase and Sanborn Hour
8:15				
8:30				
8:45		Elmer Davis, news (8:55pm)		
9pm	The Hollywood Playhouse	The Ford Summer Hour	New York Town, Ed East	The Manhattan Merry-Go-Round
9:15				
9:30	Walter Winchell's Jergens Journal		Vincent Lopez Orchestra	The American Album of Familiar Music
9:45	Irene Rich Dramas			
10pm	The Voice of Hawaii	Let's Go to the Fair	The Goodwill Hour	The Circle
10:15				
10:30	Cheerio's Musical Mosaics	H. V. Kaltenborn, news		
10:45		Public Affairs		

EVENING — SUMMER, 1939

Monday

BLUE	CBS	MBS	NBC	
Ricardo and His Caballeros	Edwin C. Hill, news	Uncle Don	Science in the News	6pm
Lee Morse, songs	Mel Allen, sports		Ford Bond, sports	6:15
Ray Perkins, piano	Uncle Jonathan	Frank Singiser, news	The Stamp Club	6:30
Lowell Thomas, news	Judith Arlen, songs	The Johnson Family	Bill Stern, sports	6:45
Orphans of Divorce	Amos 'n' Andy	Stan Lomax, sports	Chesterfield Time	7pm
	Michael Loring, songs	The Answer Man	The Luther Layman Singers	7:15
Frankie Masters Orchestra	Blondie	The Lone Ranger	Sensation and Swing	7:30
Science on the March				7:45
Order of Adventurers	The Cavalcade of America	Breezin' Along	Dick Tracy	8pm
				8:15
True or False	The Model Minstrels	Benay Venuta's Variety Program	The Voice of Firestone	8:30
	Elmer Davis, news (8:55pm)			8:45
The Magic Key of RCA	Man About Hollywood	Arthur Hale, news	Dr. I. Q., the Mental Banker	9pm
		Edwin C. Hill, news		9:15
Gray Gordon Orchestra	Guy Lombardo Orchestra	Author, Author	Horace Heidt Orchestra	9:30
				9:45
	So This is Radio	Raymond Gram Swing, news	The Carnation Contented Hour	10pm
		Love Orchestra		10:15
The National Radio Forum	The Grant Park Concerts	Pageant of Melody	Al Donahue Orchestra	10:30
				10:45

EVENING — SUMMER, 1939

Tuesday

	BLUE	CBS	MBS	NBC
6pm	Gordon Jenkins Orchestra	Edwin C. Hill, news	Uncle Don	Dol Brisette Orchestra
6:15	George Crook, organ	Mel Allen, sports		Ford Bond, sports
6:30	The Ink Spots	Michael Loring, news	Frank Singiser, news	Irving Miller Orchestra
6:45	Lowell Thomas, news	Judith Arlen, songs	The Johnson Family	Bill Stern, sports
7pm	Easy Aces	Amos 'n' Andy	Stan Lomax, sports	Chesterfield Time
7:15	Mr. Keen, Tracer of Lost Persons	That's What I Said	Elliott Roosevelt, comment	Quicksilver
7:30	Around New York	Second Husband	Everett Hoagland Orchestra	Youth vs. Age
7:45			Sam Balter, sports	
8pm	The Inside Story	The Human Adventure	The Green Hornet	Johnny Presents
8:15				
8:30	Information, Please		Benno Rabinoff, violin	Eugene Conley, songs
8:45		Elmer Davis, news (8:55pm)		
9pm	The Old Gold Program, Robert Benchley	We, the People	Arthur Hale, news	Battle of the Sexes
9:15			Edwin C. Hill, news	
9:30	True Story Time	The Camel Caravan	Help Yourself	Alec Templeton Time
9:45				
10pm	If I Had the Chance	Time to Shine	Morton Gould Orchestra	Mr. District Attorney
10:15				
10:30	Little Jack Little Orchestra	H. V. Kaltenborn, news	Dance Orchestra	Uncle Walter's Dog House
10:45		Armchair Adventures		

EVENING — SUMMER, 1939

Wednesday

BLUE	CBS	MBS	NBC	
Little Jack Little Orchestra	Edwin C. Hill, news	Uncle Don	Art in the News	*6pm*
	Mel Allen, sports		Ford Bond, sports	*6:15*
The Ink Spots	Uncle Jonathan	Frank Singiser, news	The Stamp Club	*6:30*
Lowell Thomas, news	Judith Arlen, songs	The Johnson Family	Bill Stern, sports	*6:45*
Easy Aces	Amos 'n' Andy	Stan Lomax, sports	Chesterfield Time	*7pm*
Mr. Keen, Tracer of Lost Persons	Michael Loring, songs	The Answer Man	String Quartet	*7:15*
Diversion Without Exercise	The People's Platform	The Lone Ranger	The Revelers Quartet	*7:30*
			Johnny Messner Orchestra	*7:45*
Ransom Sherman Variety	Honolulu Bound, Phil Baker	Name Three	One Man's Family	*8pm*
				8:15
Hobby Lobby	Chesterfield Presents	Edwin Franko Goldman Band	The Raleigh and Kool Show	*8:30*
	Elmer Davis, news (8:55pm)			*8:45*
Horse and Buggy Days	The Lewisohn Stadium Concerts	Arthur Hale, news	What's My Name	*9pm*
		Edwin C. Hill, news		*9:15*
Freddy Martin Orchestra		Percy Faith Orchestra	George Jessel's Celebrity Program	*9:30*
				9:45
National Symphony		Raymond Gram Swing, news	Kay Kyser's College of Musical Knowledge	*10pm*
		Harold Stokes Orchestra		*10:15*
Public Interest in Democracy	American Viewpoints	Melodies from the Skies		*10:30*
	Armchair Adventures			*10:45*

EVENING — SUMMER, 1939

Thursday

	BLUE	CBS	MBS	NBC
6pm	Ruth Peters, songs	Edwin C. Hill, news	Uncle Don	Jimmy Kemper, songs
6:15	Patricia Gilmore, songs	Mel Allen, sports		Ford Bond, sports
6:30	Ella Fitzgerald Orchestra	Mitchell Loring, songs	Frank Singiser, news	Lucille Linwood, songs
6:45	Lowell Thomas, news	Judith Arlen, songs	The Johnson Family	Bill Stern, sports
7pm	Easy Aces	Amos 'n' Andy	Stan Lomax, sports	Chesterfield Time
7:15	Mr. Keen, Tracer of Lost Persons	Music By Malneck	Elliott Roosevelt, comment	The Luther Layman Singers
7:30	Jack Joy Orchestra	The Joe E. Brown Show	The Charioteers Quartet	The Schaefer All-Star Parade
7:45			Sam Balter, sports	
8pm	Vicki Chase, songs	Buddy Clark's Summer Colony	Kay Kyser's College of Musical Knowledge	The Royal Gelatin Hour, Rudy Vallee
8:15				
8:30	It's Up to You	Music from Montreal		
8:45		Elmer Davis, news (8:55pm)		
9pm	Promenade Symphony of Toronto	Major Bowes' Original Amateur Hour	Arthur Hale, news	America's Lost Plays
9:15			Edwin C. Hill, news	
9:30			Sinfonietta	
9:45				
10pm	One Thousand and One Wives	The Columbia Workshop	Ted Fio Rito Orchestra	The Kraft Music Hall, Bob Burns
10:15				
10:30	Glen Bainum Orchestra	American Viewpoints	Busman's Holiday	
10:45		Armchair Adventures		

EVENING — SUMMER, 1939

Friday

BLUE	CBS	MBS	NBC	
Alma Kitchell's Briefcase	Edwin C. Hill, news	Uncle Don	The Four Belles	6pm
Gray Gordon Orchestra	Mel Allen, sports		Ford Bond, sports	6:15
	Uncle Jonathan	Frank Singiser, news	The Stamp Club	6:30
Lowell Thomas, news	Enoch Light Orchestra	The Johnson Family	Bill Stern, sports	6:45
Artie Shaw Orchestra	Amos 'n' Andy	Stan Lomax, sports	Chesterfield Time	7pm
	The Parker Family	The Answer Man	Jesse Crawford, organ	7:15
The Three Cheers	Michael Loring, songs	The Lone Ranger	The Revelers Quartet	7:30
ABC of Radio Broadcasting	Bob Edge's Outdoor Talks		Angler and Hunter	7:45
The National Music Camp	Under Western Skies	Welcome Neighbor	The Cities Service Concerts	8pm
				8:15
Don't Forget	Johnny Presents Dramatized Short Stories	WOR Symphony Orchestra		8:30
	Elmer Davis, news (8:55pm)			8:45
Paducah Plantation, Red Foley	The Musical Comedy Hour	Arthur Hale, news	Waltz Time	9pm
		Edwin C. Hill, news		9:15
Harry Horlick Orchestra	The First Nighter Program	Take a Note	Death Valley Days	9:30
				9:45
The Grant Park Concerts	Grand Central Station	Raymond Gram Swing, news	Guy Lombardo Orchestra	10pm
		Teddy Powell Orchestra		10:15
Horace Heidt Orchestra	Believe It or Not	Henry Weber's Musical Revue	America Unlimited	10:30
			Jan Savitt Orchestra	10:45

EVENING — SUMMER, 1939

Saturday

	BLUE	CBS	MBS	NBC
6pm	El Chico	News and Sports	Uncle Don	Kaltenmeyer's Kindergarten
6:15		Dance Orchestra		
6:30	Renfrew of the Mounted	Albert Warner, news	Frank Singiser, news	The Art of Living
6:45		Today in Europe	The Charioteers Quartet	Bill Stern, sports
7pm	Message of Israel	Americans at Work	Stan Lomax, sports	Dance Orchestra
7:15			Elliott Roosevelt, comment	
7:30	Uncle Jim's Question Bee	County Seat	Cats and Jammers	
7:45			Sam Balter, sports	
8pm	Dance Orchestra	The Melody Club	Tropical Serenade, Don Arres	Dick Tracy
8:15				
8:30	Brent House	Professor Quiz	Hawaii Calls	Avalon Variety Time, Red Skelton
8:45		Elmer Davis, news (8:55pm)		
9pm	The National Barn Dance	Your Hit Parade	George Fisher, gossip	Vox Pop
9:15			The Sons of the Pioneers	
9:30			Symphonic Strings	Arch Oboler's Plays
9:45		Saturday Night Serenade		
10pm	Barney Rapp		The Chicagoland Music Festival	Benny Goodman Orchestra
10:15		San Francisco Symphony Orchestra		
10:30	Al Donahue Orchestra		Music by Moonlight	The Cross Country Swing Concert
10:45		Armchair Adventures		

DAYTIME — SUMMER, 1939

Sunday

	BLUE	CBS	MBS	NBC
9am	The Children's Hour	From the Organ Loft	Rainbow House	Turn Back the Clock
9:15				Vagabond Adventures
9:30		Aubade for Strings		Sunday Drivers
9:45				
10am	The American Art Quartet	The CBS Church of the Air	News	Highlights of the Bible
10:15			Pauline Alpert, piano	
10:30	Russian Melodies	Wings Over Jordan	Uncle Don Reads the Comics	The Horn and Hardart Children's Hour
10:45				
11am	The Musical Story Lady	News and Rhythm	Arranged By	
11:15	Neighbor Nell			
11:30	The Southernaires Quartet	Major Bowes' Capitol Family	Chorus from the World's Fair	News
11:45				Vernon Crane's Storybook
12pm	The Radio City Music Hall		Harry Farbman, violin	Walter Logan's Musicale
12:15				
12:30		The Salt Lake Tabernacle Choir	Betty and Buddy, songs	On Your Job
12:45			Don Arres, songs	
1pm	Waterloo Junction	The CBS Church of the Air	Milton Katims Orchestra	Music for Moderns
1:15				
1:30	Continental Varieties	Walberg Brown Strings	Salvatore Mario de Stefano, harp	Sunday Symphonette
1:45			Bob Crosby Orchestra	

DAYTIME — SUMMER, 1939

Monday-Friday

BLUE	CBS	MBS	NBC	
The Woman of Tomorrow	Richard Maxwell, songs	Music / Arthur Godfrey, songs	Women in the News	*9am*
	Meet the Dixons	Music / Modern Living	The Band Goes to Town	*9:15*
The Breakfast Club	Manhattan Mother	Women Make the News	The Family Man / Isabel Manning Hewson, food	*9:30*
	Bachelor's Children	Talk and Music	Life Can Be Beautiful	*9:45*
Thunder Over Paradise	Pretty Kitty Kelly	The Career of Alice Blair	The Man I Married	*10am*
Music	The Story of Myrt and Marge	Meet Miss Julia	John's Other Wife	*10:15*
Music / The Jack Berch Show	Hilltop House	The Norman Brokenshire Show	Just Plain Bill	*10:30*
Breen and DeRose, songs	Stepmother	Music / The Album of Life	The Woman in White	*10:45*
The Story of Mary Marlin	Music / Music from Hollywood	Talk and Music	David Harum	*11am*
Vic and Sade	Scattergood Baines	Songs / The Heart of Julia Blake	Lorenzo Jones	*11:15*
Pepper Young's Family	Big Sister	Get Thin to Music	Young Widder Brown	*11:30*
Getting the Most Out of Life	Aunt Jenny's True Life Stories	Talk / The Radio Garden Club	The Road of Life	*11:45*
Songs	Joyce Jordan, Girl Intern	Music / Victor Lindlahr, health	Luigi Romanelli Orchestra	*12pm*
Music	When a Girl Marries	Talk / The Jack Berch Show	The O'Neills	*12:15*
The National Farm and Home Hour	The Romance of Helen Trent	Vincent Connolly, news	Time for Thought	*12:30*
	Our Gal Sunday	The Consumers' Quiz	Stock Market Reports	*12:45*
	The Goldbergs	Dramatized Health Talk	Music	*1pm*
	Life Can Be Beautiful	The Story of Myrt and Marge	Music / Let's Talk It Over	*1:15*
Peables Takes Charge	The Road of Life	Hilltop House	News	*1:30*
Songs	This Day is Ours	Music / Vaughn de Leath, songs	Talk / Words and Music	*1:45*

DAYTIME — SUMMER, 1939

Sunday

	BLUE	CBS	MBS	NBC
2pm	The National Music Camp	Democracy in Action	Sports	Sunday Dinner at Aunt Fanny's
2:15				
2:30	Treasure Trails of Songs	Mark Warnow Orchestra		The University of Chicago Round Table
2:45				
3pm	The Three Cheers	New York Philharmonic Orchestra		Chautauqua Symphony Orchestra
3:15	Joseph Jackson, books			
3:30	Al Roth Presents			
3:45				
4pm	National Vespers	So You Think You Know Music		John Gunther, war talk
4:15				
4:30	Vivian Della Chiesa, songs	Syncopation Piece		The World is Yours
4:45		St. Louis Orchestra		
5pm	Irving Miller Orchestra	World News Roundup	Nobody's Children	The Hall of Fun
5:15				
5:30		Chorus from the World's Fair	Teddy Powell Orchestra	Spelling Bee
5:45	Letters Home from New York World's Fair			

DAYTIME — SUMMER, 1939

Monday-Friday

BLUE	CBS	MBS	NBC	
Informational Talk	Doc Barclay's Daughters	Martha Deane, talk	Betty and Bob	2pm
	The Life and Love of Dr. Susan		Arnold Grimm's Daughter	2:15
Music / The Little Variety Show	Your Family and Mine		Valiant Lady	2:30
	Songs / Enoch Light Orchestra	David Harum	Betty Crocker, cooking / Hymns of All Churches	2:45
Music	Music	Sports	The Story of Mary Marlin	3pm
			Ma Perkins	3:15
			Pepper Young's Family	3:30
Between the Bookends			The Guiding Light	3:45
Club Matinee, Ransom Sherman			Mary Noble, Backstage Wife	4pm
			Stella Dallas	4:15
			Vic and Sade	4:30
			Midstream	4:45
Music			The O'Neills	5pm
The Trouble with Marriage			Music	5:15
The Affairs of Anthony		Music		5:30
Music	March of Games / Informational Talk		Little Orphan Annie	5:45

DAYTIME — SUMMER, 1939

Saturday

	BLUE	CBS	MBS	NBC
9am	The Breakfast Club	Richard Maxwell, songs	Betty and Buddy, songs	Texas Jim Robertson, songs
9:15		Fiddler's Fancy	Syncopators Orchestra	Annette Hastings, songs
9:30		National Hillbilly Champions	Women Make the News	Isabel Manning Hewson, food
9:45				The Crackerjack Quartet
10am	The Morin Sisters, songs	The Deep River Boys	The Marriage Clinic	The Wise Man
10:15	Amanda's Party	Leo Weber, organ		No School Today
10:30	Barry McKinley, songs	Saturday Morning Serenade	The Model Airplane Club	The Bright Idea Club
10:45	Child Grows Up		The First Offender	
11am	The Ross Trio	The Dorian String Quartet		Chautauqua Concert for Young People
11:15	Bill Stern's Sports School		Hayden Planetarium Talks	
11:30	Our Barn	The Columbia Concert Hall	The US Army Band	The Armchair Quartet
11:45				Nature Sketches
12pm	Luigi Romanelli Orchestra	Dance Orchestra	The Gloomchasers	Annette Hastings, songs
12:15		Women in the World of Tomorrow		
12:30	The National Farm and Home Hour	Let's Pretend	Vincent Connolly, news	Call to Youth
12:45			Midday	The Charioteers
			Melodies	Quartet
1pm		Enoch Light Orchestra	Xavier Cugat Orchestra	Jean Ellington, songs
1:15				The Stamp Club
1:30	The Little Variety Show	What Price America	Dance Orchestra	Words and Music
1:45				

DAYTIME — SUMMER, 1939

Saturday

	BLUE	CBS	MBS	NBC
2pm	Morton Franklin's Notes of Grace	Men Against Death	Ralph Ginsberg Orchestra	Ray Kinney Orchestra
2:15				
2:30	Indiana Indigo	The Brush Creek Follies	Dance Orchestra	Matinee in Rhythm
2:45				
3pm	Dance Orchestra	Sports	Sports	Golden Memories
3:15				
3:30	Crazy Quilt in Rhythm			Roy Eldridge Orchestra
3:45				
4pm	Club Matinee, Ransom Sherman			Paul La Valle Orchestra
4:15				
4:30				The Crawford Caravan
4:45				
5pm	Ricardo and His Caballeros	St. Louis Blues	Dance Orchestra	The National Music Camp
5:15				
5:30	Dance Orchestra	Dance Orchestra	Tommy Tucker Orchestra	Summertime Swing
5:45				Dance Orchestra

EVENING — FALL, 1939

Sunday

	BLUE	CBS	MBS	NBC
6pm	New Friends of Music	The Silver Theater	Listen, America	The Catholic Hour
6:15				
6:30		Gateway to Hollywood	The Show of the Week	The Grouch Club
6:45				
7pm	The Dinah Shore Show	European News Roundup	The Bach Cantata Series	The Jello Program, Jack Benny
7:15	European News			
7:30	Mr. District Attorney	The Gulf Screen Guild Show	Frank Singiser, news	The Fitch Bandwagon
7:45			Overseas News	
8pm	Festival of Music	The Campbell Playhouse	The American Forum of the Air	The Chase and Sanborn Hour
8:15				
8:30	Youth vs. Age			
8:45		Elmer Davis, news (8:55pm)		
9pm	Walter Winchell's Jergens Journal	The Ford Sunday Evening Hour	Benay Venuta's Variety Program	The Manhattan Merry-Go-Round
9:15	The Parker Family			
9:30	Irene Rich Dramas		Arthur Hale, news	The American Album of Familiar Music
9:45	The Colgate Sports Newsreel, Bill Stern		Jimmy Dorsey Orchestra	
10pm	William Hillman, news	The Adventures of Ellery Queen	The Goodwill Hour	The Hour of Charm
10:15	Jan Savitt Orchestra			
10:30	Cheerio's Musical Mosaics			The Primrose String Quartet
10:45				

EVENING — FALL, 1939

Monday

BLUE	CBS	MBS	NBC	
Reggie Childs Orchestra	Edwin C. Hill, news	Uncle Don	Dance Orchestra	6pm
Annette Hastings, songs	Mel Allen, sports		John Lardner, sports	6:15
Ray Perkins, piano	H. V. Kaltenborn, news	Frank Singiser, news	The Stamp Club	6:30
Lowell Thomas, news	The World Today	The Johnson Family	Dance Orchestra	6:45
Ray Kinney Orchestra	Amos 'n' Andy	Stan Lomax, sports	Chesterfield Time	7pm
Science on the March	Lum and Abner	The Answer Man	I Love a Mystery	7:15
One of the Finest	Blondie	The Lone Ranger	Sensation and Swing	7:30
Science on the March				7:45
Sherlock Holmes	Tune-Up Time	Breezin' Along	Tommy Riggs and Betty Lou	8pm
				8:15
True or False	The Model Minstrels	The Green Hornet	The Voice of Firestone	8:30
	Elmer Davis, news (8:55pm)			8:45
Allen Roth Orchestra	The Lux Radio Theater	Gabriel Heatter, news	Dr. I. Q., the Mental Banker	9pm
		Edwin C. Hill, news		9:15
Youth Questions the Headlines		Author, Author	Alex Templeton Time	9:30
				9:45
Charlie Barnett Orchestra	Guy Lombardo Orchestra	Raymond Gram Swing, news	The Carnation Contented Hour	10pm
		Fulton Lewis Jr., news		10:15
The National Radio Forum	Rosa Tentoni, songs	Pageant of Melody	Barry Winton Orchestra	10:30
				10:45

EVENING — FALL, 1939

Tuesday

	BLUE	CBS	MBS	NBC
6pm	Dinner Date	Edwin C. Hill, news	Uncle Don	The Safety Council Program
6:15		Mel Allen, sports		John Lardner, sports
6:30		H. V. Kaltenborn, news	Frank Singiser, news	Blue Barron Orchestra
6:45	Lowell Thomas, news	The World Today	The Johnson Family	Dance Orchestra
7pm	Easy Aces	Amos 'n' Andy	Stan Lomax, sports	Chesterfield Time
7:15	Mr. Keen, Tracer of Lost Persons	Jimmy Fidler, gossip	Elliott Roosevelt, comment	I Love a Mystery
7:30	Frank Novak Orchestra	Second Husband	Dance Orchestra	Around New York
7:45			Sam Balter, sports	
8pm	The Aldrich Family	Big Town	The Green Hornet	Johnny Presents
8:15				
8:30	Information, Please	The Tuesday Night Party, Walter O' Keefe	Morton Gould Orchestra	Pot o' Gold
8:45		Elmer Davis, news (8:55pm)		
9pm	The Old Gold Program, Robert Benchley	We, the People	Arthur Hale, news	Battle of the Sexes
9:15			Edwin C. Hill, news	
9:30	Letters Which Have Made History	The Camel Caravan	Help Yourself	Fibber Magee and Molly
9:45				
10pm	The Ransom Sherman Show	Time to Shine	Raymond Gram Swing, news	The Pepsodent Show, Bob Hope
10:15			Fulton Lewis Jr., news	
10:30	Fun with the Famous	Judith Arlen, songs	The Mozart Concerto Series	Uncle Walter's Dog House
10:45		Public Affairs		

EVENING — FALL, 1939

Wednesday

BLUE	CBS	MBS	NBC	
Little Jack Little Orchestra	Edwin C. Hill, news	Uncle Don	The Luther Layman Singers	6pm
	Mel Allen, sports		John Lardner, sports	6:15
The Gulden Serenaders	H. V. Kaltenborn, news	Frank Singiser, news	The Stamp Club	6:30
Lowell Thomas, news	The World Today	The Johnson Family	Dance Orchestra	6:45
Easy Aces	Amos 'n' Andy	Stan Lomax, sports	Chesterfield Time	7pm
Mr. Keen, Tracer of Lost Persons	Lum and Abner	The Answer Man	I Love a Mystery	7:15
Norman Cloutier Orchestra	Burns and Allen	The Lone Ranger	The Revelers Quartet	7:30
			Johnny Messner Orchestra	7:45
These Amazing Years	Al Pearce and His Gang	Dance Orchestra	The Hollywood Playhouse	8pm
				8:15
Quicksilver	Chesterfield Presents	Sherlock Holmes	Avalon Variety Time, Red Skelton	8:30
	Elmer Davis, news (8:55pm)			8:45
Horse and Buggy Days	The Texaco Star Theater	Gabriel Heatter, news	The Fred Allen Show	9pm
		Edwin C. Hill, news		9:15
The Radio Guild		Percy Faith Orchestra		9:30
				9:45
The Fisk Jubilee Choir	Indianapolis Symphony Orchestra	Raymond Gram Swing, news	Kay Kyser's College of Musical Knowledge	10pm
		Fulton Lewis Jr., news		10:15
Harry Kogen Orchestra		Romance in Rhythm		10:30
				10:45

EVENING — FALL, 1939

Thursday

	BLUE	CBS	MBS	NBC
6pm	Ruth Peters, songs	Edwin C. Hill, news	Uncle Don	June Hynd's Guest Book
6:15		Mel Allen, sports		John Lardner, sports
6:30	Little Jack Little Orchestra	H. V. Kaltenborn, news	Frank Singiser, news	Reggie Childs Orchestra
6:45	Lowell Thomas, news	The World Today	The Johnson Family	Dance Orchestra
7pm	Easy Aces	Amos 'n' Andy	Stan Lomax, sports	Chesterfield Time
7:15	Mr. Keen, Tracer of Lost Persons	Judith Arlen, songs	Elliott Roosevelt, comment	I Love a Mystery
7:30	One of the Finest	Vox Pop	Fables in Rhythm	The Schaefer All-Star Parade
7:45	Sports Comments		Sam Balter, sports	
8pm	Don't Forget	The Ask-It Basket	Kay Kyser's College of Musical Knowledge	One Man's Family
8:15				
8:30	The Tip Top Show, Joe Penner	Strange As It Seems		Those We Love
8:45		Elmer Davis, news (8:55pm)		
9pm	Vicki Chase, songs	Major Bowes' Original Amateur Hour	Arthur Hale, news	Good News of 1940
9:15			Edwin C. Hill, news	
9:30	America's Town Meeting of the Air		Sinfonietta	
9:45				
10pm		The Columbia Workshop	Raymond Gram Swing, news	The Kraft Music Hall, Bing Crosby
10:15			Fulton Lewis Jr., news	
10:30	The Roy Shield Revue	Americans at Work	We Want a Touchdown	
10:45				

EVENING — FALL, 1939

Friday

BLUE	CBS	MBS	NBC	
Alma Kitchell's Briefcase	Edwin C. Hill, news	Uncle Don	The Torch of Progress	6pm
Ed Dooley, sports	Mel Allen, sports		John Lardner, sports	6:15
The Gulden Serenaders	H. V. Kaltenborn, news	Frank Singiser, news	The Stamp Club	6:30
Lowell Thomas, news	The World Today	The Johnson Family	Dance Orchestra	6:45
Jean Cavall, songs	Amos 'n' Andy	Stan Lomax, sports	Chesterfield Time	7pm
Radio Magic	Lum and Abner	The Answer Man	I Love a Mystery	7:15
African Trek	Professor Quiz	The Lone Ranger	The Revelers Quartet	7:30
			Magic Waves	7:45
Order of Adventurers	The Kate Smith Hour	Quixie Doodle	The Cities Service Concerts	8pm
				8:15
Carson Robison's Buckeroos		WOR Symphony Orchestra		8:30
	Elmer Davis, news (8:55pm)			8:45
Paducah Plantation, Red Foley	Johnny Presents Dramatized Short Stories	Gabriel Heatter, news	Waltz Time	9pm
		Edwin C. Hill, news		9:15
Freddy Martin Orchestra	The First Nighter Program	Ernie Fio Rito's Studies in Contrast	For Men Only, George Jessel	9:30
				9:45
One Thousand and One Wives	Grand Central Station	Raymond Gram Swing, news	Guy Lombardo Orchestra	10pm
		Overseas News		10:15
Melody Marathon	Young Man with a Band	Fulton Lewis Jr., news	Cesar Searchinger, news	10:30
		Jimmy Dorsey Orchestra	Jan Savitt Orchestra	10:45

EVENING — FALL, 1939

Saturday

	BLUE	CBS	MBS	NBC
6pm	El Chico	Eddy Duchin Orchestra	Uncle Don	Kaltenmeyer's Kindergarten
6:15	Ed Dooley, sports	Mel Allen, sports		
6:30	Renfrew of the Mounted	What's Art to Me	Frank Singiser, news	Religion in the News
6:45		Today in Europe	The Charioteers Quartet	John Lardner, sports
7pm	Message of Israel	The People's Platform	Stan Lomax, sports	What's My Name
7:15			Elliott Roosevelt, comment	
7:30	Uncle Jim's Question Bee	The Gay Nineties Revue	Cats and Jammers	Art for Your Sake
7:45			Sam Balter, sports	
8pm	Dance Orchestra	Gangbusters	Name Three	Jimmy Dorsey Orchestra
8:15				
8:30	Brent House	Wayne King Orchestra	Hawaii Calls	Stop Me If You've Heard This One
8:45		Elmer Davis, news (8:55pm)		
9pm	The National Barn Dance	Your Hit Parade	Gabriel Heatter, news	Arch Oboler's Plays
9:15			Swing Music	
9:30			Symphonic Strings	Death Valley Days
9:45		News		
10pm	NBC Symphony Orchestra	Uncle Jonathan	Tropical Serenade, Don Arres	Benny Goodman Orchestra
10:15		Saturday Night Serenade		
10:30			Music by Moonlight	Dance Orchestra
10:45		Public Affairs		

DAYTIME — FALL, 1939

Sunday

	BLUE	CBS	MBS	NBC
9am	The Children's Hour	From the Organ Loft	Rainbow House	Turn Back the Clock
9:15		Bob Edge's Outdoor Talks		Vagabond Adventures
9:30		Wings Over Jordan		Sunday Drivers
9:45				
10am	Tone Pictures	The CBS Church of the Air	News	The National Radio Pulpit
10:15			Mildred Bailey Orchestra	
10:30	Tapestry Musicale	March of Games	Uncle Don Reads the Comics	The Horn and Hardart Children's Hour
10:45				
11am	The Musical Story Lady	News and Rhythm	Hawaii Calls	
11:15	Neighbor Nell			
11:30	The Southernaires Quartet	Major Bowes' Capitol Family	Chorus from the World's Fair	News
11:45				Vernon Crane's Storybook
12pm	The Radio City Music Hall		The Perole String Quartet	Walter Logan's Musicale
12:15				Julio Oyanguran, guitar
12:30		The Salt Lake Tabernacle Choir	Betty and Buddy, songs	On Your Job
12:45			News	
1pm	Pilgrimage of Poetry	The CBS Church of the Air	Don Arres, songs	Sunday Symphony
1:15			True to Life	
1:30	Paul La Valle Orchestra	Walberg Brown Strings	Salvatore Mario de Stefano, harp	From Hollywood Today
1:45				

DAYTIME — FALL, 1939

Monday-Friday

BLUE	CBS	MBS	NBC	
The Woman of Tomorrow	Manhattan Mother	Arthur Godfrey, songs	Happy Jack Turner, songs	9am
	The American School of the Air	Modern Living / The Lamplighter	The Band Goes to Town	9:15
The Breakfast Club		Women and the News	The Family Man / Isabel Manning Hewson, food	9:30
	Bachelor's Children	Music / Nell Vinick, beauty	Life Can Be Beautiful	9:45
Thunder Over Paradise	Pretty Kitty Kelly	The Pure Food Hour /	The Man I Married	10am
Career Wife	The Story of Myrt and Marge	Music	John's Other Wife	10:15
Music / The Jack Berch Show	Hilltop House		Just Plain Bill	10:30
Rakov Orchestra	Stepmother		The Woman in White	10:45
The Story of Mary Marlin	Music / The Lanny Ross Show	Talk and Music	David Harum	11am
The Right to Happiness	Brenda Curtis	Music	Lorenzo Jones	11:15
Pepper Young's Family	Big Sister	Talk / Get Thin to Music	Young Widder Brown	11:30
Getting the Most Out of Life	Aunt Jenny's True Life Stories	Music / The Radio Garden Club	The Road of Life	11:45
Music / Nellie Revell, talk	Kate Smith Speaks	Music / Victor Lindlahr, health	The Carters of Elm Street	12pm
Music	When a Girl Marries	Music / The Jack Berch Show	The O'Neills	12:15
The National Farm and Home Hour	The Romance of Helen Trent	Vincent Connolly, news	Time for Thought	12:30
	Our Gal Sunday	The Consumers' Quiz	Stock Market Reports	12:45
	The Goldbergs	Dramatized Health Talk	Songs	1pm
Virginia Hayes, songs	Life Can Be Beautiful	Talk and Music	The Story of Ellen Randolph	1:15
Music	The Road of Life		Music / Let's Talk It Over	1:30
	This Day is Ours	The Marriage License Bureau / The Voice of Experience	Talk / Words and Music	1:45

DAYTIME — FALL, 1939

Sunday

	BLUE	CBS	MBS	NBC
2pm	Great Plays	Democracy in Action	The Mystery History Quiz	String Symphony
2:15				
2:30		So You Think You Know Music	Sports	The University of Chicago Round Table
2:45				
3pm	The Roy Shield Revue	New York Philharmonic Orchestra		I Want a Divorce
3:15	Joseph Jackson, books			
3:30	Al Roth Presents			H. V. Kaltenborn, news
3:45				Bob Becker's Dog Talks
4pm	National Vespers		Nobody's Children	Music for Moderns
4:15				
4:30	Music from the Straw Hat Revue	The Pursuit of Happiness	Johnny McGhee Orchestra	The World is Yours
4:45				
5pm	The Moylan Sisters, songs	Hobby Lobby	The Musical Steelmakers	Enoch Light Orchestra
5:15	Four-Star News			Ranger's Serenade
5:30	The Metropolitan Opera Auditions	Ben Bernie, the Old Maestro	The Shadow	Spelling Bee
5:45				

DAYTIME — FALL, 1939

Monday-Friday

BLUE	CBS	MBS	NBC	
Music / Informational Talk	Doc Barclay's Daughters	Talk and Music	Betty and Bob	2pm
	The Life and Love of Dr. Susan	Ed Fitzgerald and Company	Arnold Grimm's Daughter	2:15
Music	Your Family and Mine	Music / Word Dramas	Valiant Lady	2:30
	My Son and I	David Harum	Betty Crocker, cooking / Hymns of All Churches	2:45
Orphans of Divorce	Joyce Jordan, Girl Intern	Martha Deane, talk	The Story of Mary Marlin	3pm
The Chase Twins	Society Girl		Ma Perkins	3:15
Music	Songs		Pepper Young's Family	3:30
Between the Bookends	Music / Richard Maxwell, songs	Music / The Heart of Julia Blake	The Guiding Light	3:45
Club Matinee, Garry Moore	Music	News	Mary Noble, Backstage Wife	4pm
		Music	Stella Dallas	4:15
	Informational Talk		Vic and Sade	4:30
	Smilin' Ed McConnell, songs	The Career of Alice Blair	Midstream	4:45
Music	By Kathleen Norris	Meet Miss Julia	Girl Alone	5pm
The Trouble with Marriage	Music	Dance Orchestra	Against the Storm	5:15
The Affairs of Anthony	It Happened in Hollywood		Jack Armstrong, the All-American Boy	5:30
The Tom Mix Ralston Straight Shooters	Scattergood Baines	The Adventures of Pinocchio	Little Orphan Annie	5:45

DAYTIME — FALL, 1939

Saturday

	BLUE	CBS	MBS	NBC
9am	The Breakfast Club	Richard Maxwell, songs	Betty And Buddy, songs	Texas Jim Robertson, songs
9:15		Fiddler's Fancy	The Orange Blossom Quartet	Annette Hastings, songs
9:30		Saturday Morning Serenade	Syncopators Orchestra	Isabel Manning Hewson, food
9:45				The Crackerjack Quartet
10am	The Morin Sisters, songs	The Chicago Student Forum	The Marriage Clinic	The Wise Man
10:15	Amanda's Party			No School Today
10:30	Barry McKinley, songs	National Hillbilly Champions	The First Offender	The Bright Idea Club
10:45	Child Grows Up			
11am	The Charioteers Quartet	Cincinnati Conservatory Recitals	The Model Airplane Club	The Ross Trio
11:15	Bill Stern's Sports School		Hayden Planetarium Talks	Smilin' Ed McConnell, songs
11:30	Our Barn	The Columbia Concert Hall	The US Army Band	Hilda Hope, MD
11:45				
12pm	The American Education Forum	Columbia's Country Journal	The Man on the Farm	Dol Brissett Orchestra
12:15				
12:30	The National Farm and Home Hour	Let's Pretend	Vincent Connolly, news	Call to Youth
12:45			Dance Orchestra	Songs
1pm		What Price America	The Gloomchasers	Dance Orchestra
1:15				The Stamp Club
1:30	Three-Quarter Time	Enoch Light Orchestra	Carter and Bowle, piano	Matinee in Rhythm
1:45			Sports	

DAYTIME — FALL, 1939

Saturday

	BLUE	CBS	MBS	NBC
2pm	Morton Franklin Orchestra	Buffalo Presents		Ray Kinney Orchestra
2:15				
2:30	Indiana Indigo	Sports		Golden Melodies
2:45	Sports			
3pm				Campus Capers
3:15				
3:30				Harry James Orchestra
3:45				
4pm				The Trytons Band at the World's Fair
4:15				
4:30				Paul La Valle Orchestra
4:45				
5pm		Dance Orchestra		Serenade Musicale
5:15				
5:30	Benny Carter Orchestra		Tommy Tucker Orchestra	Del Courtney Orchestra
5:45			Ed Thorgerson, sports	

LISTINGS FOR 1940

EVENING — WINTER, 1940

Sunday

	BLUE	CBS	MBS	NBC
6pm	New Friends of Music	The Silver Theater	Gene Krupa Orchestra	The Catholic Hour
6:15				
6:30		Gene Autry's Melody Ranch	The Show of the Week	Beat the Band
6:45				
7pm	European News	European War Roundup	The Bach Cantata Series	The Jello Program, Jack Benny
7:15				
7:30	Mr. District Attorney	The Gulf Screen Theater	Frank Singiser, news	The Fitch Bandwagon
7:45			Gabriel Heatter, news	
8pm	Festival of Music	The Campbell Playhouse	The American Forum of the Air	The Charlie McCarthy Show
8:15				
8:30	The Voice of Hawaii			One Man's Family
8:45		Elmer Davis, news (8:55pm)		
9pm	Walter Winchell's Jergens Journal	The Ford Sunday Evening Hour	The Laugh and Swing Club	The Manhattan Merry-Go-Round
9:15	The Parker Family			
9:30	Irene Rich Dramas		Arthur Hale, news	The American Album of Familiar Music
9:45	The Colgate Sports Newsreel, Bill Stern		New Voices Musicale	
10pm	William Hillman, news	The Adventures of Ellery Queen	The Goodwill Hour	The Hour of Charm
10:15	Jan Savitt Orchestra			
10:30	Cheerio's Musical Mosaics			The Primrose String Quartet
10:45				

EVENING — WINTER, 1940

Monday

BLUE	CBS	MBS	NBC	
Randy Brooks Orchestra	Edwin C. Hill, news	Uncle Don	El Chico	6pm
Annette Hastings, songs	Hedda Hopper, gossip		Jack Miley, sports	6:15
Ray Perkins, piano	Elmer Davis, news	Frank Singiser, news	The Stamp Club	6:30
Lowell Thomas, news	The World Today	The Adrian Rollini Trio	Lil' Abner	6:45
Ray Kinney Orchestra	Amos 'n' Andy	Stan Lomax, sports	Chesterfield Time	7pm
Science on the March	Lum and Abner	The Answer Man	I Love a Mystery	7:15
One of the Finest	Blondie	The Lone Ranger	Sensation and Swing	7:30
				7:45
Sherlock Holmes	Tune-Up Time	Author, Author	Tommy Riggs and Betty Lou	8pm
				8:15
True or False	The Model Minstrels	Ted Fio Rito Orchestra	The Voice of Firestone	8:30
	Elmer Davis, news (8:55pm)			8:45
Rochester Civic Orchestra	The Lux Radio Theater	Gabriel Heatter, news	Dr. I. Q., the Mental Banker	9pm
		This War		9:15
Public Affairs		Morton Gould Orchestra	Alex Templeton Time	9:30
				9:45
Little Ol' Hollywood	Guy Lombardo Orchestra	Raymond Gram Swing, news	The Carnation Contented Hour	10pm
		True to Life		10:15
The National Radio Forum	The Curtis Institute Concert	Fulton Lewis Jr., news	Barry Winton Orchestra	10:30
		Pageant of Melody		10:45

EVENING — WINTER, 1940

Tuesday

	BLUE	CBS	MBS	NBC
6pm	Dinner Date	Edwin C. Hill, news	Uncle Don	Music from Mexico
6:15	The Washington Variety Show	The Jerry Cooper Show		Jack Miley, sports
6:30	The Museum of Natural History	Albert Warner, news	Frank Singiser, news	Reggie Childs Orchestra
6:45	Lowell Thomas, news	The World Today	The Adrian Rollini Trio	Lil' Abner
7pm	Easy Aces	Amos 'n' Andy	Stan Lomax, sports	Chesterfield Time
7:15	Mr. Keen, Tracer of Lost Persons	Jimmy Fidler, gossip	John B. Kennedy, news	I Love a Mystery
7:30	Frank Novak Orchestra	Second Husband	Unsung Americans	Around New York
7:45			Sam Balter, sports	
8pm	The Aldrich Family	Big Town	The Antonini Concert Series	Johnny Presents
8:15				
8:30	Information, Please	The Court of Missing Heirs	Morton Gould Orchestra	Pot o' Gold
8:45		Elmer Davis, news (8:55pm)		
9pm	The Cavalcade of America	We, the People	Arthur Hale, news	Battle of the Sexes
9:15			Victor Lushinchi, news	
9:30	Meet Edward Weeks	Concert in Rhythm	The Mozart Concerto Series	Fibber Magee and Molly
9:45				
10pm	The Roy Shield Revue	Moonlight Serenade	Raymond Gram Swing, news	The Pepsodent Show, Bob Hope
10:15		Americans at Work	Fulton Lewis Jr., news	
10:30	Brent House		Meriwether's Minstrels	Uncle Walter's Dog House
10:45		The Four Clubmen		

EVENING — WINTER, 1940

Wednesday

BLUE	CBS	MBS	NBC	
Little Jack Little Orchestra	Edwin C. Hill, news	Uncle Don	The Luther Layman Singers	6pm
	Hedda Hopper, gossip		Jack Miley, sports	6:15
The Gulden Serenaders	Elmer Davis, news	Frank Singiser, news	The Stamp Club	6:30
Lowell Thomas, news	The World Today	The Adrian Rollini Trio	Lil' Abner	6:45
Easy Aces	Amos 'n' Andy	Stan Lomax, sports	Chesterfield Time	7pm
Mr. Keen, Tracer of Lost Persons	Lum and Abner	The Answer Man	I Love a Mystery	7:15
Paul Baron Orchestra	Burns and Allen	The Lone Ranger	The Revelers Quartet	7:30
			Johnny Messner Orchestra	7:45
Breezin' Along	Al Pearce and His Gang	Dance Orchestra	The Hollywood Playhouse	8pm
				8:15
Quicksilver	Dr. Christian	Sherlock Holmes	Avalon Variety Time, Cliff Arquette	8:30
	Elmer Davis, news (8:55pm)			8:45
The Radio Guild	The Texaco Star Theater	Gabriel Heatter, news	The Fred Allen Show	9pm
		Paul Schubert, news		9:15
Horse and Buggy Days	The Ethel Barrymore Theater	Percy Faith Orchestra		9:30
				9:45
The Roy Shield Revue	Moonlight Serenade	Raymond Gram Swing, news	Kay Kyser's College of Musical Knowledge	10pm
	Public Affairs	True to Life		10:15
Adventures in Photography	Indianapolis Symphony Orchestra	Fulton Lewis Jr., news		10:30
		Romance in Rhythm		10:45

EVENING — WINTER, 1940

Thursday

	BLUE	CBS	MBS	NBC
6pm	Dinner Date	Edwin C. Hill, news	Uncle Don	June Hynd's Guest Book
6:15	Ruth Peters, songs	Mel Allen, sports		Jack Miley, sports
6:30	Johnny McGhee Orchestra	George Fielding Eliot, news	Frank Singiser, news	Reggie Childs Orchestra
6:45	Lowell Thomas, news	The World Today	The Adrian Rollini Trio	Lil' Abner
7pm	Easy Aces	Amos 'n' Andy	Stan Lomax, sports	Chesterfield Time
7:15	Mr. Keen, Tracer of Lost Persons	Genevieve Rowe, songs	John B. Kennedy, news	I Love a Mystery
7:30	One of the Finest	Vox Pop	Unsung Americans	The Schaefer All-Star Parade
7:45			Sam Balter, sports	
8pm	The Green Hornet	The Ask-It Basket	Kay Kyser's College of Musical Knowledge	For Men Only, George Jessel
8:15				
8:30	The Tip Top Show, Joe Penner	Strange As It Seems		Those We Love
8:45		Elmer Davis, news (8:55pm)		
9pm	Rochester Philharmonic Orchestra	Major Bowes' Original Amateur Hour	Arthur Hale, news	Good News of 1940
9:15			Public Affairs	
9:30	America's Town Meeting of the Air		Ned Jordan, Secret Agent	
9:45				
10pm		Moonlight Serenade	Raymond Gram Swing, news	The Kraft Music Hall, Bing Crosby
10:15		The Columbia Workshop	Fulton Lewis Jr., news	
10:30	Florence Wyman and Tom Thomas, songs		Henry Weber's Musical Revue	
10:45		Nan Wynn, songs		

EVENING — WINTER, 1940

Friday

BLUE	CBS	MBS	NBC	
Alma Kitchell's Briefcase	Edwin C. Hill, news	Uncle Don	The Torch of Progress	6pm
Garrand Orchestra	Hedda Hopper, gossip		Jack Miley, sports	6:15
The Gulden Serenaders	Elmer Davis, news	Frank Singiser, news	The Stamp Club	6:30
Lowell Thomas, news	The World Today	The Adrian Rollini Trio	Lil' Abner	6:45
African Trek	Amos 'n' Andy	Stan Lomax, sports	Chesterfield Time	7pm
	Lum and Abner	The Answer Man	I Love a Mystery	7:15
Yesterday's Children	Professor Quiz	The Lone Ranger	The Revelers Quartet	7:30
			Ted Steele Orchestra	7:45
Don't Forget	The Kate Smith Hour	Quixie Doodle	The Cities Service Concerts	8pm
				8:15
Carson Robison's Buckeroos		Sinfonietta		8:30
	Elmer Davis, news (8:55pm)			8:45
Paducah Plantation, Red Foley	Johnny Presents Dramatized Short Stories	Gabriel Heatter, news	Waltz Time	9pm
		Al Donahue Orchestra		9:15
What Would You Have Done	The First Nighter Program	Benay Venuta's Variety Program	Cavalcade of Hits	9:30
				9:45
Madison Square Garden Boxing	Grand Central Station	Raymond Gram Swing, news	Guy Lombardo Orchestra	10pm
		John Steele, news		10:15
Melody Marathon	Young Man with a Band	Fulton Lewis Jr., news	Cesar Saerchinger, news	10:30
		Ted Steele Orchestra	Human Nature in Action	10:45

EVENING — WINTER, 1940

Saturday

	BLUE	CBS	MBS	NBC
6pm	Johnny McGhee Orchestra	Eddy Duchin Orchestra	Uncle Don	Kaltenmeyer's Kindergarten
6:15		Mel Allen, sports		
6:30	Renfrew of the Mounted	Which Way to Lasting Peace	Frank Singiser, news	Religion in the News
6:45		Today in Europe	The Charioteers Quartet	Southwestern Serenade
7pm	Message of Israel	The People's Platform	Stan Lomax, sports	What's My Name
7:15			Cats and Jammers	
7:30	Dance Orchestra	Sky Blazers	Arthur Hale, news	Art for Your Sake
7:45			Sam Balter, sports	
8pm	The Green Hornet	Gangbusters	Name Three	Arch Oboler's Plays
8:15				
8:30	Youth vs. Age	Wayne King Orchestra	Hawaii Calls	Stop Me If You've Heard This One
8:45		Elmer Davis, news (8:55pm)		
9pm	The National Barn Dance	Your Hit Parade	George Fisher, gossip	Dance Orchestra
9:15			The Sons of the Pioneers	
9:30			Symphonic Strings	Death Valley Days
9:45		Saturday Night Serenade		
10pm	NBC Symphony Orchestra		Tropical Serenade, Don Arres	The Camel Caravan
10:15		Public Affairs		
10:30		The Gay Nineties Revue	Music by Moonlight	Eddie LeBaron Orchestra
10:45				

DAYTIME — WINTER, 1940

Sunday

	BLUE	CBS	MBS	NBC
9am	The Children's Hour	News	Rainbow House	Turn Back the Clock
9:15		Bob Edge's Outdoor Talks		Vagabond Adventures
9:30		Wings Over Jordan		Sunday Drivers
9:45				
10am	Stringtime with Walberg Brown	The CBS Church of the Air	News	The National Radio Pulpit
10:15			The Lamplighter	
10:30	The Four Belles	March of Games	Uncle Don Reads the Comics	The Horn and Hardart Children's Hour
10:45	Smilin' Ed McConnell, songs			
11am	News	News and Rhythm	Al Helfer, sports	
11:15	Melodic Moods		The Northwestern Reviewing Stand	
11:30	The Southernaires Quartet	Major Bowes' Capitol Family	Chorus from the World's Fair	News
11:45				Music and American Youth
12pm	The Radio City Music Hall		The Perole String Quartet	Vernon Crane's Storybook
12:15				Julio Oyanguran, guitar
12:30		The Salt Lake Tabernacle Choir	The Sing a Song of Safety Club	On Your Job
12:45			News	
1pm	Pilgrimage of Poetry	The CBS Church of the Air	Don Arres, songs	Music for Moderns
1:15	The Vass Family, songs			
1:30	Metropolitan Moods	Grand Hotel	Milton Katims Orchestra	From Hollywood Today
1:45				

DAYTIME — WINTER, 1940

Monday-Friday

BLUE	CBS	MBS	NBC	
The Woman of Tomorrow	Woman of Courage	Music / Arthur Godfrey, songs	Happy Jack Turner, songs	*9am*
	The American School of the Air	Songs / The Lamplighter	The Band Goes to Town	*9:15*
The Breakfast Club		Women and the News	Isabel Manning Hewson, food / The Gospel Singer	*9:30*
	Bachelor's Children	Music / Nell Vinick, beauty	Life Can Be Beautiful	*9:45*
Thunder Over Paradise	Pretty Kitty Kelly	The Pure Food Hour /	The Man I Married	*10am*
This Day is Ours	The Story of Myrt and Marge	Music	John's Other Wife	*10:15*
The Story of Mary Marlin	Hilltop House		Just Plain Bill	*10:30*
Midstream	Stepmother		The Woman in White	*10:45*
Pepper Young's Family	Music / Short, Short Story	Pegeen Presents	David Harum	*11am*
Young Dr. Malone	Life Begins		The Road of Life	*11:15*
Music / The Traveling Chef	Big Sister	Talk / The Radio Garden Club / Get Thin to Music	Against the Storm	*11:30*
Music	Aunt Jenny's True Life Stories	Talk and Music	The Guiding Light	*11:45*
Music / Nellie Revell, talk	Kate Smith Speaks	Music / Victor Lindlahr, health	Music	*12pm*
Music	When a Girl Marries	Music / The Jack Berch Show	The O'Neills	*12:15*
The National Farm and Home Hour	The Romance of Helen Trent	Vincent Connolly, news	Time for Thought	*12:30*
	Our Gal Sunday	The Consumers' Quiz	Stock Market Reports	*12:45*
	The Goldbergs	Ed Fitzgerald and Company	Songs	*1pm*
Virginia Hayes, songs	Life Can Be Beautiful	Dramatized Health Talk	The Story of Ellen Randolph	*1:15*
Music	The Right to Happiness	Talk and Music	Let's Talk It Over / Words and Music	*1:30*
	The Road of Life		The Hollywood News Girl / Hollywood 10,000	*1:45*

DAYTIME — WINTER, 1940

Sunday

	BLUE	CBS	MBS	NBC
2pm	Great Plays	Democracy in Action	The Mystery History Quiz	String Symphony
2:15				
2:30		So You Think You Know Music	Manhatters Orchestra	The University of Chicago Round Table
2:45				
3pm	Mischa Mischakoff, violin	New York Philharmonic Orchestra	Meditation and Melody	I Want a Divorce
3:15	Foreign Policy Association Talks			
3:30	Tapestry Musicale		Tommy Reynolds Orchestra	H. V. Kaltenborn, news
3:45				Eddie LeBaron Orchestra
4pm	National Vespers		Nobody's Children	Al Donahue Orchestra
4:15				
4:30	Music from the Straw Hat Revue	The Pursuit of Happiness	Mischa Boer Orchestra	The World is Yours
4:45				
5pm	The Moylan Sisters, songs	Hobby Lobby	The Musical Steelmakers	Enoch Light Orchestra
5:15	Four-Star News			Bob Becker's Dog Talks
5:30	The Metropolitan Opera Auditions	Ben Bernie, the Old Maestro	The Shadow	Spelling Bee
5:45				

DAYTIME — WINTER, 1940

Monday-Friday

BLUE	CBS	MBS	NBC	
Music / Informational Talk	The Lanny Ross Show		Betty and Bob	2pm
	Music		Arnold Grimm's Daughter	2:15
Music	Your Family and Mine		Valiant Lady	2:30
	My Son and I		Betty Crocker, cooking / Hymns of All Churches	2:45
Orphans of Divorce	Joyce Jordan, Girl Intern	Martha Deane, talk	The Story of Mary Marlin	3pm
The Chase Twins	Society Girl		Ma Perkins	3:15
The Affairs of Anthony	Uncle Jonathan		Pepper Young's Family	3:30
Between the Bookends	Music / Richard Maxwell, songs	Music / The Heart of Julie Blake	Vic and Sade	3:45
Club Matinee, Garry Moore	Music	News	Mary Noble, Backstage Wife	4pm
	Informational Talk	Mischa Borr Orchestra /	Stella Dallas	4:15
	Manhattan Mother	Music	Lorenzo Jones	4:30
	Smilin' Ed McConnell, songs	The Career of Alice Blair	Young Widder Brown	4:45
Music / Name It and Take It	By Kathleen Norris	Meet Miss Julia	Girl Alone	5pm
Music / The Singing Story Lady	Billy and Betty	The Johnson Family	Midstream	5:15
Bud Barton	It Happened in Hollywood	Music	Jack Armstrong, the All-American Boy	5:30
The Tom Mix Ralston Straight Shooters	Scattergood Baines	Little Orphan Annie	Songs	5:45

DAYTIME — WINTER, 1940

Saturday

	BLUE	CBS	MBS	NBC
9am	The Breakfast Club	Richard Maxwell, songs	Betty And Buddy, songs	Texas Jim Robertson, songs
9:15		Old Vienna	The Orange Blossom Quartet	Annette Hastings, songs
9:30		Carl Hohengarten Orchestra	Syncopators Orchestra	Isabel Manning Hewson, food
9:45				The Crackerjack Quartet
10am	Al and Lee Reiser, piano	Stringtime with Walberg Brown	The Marriage Clinic	The Wise Man
10:15	Rakov Orchestra			No School Today
10:30	The Charioteers Quartet	National Hillbilly Champions	The First Offender	The Bright Idea Club
10:45	Child Grows Up			
11am	Norman Cloutier Orchestra	Cincinnati Conservatory Recitals	The Model Airplane Club	The Vass Family, songs
11:15			Hayden Planetarium Talks	Smilin' Ed McConnell, songs
11:30	Our Barn		The US Army Band	Hilda Hope, MD
11:45				
12pm	The American Education Forum	Columbia's Country Journal	The Man on the Farm	The Eastman School of Music
12:15				
12:30	The National Farm and Home Hour	Let's Pretend	Vincent Connolly, news	Call to Youth
12:45			Enoch Light Orchestra	Matinee in Rhythm
1pm		What Price America	Ed Fitzgerald and Company	Harry James Orchestra
1:15				The Stamp Club
1:30	Al Kavelin Orchestra	Songs	The University Life Forum	Lani McIntyre Orchestra
1:45		Dance Orchestra		

DAYTIME — WINTER, 1940

Saturday

	BLUE	CBS	MBS	NBC
2pm	The Metropolitan Opera	Buffalo Presents	Dance Orchestra	Ray Kinney Orchestra
2:15				
2:30		The Brush Creek Follies		Golden Melodies
2:45				
3pm		Columbia Chamber Orchestra	Manhatters Orchestra	Music Styled for You
3:15				
3:30		Vera Brodsky, piano	Dance Orchestra	Dol Brissett Orchestra
3:45				
4pm		Bull Session	Music	Campus Capers
4:15			Horse Racing	
4:30		Your Host is Buffalo	Mischa Borr Orchestra	Paul La Valle Orchestra
4:45				
5pm	Dance Orchestra	Wayne King Orchestra	Sammy Kaye Orchestra	Dance Orchestra
5:15	Magic Waves			
5:30	Sammy Hawkins Orchestra	Eddy Duchin Orchestra		
5:45	Music from Syracuse			

EVENING — SPRING, 1940

Sunday

	BLUE	CBS	MBS	NBC
6pm	Glen Gray Orchestra	The Silver Theater	Ramona and the Tune Twisters	The Catholic Hour
6:15				
6:30	Cavalcade of Hits	Gene Autry's Melody Ranch	The Show of the Week	Beat the Band
6:45				
7pm	European News	European War Roundup	The Bach Cantata Series	The Jello Program, Jack Benny
7:15				
7:30	The Fisk Jubilee Choir	The Gulf Screen Theater	Frank Singiser, news	The Fitch Bandwagon
7:45			Gabriel Heatter, news	
8pm	The Musical Comedy Revue	The Adventures of Ellery Queen	The American Forum of the Air	The Charlie McCarthy Show
8:15				
8:30	The Voice of Hawaii	So You Think You Know Music		One Man's Family
8:45		Elmer Davis, news (8:55pm)		
9pm	Walter Winchell's Jergens Journal	The Ford Sunday Evening Hour	True to Life	The Manhattan Merry-Go-Round
9:15	The Parker Family		Glenn Miller Orchestra	
9:30	Irene Rich Dramas		Arthur Hale, news	The American Album of Familiar Music
9:45	The Colgate Sports Newsreel, Bill Stern		The Song Spinners	
10pm	The Goodwill Hour	Take It or Leave It	The Symphonic Hour	The Hour of Charm
10:15				
10:30		Public Affairs		The Primrose String Quartet
10:45				

EVENING — SPRING, 1940

Monday

BLUE	CBS	MBS	NBC	
Herman Middleman Orchestra	Edwin C. Hill, news	Uncle Don	Lil' Abner	6pm
Bill Stern, sports	Hedda Hopper, gossip		Ed East's Jingles	6:15
Whispering Rhythm	Elmer Davis, news	Frank Singiser, news	The Stamp Club	6:30
Lowell Thomas, news	The World Today	George Fisher, gossip	Paul Douglas, sports	6:45
Dick Stabile Orchestra	Amos 'n' Andy	Stan Lomax, sports	Chesterfield Time	7pm
Youth in the Toils	The Lanny Ross Show	Wythe Williams, news	H. V. Kaltenborn, news	7:15
One of the Finest	Blondie	The Lone Ranger	Sensation and Swing	7:30
				7:45
Little Ol' Hollywood	Tune-Up Time	Play Broadcast	The Bell Telephone Hour	8pm
				8:15
True or False	The Model Minstrels	Let's Go to Work	The Voice of Firestone	8:30
	Elmer Davis, news (8:55pm)			8:45
The Green Hornet	The Lux Radio Theater	Gabriel Heatter, news	Dr. I. Q., the Mental Banker	9pm
		Glenn Miller Orchestra		9:15
Rochester Civic Orchestra		Morton Gould Orchestra	Alex Templeton Time	9:30
				9:45
Paul Martin Orchestra	Guy Lombardo Orchestra	Raymond Gram Swing, news	The Carnation Contented Hour	10pm
		Fulton Lewis Jr., news		10:15
The National Radio Forum	The Curtis Institute Concert	WOR Symphony Orchestra	Barry Winton Orchestra	10:30
				10:45

EVENING — SPRING, 1940

Tuesday

	BLUE	CBS	MBS	NBC
6pm	Dinner Date	Edwin C. Hill, news	Uncle Don	Lil' Abner
6:15	Bill Stern, sports	Waite Hoyt, sports		Ed East's Jingles
6:30	Richard Himber Orchestra	Albert Warner, news	Frank Singiser, news	Yvette Sings
6:45	Lowell Thomas, news	The World Today	Unsung Americans	Paul Douglas, sports
7pm	Easy Aces	Amos 'n' Andy	Stan Lomax, sports	Chesterfield Time
7:15	Mr. Keen, Tracer of Lost Persons	Jimmy Fidler, gossip	John B. Kennedy, news	H. V. Kaltenborn, news
7:30	Frank Novak Orchestra	Second Husband	Arthur Hale, sports	Around New York
7:45			Sam Balter, sports	
8pm	The Aldrich Family	Big Town	The Antonini Concert Series	Johnny Presents
8:15				
8:30	Information, Please	The Court of Missing Heirs	Cats and Jammers	Pot o' Gold
8:45		Elmer Davis, news (8:55pm)		
9pm	The Cavalcade of America	We, the People	Meet the Stars	Battle of the Sexes
9:15				
9:30	The Revuers	Public Affairs	The Laugh and Swing Club	Fibber Magee and Molly
9:45				
10pm	The Roy Shield Revue	Moonlight Serenade	Raymond Gram Swing, news	The Pepsodent Show, Bob Hope
10:15		Americans at Work	Fulton Lewis Jr., news	
10:30	Brent House		Meriwether's Minstrels	Uncle Walter's Dog House
10:45		The Four Clubmen		

EVENING — SPRING, 1940

Wednesday

BLUE	CBS	MBS	NBC	
Little Jack Little Orchestra	Edwin C. Hill, news	Uncle Don	Lil' Abner	6pm
Bill Stern, sports	Hedda Hopper, gossip		Ed East's Jingles	6:15
The Gulden Serenaders	Elmer Davis, news	Frank Singiser, news	The Stamp Club	6:30
Lowell Thomas, news	The World Today	George Fisher, gossip	Paul Douglas, sports	6:45
Easy Aces	Amos 'n' Andy	Stan Lomax, sports	Chesterfield Time	7pm
Mr. Keen, Tracer of Lost Persons	The Lanny Ross Show	Wythe Williams, news	H. V. Kaltenborn, news	7:15
Paul Baron Orchestra	Burns and Allen	The Lone Ranger	The Revelers Quartet	7:30
			Bob Howard, piano	7:45
Jingo	Ben Bernie, the Old Maestro	The Sheep and Goats Club Revue	The Hollywood Playhouse	8pm
				8:15
What Would You Have Done	Dr. Christian	Where Are You From	Avalon Variety Time, Cliff Arquette	8:30
	Elmer Davis, news (8:55pm)			8:45
The Green Hornet	The Texaco Star Theater	Gabriel Heatter, news	The Fred Allen Show	9pm
		This War		9:15
The Roy Shields Revue	The Ethel Barrymore	Percy Faith Orchestra		9:30
				9:45
Public Affairs	Moonlight Serenade	Raymond Gram Swing, news	Kay Kyser's College of Musical Knowledge	10pm
	Public Affairs	Fulton Lewis Jr., news		10:15
Prairie Folks	Indianapolis Symphony Orchestra	Pageant of Melody		10:30
				10:45

EVENING — SPRING, 1940

Thursday

	BLUE	CBS	MBS	NBC
6pm	Dinner Date	Edwin C. Hill, news	Uncle Don	Lil' Abner
6:15	Bill Stern, sports	Waite Hoyt, sports		Ed East's Jingles
6:30	Richard Himber Orchestra	George Fielding Eliot, comment	Frank Singiser, news	June Hynd's Guest Book
6:45	Lowell Thomas, news	The World Today	Unsung Americans	Paul Douglas, sports
7pm	Easy Aces	Amos 'n' Andy	Stan Lomax, sports	Chesterfield Time
7:15	Mr. Keen, Tracer of Lost Persons	The Lanny Ross Show	Dinner at Home	H. V. Kaltenborn, news
7:30	One of the Finest	Vox Pop	Arthur Hale, news	The Schaefer All-Star Parade
7:45			Sam Balter, sports	
8pm	Musical Americana	The Ask-It Basket	Kay Kyser's College of Musical Knowledge	Mr. District Attorney
8:15				
8:30	The Tip Top Show, Joe Penner	Strange As It Seems		I Love a Mystery
8:45		Elmer Davis, news (8:55pm)		
9pm	Rochester Philharmonic Orchestra	Major Bowes' Original Amateur Hour	David Rose Orchestra	Good News of 1940
9:15				
9:30	America's Town Meeting of the Air		Ned Jordan, Secret Agent	Vallee Varieties
9:45				
10pm		Moonlight Serenade	Raymond Gram Swing, news	The Kraft Music Hall, Bing Crosby
10:15		The Columbia Workshop	Fulton Lewis Jr., news	
10:30	Florence Wyman and Tom Thomas, songs		Henry Weber's Musical Revue	
10:45		Nan Wynn, songs		

EVENING — SPRING, 1940

Friday

BLUE	CBS	MBS	NBC	
Alma Kitchell's Briefcase	Edwin C. Hill, news	Uncle Don	Lil' Abner	6pm
Bill Stern, sports	Hedda Hopper, gossip		Ed East's Jingles	6:15
The Gulden Serenaders	Elmer Davis, news	Frank Singiser, news	The Stamp Club	6:30
Lowell Thomas, news	The World Today	The Adrian Rollini Trio	Paul Douglas, sports	6:45
African Trek	Amos 'n' Andy	Stan Lomax, sports	Chesterfield Time	7pm
	The Lanny Ross Show	Wythe Williams, news	H. V. Kaltenborn, news	7:15
Yesterday's Children	Professor Quiz	The Lone Ranger	The Revelers Quartet	7:30
			Ted Steele Orchestra	7:45
This Amazing America	The Kate Smith Hour	Fifth Row Center	The Cities Service Concerts	8pm
				8:15
Carson Robison's Buckaroos		Sinfonietta		8:30
	Elmer Davis, news (8:55pm)			8:45
Paducah Plantation, Red Foley	Johnny Presents Dramatized Short Stories	Gabriel Heatter, news	Waltz Time	9pm
		Red Barber, sports		9:15
The American Music Festival	The First Nighter Program	Comedy By	What's My Name	9:30
				9:45
Madison Square Garden Boxing	Grand Central Station	Raymond Gram Swing, news	The Don Ameche Variety Show	10pm
		Fulton Lewis Jr., news		10:15
Melody Marathon	Believe It or Not	The Dick Robertson Show	Cesar Saerchinger, news	10:30
		Dance Orchestra	Human Nature in Action	10:45

EVENING — SPRING, 1940

Saturday

	BLUE	CBS	MBS	NBC
6pm	Cecil Golly Orchestra	Eddy Duchin Orchestra	Uncle Don	Ted Steele Orchestra
6:15		Waite Hoyt, sports		Ed East's Jingles
6:30	Renfrew of the Mounted	Which Way to Lasting Peace	Frank Singiser, news	Religion in the News
6:45		Today in Europe	The Charioteers Quartet	Southwestern Serenade
7pm	Message of Israel	The People's Platform	Stan Lomax, sports	Art for Your Sake
7:15			Swing Session	
7:30	Dance Orchestra	Sky Blazers	Arthur Hale, news	Dance Orchestra
7:45			Sam Balter, sports	H. V. Kaltenborn, news
8pm	Woody Herman Orchestra	Gangbusters	Name Three	Landmarks of Radio
8:15				
8:30	The Radio Guild	Wayne King Orchestra	Who Knows	Dance Orchestra
8:45		Elmer Davis, news (8:55pm)	Hawaii Calls	
9pm	The National Barn Dance	Your Hit Parade	George Fisher, gossip	Youth vs. Age
9:15			The Playboys Trio	
9:30			Symphonic Strings	Death Valley Days
9:45		Truth or Consequences		
10pm	NBC Symphony Orchestra		Tropical Serenade, Don Arres	The Camel Caravan
10:15		Public Affairs		
10:30		The Gay Nineties Revue	Music by Moonlight	Freddy Martin Orchestra
10:45				

DAYTIME — SPRING, 1940

Sunday

	BLUE	CBS	MBS	NBC
9am	The Children's Hour	News	Rainbow House	The Four Showmen
9:15		Bob Edge's Outdoor Talks		Vagabond Adventures
9:30		Wings Over Jordan		Sunday Drivers
9:45				
10am	Stringtime with Walberg Brown	The CBS Church of the Air	News	The National Radio Pulpit
10:15			The Lamplighter	
10:30	The Southernaires Quartet	March of Games	Uncle Don Reads the Comics	The Horn and Hardart Children's Hour
10:45	Smilin' Ed McConnell, songs			
11am	News	News and Rhythm	Mellow Music	
11:15	Melodic Moods		Recorded Music	
11:30	Happy Jim Parsons, songs	Major Bowes' Capitol Family	Chorus from the World's Fair	News
11:45	The Four Belles			Music and American Youth
12pm	The Radio City Music Hall		Milton Katims Orchestra	Vernon Crane's Storybook
12:15				Julio Oyanguran, guitar
12:30		The Salt Lake Tabernacle Choir	The Sing a Song of Safety Club	On Your Job
12:45			News	
1pm	Pilgrimage of Poetry	The CBS Church of the Air	The Canary Pet Shop	Music for Moderns
1:15	The Vass Family, songs		Don Arres, songs	
1:30	Harry Reser Orchestra	Democracy in Action	Music	From Hollywood Today
1:45				

DAYTIME — SPRING, 1940

Monday-Friday

BLUE	CBS	MBS	NBC	
The Woman of Tomorrow	Woman of Courage	Music / Arthur Godfrey, songs	Happy Jack Turner, songs	9am
	The American School of the Air	Songs / The Heart of Julia Blake	The Band Goes to Town	9:15
The Breakfast Club		Get Thin to Music	Music / Isabel Manning Hewson, food	9:30
	Bachelor's Children	Music / Nell Vinick, beauty	The Gospel Singer	9:45
Thunder Over Paradise	Pretty Kitty Kelly	The Pure Food Hour /	The Man I Married	10am
Vic and Sade	The Story of Myrt and Marge	Music	Life Can Be Beautiful	10:15
The Story of Mary Marlin	Hilltop House		The Story of Ellen Randolph	10:30
Norman Cloutier Orchestra	Stepmother		The Woman in White	10:45
Pepper Young's Family	Music / Short, Short Story	Pegeen Presents	David Harum	11am
Young Dr. Malone	Life Begins	Martha Deane, talk	The Road of Life	11:15
Music / The Traveling Chef	Big Sister		Against the Storm	11:30
The Affairs of Anthony	Aunt Jenny's True Life Stories		The Guiding Light	11:45
Music / Nellie Revell, talk	Kate Smith Speaks	Music / Victor Lindlahr, health	Music	12pm
Music	When a Girl Marries	Music / The Jack Berch Show	The O'Neills	12:15
The National Farm and Home Hour	The Romance of Helen Trent	Vincent Connolly, news	Religious Talk	12:30
	Our Gal Sunday	The Consumers' Quiz	Stock Market Reports	12:45
Jeno Bartal Orchestra	The Goldbergs	Ed Fitzgerald and Company	Songs	1pm
Between the Bookends	Life Can Be Beautiful	Dramatized Health Talk	Ben Bernie, the Old Maestro	1:15
Maurice Spitalny Orchestra	The Right to Happiness	The Carters of Elm Street	Music / Let's Talk It Over	1:30
Music	The Road of Life	Pegeen Presents	The Hollywood News Girl / Words and Music	1:45

DAYTIME — SPRING, 1940

Sunday

	BLUE	CBS	MBS	NBC
2pm	Great Plays	Salute to the Americas	Salute to the Americas	Salute to the Americas
2:15				
2:30		Music from Pittsburgh	Music	The University of Chicago Round Table
2:45			Sports	
3pm	Mischa Mischakoff, violin	New York Philharmonic Orchestra		I Want a Divorce
3:15	Foreign Policy Association Talks			
3:30	Tapestry Musicale			European news
3:45				H. V. Kaltenborn, news
4pm	National Vespers			Glen Gray Orchestra
4:15				
4:30	The Chamber Music Society of Lower Basin Street	The Pursuit of Happiness		The World is Yours
4:45				
5pm	The Moylan Sisters, songs	Choose Up Sides	The Musical Steelmakers	Yvette Sings
5:15	The Dinah Shore Show			Bob Becker's Dog Talks
5:30	String Symphony	Flow Gently, Sweet Rhythm	Harry James Orchestra	Crossroads
5:45				

DAYTIME — SPRING, 1940

Monday-Friday

BLUE	CBS	MBS	NBC	
Music / Informational Talk	Music	The Career of Alice Blair	The Light of the World	*2pm*
	Joyce Jordan, Girl Intern	Meet Miss Julia	Arnold Grimm's Daughter	*2:15*
Music	Your Family and Mine	Sports	Valiant Lady	*2:30*
	My Son and I		Betty Crocker, cooking / Hymns of All Churches	*2:45*
Orphans of Divorce	Society Girl		The Story of Mary Marlin	*3pm*
Amanda of Honeymoon Hill	The Golden Gate Quartet		Ma Perkins	*3:15*
John's Other Wife	Uncle Jonathan		Pepper Young's Family	*3:30*
Just Plain Bill	Music / Richard Maxwell, songs		Vic and Sade	*3:45*
Club Matinee, Garry Moore	Music		Mary Noble, Backstage Wife	*4pm*
	Informational Talk		Stella Dallas	*4:15*
	Manhattan Mother		Lorenzo Jones	*4:30*
	Smilin' Ed McConnell, songs		Young Widder Brown	*4:45*
Music / Name It and Take It	By Kathleen Norris	Dick Kuhn Orchestra	Girl Alone	*5pm*
Music / The Singing Story Lady	Billy and Betty	Music / The Adventures of Superman	Midstream	*5:15*
Bud Barton	It Happened in Hollywood	The Johnson Family	Jack Armstrong, the All-American Boy	*5:30*
The Tom Mix Ralston Straight Shooters	Scattergood Baines	Little Orphan Annie	The O'Neills	*5:45*

DAYTIME — SPRING, 1940

Saturday

	BLUE	CBS	MBS	NBC
9am	The Breakfast Club	Richard Maxwell, songs	Pauline Alpert, piano	Texas Jim Robertson, songs
9:15		Old Vienna	Junior Spotlight	Watch Your Step
9:30		Carl Hohengarten Orchestra		Isabel Manning Hewson, food
9:45				The Crackerjack Quartet
10am	Al and Lee Reiser, piano	Stringtime with Walberg Brown	The Marriage Clinic	Lincoln Highway
10:15	Rakov Orchestra			
10:30	The Charioteers Quartet	National Hillbilly Champions	The First Offender	Betty Moore, talk
10:45	Child Grows Up			The Bright Idea Club
11am	Spud Murphy Orchestra	Cincinnati Conservatory Recitals	News	
11:15	The State Normal School Choir		Hayden Planetarium Talks	Smilin' Ed McConnell, songs
11:30	Our Barn		The US Army Band	Joseph Gallicchio Orchestra
11:45				
12pm	The American Education Forum	Columbia's Country Journal	The Man on the Farm	Strings That Sing
12:15				
12:30	The National Farm and Home Hour	Let's Pretend	Vincent Connolly, news	Call to Youth
12:45			Enoch Light Orchestra	Pfaender and Miles, piano
1pm		Music	Ed Fitzgerald and Company	Gordon Benedict Orchestra
1:15				The Stamp Club
1:30	Luncheon at the Waldorf	Time to Take It Easy	The University Life Forum	Ben Bernie, the Old Maestro
1:45				Matinee in Rhythm

DAYTIME — SPRING, 1940

Saturday

	BLUE	CBS	MBS	NBC
2pm	The Metropolitan Opera	The Brush Creek Follies	Carnegie Tech Symphony	Lani McIntyre Orchestra
2:15			Sports	
2:30		Music		Golden Melodies
2:45				
3pm		Sports		Music Styled for You
3:15				
3:30				Dol Brissett Orchestra
3:45				
4pm			Sweetheart Songs	Campus Capers
4:15				
4:30			Horse Racing	Dance Orchestra
4:45				
5pm	Magic Waves		Sammy Kaye Orchestra	Paul La Valle Orchestra
5:15	Gus Steck Orchestra			
5:30	Ted Powell Orchestra	The Human Adventure		Don Bestor Orchestra
5:45				

EVENING — SUMMER, 1940

Sunday

	BLUE	CBS	MBS	NBC
6pm	Gray Gordon Orchestra	Fun in Print	Tropical Serenade, Don Arres	The Catholic Hour
6:15				
6:30	The Parade of Years	Gene Autry's Melody Ranch	The Show of the Week	Beat the Band
6:45				
7pm	European News	European News Roundup	Ramona and the Tune Twisters	Name Three
7:15				
7:30	The World's Fair Band	The Adventures of Ellery Queen	Frank Singiser, news	The Fitch Bandwagon
7:45			Wythe Williams, news	
8pm	The Sunday Night Concert	The Columbia Workshop	The American Forum of the Air	The Bishop and the Gargoyle
8:15				
8:30		Crime Doctor		One Man's Family
8:45		Elmer Davis, news (8:55pm)		
9pm	Walter Winchell's Jergens Journal	The Ford Summer Hour	Overseas News	The Manhattan Merry-Go-Round
9:15	The Parker Family		Glenn Miller Orchestra	
9:30	Irene Rich Dramas		Arthur Hale, news	The American Album of Familiar Music
9:45	The Colgate Sports Newsreel, Bill Stern		The Song Spinners	
10pm	The Goodwill Hour	Take It or Leave It	The Symphonic Hour	The Hour of Charm
10:15				
10:30		The Grant Park Concerts		Human Nature in Action
10:45				The Voice That Walks Beside You

EVENING — SUMMER, 1940

Monday

BLUE	CBS	MBS	NBC	
The Dinning Sisters, songs	Edwin C. Hill, news	Uncle Don	Lil' Abner	6pm
Bill Stern, sports	Hedda Hopper, gossip		Selective Service	6:15
Jose Bethancourt Orchestra	Paul Sullivan, news	Frank Singiser, news	The Stamp Club	6:30
Lowell Thomas, news	The World Today	The Adventures of Superman	Paul Douglas, sports	6:45
Frankie Masters Orchestra	Amos 'n' Andy	Stan Lomax, sports	Chesterfield Time	7pm
Radio Magic	Joey Kearns Orchestra	Arthur Hale, news	Edward Tomlinson, news	7:15
The Coolidge String Quartet	Blondie	The Lone Ranger	Burns and Allen	7:30
				7:45
Little Ol' Hollywood	Tune-Up Time	Play Broadcast	The Bell Telephone Hour	8pm
				8:15
The Washington Merry-Go-Round	The Model Minstrels	On the Spot	The Voice of Firestone	8:30
	Elmer Davis, news (8:55pm)			8:45
The Green Hornet	Forecast	Wythe Williams, news	Dr. I. Q., the Mental Banker	9pm
		Glenn Miller Orchestra		9:15
Paul Martin Orchestra		Edwin Franko Goldman Band	The Show Boat	9:30
				9:45
T. R. Ybarra, news	Guy Lombardo Orchestra	Raymond Gram Swing, news	The Carnation Contented Hour	10pm
Gene Brown Orchestra		Who Knows		10:15
Adventures in Reading	George Fielding Eliot, comment	Fulton Lewis Jr., news	Barry Winton Orchestra	10:30
	Genevieve Rowe, songs	Tommy Reynolds Orchestra		10:45

EVENING — SUMMER, 1940

Tuesday

	BLUE	CBS	MBS	NBC
6pm	The Dinning Sisters, songs	Edwin C. Hill, news	Uncle Don	Lil' Abner
6:15	Bill Stern, sports	Michael Loring, songs		Selective Service
6:30	Jose Bethancourt Orchestra	Paul Sullivan, news	Frank Singiser, news	Yvette Sings
6:45	Lowell Thomas, news	The World Today	Tommy Reynolds Orchestra	Paul Douglas, sports
7pm	Easy Aces	Amos 'n' Andy	Stan Lomax, sports	Chesterfield Time
7:15	Mr. Keen, Tracer of Lost Persons	Joey Kearns Orchestra	Joe Venuti and the Venutians	Edward Tomlinson, news
7:30	Gordon Jenkins Orchestra	Second Husband	Arthur Hale, sports	Tony Russell, songs
7:45			Sam Balter, sports	H. V. Kaltenborn, news
8pm	The Roy Shield Revue	The Court of Missing Heirs	Symphonic Strings	Johnny Presents
8:15				
8:30	Information, Please	Lud Gluskin Orchestra	Meet the Stars	Tums Treasure Chest
8:45		Elmer Davis, news (8:55pm)		
9pm	Musical Americana	We, the People	Gabriel Heatter, news	Battle of the Sexes
9:15			Fulton Lewis Jr., news	
9:30	Your Neighbors, the Haines	Professor Quiz	The Laugh and Swing Club	Meredith Willson's Musical Revue
9:45				
10pm	T. R. Ybarra, news	Moonlight Serenade	Raymond Gram Swing, news	Summer Pastime
10:15	The Ink Spots	Public Affairs	L. H. Nason, news	
10:30	Monsieur Le Capitaine	George Fielding Eliot, comment	The Vagabonds Trail	Uncle Walter's Dog House
10:45		The Four Clubmen		

EVENING — SUMMER, 1940

	Wednesday			
BLUE	CBS	MBS	NBC	
The Dinning Sisters, songs	Edwin C. Hill, news	Uncle Don	Lil' Abner	6pm
Bill Stern, sports	Hedda Hopper, gossip		Selective Service	6:15
Jose Bethancourt Orchestra	Paul Sullivan, news	Frank Singiser, news	The Stamp Club	6:30
Lowell Thomas, news	The World Today	The Adventures of Superman	Paul Douglas, sports	6:45
Easy Aces	Amos 'n' Andy	Stan Lomax, sports	Chesterfield Time	7pm
Mr. Keen, Tracer of Lost Persons	The Lanny Ross Show	Arthur Hale, news	Edward Tomlinson, news	7:15
Paul LaValle Orchestra	Meet Mr. Meek	The Lone Ranger	The Revelers Quartet	7:30
			H. V. Kaltenborn, news	7:45
This, Our America	Uncle Jim's Question Bee	The Sheep and Goats Club Revue	Promoting Priscilla	8pm
				8:15
Manhattan at Midnight	Dr. Christian	Where Are You From	Paducah Plantation, Whitey Ford	8:30
	Elmer Davis, news (8:55pm)			8:45
The Green Hornet	The Texaco Star Theater	Gabriel Heatter, news	Abbott and Costello	9pm
		Fulton Lewis Jr., news		9:15
The Roy Shields Revue	The Lewisohn Stadium Concerts	Serenade for Strings	Mr. District Attorney	9:30
				9:45
T. R. Ybarra, news	Moonlight Serenade	Raymond Gram Swing, news	Kay Kyser's College of Musical Knowledge	10pm
The Ink Spots	Public Affairs	L. H. Nason, news		10:15
Dance Orchestra	George Fielding Eliot, comment	Pageant of Melody		10:30
	Genevieve Rowe, songs			10:45

EVENING — SUMMER, 1940

Thursday

	BLUE	CBS	MBS	NBC
6pm	The Dinning Sisters, songs	Edwin C. Hill, news	Uncle Don	Lil' Abner
6:15	Bill Stern, sports	Bob Edge's Outdoor Talks		Selective Service
6:30	Barnes Orchestra	Paul Sullivan, news	Frank Singiser, news	June Hynd's Guest Book
6:45	Lowell Thomas, news	The World Today	McFarland Twins Orchestra	Paul Douglas, sports
7pm	Easy Aces	Amos 'n' Andy	Stan Lomax, sports	Chesterfield Time
7:15	Mr. Keen, Tracer of Lost Persons	The Lanny Ross Show	Joe Venuti and the Venutians	Edward Tomlinson, news
7:30	Bob Crosby Orchestra	Vox Pop	Arthur Hale, news	The Schaefer All-Star Parade
7:45			Sam Balter, sports	
8pm	Canadian Travelogue	The Ask-It Basket	The Eddie Mayehoff Show	Good News of 1940
8:15				
8:30	Pot o' Gold	Strange As It Seems	In Chicago Tonight	The Aldrich Family
8:45		Elmer Davis, news (8:55pm)		
9pm	Singing and Swinging	Major Bowes' Original Amateur Hour	Gabriel Heatter, news	The Kraft Music Hall, Bob Burns
9:15			Fulton Lewis Jr., news	
9:30	Concert in Miniature		Morton Gould Orchestra	
9:45				
10pm	T. R. Ybarra, news	Moonlight Serenade	Raymond Gram Swing, news	Vallee Varieties
10:15	Montreal Symphony Orchestra	Public Affairs	L. H. Nason, news	
10:30		George Fielding Eliot, comment	Harold Stokes Eskimo Pie Orchestra	The Grant Park Concerts
10:45		Buddy Clark, songs		

EVENING — SUMMER, 1940

Friday

BLUE	CBS	MBS	NBC	
Alma Kitchell's Briefcase	Edwin C. Hill, news	Uncle Don	Lil' Abner	6pm
Bill Stern, sports	Hedda Hopper, gossip		Selective Service	6:15
Dance Orchestra	Paul Sullivan, news	Frank Singiser, news	The Stamp Club	6:30
Lowell Thomas, news	The World Today	The Adventures of Superman	Paul Douglas, sports	6:45
African Trek	Amos 'n' Andy	Stan Lomax, sports	Chesterfield Time	7pm
	The Lanny Ross Show	Arthur Hale, news	Edward Tomlinson, news	7:15
Russ Morgan Orchestra	Al Pearce and His Gang	The Lone Ranger	The Revelers Quartet	7:30
			Ted Steele Orchestra	7:45
Strictly Business	Man About Hollywood	Wings for America	The Cities Service Concerts	8pm
				8:15
Death Valley Days	Choose Up Sides	Sinfonietta	Hollywood Today	8:30
	Elmer Davis, news (8:55pm)			8:45
Harry Kogen Orchestra	Johnny Presents Dramatized Short Stories	Gabriel Heatter, news	Waltz Time	9pm
		Fulton Lewis Jr., news		9:15
The American Music Festival	Grand Central Station	Command Performance	Music for Moderns	9:30
				9:45
T. R. Ybarra, news	Public Affairs	Raymond Gram Swing, news	The Don Ameche Variety Show	10pm
The Dinah Shore Show		L. H. Nason, news		10:15
The Ink Spots	George Fielding Eliot, comment	The Grant Park Concerts	The Quiz Kids	10:30
Condido Bothelo, songs	The Golden Gate Quartet			10:45

EVENING — SUMMER, 1940

Saturday

	BLUE	CBS	MBS	NBC
6pm	Cecil Golly Orchestra	News	Uncle Don	El Chico
6:15		Yella Pessi, harp		
6:30	Renfrew of the Mounted	Today in Europe	Frank Singiser, news	The Art of Living
6:45		The World Today	The Profit Trio	Paul Douglas, sports
7pm	Message of Israel	The People's Platform	Stan Lomax, sports	Kaltenmeyer's Kindergarten
7:15			Dance Orchestra	
7:30	Eddy Duchin Orchestra	The Gay Nineties Revue	Arthur Hale, news	Dance Orchestra
7:45			Sam Balter, sports	H. V. Kaltenborn, news
8pm	The Radio Guild	Sky Blazers	Wythe Williams, news	Bobby Byrne Orchestra
8:15			Tommy Tucker Orchestra	
8:30	Your Marriage Club	The Human Adventure	Nobody's Children	The Listener's Playhouse
8:45		Elmer Davis, news (8:55pm)		
9pm	Gordon Jenkins Orchestra	Your Hit Parade	Gabriel Heatter, news	The National Barn Dance
9:15			Hawaii Calls	
9:30	Dance Orchestra		The American Choral Festival	
9:45		Truth or Consequences		
10pm	T. R. Ybarra, news			Uncle Ezra's Radio Station
10:15	Music	Public Affairs		
10:30	Melody in the Night	George Fielding Eliot, comment	Music by Moonlight	Public Affairs
10:45		Michael Loring, songs		

DAYTIME — SUMMER, 1940

Sunday

	BLUE	CBS	MBS	NBC
9am	News	News	Rainbow House	News
9:15	The Children's Hour	Marion Carley, piano		The Four Showmen
9:30		Richard Maxwell, songs		Sunday Drivers
9:45				
10am	Melodic Moods	The CBS Church of the Air	News	Highlights of the Bible
10:15			The Garden of Memories	
10:30	The Southernaires Quartet	Wings Over Jordan		The Horn and Hardart Children's Hour
10:45			Songs	
11am	News	News and Rhythm	Music	
11:15	The Luther Layman Singers	Yella Pessi, harp	The Northwestern Reviewing Stand	
11:30	Sidney Walton's Music	Major Bowes' Capitol Family	Pauline Alpert, piano	News
11:45	The Moylan Sisters, songs			Music and American Youth
12pm	The Radio City Music Hall		Chorus from the World's Fair	Bonnie Stewart, songs
12:15				Julio Oyanguran, guitar
12:30		The Salt Lake Tabernacle Choir	The Sing a Song of Safety Club	Wings Over America
12:45			News	
1pm	Listen and Live	The CBS Church of the Air	Music	The Cleveland Pops Concert
1:15	The Vass Family, songs			
1:30	Harry Reser Orchestra	March of Games	Jack Kilty, songs	The Silver Strings
1:45			Sports	

DAYTIME — SUMMER, 1940

Monday-Friday

BLUE	CBS	MBS	NBC	
The Woman of Tomorrow	Woman of Courage	Music / Arthur Godfrey, songs	Happy Jack Turner, songs	9am
	News	Songs / The Heart of Julia Blake	Music / The Band Goes to Town	9:15
The Breakfast Club	Music	Music	Music / Isabel Manning Hewson, food	9:30
	Bachelor's Children	Music / Nell Vinick, beauty	The Gospel Singer	9:45
Painted Dreams	Pretty Kitty Kelly	Get Thin to Music	The Man I Married	10am
Vic and Sade	The Story of Myrt and Marge	Music	Midstream	10:15
The Story of Mary Marlin	Hilltop House	Meet Mr. Morgan	The Story of Ellen Randolph	10:30
Pepper Young's Family	Stepmother	Music	The Woman in White	10:45
Linda Dale	Hollywood Dreams / Short, Short Story	News	David Harum	11am
Clark Dennis, songs	Martha Webster	Martha Deane, talk	The Road of Life	11:15
The Wife Saver	Big Sister		Against the Storm	11:30
Thunder Over Paradise	Aunt Jenny's True Life Stories		The Guiding Light	11:45
Music / Nellie Revell, talk	Kate Smith Speaks	The Consumers' Quiz	The Woman in White	12pm
Music / Nancy Booth Craig, talk	When a Girl Marries	Music	The O'Neills	12:15
The National Farm and Home Hour	The Romance of Helen Trent	Vincent Connolly, news	Music	12:30
	Our Gal Sunday	Pegeen Presents	News	12:45
	The Goldbergs	I'll Never Forget, Frank Luther	Music	1pm
Between the Bookends	Life Can Be Beautiful	Ed Fitzgerald and Company	Music / Nature Sketches	1:15
Religious Talk	The Right to Happiness	The Voice of Experience	Friendly Neighbors	1:30
Music	The Road of Life	Victor Lindlahr, health	Words and Music	1:45

DAYTIME — SUMMER, 1940

Sunday

	BLUE	CBS	MBS	NBC
2pm	Treasure Trails of Songs	Rio de Janeiro Symphony Orchestra		Southwestern Serenade
2:15				
2:30	Salon Silhouettes	Buddy Clark and the Symphonettes		The University of Chicago Round Table
2:45				
3pm	Vincente Gomez, guitar	New York Philharmonic Orchestra		I Want a Divorce
3:15	Foreign Policy Association Talks			
3:30	The National Music Camp			Yvette Sings
3:45				H. V. Kaltenborn, news
4pm	National Vespers			Chautaqua Symphony Orchestra
4:15				
4:30	The Chamber Music Society of Lower Basin Street	Invitation to Learning		
4:45				
5pm	Bobby Byrne Orchestra	World's Fair Vespers		The World is Yours
5:15				
5:30	The Voice of Hawaii	Flow Gently, Sweet Rhythm		Horace Heidt Orchestra
5:45				

DAYTIME — SUMMER, 1940

Monday-Friday

BLUE	CBS	MBS	NBC	
Music / Informational Talk	Young Dr. Malone	The Career of Alice Blair	The Light of the World	2pm
	Joyce Jordan, Girl Intern	Meet Miss Julia	Arnold Grimm's Daughter	2:15
Music	Fletcher Wiley, talk	Talk and Music	Valiant Lady	2:30
	My Son and I		Betty Crocker, cooking / Hymns of All Churches	2:45
Orphans of Divorce	Society Girl	Sports	The Story of Mary Marlin	3pm
Amanda of Honeymoon Hill	Sports		Ma Perkins	3:15
John's Other Wife			Pepper Young's Family	3:30
Just Plain Bill			Vic and Sade	3:45
Club Matinee, Garry Moore			Mary Noble, Backstage Wife	4pm
			Stella Dallas	4:15
			Lorenzo Jones	4:30
			Young Widder Brown	4:45
Uncle Mal			Girl Alone	5pm
Rocky Gordon		Waite Hoyt, sports	Life Can Be Beautiful	5:15
Music / The Singing Story Lady		Music	Jack Armstrong, the All-American Boy	5:30
Bud Barton	Scattergood Baines		The O'Neills	5:45

DAYTIME — SUMMER, 1940

Saturday

	BLUE	CBS	MBS	NBC
9am	The Breakfast Club	National Hillbilly Champions	Weekend in New York	Texas Jim Robertson, songs
9:15		News	Dance Orchestra	Watch Your Step
9:30		Let's Be Lazy	Ed Fitzgerald and Company	Peggy Harris, talk
9:45				Musical Tete-a-Tete
10am	The Traveling Chef	Honest Abe		Lincoln Highway
10:15	The Four Belles			
10:30	Rakov Orchestra	The Singing Bee	The Singing Strings	The Bright Idea Club
10:45				
11am	The Charioteers Quartet	The Old Dirt Dobber	News	Chautauqua Concert for Young People
11:15	Rosa Lee, songs		The US Army Band	
11:30	Our Barn	The Dorian String Quartet		Bill Stern's Sports School
11:45			Hayden Planetarium Talks	The Federation of Women's Clubs
12pm	Dance Orchestra	Columbia's Country Journal	Buck Rogers of the 25th Century	Strings That Sing
12:15				Julio Oyanguren, guitar
12:30	The National Farm and Home Hour	Let's Pretend	Vincent Connolly, news	Call to Youth
12:45			Zeke Manners Variety	Pfaender and Miles, piano
1pm		Keyboard Capers	Tropical Serenade, Don Arres	Howard Ropa, songs
1:15		Highways to Health		The Stamp Club
1:30	Luncheon at the Waldorf	Dance Orchestra	McFarland Twins Orchestra	Frankie Masters Orchestra
1:45				

DAYTIME — SUMMER, 1940

Saturday

	BLUE	CBS	MBS	NBC
2pm	Ray Kinney Orchestra	Vera Brodsky, piano	The World's Fair Band	I'm An American
2:15				Gardner Benedict Orchestra
2:30	The World's Fair Band	The Brush Creek Follies	Dance Orchestra	Matinee in Rhythm
2:45				
3pm	Dance Orchestra	Sports	Elinor Sherry, songs	Dance Orchestra
3:15			Sports	
3:30	The National Music Camp			Concert Orchestra
3:45				
4pm	Club Matinee, Garry Moore			Golden Melodies
4:15				
4:30				Dance Orchestra
4:45				
5pm	Gus Steck Orchestra		Waite Hoyt, sports	Tommy Dorsey Orchestra
5:15			Dance Orchestra	
5:30	Rhythms By Ricardo	Nat Brandwynne Orchestra		
5:45				

EVENING — FALL, 1940

Sunday

	BLUE	CBS	MBS	NBC
6pm	New Friends of Music	The Silver Theater	Double or Nothing	The Catholic Hour
6:15				
6:30		Gene Autry's Melody Ranch	The Show of the Week	Beat the Band
6:45				
7pm	Drew Pearson, news	News of the World	Ramona and the Tune Twisters	The Jello Program, Jack Benny
7:15	European News			
7:30	Speak Up, America	The Gulf Screen Theater	Frank Singiser, news	The Fitch Bandwagon
7:45			Wythe Williams, news	
8pm	Parade of the Years	The Helen Hayes Theater	The American Forum of the Air	The Charlie McCarthy Show
8:15				
8:30	Sherlock Holmes	Crime Doctor		One Man's Family
8:45		Elmer Davis, news (8:55pm)	Dorothy Thompson, news	
9pm	Walter Winchell's Jergens Journal	The Ford Sunday Evening Hour	Overseas News	The Manhattan Merry-Go-Round
9:15	The Parker Family		Glenn Miller Orchestra	
9:30	Irene Rich Dramas		Battle of the Burroughs	The American Album of Familiar Music
9:45	The Colgate Sports Newsreel, Bill Stern			
10pm	The Goodwill Hour	Take It or Leave It	The Symphonic Hour	The Hour of Charm
10:15				
10:30		The Columbia Workshop		The Madrigal Singers
10:45				The Voice That Walks Beside You

EVENING — FALL, 1940

Monday

BLUE	CBS	MBS	NBC	
The Escorts and Betty	Edwin C. Hill, news	Uncle Don	Dance Orchestra	6pm
Bill Stern, sports	Hedda Hopper, gossip		Selective Service	6:15
Richard Himber Orchestra	Paul Sullivan, news	Frank Singiser, news	The Stamp Club	6:30
Lowell Thomas, news	The World Today	Meet Mr. Morgan	Lil' Abner	6:45
Bob Hannon, songs	Amos 'n' Andy	Stan Lomax, sports	Chesterfield Time	7pm
Radio Magic	The Lanny Ross Show	Arthur Hale, news	John W. Vandercook, news	7:15
Glenn Miller Orchestra	Blondie	The Lone Ranger	Burns and Allen	7:30
				7:45
I Love a Mystery	Those We Love	Play Broadcast	The Bell Telephone Hour	8pm
				8:15
True or False	The Model Minstrels	The Green Hornet	The Voice of Firestone	8:30
	Elmer Davis, news (8:55pm)			8:45
The National Radio Forum	The Lux Radio Theater	Gabriel Heatter, news	Dr. I. Q., the Mental Banker	9pm
		Glenn Miller Orchestra		9:15
The Chamber Music Society		Eddy Duchin Orchestra	The Show Boat	9:30
				9:45
Story Dramas	Guy Lombardo Orchestra	Raymond Gram Swing, news	The Carnation Contented Hour	10pm
Don Pastor Orchestra		Who Knows		10:15
Adventures in Reading	Back Where I Come From	Life Can Be Beautiful	Barry Winton Orchestra	10:30
	George Fielding Eliot, comment	Dance Orchestra		10:45

EVENING — FALL, 1940

Tuesday

	BLUE	CBS	MBS	NBC
6pm	The Dinning Sisters, songs	Edwin C. Hill, news	Uncle Don	Dance Orchestra
6:15	Bill Stern, sports	The Voice of Broadway		Selective Service
6:30	The Gulden Serenaders	Paul Sullivan, news	Frank Singiser, news	The Stamp Club
6:45	Lowell Thomas, news	The World Today	Meet Mr. Morgan	Lil' Abner
7pm	Easy Aces	Amos 'n' Andy	Stan Lomax, sports	Chesterfield Time
7:15	Mr. Keen, Tracer of Lost Persons	The Lanny Ross Show	James H. R. Cromwell, talk	John W. Vandercook, news
7:30	Abe Lyman Orchestra	Second Husband	Arthur Hale, news	So You Think You Know Music
7:45	Famous Fathers		Sam Balter, sports	
8pm	Ben Bernie, the Old Maestro	The Court of Missing Heirs	Wythe Williams, news	Johnny Presents
8:15			Cats and Jammers	
8:30	Information, Please	The First Nighter Program	Symphonic Strings	Tums Treasure Chest
8:45		Elmer Davis, news (8:55pm)		
9pm	Uncle Jim's Question Bee	We, the People	News	Battle of the Sexes
9:15			Fulton Lewis Jr., news	
9:30	The Bishop and the Gargoyle	Professor Quiz	The Laugh and Swing Club	Fibber Magee and Molly
9:45				
10pm	Story Dramas	Moonlight Serenade	Raymond Gram Swing, news	The Pepsodent Show, Bob Hope
10:15	Dance Orchestra	Public Affairs	The War at Sea	
10:30	Emma Otero, songs		Life Can Be Beautiful	Uncle Walter's Dog House
10:45		George Fielding Eliot, comment	Public Affairs	

EVENING — FALL, 1940

Wednesday

BLUE	CBS	MBS	NBC	
The Vagabonds Quartet	Edwin C. Hill, news	Uncle Don	Dance Orchestra	6pm
Bill Stern, sports	Hedda Hopper, gossip		Selective Service	6:15
Richard Himber Orchestra	Paul Sullivan, news	Frank Singiser, news	The Stamp Club	6:30
Lowell Thomas, news	The World Today	Meet Mr. Morgan	Lil' Abner	6:45
Easy Aces	Amos 'n' Andy	Stan Lomax, sports	Chesterfield Time	7pm
Mr. Keen, Tracer of Lost Persons	The Lanny Ross Show	Arthur Hale, news	John W. Vandercook, news	7:15
Echoes of New York	Meet Mr. Meek	The Lone Ranger	The Cavalcade of America	7:30
				7:45
The Quiz Kids	Big Town	Where Are You From	The Hollywood Playhouse	8pm
				8:15
Manhattan at Midnight	Dr. Christian	Sherlock Holmes	Paducah Plantation, Red Foley	8:30
	Elmer Davis, news (8:55pm)			8:45
The Song of Your Life	The Texaco Star Theater, Fred Allen	Gabriel Heatter, news	Time to Smile, Eddie Cantor	9pm
		Fulton Lewis Jr., news		9:15
The Roy Shield Revue		The Sheep and Goats Club Revue	Mr. District Attorney	9:30
				9:45
Story Dramas	Moonlight Serenade	Raymond Gram Swing, news	Kay Kyser's College of Musical Knowledge	10pm
Dance Orchestra	Public Affairs	The War in the Air		10:15
Gordon Jenkins Orchestra	Back Where I Come From	The Green Hornet		10:30
	George Fielding Eliot, comment			10:45

EVENING — FALL, 1940

Thursday

	BLUE	CBS	MBS	NBC
6pm	Dance Orchestra	Edwin C. Hill, news	Uncle Don	Dance Orchestra
6:15	Bill Stern, sports	William L. Shirer, news		Selective Service
6:30	The Gulden Serenaders	Paul Sullivan, news	Frank Singiser, news	Dr. Walter Van Kirk, talk
6:45	Lowell Thomas, news	The World Today	Meet Mr. Morgan	Lil' Abner
7pm	Easy Aces	Amos 'n' Andy	Stan Lomax, sports	Chesterfield Time
7:15	Mr. Keen, Tracer of Lost Persons	The Lanny Ross Show	Public Affairs	John W. Vandercook, news
7:30	Tom Powers Life Studies	Vox Pop	Arthur Hale, news	The Camel Caravan
7:45	Music		Sam Balter, sports	
8pm	Pot o' Gold	The Ask-It Basket	Wythe Williams, news	Maxwell House Coffee Time, Brice and Morgan
8:15			Ed Dooley, sports	
8:30	Fame and Fortune	Strange As It Seems	In Chicago Tonight	The Aldrich Family
8:45		Elmer Davis, news (8:55pm)		
9pm	Singing and Swinging	Major Bowes' Original Amateur Hour	Gabriel Heatter, news	The Kraft Music Hall, Bing Crosby
9:15			Fulton Lewis Jr., news	
9:30	Concert in Miniature		The Eddie Mayehoff Show	
9:45				
10pm	The Fisk Jubilee Choir	Moonlight Serenade	Raymond Gram Swing, news	Vallee Varieties
10:15		Choose Up Sides	Arthur Mann, news	
10:30	Frank Black Orchestra		Morton Gould Orchestra	Musical Americana
10:45		George Fielding Eliot, comment		

EVENING — FALL, 1940

Friday

BLUE	CBS	MBS	NBC	
Dance Orchestra	Edwin C. Hill, news	Uncle Don	Dance Orchestra	6pm
Bill Stern, sports	Hedda Hopper, gossip		Selective Service	6:15
Richard Himber Orchestra	Paul Sullivan, news	Frank Singiser, news	The Stamp Club	6:30
Lowell Thomas, news	The World Today	Meet Mr. Morgan	Lil' Abner	6:45
African Trek	Amos 'n' Andy	Stan Lomax, sports	Chesterfield Time	7pm
	The Lanny Ross Show	Arthur Hale, news	John W. Vandercook, news	7:15
Radio Magic	Al Pearce and His Gang	The Lone Ranger	Alec Templeton Time	7:30
				7:45
Harry Kogen Orchestra	The Kate Smith Hour	Lew Loyal Orchestra	The Cities Service Concerts	8pm
				8:15
Death Valley Days		Sinfonietta	From Hollywood Today	8:30
	Elmer Davis, news (8:55pm)			8:45
Gangbusters	Johnny Presents Dramatized Short Stories	Gabriel Heatter, news	Waltz Time	9pm
		Lou Little, sports		9:15
The Vass Family, songs	Grand Central Station	I Want a Divorce	Everyman's Theater	9:30
Condido Botehlo, songs				9:45
Madison Square Garden Boxing	Believe It or Not	Raymond Gram Swing, news	Wings of Destiny	10pm
		Overseas News		10:15
	Back Where I Come From	Life Can Be Beautiful	Dance Orchestra	10:30
	George Fielding Eliot, comment	Public Affairs		10:45

EVENING — FALL, 1940

Saturday

	BLUE	CBS	MBS	NBC
6pm	Dance Orchestra	Albert Warner, sports	Uncle Don	El Chico
6:15		Music		Selective Service
6:30	Renfrew of the Mounted	Elmer Davis, news	Frank Singiser, news	Religion in the News
6:45		The World Today	Meet Mr. Morgan	Sports Round-Up
7pm	Message of Israel	The People's Platform	Stan Lomax, sports	Frankie Masters Orchestra
7:15			The Charioteers Quartet	John W. Vandercook, news
7:30	Little Ol' Hollywood	The Gay Nineties Revue	Arthur Hale, news	Yvette Sings
7:45			Sam Balter, sports	H. V. Kaltenborn, news
8pm	Dance Orchestra	Your Marriage Club	The New Jersey Schoolmaster	The Knickerbocker Playhouse
8:15			Ed Dooley, sports	
8:30	Hollywood Tomorrow	Wayne King Orchestra	Tropical Serenade, Don Arres	Truth or Consequences
8:45		Elmer Davis, news (8:55pm)		
9pm	Paul La Valle Orchestra	Your Hit Parade	Gabriel Heatter, news	The National Barn Dance
9:15			Jimmy Dorsey Orchestra	
9:30	The Listener's Playhouse		Contact Dave Elman	
9:45		Saturday Night Serenade		
10pm	NBC Symphony Orchestra		The Chicago Theater of the Air	Uncle Ezra's Radio Station
10:15		Public Affairs		
10:30		Jack Leonard, songs		Gene Krupa Orchestra
10:45		George Fielding Eliot, comment		

DAYTIME — FALL, 1940

Sunday

	BLUE	CBS	MBS	NBC
9am	News	News	Rainbow House	News
9:15	The Children's Hour	Clyde Barrie, songs		The Four Showmen
9:30		Wings Over Jordan		Sunday Drivers
9:45				
10am	Stringtime with Walberg Brown	The CBS Church of the Air	News	The National Radio Pulpit
10:15			The Lamplighter	
10:30	The Southernaires Quartet	Indianapolis Symphony Orchestra	The Smart Set	The Horn and Hardart Children's Hour
10:45				
11am	News	News and Rhythm	The Minute Men Quartet	
11:15	Sweet Land of Liberty			
11:30	Sidney Walton's Music	Major Bowes' Capitol Family	The Northwestern Reviewing Stand	News
11:45	Ahead of the Headlines			Music and American Youth
12pm	The Radio City Music Hall		Don Arres, songs	Gray Gordon Orchestra
12:15				
12:30		The Salt Lake Tabernacle Choir	The Sing a Song of Safety Club	Wings Over America
12:45			Frank Singiser, news	
1pm	I'm An American	The CBS Church of the Air	The Canary Pet Shop	The Cleveland Pops Concert
1:15	The Vass Family, songs		Jack Kilty, songs	
1:30	Vicki Chase and Tom Thomas, songs	March of Games	The Lutheran Hour	On Your Job
1:45				

LISTINGS FOR 1940

DAYTIME — FALL, 1940

Monday-Friday

BLUE	CBS	MBS	NBC	
The Woman of Tomorrow	George Bryan, news	Music / Arthur Godfrey, songs	Happy Jack Turner, songs	*9am*
	The American School of the Air	Talk and Music / The Heart of Julia Blake	Music / The Band Goes to Town	*9:15*
The Breakfast Club		Music	Isabel Manning Hewson, food	*9:30*
	Bachelor's Children		The Gospel Singer	*9:45*
Painted Dreams	By Kathleen Norris	The Pure Food Hour /	This Small Town	*10am*
Vic and Sade	The Story of Myrt and Marge	Music	Hank Lawson's Knights	*10:15*
The Story of Mary Marlin	Stepmother		The Story of Ellen Randolph	*10:30*
Pepper Young's Family	Woman of Courage		The Guiding Light	*10:45*
Linda Dale	Hollywood Dreams / Short, Short Story	News	The Man I Married	*11am*
Clark Dennis, songs	Martha Webster	Martha Deane, talk	Against the Storm	*11:15*
The Wife Saver	Big Sister		The Road of Life	*11:30*
Thunder Over Paradise	Aunt Jenny's True Life Stories		David Harum	*11:45*
Music	Kate Smith Speaks	Victor Lindlahr, health /	The Wheatena Playhouse	*12pm*
Music / Nancy Booth Craig, talk	When a Girl Marries	Talk	The O'Neills	*12:15*
The National Farm and Home Hour	The Romance of Helen Trent	Vincent Connolly, news	Songs	*12:30*
	Our Gal Sunday	The Consumers' Quiz	News	*12:45*
	Life Can Be Beautiful	I'll Never Forget, Frank Luther	Music	*1pm*
Between the Bookends	The Woman in White	Ed Fitzgerald, talk	Music / Tony Wons' Scrapbook	*1:15*
Religious Talk	The Right to Happiness	The Voice of Experience	Friendly Neighbors	*1:30*
Music	The Road of Life	The Career of Alice Blair	Words and Music	*1:45*

DAYTIME — FALL, 1940

Sunday

	BLUE	CBS	MBS	NBC
2pm	American Pilgrimage	Flow Gently, Sweet Rhythm	Sports	Washington Calling
2:15	Foreign Policy Association Talks			
2:30	Tapestry Musicale	World News Today		The University of Chicago Round Table
2:45				
3pm	Great Plays	New York Philharmonic Orchestra		String Symphony
3:15				
3:30				H. V. Kaltenborn, news
3:45				Bob Becker's Dog Talks
4pm	National Vespers			Jan Savitt Orchestra
4:15				Tony Wons' Scrapbook
4:30	The Reveurs	Invitation to Learning		The World is Yours
4:45				
5pm	The Moylan Sisters, songs	Design for Happiness	The Musical Steelmakers	Yvette Sings
5:15	Olivio Santora, yodeler			The Three Cheers
5:30	Behind the Mike	Quixie Doodles	The Shadow	Sunday Down South
5:45				

DAYTIME — FALL, 1940

Monday-Friday

BLUE	CBS	MBS	NBC	
Music / Raising a President	Young Dr. Malone	Meet Miss Julia	Betty Crocker, cooking / Hymns of All Churches	2pm
Music / The Traveling Chef	Joyce Jordan, MD	Talk / The Radio Garden Club	Arnold Grimm's Daughter	2:15
Music	Fletcher Wiley, news	News and Music	Valiant Lady	2:30
	My Son and I		The Light of the World	2:45
Orphans of Divorce	Mary Margaret McBride, talk		The Story of Mary Marlin	3pm
Amanda of Honeymoon Hill	The Squibb Golden Treasury of Song	Talk and Music	Ma Perkins	3:15
John's Other Wife	Friend in Deed		Pepper Young's Family	3:30
Just Plain Bill	Informational Talk	Pegeen Presents	Vic and Sade	3:45
Mother of Mine	Portia Faces Life	News	Mary Noble, Backstage Wife	4pm
Club Matinee, Garry Moore	We, the Abbotts	Music	Stella Dallas	4:15
	Hilltop House	Music / The Heart of Julia Blake	Lorenzo Jones	4:30
	Kate Hopkins, Angel of Mercy	The Johnson Family	Young Widder Brown	4:45
Set Sail	The Goldbergs	Talk	Girl Alone	5pm
Music / The Singing Story Lady	Music	The Adventures of Superman / The Model Airplane Club	Life Can Be Beautiful	5:15
Bud Barton		Music	Jack Armstrong, the All-American Boy	5:30
The Tom Mix Ralston Straight Shooters	Scattergood Baines	Captain Midnight	The O'Neills	5:45

DAYTIME — FALL, 1940

Saturday

	BLUE	CBS	MBS	NBC
9am	The Breakfast Club	National Hillbilly Champions	Selective Service	Texas Jim Robertson, songs
9:15				Watch Your Step
9:30		Honest Abe	Music	Peggy Harris Sees the Town
9:45				The Charioteers Quartet
10am	Al and Lee Reiser, piano	The Singing Bee	The First Offender	Lincoln Highway
10:15	The Traveling Chef			
10:30	Joseph Gallicchio Orchestra	The Old Dirt Dobber	The Singing Strings	The Bright Idea Club
10:45			Erskine Butterfield, piano	
11am	The Deep River Boys	Cincinnati Conservatory Recitals	News	Song Folks
11:15	Rosa Lee, songs		The US Army Band	The Federation of Women's Clubs
11:30	Our Barn			Music
11:45			Hayden Planetarium Talks	Smilin' Ed McConnell, songs
12pm	The American Education Forum	Columbia's Country Journal	The Man on the Farm	The Eastman School of Music
12:15				
12:30	The National Farm and Home Hour	Let's Pretend	Dance Orchestra	Call to Youth
12:45				News
1pm		Of Men and Books		Matinee in Rhythm
1:15		Highways to Health		The Stamp Club
1:30	Luncheon at the Waldorf	Sports	Sports	Sports
1:45				

DAYTIME — FALL, 1940

Saturday

	BLUE	CBS	MBS	NBC
2pm	Sports			
2:15				
2:30				
2:45				
3pm				
3:15				
3:30				
3:45				
4pm			Dance Orchestra	
4:15				
4:30	Club Matinee, Garry Moore	Keyboard and Console		
4:45			Horse Racing	
5pm		Buffalo Presents	The Passing Parade	Campus Capers
5:15				
5:30	Sports Scores	Eddy Duchin Orchestra	McFarland Twins Orchestra	The Curtis Institute Recitals
5:45				

LISTINGS FOR 1941

EVENING — WINTER, 1941

Sunday

	BLUE	CBS	MBS	NBC
6pm	New Friends of Music	The Silver Theater	Double or Nothing	The Catholic Hour
6:15				
6:30		Gene Autry's Melody Ranch	The Show of the Week	Beat the Band
6:45				
7pm	Drew Pearson, news	News of the World	The Bach Cantata Series	The Jello Program, Jack Benny
7:15	European News			
7:30	News for the Americas	The Gulf Screen Theater	Frank Singiser, news	The Fitch Bandwagon
7:45	Music for Listening		Wythe Williams, news	
8pm	The Star Spangled Theater	The Helen Hayes Theater	The American Forum of the Air	The Charlie McCarthy Show
8:15				
8:30	Sherlock Holmes	Crime Doctor		One Man's Family
8:45		Elmer Davis, news (8:55pm)	Dorothy Thompson, news	
9pm	Walter Winchell's Jergens Journal	The Ford Sunday Evening Hour	Overseas News	The Manhattan Merry-Go-Round
9:15	The Parker Family		Glenn Miller Orchestra	
9:30	Irene Rich Dramas		Johannes Steele, news	The American Album of Familiar Music
9:45	The Colgate Sports Newsreel, Bill Stern		The Song Spinners	
10pm	The Goodwill Hour	Take It or Leave It	Chicago Symphony Orchestra	The Hour of Charm
10:15				
10:30		The Columbia Workshop		Deadline Dramas
10:45				

EVENING — WINTER, 1941

Monday

BLUE	CBS	MBS	NBC	
The Escorts and Betty	Edwin C. Hill, news	Uncle Don	The American Education Forum	6pm
Bill Stern, sports	Hedda Hopper, gossip			6:15
Alma Kitchell's Brief Case	Paul Sullivan, news	Frank Singiser, news	The Stamp Club	6:30
Lowell Thomas, news	The World Today	Here's Morgan	Ford Pearson, sports	6:45
Famous Jury Trials	Amos 'n' Andy	Stan Lomax, sports	Chesterfield Time	7pm
	The Lanny Ross Show	Arthur Hale, news	John W. Vandercook, news	7:15
This is the Show	Blondie	The Lone Ranger	Burns and Allen	7:30
				7:45
I Love a Mystery	Those We Love	Play Broadcast	The Bell Telephone Hour	8pm
				8:15
True or False	The Model Minstrels	Boake Carter, news	The Voice of Firestone	8:30
	Elmer Davis, news (8:55pm)	On The Town, Eddie Mayehoff		8:45
You're in the Army Now	The Lux Radio Theater	Gabriel Heatter, news	Dr. I. Q., the Mental Banker	9pm
		Glenn Miller Orchestra		9:15
The Chamber Music Society of Lower Basin Street		Can You Top This	The Show Boat	9:30
				9:45
Story Dramas	Guy Lombardo Orchestra	Raymond Gram Swing, news	The Carnation Contented Hour	10pm
Bob Hannon, songs		Who Knows		10:15
The National Radio Forum	Back Where I Come From	The Green Hornet	Ben Cutler Orchestra	10:30
	George Fielding Eliot, comment			10:45

EVENING — WINTER, 1941

Tuesday

	BLUE	CBS	MBS	NBC
6pm	The Dinning Sisters, songs	Edwin C. Hill, news	Uncle Don	Charlie Spivak Orchestra
6:15	Bill Stern, sports	Ted Steele Orchestra		
6:30	The Gulden Serenaders	Paul Sullivan, news	Frank Singiser, news	The Reveries
6:45	Lowell Thomas, news	The World Today	Here's Morgan	Ford Pearson, sports
7pm	Easy Aces	Amos 'n' Andy	Stan Lomax, sports	Chesterfield Time
7:15	Mr. Keen, Tracer of Lost Persons	The Lanny Ross Show	Lawyer Q	John W. Vandercook, news
7:30	Tom Powers Life Studies	Second Husband	Arthur Hale, news	So You Think You Know Music
7:45	Music		Sam Balter, sports	
8pm	Ben Bernie, the Old Maestro	The Court of Missing Heirs	Wythe Williams, news	Johnny Presents
8:15			Frazier Hunt, news	
8:30	Uncle Jim's Question Bee	The First Nighter Program	The Antonini Concert Series	Tums Treasure Chest
8:45		Elmer Davis, news (8:55pm)		
9pm	Grand Central Station	We, the People	Gabriel Heatter, news	Battle of the Sexes
9:15			Fulton Lewis Jr., news	
9:30	Inner Sanctum Mysteries	Professor Quiz	Morton Gould Orchestra	Fibber Magee and Molly
9:45				
10pm	Story Dramas	Moonlight Serenade	Raymond Gram Swing, news	The Pepsodent Show, Bob Hope
10:15	Gordon Jenkins Orchestra	Invitation to Learning	The War at Sea	
10:30	Meet Edward Weeks		Dr. Stephen Wise, health	Uncle Walter's Dog House
10:45		George Fielding Eliot, comment	Sentimental Concert	

EVENING — WINTER, 1941

Wednesday

BLUE	CBS	MBS	NBC	
The Vagabonds Quartet	Edwin C. Hill, news	Uncle Don	Charlie Spivak Orchestra	6pm
Bill Stern, sports	Hedda Hopper, gossip			6:15
Dinner Date	Paul Sullivan, news	Frank Singiser, news	The Stamp Club	6:30
Lowell Thomas, news	The World Today	Here's Morgan	Ford Pearson, sports	6:45
Easy Aces	Amos 'n' Andy	Stan Lomax, sports	Chesterfield Time	7pm
Mr. Keen, Tracer of Lost Persons	The Lanny Ross Show	Arthur Hale, news	John W. Vandercook,	7:15
Echoes of New York	Meet Mr. Meek	The Lone Ranger	The Cavalcade of America	7:30
				7:45
The Quiz Kids	Big Town	Where Are You From	Tony Martin, songs	8pm
			How Did You Meet	8:15
Manhattan at Midnight	Dr. Christian	Boake Carter, news	Paducah Plantation, Red Foley	8:30
	Elmer Davis, news (8:55pm)	On The Town, Eddie Mayehoff		8:45
The Roy Shield Revue	The Texaco Star Theater, Fred Allen	Gabriel Heatter, news	Time To Smile, Eddie Cantor	9pm
		Stephen McCormick, news		9:15
Spin and Win		The Chicagoland Concert Hour	Mr. District Attorney	9:30
				9:45
Story Dramas	Moonlight Serenade	Raymond Gram Swing, news	Kay Kyser's College of Musical Knowledge	10pm
The First Piano Quartet	Public Affairs	The War in the Air		10:15
Doctors at Work	Back Where I Come From	Dance Orchestra		10:30
	George Fielding Eliot, comment			10:45

EVENING — WINTER, 1941

Thursday

	BLUE	CBS	MBS	NBC
6pm	Music	Edwin C. Hill, news	Uncle Don	Charlie Spivak Orchestra
6:15	Bill Stern, sports	Bob Edge's Outdoor Talks		
6:30	The Gulden Serenaders	Paul Sullivan, news	Frank Singiser, news	Dr. Walter Van Kirk, talk
6:45	Lowell Thomas, news	The World Today	Here's Morgan	Ford Pearson, sports
7pm	Easy Aces	Amos 'n' Andy	Stan Lomax, sports	Chesterfield Time
7:15	Mr. Keen, Tracer of Lost Persons	The Lanny Ross Show	Lawyer Q	John W. Vandercook, news
7:30	Tom Powers Life Studies	Vox Pop	Arthur Hale, news	The Cugat Rumba Revue
7:45	The Metropolitan Opera Guild		Sam Balter, sports	
8pm	Pot o' Gold	The Ask-It Basket	Wythe Williams, news	Maxwell House Coffee Time, Brice and Morgan
8:15			Frazier Hunt, news	
8:30	Fame and Fortune	City Desk	Sherlock Holmes	The Aldrich Family
8:45		Elmer Davis, news (8:55pm)		
9pm	Rochester Philharmonic Orchestra	Major Bowes' Original Amateur Hour	Gabriel Heatter, news	The Kraft Music Hall, Bing Crosby
9:15			Fulton Lewis Jr., news	
9:30	America's Town Meeting of the Air		Sinfonietta	
9:45				
10pm		Moonlight Serenade	Raymond Gram Swing, news	Vallee Varieties
10:15		Choose Up Sides	Arthur Mann, news	
10:30	Ahead of the Headlines		In Chicago Tonight	Public Affairs
10:45	Dance Orchestra	George Fielding Eliot, comment		

EVENING — WINTER, 1941

Friday

BLUE	CBS	MBS	NBC	
Music	Edwin C. Hill, news	Uncle Don	Cesar Saerchinger, news	6pm
Bill Stern, sports	Hedda Hopper, gossip		Earl Wild, piano	6:15
Dinner Date	Paul Sullivan, news	Frank Singiser, news	The Stamp Club	6:30
Lowell Thomas, news	The World Today	Here's Morgan	Ford Pearson, sports	6:45
Gordon's Rangers	Amos 'n' Andy	Stan Lomax, sports	Chesterfield Time	7pm
Radio Magic	The Lanny Ross Show	Arthur Hale, news	John W. Vandercook,	7:15
Discoveries of '41	Al Pearce and His Gang	The Lone Ranger	Alec Templeton Time	7:30
				7:45
The Army Show	The Kate Smith Hour	Symphonic Strings	The Cities Service Concerts	8pm
				8:15
Death Valley Days		The Laugh and Swing Club	Information, Please	8:30
	Elmer Davis, news (8:55pm)			8:45
Gangbusters	Johnny Presents Dramatized Short Stories	Gabriel Heatter, news	Waltz Time	9pm
		Fulton Lewis Jr., news		9:15
Your Happy Birthday	The Campbell Playhouse	I Want a Divorce	Everyman's Theater	9:30
				9:45
Madison Square Garden Boxing	Public Affairs	Raymond Gram Swing, news	Wings of Destiny	10pm
		Overseas News		10:15
	Back Where I Come From	World Affairs	Joseph Gallicchio Orchestra	10:30
	George Fielding Eliot, comment	Dance Orchestra		10:45

EVENING — WINTER, 1941

Saturday

	BLUE	CBS	MBS	NBC
6pm	Johnny Long Orchestra	Report to the Nation	Uncle Don	Dance Orchestra
6:15				
6:30	The Vass Family, songs	Elmer Davis, news	Frank Singiser, news	Religion in the News
6:45	Edward Tomlinson, news	The World Today	Here's Morgan	Dance Orchestra
7pm	Message of Israel	The People's Platform	Stan Lomax, sports	
7:15			Dance Orchestra	John W. Vandercook, news
7:30	Little Ol' Hollywood	The Gay Nineties Revue	Arthur Hale, news	Muriel Angelus, songs
7:45			Sam Balter, sports	H. V. Kaltenborn, news
8pm	Hurtado Brothers Orchestra	Your Marriage Club	Tropical Serenade, Don Arres	The Knickerbocker Playhouse
8:15	Man and the World		Frazier Hunt, news	
8:30	The Bishop and the Gargoyle	Wayne King Orchestra	Boake Carter, news	Truth or Consequences
8:45		Elmer Davis, news (8:55pm)	Jean Merrill, songs	
9pm	The Song of Your Life	Your Hit Parade	Gabriel Heatter, news finances	The National Barn Dance
9:15			H. M. Fleming,	
9:30	NBC Symphony Orchestra		Contact Dave Elman	
9:45		Saturday Night Serenade		
10pm			The Chicago Theater of the Air	Uncle Ezra's Radio Station
10:15		Public Affairs		
10:30		Songs		Dance Orchestra
10:45		George Fielding Eliot, comment		

DAYTIME — WINTER, 1941

Sunday

	BLUE	CBS	MBS	NBC
9am	News	News	Rainbow House	News
9:15	The Children's Hour	Clyde Barrie, songs		The Deep River Boys
9:30		Wings Over Jordan		Sunday Drivers
9:45				
10am	The Primrose String Quartet	The CBS Church of the Air	News	The National Radio Pulpit
10:15			The Lamplighter	
10:30	The Southernaires Quartet	Indianapolis Symphony Orchestra	Pauline Alpert, songs	The Horn and Hardart Children's Hour
10:45			Sports Diary	
11am	News	News and Rhythm	The Smart Set	
11:15	Irving Miller Orchestra			
11:30	Sweet Land of Liberty	Major Bowes' Capitol Family	Milton Katims Orchestra	News
11:45				Music and American Youth
12pm	Rex Maupin Orchestra		Alvino Rey Orchestra	Emma Otero, songs
12:15	I'm An American			
12:30	The Radio City Music Hall	The Salt Lake Tabernacle Choir	The Sing a Song of Safety Club	Wings Over America
12:45			Frank Singiser, news	
1pm		The CBS Church of the Air	The Canary Pet Shop	Sammy Kaye's Sunday Serenade
1:15			Play Safe	
1:30	African Trek	March of Games	Ramona and the Tune Twisters	On Your Job
1:45			The Charioteers Quartet	

DAYTIME — WINTER, 1941

Monday-Friday

BLUE	CBS	MBS	NBC	
The Woman of Tomorrow	George Bryan, news	Music / Arthur Godfrey, songs	Happy Jack Turner, songs	9am
	The American School of the Air	Talk and Music / The Heart of Julia Blake	Music / The Band Goes to Town	9:15
The Breakfast Club		Music	Isabel Manning Hewson, food	9:30
	Bachelor's Children		The Gospel Singer	9:45
Josh Higgins of Finchville	By Kathleen Norris	The Pure Food Hour /	This Small Town	10am
Vic and Sade	The Story of Myrt and Marge	Music	Hank Lawson's Knights	10:15
The Story of Mary Marlin	Stepmother		The Story of Ellen Randolph	10:30
Pepper Young's Family	Woman of Courage		The Guiding Light	10:45
Linda Dale	Mary Lee Taylor, cooking / Short, Short Story	News	The Man I Married	11am
Clark Dennis, songs	Martha Webster	Martha Deane, talk	Against the Storm	11:15
The Wife Saver	Big Sister		The Road of Life	11:30
Thunder Over Paradise	Aunt Jenny's True Life Stories		David Harum	11:45
Music	Kate Smith Speaks	Victor Lindlahr, health /	The Wheatena Playhouse	12pm
	When a Girl Marries	Talk	The O'Neills	12:15
The National Farm and Home Hour	The Romance of Helen Trent	News	Songs	12:30
	Our Gal Sunday	The Consumers' Quiz	News	12:45
	Life Can Be Beautiful	The Johnson Family	Music	1pm
Between the Bookends	The Woman in White	Ed Fitzgerald, talk	Music / Tony Wons' Scrapbook	1:15
Religious Talk	The Right to Happiness	Music	Words and Music	1:30
Harvey Harding, songs	The Road of Life	Cheer Up Gang	Betty and Bob	1:45

DAYTIME — WINTER, 1941

Sunday

	BLUE	CBS	MBS	NBC
2pm	American Pilgrimage	CIO Labor Talks	This is Fort Dix	String Symphony
2:15	Foreign Policy Association Talks			
2:30	Tapestry Musicale	World News Today	Cedric Fosters, news	The University of Chicago Round Table
2:45			The Troubadours	
3pm	Great Plays	New York Philharmonic Orchestra		Martha Tilton Time
3:15				H. V. Kaltenborn, news
3:30			The Sidewalk Cafe	Julio Oyanguran, guitar
3:45				Bob Becker's Dog Talks
4pm	National Vespers		Battle of the Burroughs	Muriel Angelus, songs
4:15				Tony Wons' Scrapbook
4:30	Behind the Mike	The Pause That Refreshes	Tommy Dorsey Orchestra	Pageant of Art
4:45				
5pm	The Moylan Sisters, songs	Design for Happiness	The Musical Steelmakers	The Metropolitan Opera Auditions
5:15	Olivio Santora, yodeler			
5:30	Hidden Stars, Wee Bonnie Baker	Quixie Doodles	The Shadow	Your Dream Has Come True
5:45				

DAYTIME — WINTER, 1941

Monday-Friday

BLUE	CBS	MBS	NBC	
Music / Raising a President / Mother's Adventures	Young Dr. Malone	Cedric Foster, news	Betty Crocker, cooking / Hymns of All Churches	2pm
Music / The Traveling Chef	Joyce Jordan, MD	Dramatized Health Talk	Arnold Grimm's Daughter	2:15
Music	Fletcher Wiley, news	Talk / The Radio Garden Club	Valiant Lady	2:30
	Home of the Brave	News	The Light of the World	2:45
Orphans of Divorce	Mary Margaret McBride, talk	The Three O' Clock Playhouse	The Story of Mary Marlin	3pm
Amanda of Honeymoon Hill	The Squibb Golden Treasury of Song		Ma Perkins	3:15
John's Other Wife	Friend in Deed	Talk and Music	Pepper Young's Family	3:30
Just Plain Bill	Informational Talk		Vic and Sade	3:45
Mother of Mine	Portia Faces Life	News	Mary Noble, Backstage Wife	4pm
Club Matinee, Garry Moore	We, the Abbotts	Talk and Music	Stella Dallas	4:15
	Hilltop House	Danceland	Lorenzo Jones	4:30
Songs / Musical Memories	Kate Hopkins, Angel of Mercy		Young Widder Brown	4:45
King Arthur Jr.	The Goldbergs	Little Orphan Annie	Girl Alone	5pm
Music / The Singing Story Lady	The O'Neills	Music / The Adventures of Superman	Lone Journey	5:15
Bud Barton	Music	Music / Mandrake the Magician	Jack Armstrong, the All-American Boy	5:30
The Tom Mix Ralston Straight Shooters	Scattergood Baines	Captain Midnight	Life Can Be Beautiful	5:45

DAYTIME — WINTER, 1941

Saturday

	BLUE	CBS	MBS	NBC
9am	The Breakfast Club	News	Dear Imogene	Happy Jack Turner, songs
9:15		National Hillbilly Champions	Music	Peggy Harris Sees the Town
9:30		Honest Abe		The Wise Man
9:45				The Four Showmen
10am	Al and Lee Reiser, piano	The Singing Bee	The First Offender	Lincoln Highway
10:15	The Traveling Chef			
10:30	Harry Kogen Orchestra	The Old Dirt Dobber	The Singing Strings	The Bright Idea Club
10:45			Selective Service	
11am	The Norsemen Quartet	Cincinnati Conservatory Recitals	News	Song Folks
11:15	Rosa Lee, songs		Songs	The Federation of Women's Clubs
11:30	Our Barn		The US Army Band	Music
11:45				Smilin' Ed McConnell, songs
12pm	The American Education Forum	Columbia's Country Journal	The Man on the Farm	The Eastman School of Music
12:15				
12:30	The National Farm and Home Hour	Highways to Health	Vincent Connolly, news	Call to Youth
12:45		Of Men and Books	The Charioteers Quartet	News
1pm		Let's Pretend	Hayden Planetarium Talks	Matinee in Rhythm
1:15			Music	
1:30	Luncheon at the Waldorf	The Little Congress Forum		Dance Orchestra
1:45				

DAYTIME — WINTER, 1941

Saturday

	BLUE	CBS	MBS	NBC
2pm	The Metropolitan Opera	The Brush Creek Follies		Music in a Mellow Mood
2:15				
2:30		Bull Session		Golden Melodies
2:45				
3pm		Vera Brodsky, piano		Gordon Jenkins Orchestra
3:15				
3:30		Old Vienna	Alvino Rey Orchestra	Saturday Soiree
3:45		This is My Land		
4pm		Music	Music	Campus Capers
4:15			Horse Racing	
4:30		Keyboard and Console	Danceland	A Boy, a Girl and a Band
4:45				
5pm	Cleveland Calling	News of the Americas		The World is Yours
5:15		Buffalo Presents		
5:30	Sing Before Supper		The University Life Forum	The Curtis Institute Recitals
5:45		News		

EVENING — SPRING, 1941

Sunday

	BLUE	CBS	MBS	NBC
6pm	Blue Barron Orchestra	Ed Sullivan Variety	Double or Nothing	The Catholic Hour
6:15				
6:30	Frank Black Presents	Gene Autry's Melody Ranch	Bulldog Drummond	What's Your Idea
6:45				
7pm	Drew Pearson, news	Dear Mom (6:55pm)	Russell Bennett's Notebook	The Jello Program, Jack Benny
7:15	European News	Convoys		
7:30	Music for Listening	The Gulf Screen Theater	Frank Singiser, news	The Fitch Bandwagon
7:45	Johnny Johnston, songs		Wythe Williams, news	
8pm	The Star Spangled Theater	The Helen Hayes Theater	The American Forum of the Air	The Charlie McCarthy Show
8:15				
8:30	Inner Sanctum Mysteries	Crime Doctor		One Man's Family
8:45		Elmer Davis, news (8:55pm)	Dorothy Thompson, news	
9pm	Walter Winchell's Jergens Journal	The Ford Sunday Evening Hour	Overseas News	The Manhattan Merry-Go-Round
9:15	The Parker Family		Glenn Miller Orchestra	
9:30	Irene Rich Dramas		Johannes Steele, news	The American Album of Familiar Music
9:45	The Colgate Sports Newsreel, Bill Stern		The Song Spinners	
10pm	The Goodwill Hour	Take It or Leave It	Chicago Symphony Orchestra	The Hour of Charm
10:15				
10:30		The Columbia Workshop		Deadline Dramas
10:45				

EVENING — SPRING, 1941

Monday

BLUE	CBS	MBS	NBC	
The Escorts and Betty	Edwin C. Hill, news	Uncle Don	Novelettes	6pm
Bill Stern, sports	Hedda Hopper, gossip		Music	6:15
Alma Kitchell's Brief Case	Paul Sullivan, news	Frank Singiser, news	The Stamp Club	6:30
Lowell Thomas, news	The World Today	Here's Morgan	Gasoline Alley	6:45
Famous Jury Trials	Amos 'n' Andy	Stan Lomax, sports	Chesterfield Time	7pm
	The Lanny Ross Show	Arthur Hale, news	John W. Vandercook, news	7:15
The What's New Program	Blondie	The Lone Ranger	The Cavalcade of America	7:30
				7:45
I Love a Mystery	Those We Love	The Amazing Mr. Smith	The Bell Telephone Hour	8pm
				8:15
True or False	The Gay Nineties Revue	Boake Carter, news	The Voice of Firestone	8:30
	Bob Trout, news (8:55pm)	Here's Looking at You		8:45
The Chamber Music Society of Lower Basin Street	The Lux Radio Theater	Gabriel Heatter, news	Dr. I. Q., the Mental Banker	9pm
		Red Barber, sports		9:15
Public Affairs		Can You Top This	The Show Boat	9:30
The Nickel Man (9:55pm)				9:45
Story Dramas	Guy Lombardo Orchestra	Raymond Gram Swing, news	The Carnation Contented Hour	10pm
The First Piano Quartet		Who Knows		10:15
The National Radio Forum	The Joan Edwards Show	Vic and Sade	Matty Malneck Orchestra	10:30
	George Fielding Eliot, comment	Pageant of Melody		10:45

EVENING — SPRING, 1941

Tuesday

	BLUE	CBS	MBS	NBC
6pm	Selective Service	Edwin C. Hill, news	Uncle Don	Novelettes
6:15	Bill Stern, sports	Ted Steele Orchestra		Music
6:30	The Gulden Serenaders	Paul Sullivan, news	Frank Singiser, news	The Reveries
6:45	Lowell Thomas, news	The World Today	Here's Morgan	Gasoline Alley
7pm	Easy Aces	Amos 'n' Andy	Stan Lomax, sports	Chesterfield Time
7:15	Mr. Keen, Tracer of Lost Persons	The Lanny Ross Show	The People's Playhouse	John W. Vandercook, news
7:30	Lawyer Q	Second Husband	Arthur Hale, news	So You Think You Know Music
7:45			Sam Balter, sports	
8pm	Gordon Jenkins Orchestra	The Court of Missing Heirs	Wythe Williams, news	Johnny Presents
8:15			Tropical Serenade, Don Arres	
8:30	Uncle Jim's Question Bee	The First Nighter Program	The Antonini Concert Series	Tums Treasure Chest
8:45		Bob Trout, news (8:55pm)		
9pm	Grand Central Station	We, the People	Gabriel Heatter, news	Battle of the Sexes
9:15			Red Barber, sports	
9:30	Unlimited Horizons	Invitation to Learning	Morton Gould Orchestra	Fibber Magee and Molly
9:45	The Nickel Man (9:55pm)			
10pm	Our New American Music	Moonlight Serenade	Raymond Gram Swing, news	The Pepsodent Show, Bob Hope
10:15		Public Affairs	The War at Sea	
10:30			Vic and Sade	Uncle Walter's Dog House
10:45		The Four Clubmen	Sentimental Concert	

EVENING — SPRING, 1941

Wednesday

BLUE	CBS	MBS	NBC	
The Three Romeos	Edwin C. Hill, news	Uncle Don	Novelettes	6pm
Bill Stern, sports	Hedda Hopper, gossip		Music	6:15
Dinner Date	Paul Sullivan, news	Frank Singiser, news	The Stamp Club	6:30
Lowell Thomas, news	The World Today	Here's Morgan	Gasoline Alley	6:45
Easy Aces	Amos 'n' Andy	Stan Lomax, sports	Chesterfield Time	7pm
Mr. Keen, Tracer of Lost Persons	The Lanny Ross Show	Arthur Hale, news	John W. Vandercook, news	7:15
Echoes of New York	Meet Mr. Meek	The Lone Ranger	The Fisk Jubilee Choir	7:30
				7:45
The Quiz Kids	Big Town	Where Are You From	Tony Martin, songs	8pm
			How Did You Meet	8:15
Manhattan at Midnight	Dr. Christian	Boake Carter, news	Paducah Plantation, Red Foley	8:30
	Bob Trout, news (8:55pm)	Here's Looking at You		8:45
The Roy Shield Revue	The Texaco Star Theater, Fred Allen	Gabriel Heatter, news	Time To Smile, Eddie Cantor	9pm
		Red Barber, sports		9:15
Spin and Win		Guy Lombardo Orchestra	Mr. District Attorney	9:30
The Nickel Man (9:55pm)				9:45
Story Dramas	Moonlight Serenade	Raymond Gram Swing, news	Kay Kyser's College of Musical Knowledge	10pm
The First Piano Quartet	Public Affairs	The War in the Air		10:15
Doctors at Work	The Joan Edwards Show	Life Can Be Beautiful		10:30
	George Fielding Eliot, comment	Dance Orchestra		10:45

EVENING — SPRING, 1941

Thursday

	BLUE	CBS	MBS	NBC
6pm	The Escorts and Betty	Edwin C. Hill, news	Uncle Don	Novelettes
6:15	Bill Stern, sports	Public Affairs		Music
6:30	The Gulden Serenaders	Paul Sullivan, news	Frank Singiser, news	Speaking of Liberty
6:45	Lowell Thomas, news	The World Today	Here's Morgan	Gasoline Alley
7pm	Easy Aces	Amos 'n' Andy	Stan Lomax, sports	Chesterfield Time
7:15	Mr. Keen, Tracer of Lost Persons	The Lanny Ross Show	The People's Playhouse	John W. Vandercook, news
7:30	Tom Powers Life Studies	Vox Pop	Arthur Hale, news	The Cugat Rumba Revue
7:45	Music		Sam Balter, sports	
8pm	Pot o' Gold	Spotlight	Wythe Williams, news	Maxwell House Coffee Time, Brice and Morgan
8:15			Walter Scanlon, songs	
8:30	Commentator's Round Table	City Desk	Barrel of Fun, Charlie Ruggles	The Aldrich Family
8:45		Bob Trout, news (8:55pm)		
9pm	Rochester Philharmonic Orchestra	Major Bowes' Original Amateur Hour	Gabriel Heatter, news	The Kraft Music Hall, Bing Crosby
9:15			Waite Hoyt, sports	
9:30	America's Town Meeting of the Air		Sinfonietta	
9:45				
10pm		Moonlight Serenade	Johannes Steel, comment	Vallee Varieties
10:15		Professor Quiz	Arthur Mann, news	
10:30	Ahead of the Headlines		Life Can Be Beautiful	The Listener's Playhouse
10:45	Music	George Fielding Eliot, comment	Dance Orchestra	

EVENING — SPRING, 1941

Friday

BLUE	CBS	MBS	NBC	
Music	Edwin C. Hill, news	Uncle Don	Novelettes	6pm
Bill Stern, sports	Hedda Hopper, gossip		Music	6:15
Dinner Date	Paul Sullivan, news	Frank Singiser, news	The Stamp Club	6:30
Lowell Thomas, news	The World Today	Here's Morgan	Gasoline Alley	6:45
Gordon's Rangers	Amos 'n' Andy	Stan Lomax, sports	Chesterfield Time	7pm
Radio Magic	The Lanny Ross Show	Arthur Hale, news	John W. Vandercook, news	7:15
Gene Krupa Orchestra	Al Pearce and His Gang	The Lone Ranger	The Rhyme and Rhythm Club	7:30
				7:45
John Gunther, news	The Kate Smith Hour	Symphonic Strings	The Cities Service Concerts	8pm
Jose Bethancourt Orchestra				8:15
Death Valley Days		The Laugh and Swing Club	Information, Please	8:30
	Bob Trout, news (8:55pm)			8:45
The New Army Game, Ben Bernie	Great Moments from Great Plays	Gabriel Heatter, news	Waltz Time	9pm
		Red Barber, sports		9:15
Your Happy Birthday	The Campbell Playhouse	I Want a Divorce	Everyman's Theater	9:30
The Nickel Man (9:55pm)				9:45
Madison Square Garden Boxing	Hollywood Premiere	Raymond Gram Swing, news	Wings of Destiny	10pm
		The War in the Air		10:15
	The Joan Edwards Show	Life Can Be Beautiful	Ray Kinney Orchestra	10:30
	George Fielding Eliot, comment	Cats and Jammers		10:45

EVENING — SPRING, 1941

Saturday

	BLUE	CBS	MBS	NBC
6pm	Johnny Long Orchestra	Report to the Nation	Uncle Don	Dance Orchestra
6:15				News
6:30	The Vass Family, songs	Elmer Davis, news	Frank Singiser, news	Religion in the News
6:45	Edward Tomlinson, news	The World Today	Here's Morgan	Paul Douglas, sports
7pm	Message of Israel	The People's Platform	Stan Lomax, sports	Defense for America
7:15			Jean Merrill, songs	
7:30	Little Ol' Hollywood	The Hall of Song	Arthur Hale, news	Bonnie Stewart, songs
7:45			Sam Balter, sports	H. V. Kaltenborn, news
8pm	Hurtado Brothers Orchestra	Your Marriage Club	The Green Hornet	The Knickerbocker Playhouse
8:15	Man and the World			
8:30	The Bishop and the Gargoyle	Duffy's Tavern	Boake Carter, news	Truth or Consequences
8:45		Bob Trout, news (8:55pm)	Tropical Serenade, Don Arres	
9pm	The Song of Your Life	Your Hit Parade	Gabriel Heatter, news sports	The National Barn Dance
9:15			Red Barber, sports	
9:30	NBC Spring Symphony		Contact Dave Elman	
9:45		Battle of the Burroughs		
10pm			Johannes Steel, news	Uncle Ezra's Radio Station
10:15		Public Affairs	The Chicagoland Concert Hour	
10:30		The Golden Gate Quartet		Music By Malneck
10:45		George Fielding Eliot, comment		

DAYTIME — SPRING, 1941

Sunday

	BLUE	CBS	MBS	NBC
9am	News	News	Uncle Don Reads the Comics	News
9:15	The Children's Hour	Emery Deutsch Orchestra		The Deep River Boys
9:30		Wings Over Jordan	The Natural History Quiz	Words and Music
9:45				
10am	The Primrose String Quartet	The CBS Church of the Air	News	The National Radio Pulpit
10:15			The Lamplighter	
10:30	The Southernaires Quartet	Cincinnati Conservatory Recitals	The US Navy Band	The Horn and Hardart Children's Hour
10:45				
11am	News	News and Rhythm	The Northwestern Reviewing Stand	
11:15	Front Lines of Mercy			
11:30	Sweet Land of Liberty	Major Bowes' Capitol Family	Music	News
11:45				Music and American Youth
12pm	Rex Maupin Orchestra		Quaker City Symphony Orchestra	Emma Otero, songs
12:15	I'm An American			
12:30	The Radio City Music Hall	The Salt Lake Tabernacle Choir	The Charioteers Quartet	Pageant of Art
12:45			Frank Singiser, news	
1pm		The CBS Church of the Air	The Canary Pet Shop	Sammy Kaye's Sunday Serenade
1:15			Play Safe	
1:30	African Trek	March of Games	Ramona and the Tune Twisters	On Your Job
1:45			The Charioteers Quartet	

DAYTIME — SPRING, 1941

Monday-Friday

BLUE	CBS	MBS	NBC	
The Woman of Tomorrow	George Bryan, news	Music / Arthur Godfrey, songs	Happy Jack Turner, songs	9am
	Music	Talk and Music / The Heart of Julia Blake	Music	9:15
The Breakfast Club		Music	Isabel Manning Hewson, food	9:30
	Betty Crocker, cooking / Hymns of All Churches		The Gospel Singer / The Mystery Chef	9:45
Helen Hiett, news	By Kathleen Norris	The Pure Food Hour /	Bess Johnson	10am
Midstream	The Story of Myrt and Marge	Music	The Story of Ellen Randolph	10:15
The Munros	Stepmother		Bachelor's Children	10:30
The Vagabonds Quartet	Woman of Courage		The Road of Life	10:45
Stringtime	Music / Nell Vinick, beauty	News	The Story of Mary Marlin	11am
	Martha Webster	Bessie Beatty, talk	Pepper Young's Family	11:15
Clark Dennis, songs	Big Sister		Lone Journey	11:30
The Wife Saver	Aunt Jenny's True Life Stories		David Harum	11:45
Music / The Southernaires Quartet	Kate Smith Speaks	Songs / Victor Lindlahr, health	Words and Music	12pm
	When a Girl Marries		The O'Neills	12:15
The National Farm and Home Hour	The Romance of Helen Trent	Vincent Connolly, news	Songs	12:30
	Our Gal Sunday	The Consumers' Quiz	News	12:45
	Life Can Be Beautiful	We Are Always Young	Music	1pm
Between the Bookends	The Woman in White	Edith Adams		1:15
Religious Talk	The Right to Happiness	Helen Holden, Government Girl		1:30
Harvey Harding, songs	The Road of Life	I'll Find My Way	Betty and Bob	1:45

DAYTIME — SPRING, 1941

Sunday

	BLUE	CBS	MBS	NBC
2pm	American Pilgrimage	The Free Company	This is Fort Dix	String Symphony
2:15	Foreign Policy Association Talks			
2:30	Tapestry Musicale	Meet the Music	Sports	The University of Chicago Round Table
2:45				
3pm	Great Plays	New York Philharmonic Orchestra		Martha Tilton Time
3:15				H. V. Kaltenborn, news
3:30				Lee Gordon Orchestra
3:45				
4pm	National Vespers			Lavender and New Lace
4:15				Tony Wons' Scrapbook
4:30	Behind the Mike	The Pause That Refreshes		Sunday Down South
4:45				
5pm	The Moylan Sisters, songs		The Musical Steelmakers	Joe and Mabel
5:15	Olivio Santora, yodeler	Public Affairs		
5:30	Macklin Marrow Orchestra	Ned Sparks Variety	The Shadow	Your Dream Has Come True
5:45				

DAYTIME — SPRING, 1941

Monday-Friday

BLUE	CBS	MBS	NBC	
Music / Raising a President / Mother's Adventures	Young Dr. Malone	Ed Fitzgerald, talk	The Light of the World	2pm
Songs / The Traveling Chef	Joyce Jordan, MD	Dramatized Health Talk	The Mystery Man	2:15
Music	Fletcher Wiley, news	Music / The Radio Garden Club	Valiant Lady	2:30
	Kate Hopkins, Angel of Mercy	News	Arnold Grimm's Daughter	2:45
Orphans of Divorce	Mary Margaret McBride, talk		Against the Storm	3pm
Amanda of Honeymoon Hill	The Squibb Golden Treasury of Song	Talk and Music	Ma Perkins	3:15
John's Other Wife	Friend in Deed		The Guiding Light	3:30
Just Plain Bill	Informational Talk		Vic and Sade	3:45
Mother of Mine	Talk and Music	News	Mary Noble, Backstage Wife	4pm
Club Matinee, Garry Moore	We, the Abbotts	Talk and Music	Stella Dallas	4:15
	Bess Johnson	Danceland	Lorenzo Jones	4:30
We Men, We Women	Music		Young Widder Brown	4:45
Music / The Singing Story Lady	The Story of Mary Marlin	Little Orphan Annie	Home of the Brave	5pm
Bud Barton	The Goldbergs	Music	Portia Faces Life	5:15
Drama Behind the News	The O'Neills	Music / Mandrake, the Magician	Jack Armstrong, the All-American Boy	5:30
The Tom Mix Ralston Straightshooters	Scattergood Baines	Captain Midnight	The Three Suns	5:45

DAYTIME — SPRING, 1941

Saturday

	BLUE	CBS	MBS	NBC
9am	The Breakfast Club	News	Dear Imogene	Texas Jim Robertson, songs
9:15		National Hillbilly Champions	Selective Service	Isabel Manning Hewson, food
9:30		The Old Dirt Dobber	Music	Weekend Whimsey
9:45				
10am	The Traveling Chef	The Life of Riley	Rainbow House	The Bright Idea Club
10:15	The Andrini Continentals			
10:30		Gold is Where You Find It		Betty Moore, talk
10:45	Rosa Lee, songs			Lincoln Highway
11am	The Band Played On	Honest Abe	News	
11:15			Songs	Consumer Time
11:30	Our Barn	The Voice of Broadway	The US Army Band	String Ensemble
11:45		The Burl Ives Show		
12pm	Reflections in Rhythm	Columbia's Country Journal	The Man on the Farm	New England to You
12:15				
12:30	The National Farm and Home Hour	Highways to Health	Vincent Connolly, news	Call to Youth
12:45		Jobs for Defense	The Charioteers Quartet	News
1pm		Let's Pretend	We Are Always Young	Matinee in Rhythm
1:15			Edith Adams	Your Hollywood News Girl
1:30	Luncheon at the Waldorf	No Politics	Helen Holden, Government Girl	Frankie Masters Orchestra
1:45			I'll Find My Way	News

DAYTIME — SPRING, 1941

Saturday

	BLUE	CBS	MBS	NBC
2pm	Indiana Indigo	The Brush Creek Follies	Ed Fitzgerald, talk	Readin', Writin' and Rhythm
2:15			Sports	
2:30		Of Men and Books		Golden Melodies
2:45				
3pm	Bobby Bryne Orchestra	The League of Composers Concert		Gordon Jenkins Orchestra
3:15				
3:30	Music of the Americas			The Gay Hedlund Players
3:45				
4pm	Club Matinee, Garry Moore	Dance Orchestra		Campus Capers
4:15				
4:30	Horse Racing			A Boy, a Girl and a Band
4:45				
5pm	Cleveland Calling	News of the Americas		The World is Yours
5:15		F. O. B. Detroit	Waite Hoyt, sports	
5:30	Sing Before Supper		The University Life Forum	The Curtis Institute Recitals
5:45		News		

EVENING — SUMMER, 1941

Sunday

	BLUE	CBS	MBS	NBC
6pm	The National Music Camp	Ed Sullivan Variety	Cats and Jammers	The Catholic Hour
6:15				
6:30	Gordon Jenkins Orchestra	Gene Autry's Melody Ranch	Bulldog Drummond	Dr. I. Q. Jr.
6:45				
7pm	European News	Dear Mom (6:55pm)	The Rookies	Reg'lar Fellers
7:15		Convoys		
7:30	Drew Pearson, news	World News Tonight	Frank Singiser, news	The Fitch Bandwagon
7:45	Jean Cavall, songs		Wythe Williams, news	
8pm	The Star Spangled Theater	The Pause That Refreshes	The American Forum of the Air	What's My Name
8:15				
8:30	Inner Sanctum Mysteries	Crime Doctor		One Man's Family
8:45		Elmer Davis, news (8:55pm)	Gabriel Heatter, news	
9pm	William L. Shirer, news	The Ford Summer Hour	Overseas News	The Manhattan Merry-Go-Round
9:15	The Parker Family		Dance Orchestra	
9:30	Irene Rich Dramas			The American Album of Familiar Music
9:45	The Colgate Sports Newsreel, Bill Stern			
10pm	The Goodwill Hour	Take It or Leave It	Symphonic Strings	The Hour of Charm
10:15				
10:30		Twenty-Six By Corwin	Cab Calloway's Quizzicale	Studio X, Dumke and Hulick
10:45				

EVENING — SUMMER, 1941

Monday

BLUE	CBS	MBS	NBC	
Defense News	Edwin C. Hill, news	Uncle Don	Music	6pm
Bill Stern, sports	Hedda Hopper, gossip		News	6:15
Jose Bethancourt Orchestra	Bill Henry, news	Frank Singiser, news	Brad Reynolds, songs	6:30
Lowell Thomas, news	The World Today	Here's Morgan	Jack McCarthy, sports	6:45
The Best of the Week	Amos 'n' Andy	Stan Lomax, sports	Chesterfield Time	7pm
	The Lanny Ross Show	Arthur Hale, news	John W. Vandercook, news	7:15
Rex Maupin Orchestra	Blondie	The Lone Ranger	The Cavalcade of America	7:30
				7:45
The World's Best Dramas	Vox Pop	Cal Tinney, news	The Bell Telephone Hour	8pm
		Contact Dave Elman		8:15
True or False	The Gay Nineties Revue	Boake Carter, news	The Voice of Firestone	8:30
	Elmer Davis, news (8:55pm)	Eddy Brown Orchestra		8:45
The Chamber Music Society of Lower Basin Street	Forecast	Gabriel Heatter, news	Dr. I. Q., the Mental Banker	9pm
		Red Barber, sports		9:15
Hillman and Durno, news		Russell Bennett's Notebook	Mr. Pertwee	9:30
Ted Steele Orchestra			Josef Hontis Orchestra	9:45
Famous Jury Trials	Freddy Martin Orchestra	Raymond Gram Swing, news	The Carnation Contented Hour	10pm
		Imperial Time, Mary Small		10:15
The National Radio Forum	Juan Arvizu, songs	Vic and Sade	Chicago Symphony Orchestra	10:30
	War News	Ramona and the Tune Twisters		10:45

EVENING — SUMMER, 1941

Tuesday

	BLUE	CBS	MBS	NBC
6pm	Defense News	Albert Warner, news	Uncle Don	Music
6:15	Bill Stern, sports	The Voice of Broadway		News
6:30	Jose Bethancourt Orchestra	Paul Sullivan, news	Frank Singiser, news	Brad Reynolds, songs
6:45	Lowell Thomas, news	The World Today	Here's Morgan	Jack McCarthy, sports
7pm	Easy Aces	Amos 'n' Andy	Stan Lomax, sports	Chesterfield Time
7:15	Mr. Keen, Tracer of Lost Persons	The Lanny Ross Show	Bob Chester Orchestra	John W. Vandercook, news
7:30	Get Goin'	Second Husband	Arthur Hale, news	Colonel Stoopnagle's Stump Club
7:45			Sam Balter, sports	
8pm	Gordon Jenkins Orchestra	The Court of Missing Heirs	Wythe Williams, news	Johnny Presents
8:15			Sonny Dunham Orchestra	
8:30	For America We Sing	The First Nighter Program	Can You Top This	Tums Treasure Chest
8:45		Elmer Davis, news (8:55pm)		
9pm	Bringing Up Father	We, the People	Gabriel Heatter, news	Battle of the Sexes
9:15			Red Barber, sports	
9:30	Hillman and Durno, news	Report to the Nation	The People's Playhouse	Hap Hazard
9:45	Ted Steele Orchestra			
10pm	Public Affairs	Moonlight Serenade	Raymond Gram Swing, news	A Date with Judy
10:15		Public Affairs	The War at Sea	
10:30	The Grant Park Concerts		Vic and Sade	College Humor, Marlin Hurt
10:45		War News	Ramona and the Tune Twisters	

EVENING — SUMMER, 1941

Wednesday

BLUE	CBS	MBS	NBC	
Defense News	Edwin C. Hill, news	Uncle Don	Music	6pm
Bill Stern, sports	Bill Henry, news		News	6:15
Jose Bethancourt Orchestra	Paul Sullivan, news	Frank Singiser, news	Hollywood News	6:30
Lowell Thomas, news	The World Today	Here's Morgan	Jack McCarthy, sports	6:45
Easy Aces	Amos 'n' Andy	Stan Lomax, sports	Chesterfield Time	7pm
Mr. Keen, Tracer of Lost Persons	The Lanny Ross Show	Arthur Hale, news	John W. Vandercook, news	7:15
Marion Mann, songs	Meet Mr. Meek	The Lone Ranger	We Present	7:30
Upton Close, news				7:45
The Quiz Kids	Grand Central Station	Cal Tinney, news	The Adventures of the Thin Man	8pm
		The Song Spinners		8:15
Manhattan at Midnight	Dr. Christian	Boake Carter, news	Paducah Plantation, Red Foley	8:30
	Elmer Davis, news (8:55pm)	Charlie Spivak Orchestra		8:45
The Hemisphere Revue	The Treasury Hour	Gabriel Heatter, news	Quizzer Baseball	9pm
		Red Barber, sports		9:15
Hillman and Durno, news		David Rose Orchestra	Mr. District Attorney	9:30
Ted Steele Orchestra				9:45
Author's Playhouse	Moonlight Serenade	Raymond Gram Swing, news	Kay Kyser's College of Musical Knowledge	10pm
	Public Affairs	Danger is My Business		10:15
Ray Kinney Orchestra	Juan Arvizu, songs			10:30
	War News	Ramona and the Tune Twisters		10:45

EVENING — SUMMER, 1941

Thursday

	BLUE	CBS	MBS	NBC
6pm	Defense News	Albert Warner, news	Uncle Don	Music
6:15	Bill Stern, sports	Bob Edge's Outdoor Talks		News
6:30	Donald Lindley Orchestra	Paul Sullivan, news	Frank Singiser, news	Speaking of Liberty
6:45	Lowell Thomas, news	The World Today	Here's Morgan	Jack McCarthy, sports
7pm	Easy Aces	Amos 'n' Andy	Stan Lomax, sports	Chesterfield Time
7:15	Mr. Keen, Tracer of Lost Persons	The Lanny Ross Show	Sonny Dunham Orchestra	John W. Vandercook, news
7:30	Joseph Gallichio Orchestra	Maudie's Diary	Arthur Hale, news	The Cugat Rumba Revue
7:45			Sam Balter, sports	
8pm	This is Judy Jones	Death Valley Days	Wythe Williams, news	Housewarming Time
8:15			Sky Over Britain	
8:30	Ricardo and His Caballeros	The Lewisohn Stadium Concerts	Barrel of Fun, Charlie Ruggles	The Aldrich Family
8:45		Elmer Davis, news (8:55pm)		
9pm	The Grant Park Concerts	Major Bowes' Original Amateur Hour	Gabriel Heatter, news	The Kraft Music Hall, Bob Burns
9:15			Waite Hoyt, sports	
9:30	Hillman and Durno, news		Sinfonietta	
9:45	Ted Steele Orchestra			
10pm	Promenade Orchestra of Toronto	Moonlight Serenade	Frank Singiser, news	Vallee Varieties
10:15		Professor Quiz	John Paul Dickson, news	
10:30	Ahead of the Headlines		Vic and Sade	Public Affairs
10:45	Story Drama	War News	Ramona and the Tune Twisters	

EVENING — SUMMER, 1941

Friday

BLUE	CBS	MBS	NBC	
Defense News	Edwin C. Hill, news	Uncle Don	Music	6pm
Bill Stern, sports	Bill Henry, news		News	6:15
Neff Orchestra	Paul Sullivan, news	Frank Singiser, news	Music	6:30
Lowell Thomas, news	The World Today	Here's Morgan	Jack McCarthy, sports	6:45
Gordon's Rangers	Amos 'n' Andy	Stan Lomax, sports	Chesterfield Time	7pm
Radio Magic	The Lanny Ross Show	Arthur Hale, news	John W. Vandercook, news	7:15
Will Bradley Orchestra	American Cruise	The Lone Ranger	The Rhyme and Rhythm Club	7:30
				7:45
Jean Cavall, songs	Claudia and David	Double or Nothing	The Cities Service Concerts	8pm
Jose Bethancourt Orchestra				8:15
Death Valley Days	Proudly We Hail	Fight Camp	Information, Please	8:30
	Elmer Davis, news (8:55pm)			8:45
Vox Pop	Great Moments from Great Plays	Gabriel Heatter, news	Waltz Time	9pm
		Red Barber, sports		9:15
Hillman and Durno, news	The Lewisohn Stadium Concerts	Elizabeth Rethberg, songs	Uncle Walter's Dog House	9:30
Ted Steele Orchestra				9:45
Charles Dant Orchestra	Penthouse Party	Raymond Gram Swing, news	Wings of Destiny	10pm
		Who Knows		10:15
The First Piano Quartet	The Symphonettes	Vic and Sade	Listen, America	10:30
Story Drama	War News	Ramona and the Tune Twisters		10:45

EVENING — SUMMER, 1941

Saturday

	BLUE	CBS	MBS	NBC
6pm	Concert Musicale (5:30pm)	Report to the Nation	Uncle Don	Music
6:15				News
6:30	Jean Cavall, songs	Elmer Davis, news	Frank Singiser, news	The Art of Living
6:45	Edward Tomlinson, news	The World Today	Here's Morgan	Jack McCarthy, sports
7pm	Message of Israel	The People's Platform	Stan Lomax, sports	Defense for America
7:15			Music	
7:30	Little Ol' Hollywood	The Hall of Song	Arthur Hale, news	The Aristocrats Trio
7:45			Sam Balter, sports	H. V. Kaltenborn, news
8pm	Boy Meets Band	Guy Lombardo Orchestra	The Green Hornet	Latitude Zero
8:15				
8:30	The Bishop and the Gargoyle	City Desk	Boake Carter, news	Truth or Consequences
8:45		Elmer Davis, news (8:55pm)	John Duggan, songs	
9pm	Spin and Win	Your Hit Parade	Gabriel Heatter, news sports	The National Barn Dance
9:15			Red Barber,	
9:30	NBC Summer Symphony		Morton Gould Orchestra	
9:45		Battle of the Burroughs		
10pm			The Chicagoland Concert Hour	The Grant Park Concerts
10:15		Public Affairs		
10:30	Sweet and Rhythmic	The Four Clubmen		The Open House, Helen Morgan
10:45		War News		

DAYTIME — SUMMER, 1941

Sunday

	BLUE	CBS	MBS	NBC
9am	News	News	Uncle Don Reads the Comics	News
9:15	The Children's Hour	From the Organ Loft		The Deep River Boys
9:30			The Natural History Quiz	Words and Music
9:45		Gypsy Caravan		
10am	Fantasy in Melody	The CBS Church of the Air	News	Highlights of the Bible
10:15			BBC News	
10:30	The Southernaires Quartet	Wings Over Jordan	The US Navy Band	The Horn and Hardart Children's Hour
10:45				
11am	News	News	The Northwestern Reviewing Stand	
11:15	The First Piano Quartet	Emery Deutsch Orchestra		
11:30	Treasure Trails of Song	What's New at the Zoo	The Perole String Quartet	News
11:45				Lee Gordon Orchestra
12pm	Rex Maupin Orchestra	Syncopated Piece	America Preferred	Emma Otero, songs
12:15	I'm An American			
12:30	The Radio City Music Hall	The Salt Lake Tabernacle Choir	Cy Walter, piano	Sunday Down South
12:45			Frank Singiser, news	
1pm		The CBS Church of the Air	This is Fort Dix	The Silver Strings
1:15				
1:30	Matinee with Lytell	You Decide	Bob Chester Orchestra	Charles Dant Orchestra
1:45				

DAYTIME — SUMMER, 1941

Monday-Friday

BLUE	CBS	MBS	NBC	
The Woman of Tomorrow	George Bryan, news	Music / Arthur Godfrey, songs	Happy Jack Turner, songs	9am
	Music	Talk and Music / The Heart of Julia Blake	Music	9:15
The Breakfast Club		The Shoppers Club	Isabel Manning Hewson, food	9:30
	Betty Crocker, cooking / Hymns of All Churches		The Gospel Singer / The Mystery Chef	9:45
Helen Hiett, news	By Kathleen Norris	Talk / The Pure Food Forum	Bess Johnson	10am
Buck Private and His Girl	The Story of Myrt and Marge	Happy Jim Parsons, songs	The Story of Ellen Randolph	10:15
Clark Dennis, songs	Stepmother		Bachelor's Children	10:30
Prescott Presents	Woman of Courage		The Road of Life	10:45
	Music / Treat Time, Buddy Clark	News	The Story of Mary Marlin	11am
Stringtime	The Man I Married	Bessie Beatty, talk	Pepper Young's Family	11:15
Talk and Music	Big Sister		The Goldbergs	11:30
	Aunt Jenny's True Life Stories		David Harum	11:45
	Kate Smith Speaks	John B. Hughes, news	Words and Music	12pm
	When a Girl Marries	Songs / The Consumers' Quiz	The O'Neills	12:15
The National Farm and Home Hour	The Romance of Helen Trent	Vincent Connolly, news	Songs	12:30
	Our Gal Sunday	Judy and Jane	News	12:45
	Life Can Be Beautiful	We Are Always Young	Music	1pm
Between the Bookends	The Woman in White	Helen Holden, Government Girl	Vincent Lopez Orchestra	1:15
Religious Talk	The Right to Happiness	Front Page Farrell		1:30
Music	The Road of Life	I'll Find My Way	Betty and Bob	1:45

DAYTIME — SUMMER, 1941

Sunday

	BLUE	CBS	MBS	NBC
2pm	Hidden History	Invitation to Learning	Sports	Upton Close, news
2:15	Public Affairs			
2:30	Tapestry Musicale	St. Louis Orchestra		The University of Chicago Round Table
2:45				
3pm	African Trek	New York Philharmonic Orchestra		Charles Dant Orchestra
3:15				H. V. Kaltenborn, news
3:30	Weekend Cruise			Sammy Kaye's Sunday Serenade
3:45				
4pm	National Vespers	Walter Gross Orchestra		Chautauqua Symphony Orchestra
4:15				
4:30	Behind the Mike	The Spirit of '41		
4:45				
5pm	The Moylan Sisters, songs	Young Ideas		Joe and Mabel
5:15	Olivio Santora, yodeler			
5:30	Rhythms By Ricardo	The Golden Gate Quartet		The Roy Shield Revue
5:45		Ted Husing, sports		

DAYTIME — SUMMER, 1941

Monday-Friday

BLUE	CBS	MBS	NBC	
	Young Dr. Malone	Martha Deane, talk	The Light of the World	2pm
	Joyce Jordan, MD		The Mystery Man	2:15
Into the Light	Fletcher Wiley, news	Music	Valiant Lady	2:30
Midstream	Kate Hopkins, Angel of Mercy		Arnold Grimm's Daughter	2:45
Orphans of Divorce	Mary Margaret McBride, talk	Sports	Against the Storm	3pm
Amanda of Honeymoon Hill	The Squibb Golden Treasury of Song		Ma Perkins	3:15
John's Other Wife	Renfro Valley Folks		The Guiding Light	3:30
Just Plain Bill	Informational Talk		Vic and Sade	3:45
Club Matinee, Garry Moore	Richard Maxwell, songs		Mary Noble, Backstage Wife	4pm
	Music		Stella Dallas	4:15
			Lorenzo Jones	4:30
			Young Widder Brown	4:45
Music / The Singing Story Lady	The Story of Mary Marlin		Home of the Brave	5pm
Bud Barton	The Goldbergs	Waite Hoyt, sports	Portia Faces Life	5:15
Drama Behind the News	The O'Neills	Music	We, the Abbotts	5:30
Wings on Watch	The Ben Bernie War Workers' Program	Music / Mandrake, the Magician	Jack Armstrong, the All-American Boy	5:45

DAYTIME — SUMMER, 1941

Saturday

	BLUE	CBS	MBS	NBC
9am	The Breakfast Club	News	Dear Imogene	Music
9:15		Melodic Moments	Selective Service	Isabel Manning Hewson, food
9:30		The Old Dirt Dobber	Music	New England to You
9:45				
10am	The Andrini Continentals	The Burl Ives Coffee Club	Rainbow House	Music
10:15	The Cadet's Quartet			Happy Jack Turner, songs
10:30	The Four Polka Dots	Gold is Where You Find It		America, the Free
10:45	Rosa Lee, songs			
11am	The Band Played On	The Life of Riley	News	Lincoln Highway
11:15			Music	
11:30	Our Barn	The Voice of Broadway	The US Army Band	Saturday Morning Vaudeville Theater
11:45		National Hillbilly Champions		
12pm	Reflections in Rhythm	Columbia's Country Journal	Music	Consumer Time
12:15				Bonnie Stewart, songs
12:30	The National Farm and Home Hour	Stars Over Hollywood	Vincent Connolly, news	Call to Youth
12:45			The Charioteers Quartet	News
1pm		Let's Pretend	We Are Always Young	Matinee in Rhythm
1:15			Helen Holden, Government Girl	Billy Grant, songs
1:30	Cleveland Calling	The Brush Creek Follies	Music	Vincent Lopez Orchestra
1:45			I'll Find My Way	

DAYTIME — SUMMER, 1941

Saturday

	BLUE	CBS	MBS	NBC
2pm	Johnny Long Orchestra	Buffalo Presents	Ed Fitzgerald, talk	Campus Capers
2:15			Dance Orchestra	
2:30	Ray Kinney Orchestra	Of Men and Books	Sports	The Bright Idea Club
2:45				
3pm	Howard Ropa, songs	The Dorian String Quartet		Nature Sketches
3:15	The Singing Powers Models			Patti Chapin, songs
3:30	Music of the Americas	Vera Brodsky, piano		String Ensemble
3:45				
4pm	Club Matinee, Garry Moore	Calling Pan-America		Weekend Whimsey
4:15				
4:30		The Symphonettes		A Boy, a Girl and a Band
4:45				
5pm	Dolly Dawn Orchestra	Sonny Dunham Orchestra		The World is Yours
5:15			Waite Hoyt, sports	
5:30	Concert Musicale		Charlie Spivak Orchestra	Recital Period
5:45				Desi Halban, songs

EVENING — FALL, 1941

Sunday

	BLUE	CBS	MBS	NBC
6pm	| New Friends of Music	The Silver Theater	Double or Nothing	The Catholic Hour
6:15				
6:30	Drew Pearson, news	Gene Autry's Melody Ranch	Bulldog Drummond	The Great Gildersleeve
6:45	Over Our Coffee Cups			
7pm	Edward Tomlinson, news	Dear Mom (6:55pm)	Symphonic Strings	The Jello Program, Jack Benny
7:15		Public Affairs		
7:30	Captain Flagg and Sergeant Quirt	The Gulf Screen Theater	Frank Singiser, news	The Fitch Bandwagon
7:45			The Song Parade	
8pm	Blue Echoes	The Helen Hayes Theater	The American Forum of the Air	The Charlie McCarthy Show
8:15				
8:30	Inner Sanctum Mysteries	Crime Doctor		One Man's Family
8:45		Elmer Davis, news (8:55pm)	Gabriel Heatter, news	
9pm	Walter Winchell's Jergens Journal	The Ford Sunday Evening Hour	Dance Orchestra	The Manhattan Merry-Go-Round
9:15	The Parker Family			
9:30	Irene Rich Dramas		The Timid Soul	The American Album of Familiar Music
9:45	Songs By Dinah Shore			
10pm	The Goodwill Hour	Take It or Leave It	Dance Orchestra	The Hour of Charm
10:15				
10:30		Twenty-Six By Corwin	Keep 'Em Rolling	Sherlock Holmes
10:45				

EVENING — FALL, 1941

Monday

BLUE	CBS	MBS	NBC	
Music By Shrednik	Edwin C. Hill, news	Uncle Don	Sketches in Melody	6pm
Bill Stern, sports	Hedda Hopper, gossip		Robert St. John, news	6:15
Lum and Abner	The Squibb Golden Treasury of Song	Frank Singiser, news	Brad Reynolds, songs	6:30
Lowell Thomas, news	The World Today	Here's Morgan	The Three Suns	6:45
The Best of the Week	Amos 'n' Andy	Stan Lomax, sports	Chesterfield Time	7pm
	The Lanny Ross Show	Arthur Hale, news	John W. Vandercook, news	7:15
America Prepares	Blondie	The Lone Ranger	The Cavalcade of America	7:30
				7:45
I Love a Mystery	Vox Pop	Cal Tinney, news	The Bell Telephone Hour	8pm
		Sky Over Britain		8:15
True or False	The Gay Nineties Revue	Boake Carter, news	The Voice of Firestone	8:30
	Elmer Davis, news (8:55pm)	The Bert Shefter Octet		8:45
The National Radio Forum	The Lux Radio Theater	Gabriel Heatter, news	Dr. I. Q., the Mental Banker	9pm
		Imperial Time, Mary Small		9:15
For America We Sing		Russell Bennett's Notebook	That Brewster Boy	9:30
				9:45
The Monday Merry-Go-Round	The Orson Welles Theater	Raymond Gram Swing, news	The Carnation Contented Hour	10pm
		Spotlight Bands		10:15
News	Juan Arvizu, songs	Kaye Brinker, talk	Percy Faith Orchestra	10:30
Ted Steele Orchestra	Mark Hawley, news	Ramona and the Tune Twisters		10:45

EVENING — FALL, 1941

Tuesday

	BLUE	CBS	MBS	NBC
6pm	Music By Shrednik	Edwin C. Hill, news	Uncle Don	Sketches in Melody
6:15	Bill Stern, sports	The Voice of Broadway		Robert St. John, news
6:30	Lum and Abner	Hughesreel	Frank Singiser, news	Patti Chapin, songs
6:45	Lowell Thomas, news	The World Today	Here's Morgan	The Three Suns
7pm	Easy Aces	Amos 'n' Andy	Stan Lomax, sports	Chesterfield Time
7:15	Mr. Keen, Tracer of Lost Persons	The Lanny Ross Show	The Adrian Rollini Trio	John W. Vandercook, news
7:30	Vincent Lopez Orchestra	Second Husband	Arthur Hale, news	Burns and Allen
7:45			Sam Balter, sports	
8pm	The Treasury Hour	The Court of Missing Heirs	Tropical Serenade, Don Arres	Johnny Presents
8:15				
8:30		The Bob Burns Show	Can You Top This	Tums Treasure Chest
8:45		Elmer Davis, news (8:55pm)		
9pm	Famous Jury Trials	We, the People	Gabriel Heatter, news	Battle of the Sexes
9:15			Claude Thornhill Orchestra	
9:30	NBC Symphony Orchestra	Report to the Nation	Sinfonietta	Fibber Magee and Molly
9:45				
10pm		Moonlight Serenade	Raymond Gram Swing, news	The Pepsodent Show, Bob Hope
10:15		John Public's Pocketbook	Spotlight Bands	
10:30	William Hillman, news	Juan Arvizu, songs	Kaye Brinker, talk	The Raleigh Cigarette Program, Red Skelton
10:45	Ted Steele Orchestra	Mark Hawley, news	Ramona and the Tune Twisters	

EVENING — FALL, 1941

Wednesday

BLUE	CBS	MBS	NBC	
Music By Shrednik	Edwin C. Hill, news	Uncle Don	Sketches in Melody	6pm
Bill Stern, sports	Hedda Hopper, gossip		Robert St. John, news	6:15
Musical Appetizer	The Squibb Golden Treasury of Song	Frank Singiser, news	Hollywood News	6:30
Lowell Thomas, news	The World Today	Here's Morgan	The Three Suns	6:45
Easy Aces	Amos 'n' Andy	Stan Lomax, sports	Chesterfield Time	7pm
Mr. Keen, Tracer of Lost Persons	The Lanny Ross Show	Arthur Hale, news	John W. Vandercook, news	7:15
Muggsy Spanier Orchestra	Meet Mr. Meek	The Lone Ranger	Bert Burhman Orchestra	7:30
Upton Close, news				7:45
The Quiz Kids	Big Town	Cal Tinney, news	The Adventures of the Thin Man	8pm
		Go Get It		8:15
Manhattan at Midnight	Dr. Christian		Paducah Plantation, Red Foley	8:30
	Elmer Davis, news (8:55pm)	Red Barber, sports		8:45
The Chamber Music Society of Lower Basin Street	The Texaco Star Theater, Fred Allen	Gabriel Heatter, news	Time to Smile, Eddie Cantor	9pm
		Danger is My Business		9:15
Penthouse Party		David Rose Orchestra	Mr. District Attorney	9:30
				9:45
The American Melody Hour	Moonlight Serenade	Raymond Gram Swing, news	Kay Kyser's College of Musical Knowledge	10pm
	Public Affairs	Spotlight Bands		10:15
Ahead of the Headlines	Juan Arvizu, songs	Kaye Brinker, talk		10:30
Ted Steele Orchestra	Mark Hawley, news	Ramona and the Tune Twisters		10:45

EVENING — FALL, 1941

Thursday

	BLUE	CBS	MBS	NBC
6pm	Music By Shrednik	Edwin C. Hill, news	Uncle Don	Sketches in Melody
6:15	Bill Stern, sports	William L. Shirer, news		Robert St. John, news
6:30	Lum and Abner	Hughesreel	Frank Singiser, news	Heirs of Liberty
6:45	Lowell Thomas, news	The World Today	Here's Morgan	The Three Suns
7pm	Easy Aces	Amos 'n' Andy	Stan Lomax, sports	Chesterfield Time
7:15	Mr. Keen, Tracer of Lost Persons	The Lanny Ross Show	The Adrian Rollini Trio	John W. Vandercook, news
7:30	Savoy and Brown	Maudie's Diary	Arthur Hale, news	The Cugat Rumba Revue
7:45			Sam Balter, sports	
8pm	The March of Time	Death Valley Days	The Rookies	Maxwell House Coffee Time, Brice and Morgan
8:15				
8:30	The Army Show	Duffy's Tavern	Benny Goodman Orchestra	The Aldrich Family
8:45		Elmer Davis, news (8:55pm)		
9pm	Hillman and Clapper, news	Major Bowes' Original Amateur Hour	Gabriel Heatter, news	The Kraft Music Hall, Bing Crosby
9:15	America's Town Meeting of the Air		Claude Thornhill Orchestra	
9:30			America Preferred	
9:45				
10pm		Moonlight Serenade	Raymond Gram Swing, news	Vallee Varieties
10:15	The First Piano Quartet	Public Affairs	Spotlight Bands	
10:30	The Dinning Sisters, songs	Juan Arvizu, songs	Kaye Brinker, talk	The Tums Show, Frank Fay
10:45	Ted Steele Orchestra	Mark Hawley, news	Ramona and the Tune Twisters	

EVENING — FALL, 1941

Friday

BLUE	CBS	MBS	NBC	
Music By Shrednik	Edwin C. Hill, news	Uncle Don	Sketches in Melody	6pm
Bill Stern, sports	Hedda Hopper, gossip		Robert St. John, news	6:15
Musical Appetizer	The Squibb Golden Treasury of Song	Frank Singiser, news	Touchdown Tips	6:30
Lowell Thomas, news	The World Today	Here's Morgan	The Three Suns	6:45
Jean Cavall, songs	Amos 'n' Andy	Stan Lomax, sports	Chesterfield Time	7pm
Radio Magic	The Lanny Ross Show	Arthur Hale, news	John W. Vandercook, news	7:15
Glenn Miller Orchestra	Al Pearce and His Gang	The Lone Ranger	Grand Central Station	7:30
				7:45
Edward Tomlinson, news	The Kate Smith Hour	Cal Tinney, news	The Cities Service Concerts	8pm
Jose Bethancourt Orchestra		The People's Playhouse		8:15
Romance and Rhythm			Information, Please	8:30
	Elmer Davis, news (8:55pm)	Red Barber, sports		8:45
Gangbusters	The Phillip Morris Playhouse	Gabriel Heatter, news	Waltz Time	9pm
		America's Famous Fathers		9:15
Michael and Kitty	The First Nighter Program	Three Ring Time, Milton Berle	Uncle Walter's Dog House	9:30
				9:45
Rochester Civic Orchestra	Hollywood Premiere	Madison Square Garden Boxing	Wings of Destiny	10pm
				10:15
John Gunther, news	Juan Arvizu, songs		Studio X, Dumke and Hulick	10:30
Ted Steele Orchestra	Mark Hawley, news	Spotlight Bands		10:45

EVENING — FALL, 1941

Saturday

	BLUE	CBS	MBS	NBC
6pm	Carmen Cavaliero Orchestra	Calling Pan-America	Uncle Don	The Rhythmnaires
6:15				Robert St. John, news
6:30	Lum and Abner	Elmer Davis, news	Frank Singiser, news	Religion in the News
6:45	Edward Tomlinson, news	The World Today	Here's Morgan	Frankie Frisch, sports
7pm	Message of Israel	The People's Platform	Stan Lomax, sports	Defense for America
7:15			Music	
7:30	Little Ol' Hollywood	Wayne King Orchestra	Arthur Hale, news	Emma Otero, songs
7:45			Sam Balter, sports	H. V. Kaltenborn, news
8pm	Boy Meets Band	Guy Lombardo Orchestra	Dance Orchestra	The Knickerbocker Playhouse
8:15				
8:30	The Bishop and the Gargoyle	Hobby Lobby	The Song Spinners	Truth or Consequences
8:45		Elmer Davis, news (8:55pm)	Red Barber, sports	
9pm	Spin and Win	Your Hit Parade	The Chicago Theater of the Air	The National Barn Dance
9:15				
9:30	NBC Symphony Orchestra			
9:45		Battle of the Burroughs		
10pm	Hemisphere Revue		Cedric Foster, news	The Colgate Sports Newsreel, Bill Stern
10:15		Public Affairs	Spotlight Bands	Joseph Gallicchio Orchestra
10:30	Sweet and Rhythmic	Juan Arvizu, songs		Hot Copy
10:45		Mark Hawley, news	Ramona and the Tune Twisters	

DAYTIME — FALL, 1941

Sunday

	BLUE	CBS	MBS	NBC
9am	News	News	BBC News	News
9:15	The Children's Hour	From the Organ Loft	Music	The Deep River Boys
9:30			The Natural History Quiz	Words and Music
9:45		Gypsy Caravan		
10am	Fantasy in Melody	The CBS Church of the Air	News	The National Radio Pulpit
10:15			Elton Britt, songs	
10:30	The Southernaires Quartet	Wings Over Jordan	The Green Hornet	The Horn and Hardart Children's Hour
10:45				
11am	News	The Budapest String Quartet	Hawaii Calls	
11:15	Hidden History			
11:30	Maurice Spitalny Orchestra		The Mutual Radio Chapel	George Putnam, news
11:45				Sunday Down South
12pm	Foreign Policy Association Talks	Columbia's Country Journal	The Perole String Quartet	Football Second Guessers
12:15	I'm An American			
12:30	The Radio City Music Hall	The Salt Lake Tabernacle Choir	The Sing a Song of Safety Club	Emma Otero, songs
12:45			Frank Singiser, news	
1pm		The CBS Church of the Air	The Canary Pet Shop	Upton Close, news
1:15			George Fisher, gossip	The Silver Strings
1:30	African Trek	This is the Life	This is Fort Dix	The World is Yours
1:45				

DAYTIME — FALL, 1941

Monday-Friday

BLUE	CBS	MBS	NBC	
The Woman of Tomorrow	George Bryan, news	Dear Imogene	Songs	9am
	The American School of the Air	Victor Lindlahr, health	Hank Lawson's Knights	9:15
The Breakfast Club		Talk and Music	Isabel Manning Hewson, food	9:30
	Stories America Loves		The Gospel Singer / The Mystery Chef	9:45
The Dick Dinsmore Trio	Betty Crocker, cooking / Hymns of All Churches	Alfred W. McCann, food	Bess Johnson	10am
A House in the Country	The Story of Myrt and Marge		Bachelor's Children	10:15
Clark Dennis, songs	Stepmother	The Consumers' Quiz	Helpmate	10:30
Prescott Presents	Woman of Courage		The Road of Life	10:45
	Treat Time, Buddy Clark	Bessie Beatty, talk	The Story of Mary Marlin	11am
Stringtime	The Man I Married		Pepper Young's Family	11:15
Talk / Raising a President	Bright Horizon		The Goldbergs	11:30
Music	Aunt Jenny's True Life Stories		David Harum	11:45
Nancy Booth Craig, talk	Kate Smith Speaks	John B. Hughes, news	Don Goddard, news	12pm
Music	Big Sister	This is Life / Arthur Godfrey, songs	The O'Neills	12:15
The National Farm and Home Hour	The Romance of Helen Trent	Alois Havrilla, news	Words and Music	12:30
	Our Gal Sunday	Judy and Jane		12:45
	Life Can Be Beautiful	We are Always Young	Mary Margaret McBride, talk	1pm
Between the Bookends	The Woman in White	Helen Holden, Government Girl		1:15
Religious Talk	The Right to Happiness	Front Page Farrell		1:30
News	The Road of Life	I'll Find My Way	Betty and Bob	1:45

DAYTIME — FALL, 1941

Sunday

	BLUE	CBS	MBS	NBC
2pm	Wake Up, America	The Spirit of '41	Succoth Service	Sammy Kaye's Sunday Serenade
2:15				
2:30		World News Today	Bob Chester Orchestra	The University of Chicago Round Table
2:45				
3pm	Buddy Rogers Orchestra	New York Philharmonic Orchestra	Sports	Bob Carroll, songs
3:15				H. V. Kaltenborn, news
3:30	Tapestry Musicale			The Roy Shield Revue
3:45				
4pm	National Vespers			Lavender and New Lace
4:15				Tony Wons' Scrapbook
4:30	Behind the Mike	The Pause That Refreshes		String Symphony
4:45				
5pm	The Moylan Sisters, songs	The Prudential Family Hour	Blue Barron Orchestra	The Metropolitan Opera Auditions
5:15	Olivio Santora, yodeler			
5:30	The Musical Steelmakers		The Shadow	The Nickels Family of Five
5:45		William L. Shirer, news		

DAYTIME — FALL, 1941

Monday-Friday

BLUE	CBS	MBS	NBC	
Music	Young Dr. Malone	Martha Deane, talk	The Light of the World	*2pm*
	Joyce Jordan, MD		The Mystery Man	*2:15*
Into the Light	Fletcher Wiley, news	Music	Valiant Lady	*2:30*
Midstream	Kate Hopkins, Angel of Mercy		Arnold Grimm's Daughter	*2:45*
Orphans of Divorce	Of Men and Books / News for Women	Richard Willis, beauty	Against the Storm	*3pm*
Amanda of Honeymoon Hill	A Helping Hand	Talk and Music	Ma Perkins	*3:15*
John's Other Wife	Renfro Valley Folks	Music	The Guiding Light	*3:30*
Just Plain Bill	Informational Talk		Vic and Sade	*3:45*
Club Matinee, Garry Moore	Music	Arthur Van Horn, news	Mary Noble, Backstage Wife	*4pm*
		The Rains Came / My Man Godfrey	Stella Dallas	*4:15*
	The Landt Trio and Curley	Happy Jim Parsons, songs	Lorenzo Jones	*4:30*
	Mark Hawley, news		Young Widder Brown	*4:45*
Captain Tim Healy's Adventure Stories	The Story of Mary Marlin	Little Orphan Annie	When a Girl Marries	*5pm*
Bud Barton	The Goldbergs	Music / Mandrake, the Magician	Portia Faces Life	*5:15*
The Flying Patrol	The O'Neills	Jack Armstrong, the All-American Boy	We, the Abbotts	*5:30*
The Tom Mix Ralston Straight Shooters	The Ben Bernie War Workers' Program	Captain Midnight	The Three Suns	*5:45*

DAYTIME — FALL, 1941

Saturday

	BLUE	CBS	MBS	NBC
9am	The Breakfast Club	George Bryan, news	Dear Imogene	Happy Jack Turner, songs
9:15		Melodic Moments	Health Talk	Isabel Manning Hewson, food
9:30		The Old Dirt Dobber	Music	Hank Lawson's Knights
9:45			Ed Fitzgerald and Company	
10am	The Andrini Continentals	The Burl Ives Coffee Club	Rainbow House	The Don Carper Quartet
10:15	The Cadet's Quartet			The Deep River Boys
10:30	The Four Polka Dots	Jones and I		America, the Free
10:45	Rosa Lee, songs			
11am	The Band Played On	The Kay Thompson Show	Prescott Robinson, news	Lincoln Highway
11:15			Ramona and the Tune Twisters	
11:30	Our Barn	The Voice of Broadway	The US Army Band	Saturday Morning Vaudeville Theater
11:45		National Hillbilly Champions		
12pm	Al and Lee Reiser, piano	The Armstrong Theater of Today	The Man on the Farm	Don Goddard, news
12:15	Howard Ropa, songs			Consumer Time
12:30	The National Farm and Home Hour	Stars Over Hollywood	Alois Havrilla, news	Call to Youth
12:45			Happy Jim Parsons, songs	Matinee in Rhythm
1pm		Let's Pretend	We Are Always Young	
1:15			Helen Holden, Government Girl	New England to You
1:30	Vincent Lopez Orchestra	Buffalo Presents	Frank Forrest, songs	
1:45	Sports	Sports	Sports	Sports

DAYTIME — FALL, 1941

Saturday

	BLUE	CBS	MBS	NBC
2pm				
2:15				
2:30				
2:45				
3pm				
3:15				
3:30				
3:45				
4pm				Campus Capers
4:15				
4:30	Club Matinee, Garry Moore	Music		Music of the Americas
4:45				
5pm	Sunset Serenade	Matinee at the Meadowbrook		Weekend Whimsey
5:15				
5:30			Dance Orchestra	Recital Period
5:45				Desi Halban, songs

LISTINGS FOR 1942

EVENING — WINTER, 1942

Sunday

	BLUE	CBS	MBS	NBC
6pm	Mart Kenny Orchestra	The Silver Theater	Double or Nothing	The Catholic Hour
6:15				
6:30	Drew Pearson, news	Gene Autry's Melody Ranch	Bulldog Drummond	The Great Gildersleeve
6:45	Over Our Coffee Cups			
7pm	European News		Symphonic Strings	The Jello Program, Jack Benny
7:15		Public Affairs		
7:30	Captain Flagg and Sergeant Quirt	The Gulf Screen Theater	Frank Singiser, news	The Fitch Bandwagon
7:45			Short, Short Story	
8pm	Blue Echoes	The Helen Hayes Theater	The American Forum of the Air	The Charlie McCarthy Show
8:15				
8:30	Inner Sanctum Mysteries	Crime Doctor		One Man's Family
8:45		Elmer Davis, news (8:55pm)	Gabriel Heatter, news	
9pm	Walter Winchell's Jergens Journal	The Ford Sunday Evening Hour	Dance Orchestra	The Manhattan Merry-Go-Round
9:15	The Parker Family			
9:30	Irene Rich Dramas		The Timid Soul	The American Album of Familiar Music
9:45	Songs By Dinah Shore			
10pm	The Goodwill Hour	Take It or Leave It	Dance Orchestra	The Hour of Charm
10:15				
10:30		They Live Forever	Keep 'Em Rolling	Sherlock Holmes
10:45				

LISTINGS FOR 1942

EVENING — WINTER, 1942

Monday

BLUE	CBS	MBS	NBC	
Music By Shrednik	Edwin C. Hill, news	Uncle Don	Sketches in Melody	6pm
Bill Stern, sports	Hedda Hopper, gossip		Robert St. John, news	6:15
Lum and Abner	The Squibb Golden Treasury of Song	Frank Singiser, news	Brad Taylor, songs	6:30
Lowell Thomas, news	The World Today	Here's Morgan	The Three Suns	6:45
The New Old Gold Program	Amos 'n' Andy	Stan Lomax, sports	Chesterfield Time	7pm
	The Lanny Ross Show	Arthur Hale, news	John W. Vandercook, news	7:15
Rochester Civic Orchestra	Blondie	The Lone Ranger	The Cavalcade of America	7:30
				7:45
I Love a Mystery	Vox Pop	Cal Tinney, news	The Bell Telephone Hour	8pm
		Ted Weems Orchestra		8:15
True or False	The Gay Nineties Revue	Boake Carter, news	The Voice of Firestone	8:30
	Elmer Davis, news (8:55pm)	Carl Hoff Orchestra		8:45
The National Radio Forum	The Lux Radio Theater	Gabriel Heatter, news	Dr. I. Q., the Mental Banker	9pm
		The Answer Man		9:15
For America We Sing		WOR Symphony Orchestra	That Brewster Boy	9:30
				9:45
The Monday Merry-Go-Round	The Orson Welles Theater	Raymond Gram Swing, news	The Carnation Contented Hour	10pm
		Spotlight Bands		10:15
Hillman and Clapper, news	Olga Coehlo, songs	The Jerry Wayne Show	Percy Faith Orchestra	10:30
Public Affairs	Mark Hawley, news	Ramona and the Tune Twisters		10:45

EVENING — WINTER, 1942

Tuesday

	BLUE	CBS	MBS	NBC
6pm	Music By Shrednik	Edwin C. Hill, news	Uncle Don	Sketches in Melody
6:15	Bill Stern, sports	The Voice of Broadway		Robert St. John, news
6:30	Lum and Abner	Eric Severeid, news	Frank Singiser, news	Patti Chapin, songs
6:45	Lowell Thomas, news	The World Today	Here's Morgan	The Three Suns
7pm	Easy Aces	Amos 'n' Andy	Stan Lomax, sports	Chesterfield Time
7:15	Mr. Keen, Tracer of Lost Persons	The Lanny Ross Show	The Adrian Rollini Trio	John W. Vandercook, news
7:30	Vincent Lopez Orchestra	Second Husband	Arthur Hale, news	Burns and Allen
7:45			Sam Balter, sports	
8pm	Rumba Revue	The Court of Missing Heirs	What's My Name	Johnny Presents
8:15				
8:30	Meet Your Navy	The Bob Burns Show	Can You Top This	Tums Treasure Chest
8:45		Elmer Davis, news (8:55pm)		
9pm	Famous Jury Trials	We, the People	Gabriel Heatter, news	Battle of the Sexes
9:15			Alvino Rey Orchestra	
9:30	NBC Symphony Orchestra	Report to the Nation	Morton Gould Orchestra	Fibber Magee and Molly
9:45				
10pm		Moonlight Serenade	Raymond Gram Swing, news	The Pepsodent Show, Bob Hope
10:15		John Public's Pocketbook	Spotlight Bands	
10:30	Hillman and Clapper, news	Olga Coehlo, songs	The Jerry Wayne Show	The Raleigh Cigarette Program, Red Skelton
10:45	Joseph Sudy Orchestra	Mark Hawley, news	Ramona and the Tune Twisters	

EVENING — WINTER, 1942

Wednesday

BLUE	CBS	MBS	NBC	
Music By Shrednik	Edwin C. Hill, news	Uncle Don	Sketches in Melody	6pm
Bill Stern, sports	Hedda Hopper, gossip		Robert St. John, news	6:15
Musical Appetizer	The Squibb Golden Treasury of Song	Frank Singiser, news	Hollywood News	6:30
Lowell Thomas, news	The World Today	Here's Morgan	The Three Suns	6:45
Easy Aces	Amos 'n' Andy	Stan Lomax, sports	Chesterfield Time	7pm
Mr. Keen, Tracer of Lost Persons	The Lanny Ross Show	Arthur Hale, news	John W. Vandercook, news	7:15
Muggsy Spanier Orchestra	The Kay Thompson Show	The Lone Ranger	Allen Roth Orchestra	7:30
Upton Close, news				7:45
The Quiz Kids	Meet Mr. Meek	Cal Tinney, news	The Adventures of the Thin Man	8pm
		Go Get It		8:15
Manhattan at Midnight	Dr. Christian		Paducah Plantation, Red Foley	8:30
	Elmer Davis, news (8:55pm)	Red Barber, sports		8:45
The Chamber Music Society of Lower Basin Street	The Texaco Star Theater, Fred Allen	Gabriel Heatter, news	Time to Smile, Eddie Cantor	9pm
		The Answer Man		9:15
Cab Calloway's Quizzicale		David Rose Orchestra	Mr. District Attorney	9:30
				9:45
The American Melody Hour	Moonlight Serenade	Raymond Gram Swing, news	Kay Kyser's College of Musical Knowledge	10pm
	Great Moments in Music	Spotlight Bands		10:15
Hillman and Clapper, news		The Jerry Wayne Show		10:30
Ted Steele Orchestra	Mark Hawley, news	Ramona and the Tune Twisters		10:45

EVENING — WINTER, 1942

Thursday

	BLUE	CBS	MBS	NBC
6pm	Music By Shrednik	Edwin C. Hill, news	Uncle Don	Sketches in Melody
6:15	Bill Stern, sports	William L. Shirer, news		Robert St. John, news
6:30	Lum and Abner	Olga Coehlo, songs	Frank Singiser, news	Heirs of Liberty
6:45	Lowell Thomas, news	The World Today	Here's Morgan	The Three Suns
7pm	Easy Aces	Amos 'n' Andy	Stan Lomax, sports	Chesterfield Time
7:15	Mr. Keen, Tracer of Lost Persons	The Lanny Ross Show	The Adrian Rollini Trio	John W. Vandercook, news
7:30	Rochester Philharmonic Orchestra	Maudie's Diary	Arthur Hale, news	Al Pearce and His Gang
7:45			Sam Balter, sports	
8pm	The March of Time	Death Valley Days	Morton Gould Orchestra	Maxwell House Coffee Time, Brice and Morgan
8:15				
8:30	The Army Show	Duffy's Tavern	Blue Barron Orchestra	The Aldrich Family
8:45		Elmer Davis, news (8:55pm)		
9pm	America's Town Meeting of the Air	Major Bowes' Original Amateur Hour	Gabriel Heatter, news	The Kraft Music Hall, Bing Crosby
9:15			Overseas News	
9:30		Big Town	Sinfonietta	
9:45				
10pm		Moonlight Serenade	Cedric Foster, news	Vallee Varieties
10:15	The First Piano Quartet	The First Line of Defense	Spotlight Bands	
10:30	Hillman and Clapper, news		Fulton Lewis Jr., news	The Tums Show, Frank Fay
10:45	Public Affairs	Mark Hawley, news	Ramona and the Tune Twisters	

EVENING — WINTER, 1942

Friday

BLUE	CBS	MBS	NBC	
Music By Shrednik	Edwin C. Hill, news	Uncle Don	Sketches in Melody	6pm
Bill Stern, sports	Hedda Hopper, gossip		Robert St. John, news	6:15
Musical Appetizer	The Squibb Golden Treasury of Song	Frank Singiser, news	Desi Halban, songs	6:30
Lowell Thomas, news	The World Today	Here's Morgan	The Three Suns	6:45
Jean Cavall, songs	Amos 'n' Andy	Stan Lomax, sports	Chesterfield Time	7pm
Radio Magic	The Lanny Ross Show	Arthur Hale, news	John W. Vandercook, news	7:15
Charlie Spivak Orchestra	How'm I Doin'	The Lone Ranger	Grand Central Station	7:30
				7:45
Edward Tomlinson, news	The Kate Smith Hour	Cal Tinney, news	The Cities Service Concerts	8pm
Jose Bethancourt Orchestra		Don Arres, songs		8:15
Three Ring Time, Milton Berle		Russell Bennett's Notebook	Information, Please	8:30
	Elmer Davis, news (8:55pm)			8:45
Gangbusters	The Phillip Morris Playhouse	Gabriel Heatter, news	Waltz Time	9pm
		The War at Sea		9:15
Michael Piper, Private Detective	The First Night Program	America Preferred	Uncle Walter's Dog House	9:30
				9:45
Elsa Maxwell's Party Line	The Ransom Sherman Show	Madison Square Garden Boxing	Wings of Destiny	10pm
Vladimir Horowitz, piano				10:15
Hillman and Clapper, news	Public Affairs		Studio X, Dumke and Hulick	10:30
Ted Steele Orchestra	Mark Hawley, news	Spotlight Bands		10:45

EVENING — WINTER, 1942

Saturday

	BLUE	CBS	MBS	NBC
6pm	Music By Shrednik	Calling Pan-America	Uncle Don	Sketches in Melody
6:15				Robert St. John, news
6:30	Lum and Abner	Elmer Davis, news	Frank Singiser, news	Religion in the News
6:45	Edward Tomlinson, news	The World Today	Here's Morgan	The Three Suns
7pm	Message of Israel	The People's Platform	Stan Lomax, sports	Defense for America
7:15			Talk and Music	
7:30	Little Ol' Hollywood	Wayne King Orchestra	Arthur Hale, news	The Adventures of Ellery Queen
7:45			Sam Balter, sports	
8pm	The Green Hornet	Guy Lombardo Orchestra	The Treasure Hour of Song	The Knickerbocker Playhouse
8:15				
8:30	Boy Meets Band	Hobby Lobby	California Melodies	Truth or Consequences
8:45		Elmer Davis, news (8:55pm)		
9pm	NBC Symphony Orchestra	Your Hit Parade	The Chicago Theater of the Air	The National Barn Dance
9:15				
9:30				
9:45		Saturday Night Serenade		
10pm	Believe It or Not		Cedric Foster, news	The Colgate Sports Newsreel, Bill Stern
10:15		Public Affairs	Spotlight Bands	The Ink Spots
10:30	Carmen Cavallero Orchestra	Olga Coehlo, songs		Hot Copy
10:45		Mark Hawley, news	Ramona and the Tune Twisters	

DAYTIME — WINTER, 1942

Sunday

	BLUE	CBS	MBS	NBC
9am	News	News	BBC News	News
9:15	The Children's Hour	From the Organ Loft	Pauline Alpert, piano	The Deep River Boys
9:30			The Natural History Quiz	Words and Music
9:45		Gypsy Caravan		
10am	Fantasy in Melody	The CBS Church of the Air	News	The National Radio Pulpit
10:15			Elton Britt, songs	
10:30	The Southernaires Quartet	Wings Over Jordan	Ned Jordan, Secret Agent	The Horn and Hardart Children's Hour
10:45				
11am	News	Vera Brodsky, piano	The Song Spinners	
11:15	Al and Lee Reiser, piano			
11:30	Paul La Valle Orchestra	Invitation to Learning	The Mutual Radio Chapel	George Putnam, news
11:45				Kathleen McLaughlin, talk
12pm	Foreign Policy Association Talks	Syncopated Piece	The Perole String Quartet	Sunday Down South
12:15	I'm An American			
12:30	The Radio City Music Hall	The Salt Lake Tabernacle Choir	The Sing a Song of Safety Club	Tapestry Musicale
12:45			Frank Singiser, news	
1pm		The CBS Church of the Air	The Canary Pet Shop	Upton Close, news
1:15			George Fisher, gossip	The Silver Strings
1:30	African Trek	This is the Life	This is Fort Dix	The World is Yours
1:45				

DAYTIME — WINTER, 1942

Monday-Friday

BLUE	CBS	MBS	NBC	
The Woman of Tomorrow	George Bryan, news	Dear Imogene	Songs	9am
	The American School of the Air	Victor Lindlahr, health	Hank Lawson's Knights	9:15
The Breakfast Club		Talk and Music	Isabel Manning Hewson, food	9:30
	Stories America Loves		The Gospel Singer	9:45
Clark Dennis, songs	Betty Crocker, cooking / Hymns of All Churches	Alfred W. McCann, food	Bess Johnson	10am
Helen Hiett, news	The Story of Myrt and Marge		Bachelor's Children	10:15
A House in the Country	Stepmother	The Consumers' Quiz	Helpmate	10:30
Stringtime	Woman of Courage		The Road of Life	10:45
Talk / The Traveling Chef	Mary Lee Taylor, cooking / Treat Time, Buddy Clark	Bessie Beatty, talk	The Story of Mary Marlin	11am
Talk and Music	The Man I Married		The Right to Happiness	11:15
Prescott Presents	Bright Horizon		Bud Barton	11:30
	Aunt Jenny's True Life Stories		David Harum	11:45
Nancy Booth Craig, talk	Kate Smith Speaks	John B. Hughes, news	Don Goddard, news	12pm
Civilian Defense Information	Big Sister	Music / Arthur Godfrey, songs	Words and Music	12:15
The National Farm and Home Hour	The Romance of Helen Trent	Alois Havrilla, news	The Deep River Boys	12:30
	Our Gal Sunday	Judy and Jane	Stock Market Reports	12:45
	Life Can Be Beautiful	Music / This is Life	Mary Margaret McBride, talk	1pm
Between the Bookends	The Woman in White	Helen Holden, Government Girl		1:15
Religious Talk	Vic and Sade	Front Page Farrell		1:30
Talk and Music	The Road of Life	I'll Find My Way	John W. Vandercook, news	1:45

DAYTIME — WINTER, 1942

Sunday

	BLUE	CBS	MBS	NBC
2pm	Great Plays	The Spirit of '42	Anchors Aweigh	Sammy Kaye's Sunday Serenade
2:15				
2:30		The Columbia Workshop	Bob Chester Orchestra	The University of Chicago Round Table
2:45				
3pm	Wake Up, America	New York Philharmonic Orchestra	The Americas Speak	Bob Becker's Dog Talks
3:15				H. V. Kaltenborn, news
3:30			The Mutual Forum	Listen, America
3:45				
4pm	National Vespers		Blue Barron Orchestra	Music from Brazil
4:15				Tony Wons' Scrapbook
4:30	Behind the Mike	The Pause That Refreshes		Plays for Americans
4:45				
5pm	The Moylan Sisters, songs	The Prudential Family Hour	Battle of the Burroughs	The Metropolitan Opera Auditions
5:15	Olivio Santoro, yodeler			
5:30	The Musical Steelmakers		The Shadow	The Nickels Family of Five
5:45		William L. Shirer, news		

DAYTIME — WINTER, 1942

Monday-Friday

BLUE	CBS	MBS	NBC	
Music	Young Dr. Malone	Martha Deane, talk	The Light of the World	2pm
Talk and Music	Joyce Jordan, MD		The Mystery Man	2:15
Into the Light	Fletcher Wiley, news	Prescott Robinson, news	Valiant Lady	2:30
In Care of Aggie Horn	Kate Hopkins, Angel of Mercy	Richard Willis, beauty	Arnold Grimm's Daughter	2:45
Orphans of Divorce	A Helping Hand	Music	Against the Storm	3pm
Amanda of Honeymoon Hill	Music		Ma Perkins	3:15
John's Other Wife	Renfro Valley Folks / Nell Vinick, beauty	Music / The Johnson Family	The Guiding Light	3:30
Just Plain Bill	Informational Talk	Music / Rambling with Gambling	Vic and Sade	3:45
Club Matinee, Garry Moore	Music	News	Mary Noble, Backstage Wife	4pm
		Love Affair / Jane Eyre	Stella Dallas	4:15
	The Landt Trio and Curley	Happy Jim Parsons, songs	Lorenzo Jones	4:30
	Mark Hawley, news		Young Widder Brown	4:45
Captain Tim Healy's Adventure Stories	The Story of Mary Marlin	Little Orphan Annie	When a Girl Marries	5pm
Secret City	The Goldbergs	Music / Mandrake the Magician	Portia Faces Life	5:15
The Flying Patrol	The O'Neills	Jack Armstrong, the All-American Boy	We, the Abbotts	5:30
The Tom Mix Ralston Straight Shooters	The Ben Bernie War Workers' Program	Captain Midnight	Music	5:45

DAYTIME — WINTER, 1942

Saturday

	BLUE	CBS	MBS	NBC
9am	The Breakfast Club	George Bryan, news	Dear Imogene	Happy Jack Turner, songs
9:15		Kenneth Spencer, songs	Health Talk	Isabel Manning Hewison, food
9:30		The Old Dirt Dobber	The US Navy Band	Any Bonds Today
9:45				Hank Lawson's Knights
10am	The Andrini Continentals	The US Marine Band	Rainbow House	The Carnation Family Party
10:15	The Cadet's Quartet			
10:30	The Four Polka Dots	Jones and I		The Prescott Variety Show
10:45	Rosa Lee, songs			New England to You
11am	The Band Played On	National Hillbilly Champions	Prescott Robinson, news	Lincoln Highway
11:15		God's Country, Burl Ives	Ramona and the Tune Twisters	
11:30	Ask Young America	Let's Pretend	The US Army Band	America, the Free
11:45	Fables for Fun			
12pm	The Four Belles	The Armstrong Theater of Today	The Man on the Farm	Don Goddard, news
12:15				Consumer Time
12:30	The National Farm and Home Hour	Stars Over Hollywood	Alois Havrilla, news	Ilka Chase Entertains
12:45			Our City Cousins	
1pm		Buffalo Presents	Ray Kinney Orchestra	Matinee in Rhythm
1:15			Frank Forrest, songs	
1:30	The Show Shop	Adventures in Science	Irving Jacobson Orchestra	Dr. Alfred C. Walton, health
1:45		The Golden Gate Quartet		The US Marine Band

DAYTIME — WINTER, 1942

Saturday

	BLUE	CBS	MBS	NBC
2pm	The Metropolitan Opera	Of Men and Books	Benny Goodman Orchestra	
2:15				
2:30		The Brush Creek Follies	Prescott Robinson, news	Whatcha Know, Joe
2:45			Red Norvo Orchestra	
3pm		Columbia's Country Journal	The University Life Forum	Patti Chapin, songs
3:15				On the Home Front
3:30		Detroit Musicale	The Johnson Family	Music for Everyone
3:45			Rambling with Gambling	
4pm		Johnny Long Orchestra	Blue Barron Orchestra	Campus Capers
4:15				
4:30				Air Youth of America
4:45			Horse Racing	Melody Strings
5pm	Tommy Dorsey Orchestra	Cleveland Symphony Orchestra	Sunset Serenade	Doctors at Work
5:15				
5:30	Lucky Millinder Orchestra			Music
5:45				War Correspondent

EVENING — SPRING, 1942

Sunday

	BLUE	CBS	MBS	NBC
6pm	Mart Kenny Orchestra	The Silver Theater	Double or Nothing	The Catholic Hour
6:15				
6:30	Drew Pearson, news	Gene Autry's Melody Ranch	Bulldog Drummond	The Great Gildersleeve
6:45	The Ink Spots			
7pm	European News		Symphonic Strings	The Jello Program, Jack Benny
7:15		Public Affairs		
7:30	Alias John Freedom	The Gulf Screen Theater	Frank Singiser, news	The Fitch Bandwagon
7:45			Short, Short Story	
8pm	The Daughters of Uncle Sam, Mary Small	The Helen Hayes Theater	The American Forum of the Air	The Charlie McCarthy Show
8:15				
8:30	Inner Sanctum Mysteries	Crime Doctor		One Man's Family
8:45		Elmer Davis, news (8:55pm)	Gabriel Heatter, news	
9pm	Walter Winchell's Jergens Journal	The Texaco Star Theater, Fred Allen	The Better Half	The Manhattan Merry-Go-Round
9:15	The Parker Family			
9:30	Irene Rich Dramas		California Melodies	The American Album of Familiar Music
9:45	Songs By Dinah Shore			
10pm	The Goodwill Hour	Take It or Leave It	John Gunther, news	The Hour of Charm
10:15			Overseas News	
10:30		They Live Forever	Keep 'Em Rolling	Joe and Mabel
10:45				

EVENING — SPRING, 1942

Monday

BLUE	CBS	MBS	NBC	
Music By Shrednik	Edwin C. Hill, news	Uncle Don	The Funny Money Man	6pm
Joe Hasel, sports	Hedda Hopper, gossip		George Putnam, news	6:15
Lum and Abner	The Squibb Golden Treasury of Song	Frank Singiser, news	Brad Taylor, songs	6:30
Lowell Thomas, news	The World Today	Here's Morgan	Bill Stern, sports	6:45
Jimmy Fidler, gossip	Amos 'n' Andy	Stan Lomax, sports	Chesterfield Time	7pm
Belen Ortega, songs	The Lanny Ross Show	Arthur Hale, news	John W. Vandercook, news	7:15
Hillman and Linley, news	Blondie	The Lone Ranger	Rochester Civic Orchestra	7:30
Diane Courtney and the Jesters				7:45
I Love a Mystery	Vox Pop	Cal Tinney, news	The Cavalcade of America	8pm
		Music for America		8:15
True or False	The Gay Nineties Revue		The Voice of Firestone	8:30
	Elmer Davis, news (8:55pm)			8:45
The National Radio Forum	The Lux Radio Theater	Gabriel Heatter, news	The Bell Telephone Hour	9pm
		Red Barber, sports		9:15
For America We Sing		Spotlight Bands	Dr. I. Q., the Mental Banker	9:30
		Miss Meade's Children		9:45
Vic Arden Orchestra	Lady Esther Serenade	John Gunther, news	The Carnation Contented Hour	10pm
		Public Affairs		10:15
Symphonic Music	Olga Coelho, songs	Paul Schubert, news	Hot Copy	10:30
	Mark Hawley, news	The Answer Man		10:45

EVENING — SPRING, 1942

Tuesday

	BLUE	CBS	MBS	NBC
6pm	Music By Shrednik	Edwin C. Hill, news	Uncle Don	The Funny Money Man
6:15	Joe Hasel, sports	The Voice of Broadway		George Putnam, news
6:30	Lum and Abner	The Vera Burton Show	Frank Singiser, news	Ted Steele Orchestra
6:45	Lowell Thomas, news	The World Today	Here's Morgan	Bill Stern, sports
7pm	Easy Aces	Amos 'n' Andy	Stan Lomax, sports	Chesterfield Time
7:15	Mr. Keen, Tracer of Lost Persons	The Lanny Ross Show	Hank Keene, songs	John W. Vandercook, news
7:30	Hillman and Linley, news	Rochester Philharmonic Orchestra	Arthur Hale, news	Burns and Allen
7:45	Sylvia Marlowe, songs		Sam Balter, sports	
8pm	Rumba Revue	The Court of Missing Heirs	What's My Name	Johnny Presents
8:15				
8:30	Three Ring Time, Milton Berle	The Bob Burns Show	Can You Top This	Tums Treasure Chest
8:45		Elmer Davis, news (8:55pm)		
9pm	Famous Jury Trials	Duffy's Tavern	Gabriel Heatter, news	Battle of the Sexes
9:15			Red Barber, sports	
9:30	NBC Symphony Orchestra	Report to the Nation	Spotlight Bands	Fibber Magee and Molly
9:45			Miss Meade's Children	
10pm		Milton Gross Orchestra	John B. Hughes, news	The Pepsodent Show, Bob Hope
10:15			Raymond Scott Orchestra	
10:30	Morgan Beatty, news	The Jerry Wayne Show	Paul Schubert, news	The Raleigh Cigarette Program, Red Skelton
10:45	Public Affairs	Mark Hawley, news	The Answer Man	

EVENING — SPRING, 1942

Wednesday

BLUE	CBS	MBS	NBC	
Music By Shrednik	Edwin C. Hill, news	Uncle Don	The Funny Money Man	6pm
Joe Hasel, sports	Hedda Hopper, gossip		George Putnam, news	6:15
Musical Appetizer	The Squibb Golden Treasury of Song	Frank Singiser, news	Stella Unger, gossip	6:30
Lowell Thomas, news	The World Today	Here's Morgan	Bill Stern, sports	6:45
Easy Aces	Amos 'n' Andy	Stan Lomax, sports	Chesterfield Time	7pm
Mr. Keen, Tracer of Lost Persons	The Lanny Ross Show	Arthur Hale, news	John W. Vandercook, news	7:15
Hillman and Linley, news	That Brewster Boy	The Lone Ranger	Allen Roth Orchestra	7:30
Sylvia Marlowe, songs				7:45
The Quiz Kids	Raymond Scott Orchestra	Cal Tinney, news	The Adventures of the Thin Man	8pm
		Go Get It		8:15
Manhattan at Midnight	Dr. Christian		Uncle Walter's Dog House	8:30
	Elmer Davis, news (8:55pm)	Hank Keene, songs		8:45
The Chamber Music Society of Lower Basin Street	Junior Miss	Gabriel Heatter, news	Time to Smile, Eddie Cantor	9pm
		Red Barber, sports		9:15
Cab Calloway's Quizzicale	The Ransom Sherman Show	Spotlight Bands	Mr. District Attorney	9:30
		Miss Meade's Children		9:45
Three-Thirds of the Nation	Moonlight Serenade	John B. Hughes, news	Kay Kyser's College of Musical Knowledge	10pm
	Great Moments in Music	Shep Fields Orchestra		10:15
Morgan Beatty, news		Paul Schubert, news		10:30
Jean Couvall, songs	Mark Hawley, news	The Answer Man		10:45

EVENING — SPRING, 1942

Thursday

	BLUE	CBS	MBS	NBC
6pm	Music By Shrednik	Edwin C. Hill, news	Uncle Don	The Funny Money Man
6:15	Joe Hasel, sports	Our Allies		George Putnam, news
6:30	Lum and Abner	The Vera Burton Show	Frank Singiser, news	Patti Chapin, songs
6:45	Lowell Thomas, news	The World Today	Here's Morgan	Bill Stern, sports
7pm	Easy Aces	Amos 'n' Andy	Stan Lomax, sports	Chesterfield Time
7:15	Mr. Keen, Tracer of Lost Persons	The Lanny Ross Show	Hank Keene, songs	John W. Vandercook, news
7:30	Hillman and Linley, news	Maudie's Diary	Arthur Hale, news	Al Pearce and His Gang
7:45	Diane Courtney and the Jesters		Sam Balter, sports	
8pm	Tommy Tucker Orchestra	Death Valley Days	Sinfonietta	Maxwell House Coffee Time, Brice and Morgan
8:15				
8:30	Canadian Musicale	The People's Platform	Woody Herman Orchestra	The Aldrich Family
8:45	Dorothy Thompson, news	Elmer Davis, news (8:55pm)		
9pm	America's Town Meeting of the Air	Major Bowes' Original Amateur Hour	Gabriel Heatter, news	The Kraft Music Hall, Bing Crosby
9:15			Red Barber, sports	
9:30		Big Town	Spotlight Bands	
9:45			Miss Meade's Children	
10pm	Tommy Dorsey's Variety Show	Moonlight Serenade	John Gunther, news	Vallee Varieties
10:15		The First Line of Defense	Raymond Scott Orchestra	
10:30	Morgan Beatty, news		Paul Schubert, news	The Tums Show, Frank Fay
10:45	The Treasury Star Parade	Mark Hawley, news	The Answer Man	

EVENING — SPRING, 1942

Friday

BLUE	CBS	MBS	NBC	
Music By Shrednik	Edwin C. Hill, news	Uncle Don	The Funny Money Man	6pm
Joe Hasel, sports	Hedda Hopper, gossip		George Putnam, news	6:15
Musical Appetizer	The Squibb Golden Treasury of Song	Frank Singiser, news	Ted Steele Orchestra	6:30
Lowell Thomas, news	The World Today	Here's Morgan	Bill Stern, sports	6:45
The Ontario Show	Amos 'n' Andy	Stan Lomax, sports	Chesterfield Time	7pm
	The Lanny Ross Show	Arthur Hale, news	John W. Vandercook, news	7:15
Hillman and Linley, news	How'm I Doin'	The Lone Ranger	Grand Central Station	7:30
Tommy Dorsey Orchestra				7:45
The New Old Gold Program	The Kate Smith Hour	Cal Tinney, news	The Cities Service Concerts	8pm
		What Price Victory		8:15
Meet Your Navy		Music	Information, Please	8:30
	Elmer Davis, news (8:55pm)			8:45
The March of Time	The Phillip Morris Playhouse	Gabriel Heatter, news	Waltz Time	9pm
		Red Barber, sports		9:15
Celebrity Theater	The First Nighter Program	Spotlight Bands	Paducah Plantation, Red Foley	9:30
	Ginny Simms, songs (9:55pm)	Miss Meade's Children		9:45
Elsa Maxwell's Party Line	Moonlight Serenade	Cedric Foster, news	People Are Funny	10pm
The First Piano Quartet	Public Affairs	Dance Orchestra		10:15
Symphonic Music	The Jerry Wayne Show	Paul Schubert, news	Studio X, Dumke and Hulick	10:30
	Mark Hawley, news	The Answer Man		10:45

EVENING — SPRING, 1942

Saturday

	BLUE	CBS	MBS	NBC
6pm	Music By Shrednik	Frazier Hunt, news	Uncle Don	Bill Stern, golf
6:15	Joe Hasel, sports	Calling Pan-America		Robert St. John, news
6:30	Lum and Abner	Elmer Davis, news	Frank Singiser, news	Religion in the News
6:45	Edward Tomlinson, news	The World Today	Stan Lomax, sports	The Three Suns
7pm	This is War	This is War	This is War	This is War
7:15				
7:30	Message of Israel	Tillie the Toiler	Arthur Hale, news	The Adventures of Ellery Queen
7:45			Sam Balter, sports	
8pm	The Green Hornet	Guy Lombardo Orchestra	The Treasure Hour of Song	Abie's Irish Rose
8:15				
8:30	SWOP Night	Hobby Lobby	Jack Dempsey's Sports Quiz	Truth or Consequences
8:45		Elmer Davis, news (8:55pm)		
9pm	The Call of the West	Your Hit Parade	Anchors Aweigh	The National Barn Dance
9:15				
9:30	NBC Symphony Orchestra		Spotlight Bands	
9:45		Saturday Night Serenade		
10pm	Believe It or Not		John Gunther, news	The Colgate Sports Newsreel, Bill Stern
10:15		Public Affairs	America Preferred	Labor for Victory
10:30	Stag Party	Bobby Tucker, songs		Ted Steele Orchestra
10:45		Mark Hawley, news	The Bert Schefter Octet	

DAYTIME — SPRING, 1942

Sunday

	BLUE	CBS	MBS	NBC
9am	News	News	BBC News	News
9:15	The Children's Hour	From the Organ Loft	Pauline Alpert, piano	The Eton Boys Quartet
9:30			The Natural History Quiz	Words and Music
9:45		Gypsy Caravan		
10am	Fantasy in Melody	The CBS Church of the Air	News	The National Radio Pulpit
10:15			The Charioteers Quartet	
10:30	The Southernaires Quartet	Wings Over Jordan	The Chicago Theater of the Air	The Horn and Hardart Children's Hour
10:45				
11am	News	Gene Brown Orchestra	The Song Spinners	
11:15	The Blaisdell Woodwinds			
11:30	Tapestry Musicale	Invitation to Learning	The Mutual Radio Chapel	George Putnam, news
11:45				Kathleen McLaughlin, talk
12pm	Foreign Policy Association Talks	Eric Sevareid, news	The University Glee Clubs	Freedom's People
12:15	The First Piano Quartet	Syncopated Piece		
12:30	The Radio City Music Hall	The Salt Lake Tabernacle Choir	The Sing a Song of Safety Club	
12:45			Frank Singiser, news	
1pm		The CBS Church of the Air	The Canary Pet Shop	Upton Close, news
1:15			George Fisher, gossip	Bob Becker's Dog Talks
1:30	African Trek	What's New at the Zoo	Recorded Music	The World is Yours
1:45			This Week of War	

DAYTIME — SPRING, 1942

Monday-Friday

BLUE	CBS	MBS	NBC	
The Woman of Tomorrow	George Bryan, news	Dear Imogene / Pegeen Presents	Songs	9am
	The American School of the Air	Victor Lindlahr, health	Hank Lawson's Knights	9:15
The Breakfast Club		Talk and Music	Isabel Manning Hewson, food	9:30
	Harvey and Dell		Songs	9:45
Music	Valiant Lady	Alfred W. McCann, food	Bess Johnson	10am
Helen Hiett, news	Stories America Loves		Bachelor's Children	10:15
A House in the Country	Stepmother	Happy Jim Parsons, songs	Helpmate	10:30
Chaplain Jim, USA	Woman of Courage	Richard Willis, beauty / The Consumers' Quiz	The Story of Mary Marlin	10:45
Second Husband	Mary Lee Taylor, cooking / Victory Begins at Home	Bessie Beatty, talk	Bud Barton	11am
Amanda of Honeymoon Hill	Folk Music		Vic and Sade	11:15
John's Other Wife	Bright Horizon		The Road of Life	11:30
Just Plain Bill	Aunt Jenny's True Life Stories		David Harum	11:45
Jim Robertson, songs	Kate Smith Speaks	Boake Carter, news	Don Goddard, news	12pm
Nancy Booth Craig, talk	Big Sister	Music	Words and Music	12:15
The National Farm and Home Hour	The Romance of Helen Trent	Alois Havrilla, news	Songs / Nellie Revell, talk	12:30
	Our Gal Sunday	Judy and Jane	Stock Market Reports	12:45
H. R. Baukhage, news	Life Can Be Beautiful	Music / This is Life	Mary Margaret McBride, talk	1pm
The Gospel Singer	The Woman in White	I'll Find My Way		1:15
Religious Talk	Vic and Sade	The Johnson Family		1:30
Music	The Road of Life	Your Date with Don Norman	John W. Vandercook, news	1:45

DAYTIME — SPRING, 1942

Sunday

	BLUE	CBS	MBS	NBC
2pm	Great Plays	The Spirit of '42	Ned Jordan, Secret Agent	Sammy Kaye's Sunday Serenade
2:15				
2:30	Yesterday and Today	The Columbia Workshop	This is Fort Dix	The University of Chicago Round Table
2:45				
3pm	Wake Up, America	New York Philharmonic Orchestra	Sports	Music from Brazil
3:15				H. V. Kaltenborn, news
3:30				The Army Hour
3:45				
4pm	National Vespers			
4:15				
4:30	Nothing But the Truth	The Pause That Refreshes		Listen, America
4:45				
5pm	The Moylan Sisters, songs	The Prudential Family Hour	I Hear America Singing	Ports of the Pacific
5:15	Olivio Santoro, yodeler			
5:30	The Musical Steelmakers		Marines in Revue	Plays for Americans
5:45		William L. Shirer, news		

DAYTIME — SPRING, 1942

Monday-Friday

BLUE	CBS	MBS	NBC	
	Young Dr. Malone	Martha Deane, talk	The Light of the World	2pm
Between the Bookends	Joyce Jordan, MD		Arnold Grimm's Daughter	2:15
Bill Spargrove, news	We Love and Learn	Prescott Robinson, news	The Guiding Light	2:30
In Care of Aggie Horn	The Goldbergs	Richard Willis, beauty	Betty Crocker, cooking / Hymns of All Churches	2:45
Prescott Presents	David Harum	Sports	Against the Storm	3pm
	Music		Ma Perkins	3:15
Music			Pepper Young's Family	3:30
			The Right to Happiness	3:45
Club Matinee, Garry Moore			Mary Noble, Backstage Wife	4pm
	Informational Talk		Stella Dallas	4:15
	Songs		Lorenzo Jones	4:30
The Face of the War	Mark Hawley, news		Young Widder Brown	4:45
Music	Are You a Genius	Little Orphan Annie	When a Girl Marries	5pm
		Music / Rambling with Gambling	Portia Faces Life	5:15
The Flying Patrol	The Landt Trio and Curley	Jack Armstrong, the All-American Boy	The Andersons	5:30
Secret City	Scattergood Baines	Captain Midnight	The Three Suns	5:45

DAYTIME — SPRING, 1942

Saturday

	BLUE	CBS	MBS	NBC
9am	The Breakfast Club	George Bryan, news	Dear Imogene	Happy Jack Turner, songs
9:15		Caucasian Melodies	Health Talk	Isabel Manning Hewison, food
9:30		The Garden Gate	Talk and Music	Any Bonds Today
9:45				Hank Lawson's Knights
10am	The Andrini Continentals	The US Marine Band	Rainbow House	The Carnation Family Party
10:15	The Treasury Star Parade			
10:30		National Hillbilly Champions		The Prescott Variety Show
10:45	The Billy Moore Trio			Betty Moore, talk
11am	The Band Played On	News	Prescott Robinson, news	Lincoln Highway
11:15		God's Country, Burl Ives	Ramona and the Tune Twisters	
11:30	The Little Blue Playhouse	Let's Pretend	The US Army Band	America, the Free
11:45				
12pm	The Four Belles	The Armstrong Theater of Today	The Man on the Farm	Don Goddard, news
12:15				Consumer Time
12:30	The National Farm and Home Hour	Stars Over Hollywood	Alois Havrilla, news	Ilka Chase Entertains
12:45			Lani McIntyre Orchestra	
1pm	Vincent Lopez Orchestra	Buffalo Presents		Joseph Gallicchio Orchestra
1:15			Frank Forrest, songs	
1:30	The Show Shop	Adventures in Science	Irving Jacobson Orchestra	Rex Maupin Orchestra
1:45		The Golden Gate Quartet		John W. Vandercook, news

DAYTIME — SPRING, 1942

Saturday

	BLUE	CBS	MBS	NBC
2pm	Fantasy in Melody	Of Men and Books	Woody Herman Orchestra	The Metropolitan Opera
2:15				
2:30	Elwood Gary, songs	The Brush Creek Follies	Sports	
2:45	Maples Orchestra			
3pm	Royal Canadian Air Force Band	Columbia's Country Journal		New England to You
3:15				Air Youth for Victory
3:30	Clyde Lucas Orchestra	Detroit Musicale		Campus Capers
3:45				
4pm	Club Matinee, Garry Moore	Glen Gray Orchestra		Down Mexico Way
4:15				
4:30		Horse Racing		Number, Please
4:45				
5pm	Tommy Dorsey Orchestra	Matinee at the Meadowbrook	Sunset Serenade	Doctors at Work
5:15				
5:30	Lucky Millinder Orchestra			Civilian Defense Information
5:45				War Correspondent

EVENING — SUMMER, 1942

Sunday

	BLUE	CBS	MBS	NBC
6pm	Mart Kenny Orchestra	Edward R. Murrow, news	Sports (4pm)	The Catholic Hour
6:15		Public Affairs		
6:30	Drew Pearson, news	Gene Autry's Melody Ranch		The Victory Parade
6:45	Edward Tomlinson, news			
7pm	Tommy Dorsey's Variety Show	Public Affairs	Symphonic Strings	The Remarkable Miss Tuttle
7:15		The Laugh Club, Lou Holtz		
7:30	The Quiz Kids	We, the People	Frank Singiser, news	The Fitch Bandwagon
7:45			Pierre Huss, news	
8pm	Earl Godwin, news	World News Tonight	The American Forum of the Air	Star-Spangled Vaudeville, Walter O'Keefe
8:15	Gibbs and Finney, General Delivery			
8:30	Inner Sanctum Mysteries	Crime Doctor		One Man's Family
8:45		Eric Sevareid, news (8:55pm)	Gabriel Heatter, news	
9pm	Clair Boothe Luce, talk	Mischa the Magnificent	Stars and Stripes in Britain	The Manhattan Merry-Go-Round
9:15	The Parker Family			
9:30	Jimmy Fidler, gossip	The Texaco Star Theater, Jane Froman	Nothing Serious / Starlight and Music	The American Album of Familiar Music
9:45	Diane Courtney and the Jesters			
10pm	The Goodwill Hour	Take It or Leave It	John B. Hughes, news	The Hour of Charm
10:15			Overseas News	
10:30		They Live Forever	This is Our Enemy	Joe and Mabel
10:45				

EVENING — SUMMER, 1942

Monday

BLUE	CBS	MBS	NBC	
Peter Hayward, stories	John Daly, news	Uncle Don	The Funny Money Man	6pm
Joe Hasel, sports	Hedda Hopper, gossip		George Putnam, news	6:15
The Song Clinic	The Squibb Golden Treasury of Song	Frank Singiser, news	Music from Brazil	6:30
Lowell Thomas, news	The World Today	Here's Morgan	Bill Stern, sports	6:45
Major Hoople	Amos 'n' Andy	Stan Lomax, sports	Chesterfield Time	7pm
	Mary Small, songs	Arthur Hale, news	John W. Vandercook, news	7:15
Fiesta Time	Vaughn Monroe Orchestra	Red Ryder	Allen Roth Orchestra	7:30
Diane Courtney and the Jesters			H. V. Kaltenborn, news	7:45
Roy Porter, news	Vox Pop	Cal Tinney, news	The Cavalcade of America	8pm
Lum and Abner		Alvino Rey Orchestra		8:15
True or False	The Gay Nineties Revue	Bulldog Drummond	The Voice of Firestone	8:30
	Cecil Brown, news (8:55pm)			8:45
Edwin Franko Goldman Band	The Victory Theater	Gabriel Heatter, news	The Bell Telephone Hour	9pm
		Red Barber, sports		9:15
The National Radio Forum	Lady Esther Serenade	The Better Half	Dr. I. Q., the Mental Banker	9:30
Molasses and January (9:55pm)				9:45
Counterspy	An American in England	Raymond Gram Swing, news	The Carnation Contented Hour	10pm
		The Radio Vaudeville Theater		10:15
Morgan Beatty, news	The Will to Freedom	Paul Schubert, news	Lands of the Free	10:30
Freddie Stewart, songs		The Answer Man		10:45

EVENING — SUMMER, 1942

Tuesday

	BLUE	CBS	MBS	NBC
6pm	Peter Hayward, stories	Frazier Hunt, news	Uncle Don	The Funny Money Man
6:15	Joe Hasel, sports	The Voice of Broadway		George Putnam, news
6:30	The Milt Herth Trio	The Vera Burton Show	Frank Singiser, news	Music
6:45	Lowell Thomas, news	The World Today	Here's Morgan	Bill Stern, sports
7pm	Easy Aces	Amos 'n' Andy	Stan Lomax, sports	Chesterfield Time
7:15	Mr. Keen, Tracer of Lost Persons	Moonlight Serenade	Dance Orchestra	John W. Vandercook, news
7:30	The Lone Ranger	Rochester Philharmonic Orchestra	Arthur Hale, news	Emma Otero, songs
7:45			Dance Orchestra	H. V. Kaltenborn, news
8pm	Roy Porter, news	The Court of Missing Heirs	Morton Gould Orchestra	Johnny Presents
8:15	Lum and Abner			
8:30	Sing for Dough	Hobby Lobby / Nature of the Enemy	Can You Top This	Tums Treasure Chest
8:45		Cecil Brown, news (8:55pm)		
9pm	Famous Jury Trials	Tommy Riggs and Betty Lou	Gabriel Heatter, news	Battle of the Sexes
9:15			Red Barber, sports	
9:30	This Nation at War	Cheers from the Camps	Murder Clinic	Meredith Willson's Musical Revue
9:45	Molasses and January (9:55pm)			
10pm	Cab Callaway's Quizzicale		John B. Hughes, news	A Date with Judy
10:15			The Radio Vaudeville Theater	
10:30	Morgan Beatty, news	Public Affairs	Paul Schubert, news	Tommy Dorsey's Variety Show
10:45	Freddie Stewart, songs	Mary Small, songs	The Answer Man	

EVENING — SUMMER, 1942

Wednesday

BLUE	CBS	MBS	NBC	
Peter Hayward, stories	John Daly, news	Uncle Don	The Funny Money Man	6pm
Joe Hasel, sports	Hedda Hopper, gossip		George Putnam, news	6:15
The Milt Herth Trio	The Squibb Golden Treasury of Song	Frank Singiser, news	Hollywood News	6:30
Lowell Thomas, news	The World Today	Here's Morgan	Bill Stern, sports	6:45
Easy Aces	Amos 'n' Andy	Stan Lomax, sports	Chesterfield Time	7pm
Mr. Keen, Tracer of Lost Persons	Moonlight Serenade	Arthur Hale, news	John W. Vandercook, news	7:15
The Lone Ranger	Green Valley, USA	Go Get It	Allen Roth Orchestra	7:30
			H. V. Kaltenborn, news	7:45
Earl Godwin, news	The New Old Gold Program, Nelson Eddy	Cal Tinney, news	The Adventures of the Thin Man	8pm
Lum and Abner		Alvino Rey Orchestra		8:15
Manhattan at Midnight	Dr. Christian	Red Ryder	Dough Re Mi	8:30
	Cecil Brown, news (8:55pm)			8:45
The Chamber Music Society of Lower Basin Street	Junior Miss	Gabriel Heatter, news	Those We Love	9pm
		Red Barber, sports		9:15
Edwin Franko Goldman Band	Suspense	Pass in Review	Mr. District Attorney	9:30
Molasses and January (9:55pm)				9:45
The Garry Moore Variety Show / The Danny Thomas Show	Great Moments in Music	John B. Hughes, news	The Kay Kyser's College of Musical Knowledge	10pm
		The Radio Vaudeville Theater		10:15
Morgan Beatty, news	The Twenty-Second Letter	Paul Schubert, news		10:30
Freddie Stewart, songs		The Answer Man		10:45

EVENING — SUMMER, 1942

Thursday

	BLUE	CBS	MBS	NBC
6pm	Peter Hayward, stories	Frazier Hunt, news	Uncle Don	The Funny Money Man
6:15	Joe Hasel, sports	Music		George Putnam, news
6:30	The Milt Herth Trio	The Vera Burton Show	Frank Singiser, news	The Engineer at War
6:45	Lowell Thomas, news	The World Today	Here's Morgan	Bill Stern, sports
7pm	Easy Aces	Amos 'n' Andy	Stan Lomax, sports	Chesterfield Time
7:15	Mr. Keen, Tracer of Lost Persons	Moonlight Serenade	Victory is Our Business	John W. Vandercook, news
7:30	Ted Straeter Orchestra	Maudie's Diary	Arthur Hale, news	How'm I Doin'
7:45	Diane Courtney and the Jesters		Dance Orchestra	
8pm	Earl Godwin, news	Thirty Minutes to Play	Sinfonietta	Post Toasties Time, Frank Morgan
8:15	Lum and Abner			
8:30	Canadian Musicale	Death Valley Days	It Pays to Be Ignorant	The Aldrich Family
8:45		Cecil Brown, news (8:55pm)		
9pm	America's Town Meeting of the Air	Major Bowes' Original Amateur Hour	Gabriel Heatter, news	The Kraft Music Hall, Mary Martin
9:15			Red Barber, sports	
9:30		Stage Door Canteen	The WOR Summer Theater	
9:45	Molasses and January (9:55pm)			
10pm	Those Good Old Days	The First Line of Defense	Raymond Gram Swing, news	Vallee Varieties
10:15			The Radio Vaudeville Theater	
10:30	Morgan Beatty, news	Public Affairs	Paul Schubert, news	The March of Time
10:45	Freddie Stewart, songs	Mary Small, songs	Overseas News	

EVENING — SUMMER, 1942

Friday

BLUE	CBS	MBS	NBC	
Peter Hayward, stories	John Daly, news	Uncle Don	The Funny Money Man	6pm
Joe Hasel, sports	Hedda Hopper, gossip		George Putnam, news	6:15
The Milt Herth Trio	The Squibb Golden Treasury of Song	Frank Singiser, news	Caridad Garcia, songs	6:30
Lowell Thomas, news	The World Today	Here's Morgan	Bill Stern, sports	6:45
Scramble	Amos 'n' Andy	Stan Lomax, sports	Chesterfield Time	7pm
	Irene Rich Dramas	Arthur Hale, news	John W. Vandercook, news	7:15
The Lone Ranger	Report to the Nation	Red Ryder	Neighborhood Call	7:30
			H. V. Kaltenborn, news	7:45
Earl Godwin, news	The Lewisohn Stadium Concerts	Cal Tinney, news	The Cities Service Concerts	8pm
Gibbs and Finney, General Delivery		Alvino Rey Orchestra		8:15
Listen, America		Songs for Marching Men	Information, Please	8:30
	Cecil Brown, news (8:55pm)			8:45
Gangbusters	The Phillip Morris Playhouse	Gabriel Heatter, news	Waltz Time	9pm
		Red Barber, sports		9:15
In Person, Dinah Shore	That Brewster Boy	Double or Nothing	Paducah Plantation, Red Foley	9:30
Sea Stories / Molasses and January (9:55pm)				9:45
Meet Your Navy	The Camel Comedy Caravan, Herb Shriner	Madison Square Garden Boxing	People Are Funny	10pm
				10:15
Men, Machines and Victory			Tent Show Tonite	10:30
Freddie Stewart, songs		The Answer Man		10:45

EVENING — SUMMER, 1942

Saturday

	BLUE	CBS	MBS	NBC
6pm	Dinner Music	Frazier Hunt, news	Uncle Don	Horse Racing
6:15	Joe Hasel, sports	Calling Pan-America		George Putnam, news
6:30	The Jester's Trio		Frank Singiser, news	The Art of Living
6:45	Edward Tomlinson, news	The World Today	The Lenox Avenue Record Man	The Funny Money Man
7pm	Message of Israel	The People's Platform	Stan Lomax, sports	Noah Webster Says
7:15			Dick Robertson Orchestra	
7:30	SWOP Night	Tillie the Toiler	Arthur Hale, news	Musiciana
7:45			Alvino Rey Orchestra	The War in the Air
8pm	Earl Godwin, news	Soldiers With Wings	The AEF Speaks to London	Keeping Up with Rosemary
8:15	Gibbs and Finney, General Delivery			
8:30	The Green Hornet	Commandos	Jack Dempsey's Sports Quiz	Freddy Martin Orchestra
8:45		Eric Severeid, news (8:55pm)		
9pm	NBC Summer Symphony	Your Hit Parade	America Loves a Melody	The National Barn Dance
9:15				
9:30				The Grant Park Concerts
9:45	James G. McDonald, news	Saturday Night Serenade		
10pm	The Prescott Variety Show		John B. Hughes, news	The Colgate Sports Newsreel, Bill Stern
10:15		Public Affairs	Tropical Serenade, Don Arres	Labor for Victory
10:30	Stag Party	Music		Ted Steele's Studio Club
10:45			The Answer Man	

DAYTIME — SUMMER, 1942

Sunday

	BLUE	CBS	MBS	NBC
9am	News	News	Americans Calling Home	News
9:15	Recorded Music	From the Organ Loft	Pauline Alpert, piano	The Deep River Boys
9:30			The Natural History Quiz	Words and Music
9:45		Gypsy Caravan		
10am	The Children's Hour	The CBS Church of the Air	Frank Singiser, news	The National Radio Pulpit
10:15			Hawaii Calls	
10:30	The Southernaires Quartet	Wings Over Jordan		The Horn and Hardart Children's Hour
10:45			Walter Compton, news	
11am	The Sunday Morning Review	Egon Petri, piano	Marines in Review	
11:15				
11:30		Invitation to Learning	The Mutual Radio Chapel	George Putnam, news
11:45				Commando, Mary
12pm	The Weekly War Journal	John Daly, news	Salute to the States	Sunday Down South
12:15		Woman Power		
12:30	The Radio City Music Hall	The Salt Lake Tabernacle Choir	The Sing a Song of Safety Club	Tapestry Musicale
12:45			Melody Lane	
1pm		The CBS Church of the Air		Robert St. John, news
1:15			Anchors Aweigh	Silver Strings
1:30	African Trek	Green Valley, USA		Modern Music
1:45			Dance Orchestra	

DAYTIME — SUMMER, 1942

Monday-Friday

BLUE	CBS	MBS	NBC	
The Woman of Tomorrow	George Bryan, news	Dear Imogene / Pegeen Presents	Talk and Music	9am
	The Radio Reader			9:15
The Breakfast Club	Music	Talk and Music	Songs	9:30
	Harvey and Dell / Hymns of All Churches		Talk and Music	9:45
Recorded Music	Valiant Lady	BBC News	Bess Johnson	10am
Helen Hiett, news	Stories America Loves	The Johnson Family	Bachelor's Children	10:15
A House in the Country	Hillbilly Music	Happy Jim Parsons, songs	Helpmate	10:30
Chaplain Jim, USA	Music	Richard Willis, beauty / The Consumers' Quiz	Carey Longmire, news	10:45
Second Husband	Music / Mary Lee Taylor, cooking	Bessie Beatty, talk	The Road of Life	11am
Amanda of Honeymoon Hill	Fletcher Wiley, news		Vic and Sade	11:15
John's Other Wife	Bright Horizon		Against the Storm	11:30
Just Plain Bill	Aunt Jenny's True Life Stories		David Harum	11:45
The Texas Rangers Quartet	Kate Smith Speaks	Boake Carter, news	Don Goddard, news	12pm
Nancy Booth Craig, talk	Big Sister	Music	Words and Music	12:15
The National Farm and Home Hour	The Romance of Helen Trent	Alois Havrilla, news		12:30
	Our Gal Sunday	Judy and Jane		12:45
H. R. Baukhage, news	Life Can Be Beautiful	The Legion of Friends	Mary Margaret McBride, talk	1pm
The Gospel Singer	The Woman in White			1:15
Religious Talk	Vic and Sade	Talk		1:30
Music	The Goldbergs	Your Date with Don Norman	John W. Vandercook, news	1:45

DAYTIME — SUMMER, 1942

Sunday

	BLUE	CBS	MBS	NBC
2pm	Great Plays	The Spirit of '42	Ned Jordan, Secret Agent	Sammy Kaye's Sunday Serenade
2:15				
2:30	Yesterday and Today	St. Louis Municipal Opera	This is Fort Dix	The University of Chicago Round Table
2:45				
3pm	Roy Porter, news	Columbia Symphony Orchestra	Dance Orchestra	Music for Neighbors
3:15	Wake Up, America			Upton Close, news
3:30			California Melodies	The Army Hour
3:45				
4pm	National Vespers		Sports	
4:15				
4:30	The Army-Navy Game	The Pause That Refreshes		We Believe
4:45				
5pm	The Moylan Sisters, songs	The Prudential Family Hour		Dear Adolf
5:15	Olivio Santoro, yodeler			
5:30	Alias John Freedom			Britain to America
5:45		William L. Shirer, news		

DAYTIME — SUMMER, 1942

Monday-Friday

BLUE	CBS	MBS	NBC	
	Young Dr. Malone	Martha Deane, talk	The Light of the World	2pm
Between the Bookends	Joyce Jordan, MD		Lonely Women	2:15
James G. McDonald, news	We Love and Learn	Prescott Robinson, news	The Guiding Light	2:30
The Jack Baker Show	Pepper Young's Family	Sports	Betty Crocker, cooking / Hymns of All Churches	2:45
Prescott Presents	David Harum		The Story of Mary Marlin	3pm
	Music		Ma Perkins	3:15
Music			Pepper Young's Family	3:30
			The Right to Happiness	3:45
Club Matinee, Garry Moore			Mary Noble, Backstage Wife	4pm
			Stella Dallas	4:15
	Informational Talk		Lorenzo Jones	4:30
	Music		Young Widder Brown	4:45
Music	Are You a Genius		When a Girl Marries	5pm
The Sea Hound	Mother and Dad	Don Dunphy, talk	Portia Faces Life	5:15
The Flying Patrol	The Landt Trio and Curley	Rambling with Gambling	You and the War	5:30
Secret City	The Ben Bernie War Workers' Program	Music	Bud Barton	5:45

DAYTIME — SUMMER, 1942

Saturday

	BLUE	CBS	MBS	NBC
9am	The Breakfast Club	George Bryan, news	Dear Imogene	Happy Jack Turner, songs
9:15		Caucasian Melodies	Health Talk	Ruth Chorpenning, talk
9:30		The Garden Gate	Troman Harper, news	Hank Lawson's Knights
9:45			Claire Wilson, news	
10am	The Andrini Continentals	Youth on Parade	Rainbow House	The US Navy Band
10:15	The Treasury Star Parade			
10:30	The Billy Moore Trio	National Hillbilly Champions		String Serenade
10:45				Arthur Hinette, organ
11am	The Band Played On	The Golden Gate Quartet	Ed Fitzgerald, talk	The Creightons
11:15		Milton Bacon, stories	BBC News	
11:30	The Little Blue Playhouse	Let's Pretend	The US Army Band	America, the Free
11:45				
12pm	Music By Black	The Armstrong Theater of Today	The Army-Navy House Party	Don Goddard, news
12:15				Consumer Time
12:30	The National Farm and Home Hour	Stars Over Hollywood	Alois Havrilla, news	Golden Melodies
12:45			Charlie Davis Orchestra	
1pm	Vincent Lopez Orchestra	Columbia's Country Journal	The Legion of Friends	Joseph Gallicchio Orchestra
1:15				
1:30	The Show Shop	Adventures in Science	Talk	All Out for Victory
1:45		The Symphonettes	Music	John W. Vandercook, news

DAYTIME — SUMMER, 1942

Saturday

	BLUE	CBS	MBS	NBC
2pm	Fantasy in Melody	Of Men and Books		Summer Strings
2:15				
2:30	Malcolm Claire, stories	The Brush Creek Follies	Sports	The US Marine Band
2:45				
3pm	Royal Canadian Air Force Band	The University Trio		Nature Sketches
3:15				Paul La Valle Orchestra
3:30	Clyde Lucas Orchestra	Detroit Musicale		Charles Dant Orchestra
3:45				
4pm	Club Matinee, Garry Moore	Hello from Hawaii		Down Mexico Way
4:15				
4:30		Horse Racing		Number, Please
4:45				
5pm	Mitchell Ayres Orchestra	Matinee at the Meadowbrook	Jimmy Dorsey Orchestra	The National Music Camp
5:15				
5:30	Lucky Millinder Orchestra			The Three Suns
5:45				Alex Dreier, news

EVENING — FALL, 1942

Sunday

	BLUE	CBS	MBS	NBC
6pm	Britain to America	Edward R. Murrow, news	The First Nighter Program	The Catholic Hour
6:15		Irene Rich Dramas		
6:30	Drew Pearson, news	Gene Autry's Melody Ranch	Anchors Aweigh	The Great Gildersleeve
6:45	Edward Tomlinson, news			
7pm	Josephine Houston, songs	Our Secret Weapon	Symphonic Strings	The Grape Nuts Program, Jack Benny
7:15		The Laugh Club, Lou Holtz		
7:30	The Quiz Kids	We, the People	Frank Singiser, news	The Fitch Bandwagon
7:45			The Song Spinners	
8pm	Earl Godwin, news	Commandos	The American Forum of the Air	The Charlie McCarthy Show
8:15	Gibbs and Finney, General Delivery			
8:30	Inner Sanctum Mysteries	Crime Doctor		One Man's Family
8:45		Elmer Davis, news (8:55pm)	Gabriel Heatter, news	
9pm	Walter Winchell's Jergens Journal	The Radio Reader's Digest	Stars and Stripes in Britain	The Manhattan Merry-Go-Round
9:15	The Parker Family			
9:30	Jimmy Fidler, gossip	The Texaco Star Theater,	Starlight and Music	The American Album of Familiar Music
9:45	Dorothy Thompson, news			
10pm	The Goodwill Hour	Take It or Leave It	John B. Hughes, news	The Hour of Charm
10:15			Leo Cherne, news	
10:30		They Live Forever	This is Our Enemy	String Symphony
10:45				

EVENING — FALL, 1942

Monday

BLUE	CBS	MBS	NBC	
Joe Hasel, sports	Quincy Howe, news	Uncle Don	The Funny Money Man	6pm
Don Winslow of the Navy	Hedda Hopper, gossip		George Putnam, news	6:15
Al and Lee Reiser, piano	The Squibb Golden Treasury of Song	Frank Singiser, news	Bill Stern, sports	6:30
Lowell Thomas, news	The World Today	Here's Morgan	Let's Fight	6:45
The Andrini Continentals	Amos 'n' Andy	Stan Lomax, sports	Chesterfield Time	7pm
Thomas Dewey's Campaign Talk	Chesterfield Time	Arthur Hale, news	John W. Vandercook, news	7:15
Fiesta Time	Blondie	Red Ryder	Allen Roth Orchestra	7:30
Diane Courtney and the Jesters			H. V. Kaltenborn, news	7:45
Earl Godwin, news	Vox Pop	Cal Tinney, news	The Cavalcade of America	8pm
Lum and Abner		The Barrie Sisters, songs		8:15
True or False	The Gay Nineties Revue	Bulldog Drummond	The Voice of Firestone	8:30
	Cecil Brown, news (8:55pm)			8:45
Counterspy	The Lux Radio Theater	Gabriel Heatter, news	The Bell Telephone Hour	9pm
		The Song Spinners		9:15
Spotlight Bands		The Better Half	Dr. I. Q., the Mental Banker	9:30
The Gracie Fields Show (9:55pm)				9:45
Raymond Gram Swing, news	The Lady Esther Screen Guild Theater	Raymond Clapper, news	The Carnation Contented Hour	10pm
Alias John Freedom		The Radio Vaudeville Theater		10:15
	The Columbia Workshop	Paul Schubert, news	Lands of the Free	10:30
The Texas Rangers Quartet		Daddy and Rollo		10:45

EVENING — FALL, 1942

Tuesday

	BLUE	CBS	MBS	NBC
6pm	Joe Hasel, sports	Frazier Hunt, news	Uncle Don	The Funny Money Man
6:15	Don Winslow of the Navy	Edwin C. Hill, news		George Putnam, news
6:30	The Milt Herth Trio	The Frank Sinatra Show	Frank Singiser, news	Bill Stern, sports
6:45	Lowell Thomas, news	The World Today	Here's Morgan	Phyllis Creore, songs
7pm	Easy Aces	Amos 'n' Andy	Stan Lomax, sports	Chesterfield Time
7:15	Mr. Keen, Tracer of Lost Persons	Chesterfield Time	George Hogan, talk	John W. Vandercook, news
7:30	The Lone Ranger	The American Melody Hour	Arthur Hale, news	Allen Roth Orchestra
7:45			The Answer Man	H. V. Kaltenborn, news
8pm	Earl Godwin, news	Lights Out	Can You Top This	The Purple Heart Show, Ginny Simms
8:15	Lum and Abner			
8:30	Duffy's Tavern	The Colgate Program, Al Jolson	Battle of the Burroughs	Tums Treasure Chest
8:45		Cecil Brown, news (8:55pm)		
9pm	Famous Jury Trials	Burns and Allen	Gabriel Heatter, news	Battle of the Sexes
9:15			Alvino Rey Orchestra	
9:30	Spotlight Bands	Suspense	Murder Clinic	Fibber Magee and Molly
9:45	The Gracie Fields Show (9:55pm)			
10pm	Raymond Gram Swing, news	Public Affairs	John B. Hughes, news	The Pepsodent Show, Bob Hope
10:15	This Nation at War		The Wax Museum	
10:30		Dr. Harry S. Gradle, talk	Paul Schubert, news	The Raleigh Cigarette Program, Red Skelton
10:45	The Texas Rangers Quartet	Mary Small, songs	Buddy Rogers Orchestra	

EVENING — FALL, 1942

Wednesday

BLUE	CBS	MBS	NBC	
Joe Hasel, sports	Quincy Howe, news	Uncle Don	The Funny Money Man	6pm
Don Winslow of the Navy	Hedda Hopper, gossip		George Putnam, news	6:15
The Milt Herth Trio	The Squibb Golden Treasury of Song	Frank Singiser, news	Bill Stern, sports	6:30
Lowell Thomas, news	The World Today	Here's Morgan	Let's Fight	6:45
Easy Aces	Amos 'n' Andy	Stan Lomax, sports	Chesterfield Time	7pm
Mr. Keen, Tracer of Lost Persons	Chesterfield Time	Arthur Hale, news	John W. Vandercook, news	7:15
The Lone Ranger	Green Valley, USA	Go Get It	Allen Roth Orchestra	7:30
			H. V. Kaltenborn, news	7:45
Earl Godwin, news	The New Old Gold Program, Nelson Eddy	Cal Tinney, news	The Adventures of the Thin Man	8pm
Lum and Abner		The Barrie Sisters, songs		8:15
Manhattan at Midnight	Dr. Christian	The True Story Theater of the Air	Tommy Dorsey's Variety Show	8:30
	Cecil Brown, news (8:55pm)			8:45
The Chamber Music Society of Lower Basin Street	The Bob Burns Show	Gabriel Heatter, news	Time to Smile, Eddie Cantor	9pm
		The Cresta Blanca Carnival		9:15
Spotlight Bands	The Mayor of the Town		Mr. District Attorney	9:30
The Gracie Fields Show (9:55pm)				9:45
Raymond Gram Swing, news	Great Moments in Music	John B. Hughes, news	Kay Kyser's College of Musical Knowledge	10pm
The National Radio Forum		The Wax Museum		10:15
	The Man Behind the Gun	Paul Schubert, news		10:30
Men's Store News		Daddy and Rollo		10:45

EVENING — FALL, 1942

Thursday

	BLUE	CBS	MBS	NBC
6pm	Joe Hasel, sports	Frazier Hunt, news	Uncle Don	The Funny Money Man
6:15	Don Winslow of the Navy	Don't You Believe It		George Putnam, news
6:30	The Milt Herth Trio	The Frank Sinatra Show	Frank Singiser, news	Bill Stern, sports
6:45	Lowell Thomas, news	The World Today	Here's Morgan	Neighborhood Call
7pm	Easy Aces	Amos 'n' Andy	Stan Lomax, sports	Chesterfield Time
7:15	Mr. Keen, Tracer of Lost Persons	Chesterfield Time	Victory is Our Business	John W. Vandercook, news
7:30	That's a Fact	The Voice of Hawaii	Arthur Hale, news	Abbott and Costello
7:45	Diane Courtney and the Jesters		The Answer Man	
8pm	Earl Godwin, news	Reflections	Sinfonietta	Maxwell House Coffee Time, Brice and Morgan
8:15	Lum and Abner			
8:30	America's Town Meeting of the Air	Death Valley Days	It Pays to Be Ignorant	The Aldrich Family
8:45		Cecil Brown, news (8:55pm)		
9pm		Major Bowes' Original Amateur Hour	Gabriel Heatter, news	The Kraft Music Hall, Bing Crosby
9:15			Stan Lomax, sports	
9:30	Spotlight Bands	Stage Door Canteen	Vaudeville	
9:45	The Gracie Fields Show (9:55pm)			
10pm	Raymond Gram Swing, news	The First Line of Defense	Raymond Clapper, news	Vallee Varieties
10:15	White Stars to Victory		The Wax Museum	
10:30	Sing for Dough	Public Affairs	Paul Schubert, news	The March of Time
10:45	The Texas Rangers Quartet	The Vera Burton Show	Daddy and Rollo	

EVENING — FALL, 1942

Friday

BLUE	CBS	MBS	NBC	
Joe Hasel, sports	Quincy Howe, news	Uncle Don	The Funny Money Man	6pm
Don Winslow of the Navy	Hedda Hopper, gossip		George Putnam, news	6:15
The Milt Herth Trio	The Squibb Golden Treasury of Song	Frank Singiser, news	Bill Stern, sports	6:30
Lowell Thomas, news	The World Today	Here's Morgan	Let's Fight	6:45
Scramble	Amos 'n' Andy	Stan Lomax, sports	Chesterfield Time	7pm
	Mary Small, songs	Arthur Hale, news	John W. Vandercook, news	7:15
The Lone Ranger	Report to the Nation	Red Ryder	Tommy Riggs and Betty Lou	7:30
				7:45
Earl Godwin, news	The Kate Smith Hour	Cal Tinney, news	The Cities Service Concerts	8pm
In Person, Dinah Shore		The Barrie Sisters, songs		8:15
Those Good Old Days		The Cisco Kid	Information, Please	8:30
	Cecil Brown, news (8:55pm)			8:45
Gangbusters	The Phillip Morris Playhouse	Gabriel Heatter, news	Waltz Time	9pm
		Stan Lomax, sports		9:15
Spotlight Bands	That Brewster Boy	Double or Nothing	Paducah Plantation, Red Foley	9:30
The Gracie Fields Show (9:55pm)				9:45
Meet Your Navy	The Camel Caravan, Herb Shriner	Madison Square Garden Boxing	People Are Funny	10pm
				10:15
John Gunther, news			The Propeller Club of the US	10:30
The Texas Rangers Quartet				10:45

EVENING — FALL, 1942

Saturday

	BLUE	CBS	MBS	NBC
6pm	Dinner Music	Frazier Hunt, news	Uncle Don	The Funny Money Man
6:15		Calling Pan-America		George Putnam, news
6:30	Ella Fitzgerald and the Four Keys		Frank Singiser, news	Religion in the News
6:45	Edward Tomlinson, news	The World Today	The Lenox Avenue Record Man	Sports Round-Up
7pm	Message of Israel	The People's Platform	Stan Lomax, sports	Noah Webster Says
7:15			Time to Muse	
7:30	SWOP Night	Thanks to the Yanks	Arthur Hale, news	The Adventures of Ellery Queen
7:45			The Answer Man	
8pm	Roy Porter, news	The Crumit and Sanderson Quiz	Dark Destiny	Abie's Irish Rose
8:15	Gibbs and Finney, General Delivery			
8:30	The Danny Thomas Show	Hobby Lobby	Our Secret World	Truth or Consequences
8:45		Eric Sevareid, news (8:55pm)		
9pm	The Green Hornet	Your Hit Parade	The Chicago Theater of the Air	The National Barn Dance
9:15				
9:30	Spotlight Bands			Can You Top This
9:45	Lanny and Ginger, songs (9:55PM)	Saturday Night Serenade		
10pm	The Prescott Variety Show		John B. Hughes, news	The Colgate Sports Newsreel, Bill Stern
10:15		Public Affairs	Saturday Night Bandwagon	Campana Serenade, Dick Powell
10:30	John Gunther, news	Eileen Farrell, songs		Grand Ole Opry
10:45	Del Casino Orchestra		Henry Jerome Orchestra	

DAYTIME — FALL, 1942

Sunday

	BLUE	CBS	MBS	NBC
9am	News	News	News	News
9:15	Coast-to-Coast on a Bus	From the Organ Loft	Pauline Alpert, piano	The Deep River Boys
9:30			The Federal Ace	Words and Music
9:45		Faith, Hope and Victory		
10am	Fantasy in Melody	The CBS Church of the Air	Connie Desmond, news	The National Radio Pulpit
10:15			The US Navy Band	
10:30	The Southernaires Quartet	Wings Over Jordan		The Horn and Hardart Children's Hour
10:45			Walter Compton, news	
11am	Glen Gray Orchestra	Warren Sweeney, news	Pass in Review	
11:15		The Budapest String Quartet		
11:30	African Trek		The Mutual Radio Chapel	George Putnam, news
11:45				Olivio Santora, yodeler
12pm	The Weekly War Journal	Quincy Howe, news	Candle Tabernacle	Hospitality Time
12:15		Woman Power		
12:30	To the President	The Salt Lake Tabernacle Choir	The Sing a Song of Safety Club	Tapestry Musicale
12:45			Frank Singiser, news	
1pm	The Sunday Morning Review	The CBS Church of the Air	The Canary Pet Shop	Robert St. John, talk
1:15			This is Fort Dix	Labor for Victory
1:30		Invitation to Learning		Modern Music
1:45			California Melodies	

DAYTIME — FALL, 1942

Monday-Friday

BLUE	CBS	MBS	NBC	
The Woman of Tomorrow	Joe King, news	Songs / Dear Imogene	The Show Without a Name, Garry Moore	9am
	The American School of the Air	Victor Lindlahr, health		9:15
The Breakfast Club		Troman Harper, news	Josef Stopak Orchestra	9:30
	The Victory Front	Music	Songs / Richard Liebert, organ	9:45
Isabel Manning Hewson, food	Valiant Lady	Alfred W. McCann, food	Victory Volunteers	10am
Roy Porter, news	Kitty Foyle		The O'Neills	10:15
Hank Lawson's Knights	Amanda of Honeymoon Hill	Happy Jim Parsons, songs	Helpmate	10:30
Stringtime	Bachelor's Children	Talk / The Consumers' Quiz	Young Dr. Malone	10:45
Breakfast at Sardi's	Music / Mary Lee Taylor, cooking	Bessie Beatty, talk	The Road of Life	11am
	Second Husband		Vic and Sade	11:15
Music	Bright Horizon		Against the Storm	11:30
	Aunt Jenny's True Life Stories		David Harum	11:45
	Kate Smith Speaks	Boake Carter, news	Don Goddard, news	12pm
Nancy Boothe Craig, talk	Big Sister	Music	Words and Music	12:15
The Farm and Home Hour	The Romance of Helen Trent	Alois Havrilla, news		12:30
	Our Gal Sunday	Fashion Talk / Bill Hay's Bible Readings	Carey Longmire, news	12:45
H. R. Baukhage, news	Life Can Be Beautiful	The Johnson Family	Mary Margaret McBride, talk	1pm
The Gospel Singer	Ma Perkins	I'll Find My Way		1:15
Religious Talk	Vic and Sade	Pegeen Presents		1:30
Vincent Lopez Orchestra /	The Goldbergs	Music	Morgan Beatty, news	1:45

DAYTIME — FALL, 1942

Sunday

	BLUE	CBS	MBS	NBC
2pm	Chaplain Jim, USA	Those We Love		Sammy Kaye's Sunday Serenade
2:15			Al Trace Orchestra	
2:30	Yesterday and Today	World News Today	Sports	The University of Chicago Round Table
2:45				
3pm	John W. Vandercook, news	New York Philharmonic Orchestra		Music for Neighbors
3:15	Wake Up, America			Upton Close, news
3:30				The Army Hour
3:45				
4pm	National Vespers			
4:15				
4:30	Toastchee Time, Edward McHugh	The Pause That Refreshes		We Believe
4:45				
5pm	The Moylan Sisters, songs	The Prudential Family Hour	This is Our War	NBC Symphony Orchestra
5:15	Ella Fitzgerald and the Four Keys			
5:30	The Musical Steelmakers		The Shadow	
5:45		William L. Shirer, news		

DAYTIME — FALL, 1942

Monday-Friday

BLUE	CBS	MBS	NBC	
Music	Young Dr. Malone	Martha Deane, talk	The Light of the World	2pm
Between the Bookends	Joyce Jordan, MD		Lonely Women	2:15
James G. McDonald, news	We Love and Learn	Prescott Robinson, news (Monday only) /	The Guiding Light	2:30
Music	Pepper Young's Family	Mutual Matinee / Philadelphia Symphony Orchestra	Betty Crocker, cooking / Hymns of All Churches	2:45
Prescott Presents	David Harum		The Story of Mary Marlin	3pm
	Music / Missus Goes A Shopping		Ma Perkins	3:15
Talk	Music		Pepper Young's Family	3:30
A House in the Country			The Right to Happiness	3:45
Club Matinee, Garry Moore	News		Mary Noble, Backstage Wife	4pm
	Music		Stella Dallas	4:15
	Informational Talk	Dr. Eddy's Food Forum	Lorenzo Jones	4:30
Music			Young Widder Brown	4:45
The Sea Hound	Are You a Genius	Al Trace Orchestra	When a Girl Marries	5pm
Hop Harrigan	Mother and Dad	Rambling with Gambling	Portia Faces Life	5:15
Jack Armstrong, the All-American Boy	The Landt Trio and Curley	The Adventures of Superman	Just Plain Bill	5:30
Captain Midnight	The Ben Bernie War Workers' Program	Music	Front Page Farrell	5:45

DAYTIME — FALL, 1942

Saturday

	BLUE	CBS	MBS	NBC
9am	The Breakfast Club	Joe King, news	Dear Imogene	The Show Without a Name, Garry Moore
9:15		Caucasian Melodies	Health Talk	
9:30		The Garden Gate	Troman Harper, news	
9:45			Claire Wilson, news	
10am	The Blackhawk Valley Boys	Youth on Parade	Rainbow House	The Prescott Variety Show
10:15	The Treasury Star Parade			
10:30	Hank Lawson's Knights	National Hillbilly Champions		Nellie Revell Presents
10:45				String Serenade
11am	The Band Played On	The Golden Gate Quartet	Arthur Van Horn, news	The Creightons
11:15		Milton Bacon, stories	BBC News	
11:30	The Little Blue Playhouse	Let's Pretend	The US Army Band	The Coast Guard Academy Band
11:45			Our City Cousins	
12pm	Music By Black	The Armstrong Theater of Today	The Man on the Farm	Don Goddard, news
12:15				Consumer Time
12:30	The Farm and Home Hour	Stars Over Hollywood	Alois Havrilla, news	Golden Melodies
12:45			Alvino Rey Orchestra	
1pm	Vincent Lopez Orchestra	Columbia's Country Journal		Pan-American Holiday
1:15			The Coast Guard Program	
1:30	Washington Luncheon	Adventures in Science	Treasury Varieties	All Out for Victory
1:45	Sports	Sports		Sports

DAYTIME — FALL, 1942

Saturday

	BLUE	CBS	MBS	NBC
2pm			Sports	
2:15				
2:30				
2:45				
3pm				
3:15				
3:30				
3:45				
4pm				
4:15				
4:30	Club Matinee, Garry Moore			
4:45				
5pm	Opie Cates Orchestra	Matinee at the Meadowbrook		Charlie Dant Orchestra
5:15			Rambling with Gambling	
5:30	Carl Hoff Orchestra		Horse Racing	The Three Suns
5:45				Upton Close, news

LISTINGS FOR 1943

EVENING — WINTER, 1943

Sunday

	BLUE	CBS	MBS	NBC
6pm	Lou Bring Orchestra	Edward R. Murrow, news	The First Nighter Program	The Catholic Hour
6:15		Irene Rich Dramas		
6:30	The Metropolitan Opera Auditions	Gene Autry's Melody Ranch	Troman Harper, Rumor Detective	The Great Gildersleeve
6:45			News	
7pm	Drew Pearson, news	Commandos	Symphonic Strings	The Grape Nuts Program, Jack Benny
7:15	Songs America Loves			
7:30	The Quiz Kids	We, the People	Frank Singiser, news	The Fitch Bandwagon
7:45			Samuel Grafton, news	
8pm	Earl Godwin, news	Hello Americans	The American Forum of the Air	The Charlie McCarthy Show
8:15	Ella Fitzgerald, songs			
8:30	Inner Sanctum Mysteries	Crime Doctor		One Man's Family
8:45		Eric Severeid, news (8:55pm)	Gabriel Heatter, news	
9pm	Walter Winchell's Jergens Journal	The Radio Reader's Digest	The Better Half	The Manhattan Merry-Go-Round
9:15	The Parker Family			
9:30	Jimmy Fidler, gossip	The Texaco Star Theater, Fred Allen	Starlight and Music	The American Album of Familiar Music
9:45	Dorothy Thompson, news			
10pm	The Goodwill Hour	Take It or Leave It	John B. Hughes, news	The Hour of Charm
10:15			Leo Cherne, news	
10:30		Report to the Nation	This is Our Enemy	String Symphony
10:45				

EVENING — WINTER, 1943

Monday

BLUE	CBS	MBS	NBC	
Joe Hasel, sports	John B. Kennedy, news	Uncle Don	Family Time Music	6pm
Terry and the Pirates	Today at the Duncans		George Putnam, news	6:15
Joe Rines Orchestra	Keep Working, America	Frank Singiser, news	Joe Rines Orchestra	6:30
Lowell Thomas, news	The World Today	The Budd Hulick Show	Bill Stern, sports	6:45
Major Hoople	Amos 'n' Andy	Stan Lomax, sports	Chesterfield Time	7pm
	Ceiling Unlimited	Arthur Hale, news	John W. Vandercook, news	7:15
The Lone Ranger	Blondie	It Pays to Be Ignorant	Allen Roth Orchestra	7:30
			H. V. Kaltenborn, news	7:45
Earl Godwin, news	Vox Pop	Cal Tinney, news	The Cavalcade of America	8pm
Lum and Abner		The Jerry Wayne Show		8:15
True or False	The Gay Nineties Revue	Bulldog Drummond	The Voice of Firestone	8:30
	Cecil Brown, news (8:55pm)			8:45
Counterspy	The Lux Radio Theater	Gabriel Heatter, news	The Bell Telephone Hour	9pm
		A. L. Alexander's Mediation Board		9:15
Spotlight Bands			Dr. I. Q., the Mental Banker	9:30
Dale Carnegie, inspirational (9:55PM)				9:45
Raymond Gram Swing, news	The Lady Esther Screen Guild Theater	Raymond Clapper, news	The Carnation Contented Hour	10pm
The Gracie Fields Show		The Wax Museum		10:15
The Chamber Music Society of Lower Basin Street	Daytime Showcase	Paul Schubert, news	Lands of the Free	10:30
		Daddy and Rollo		10:45

EVENING — WINTER, 1943

Tuesday

	BLUE	CBS	MBS	NBC
6pm	Joe Hasel, sports	Frazier Hunt, news	Uncle Don	Family Time Music
6:15	Terry and the Pirates	Edwin C. Hill, news		George Putnam, news
6:30	The Korn Kobblers	Keep Working, America	Frank Singiser, news	String Ensemble
6:45	Lowell Thomas, news	The World Today	The Budd Hulick Show	Bill Stern, sports
7pm	Josephine Houston, songs	Amos 'n' Andy	Stan Lomax, sports	Chesterfield Time
7:15		Chesterfield Time	George Hogan, talk	John W. Vandercook, news
7:30	That's a Fact	The American Melody Hour	Arthur Hale, news	Allen Roth Orchestra
7:45	Diane Courtney and the Jesters		The Answer Man	H. V. Kaltenborn, news
8pm	Earl Godwin, news	Lights Out	Can You Top This	The Purple Heart Show, Ginny Simms
8:15	Lum and Abner			
8:30	Duffy's Tavern	The Colgate Program, Al Jolson	Battle of the Burroughs	Tums Treasure Chest
8:45		Cecil Brown, news (8:55pm)		
9pm	Famous Jury Trials	Burns and Allen	Gabriel Heatter, news	Battle of the Sexes
9:15			Alvino Rey Orchestra	
9:30	Spotlight Bands	Suspense	Murder Clinic	Fibber Magee and Molly
9:45	Dale Carnegie, inspirational (9:55PM)			
10pm	Raymond Gram Swing, news	Only Yesterday, Benny Rubin	John B. Hughes, news	The Pepsodent Show, Bob Hope
10:15	The Gracie Fields Show		Singin' Sam, the Barbasol Man	
10:30	This Nation at War	Public Affairs	Paul Schubert, news	The Raleigh Cigarette Program, Red Skelton
10:45		The Frank Sinatra Show	Buddy Rogers Orchestra	

EVENING — WINTER, 1943

Wednesday

BLUE	CBS	MBS	NBC	
Joe Hasel, sports	John B. Kennedy, news	Uncle Don	Family Time Music	6pm
Terry and the Pirates	Today at the Duncans		George Putnam, news	6:15
The Korn Kobblers	Keep Working, America	Frank Singiser, news	The First Piano Quartet	6:30
Lowell Thomas, news	The World Today	The Budd Hulick Show	Bill Stern, sports	6:45
What's Your War Job	Amos 'n' Andy	Stan Lomax, sports	Chesterfield Time	7pm
	Chesterfield Time	Arthur Hale, news	John W. Vandercook, news	7:15
The Lone Ranger	Easy Aces	Go Get It	Allen Roth Orchestra	7:30
	Mr. Keen, Tracer of Lost Persons		H. V. Kaltenborn, news	7:45
Earl Godwin, news	The New Old Gold Program, Monty Wooley	Cal Tinney, news	Mr. and Mrs. North	8pm
Lum and Abner		Alvino Rey Orchestra		8:15
Manhattan at Midnight	Dr. Christian	Just Five Lines	Tommy Dorsey's Variety Show	8:30
	Cecil Brown, news (8:55pm)			8:45
Alias John Freedom	The Mayor of the Town	Gabriel Heatter, news	Time to Smile, Eddie Cantor	9pm
		The Cresta Blanca Carnival		9:15
Spotlight Bands	Good Listening		Mr. District Attorney	9:30
Dale Carnegie, inspirational (9:55PM)				9:45
Raymond Gram Swing, news	Great Moments in Music	John B. Hughes, news	Kay Kyser's College of Musical Knowledge	10pm
The Gracie Fields Show		The Wax Museum		10:15
The National Radio Forum	The Man Behind the Gun	Paul Schubert, news		10:30
		Daddy and Rollo		10:45

EVENING — WINTER, 1943

Thursday

	BLUE	CBS	MBS	NBC
6pm	Joe Hasel, sports	Frazier Hunt, news	Uncle Don	Family Music Time
6:15	Terry and the Pirates	Don't You Believe It		George Putnam, news
6:30	The Korn Kobblers	Keep Working, America	Frank Singiser, news	String Ensemble
6:45	Lowell Thomas, news	The World Today	The Budd Hulick Show	Bill Stern, sports
7pm	Those Good Old Days	Amos 'n' Andy	Stan Lomax, sports	Chesterfield Time
7:15		Chesterfield Time	Victory is Our Business	John W. Vandercook, news
7:30	That's a Fact	Easy Aces	Arthur Hale, news	The Bob Burns Show
7:45	Diane Courtney and the Jesters	Mr. Keen, Tracer of Lost Persons	The Answer Man	
8pm	Earl Godwin, news	Meet Corliss Archer	Singin' Sam, the Barbasol Man	Maxwell House Coffee Time, Brice and Morgan
8:15	Lum and Abner		Our Headliners	
8:30	America's Town Meeting of the Air	Death Valley Days	Dark Destiny	The Aldrich Family
8:45		Cecil Brown, news (8:55pm)		
9pm		Major Bowes' Original Amateur Hour	Gabriel Heatter, news	The Kraft Music Hall, Bing Crosby
9:15			Abe Lyman Orchestra	
9:30	Spotlight Bands	Stage Door Canteen	The Treasure Hour of Song	Vallee Varieties
9:45	Dale Carnegie, inspirational (9:55PM)			
10pm	Raymond Gram Swing, news	The First Line of Defense	Raymond Clapper, news	Abbott and Costello
10:15	The Gracie Fields Show		The Wax Museum	
10:30	Wings to Victory	Public Affairs	Paul Schubert, news	The March of Time
10:45		The Frank Sinatra Show	Daddy and Rollo	

EVENING — WINTER, 1943

Friday

BLUE	CBS	MBS	NBC	
Joe Hasel, sports	John B. Kennedy, news	Uncle Don	Family Music Time	6pm
Terry and the Pirates	Today at the Duncans		George Putnam, news	6:15
The Korn Kobblers	Keep Working, America	Frank Singiser, news	Neighborhood Call	6:30
Lowell Thomas, news	The World Today	The Budd Hulick Show	Bill Stern, sports	6:45
Scramble	Amos 'n' Andy	Stan Lomax, sports	Chesterfield Time	7pm
	Our Secret Weapon	Arthur Hale, news	John W. Vandercook, news	7:15
The Lone Ranger	Easy Aces	Variety Musicale	Neighborhood Call	7:30
	Mr. Keen, Tracer of Lost Persons		H. V. Kaltenborn, news	7:45
Earl Godwin, news	The Kate Smith Hour	Cal Tinney, news	The Cities Service Concerts	8pm
In Person, Dinah Shore		The Song Spinners		8:15
Meet Your Navy	The Adventures of the Thin Man	The Cisco Kid	Information, Please	8:30
	Cecil Brown, news (8:55pm)			8:45
Gangbusters	The Phillip Morris Playhouse	Gabriel Heatter, news	Waltz Time	9pm
		Chuck Acres, talk		9:15
Spotlight Bands	That Brewster Boy	Double or Nothing	People Are Funny	9:30
Dale Carnegie, inspirational (9:55PM)				9:45
John Gunther, news	The Camel Caravan, Herb Shriner	Madison Square Garden Boxing	Tommy Riggs and Betty Lou	10pm
The Gracie Fields Show				10:15
J. K. Lasser, economics			Public Affairs	10:30
Men, Machines and Victory	Joe and Ethel Turp			10:45

EVENING — WINTER, 1943

Saturday

	BLUE	CBS	MBS	NBC
6pm	Dinner Music	Frazier Hunt, news	Uncle Don	Joseph Gallichio Orchestra
6:15		An American in Russia /		George Putnam, news
6:30	Message of Israel	Guy Lombardo Orchestra	Frank Singiser, news	Religion in the News
6:45		The World Today	The Lenox Avenue Record Man	Paul La Valle Orchestra
7pm	The Danny Thomas Show	The People's Platform	Stan Lomax, sports	Noah Webster Says
7:15			Time to Muse	
7:30	The Strange Dr. Karnac	Thanks to the Yanks	Arthur Hale, news	The Adventures of Ellery Queen
7:45			The Answer Man	
8pm	Roy Porter, news	The Crumit and Sanderson Quiz	The American Eagle Club	Abie's Irish Rose
8:15	Boston Symphony Orchestra			
8:30		Hobby Lobby	Our Secret World	Truth or Consequences
8:45		Eric Sevareid, news (8:55pm)		
9pm		Your Hit Parade	The Chicago Theater of the Air	The National Barn Dance
9:15	Edward Tomlinson, news			
9:30	Spotlight Bands			Can You Top This
9:45	Lanny and Ginger, songs (9:55PM)	Saturday Night Serenade		
10pm	John Gunther, news		John B. Hughes, news	The Colgate Sports Newsreel, Bill Stern
10:15	Public Affairs	Soldiers With Wings	Saturday Night Bandwagon	Campana Serenade, Dick Powell
10:30				Let's Play Reporter
10:45	Betty Rann, songs	Eileen Farrell, songs	Henry Jerome Orchestra	

DAYTIME — WINTER, 1943

Sunday

	BLUE	CBS	MBS	NBC
9am	News	News	News	News
9:15	Coast-to-Coast on a Bus	From the Organ Loft	Pauline Alpert, piano	The Deep River Boys
9:30			The Army-Navy House Party	Marsha Nell, songs
9:45		English Melodies		
10am	Fantasy in Melody	The CBS Church of the Air	Arthur Van Horn, news	The National Radio Pulpit
10:15			Mystery Hall	
10:30	The Southernaires Quartet	Wings Over Jordan		The Horn and Hardart Children's Hour
10:45			Walter Compton, news	
11am	Don Pastor Orchestra	Warren Sweeney, news	Marines in Review	
11:15		Vera Brodsky, piano		
11:30	African Trek	Invitation to Learning	The Mutual Radio Chapel	George Putnam, news
11:45				Olivio Santora, yodeler
12pm	The Weekly War Journal	Transatlantic Call	Candle Tabernacle	Tapestry Musicale
12:15		Woman Power		
12:30	Stars from the Blue	The Salt Lake Tabernacle Choir	The Sing a Song of Safety Club	That They May Live
12:45			Frank Singiser, news	
1pm	The Sunday Morning Review	The CBS Church of the Air	The Canary Pet Shop	Robert St. John, news
1:15			Henry Jerome Orchestra	Labor for Victory
1:30		Quincy Howe, news	This is Fort Dix	Sammy Kaye's Sunday Serenade
1:45		Stoopnagle's Schutter		

DAYTIME — WINTER, 1943

Monday-Friday

BLUE	CBS	MBS	NBC	
The Breakfast Club	Joe King, news	Linda Marvin / Dear Imogene	The Show Without a Name, Garry Moore	9am
	The American School of the Air	Victor Lindlahr, health		9:15
		Troman Harper, news	Josef Stopak Orchestra	9:30
	Songs	Music	March of Mercy / Richard Liebert, organ	9:45
Isabel Manning Hewson, food	Valiant Lady	Alfred W. McCann, food	Robert St. John, news	10am
Roy Porter, news	Kitty Foyle		The O'Neills	10:15
The Baby Institute	Amanda of Honeymoon Hill	Jimmy Fidler, gossip / Ted Steele Orchestra	Helpmate	10:30
Gene and Glenn	Bachelor's Children		A Woman of America	10:45
Breakfast at Sardi's	Mary Lee Taylor, cooking / Joe and Ethel Turp	Bessie Beatty, talk	The Road of Life	11am
	Second Husband		Vic and Sade	11:15
Music	Bright Horizon		Snow Village Sketches	11:30
	Aunt Jenny's True Life Stories		David Harum	11:45
	Kate Smith Speaks	Boake Carter, news	Don Goddard, news	12pm
	Big Sister	Music / Fashion Talk	Music	12:15
The Farm and Home Hour	The Romance of Helen Trent	Alois Havrilla, news		12:30
	Our Gal Sunday	Judy and Jane	W. W. Chaplin, news	12:45
H. R. Baukhage, news	Life Can Be Beautiful	Music	Mary Margaret McBride, talk	1pm
The Gospel Singer	Ma Perkins			1:15
Religious Talk	Vic and Sade	Pegeen Presents		1:30
Vincent Lopez Orchestra /	The Goldbergs	The Johnson Family	Carey Longmire, news	1:45

DAYTIME — WINTER, 1943

Sunday

	BLUE	CBS	MBS	NBC
2pm	Chaplain Jim, USA	Those We Love	The Federal Ace	The University of Chicago Round Table
2:15				
2:30	Yesterday and Today	World News Today	Prescott Robinson, news	The Westinghouse Program, John C. Thomas
2:45			Mutual Matinee	
3pm	John W. Vandercook, news	New York Philharmonic Orchestra		Music for Neighbors
3:15	Wake Up, America			Upton Close, news
3:30				The Army Hour
3:45				
4pm	National Vespers			
4:15				
4:30	The Green Hornet	The Pause That Refreshes	Henry Jerome Orchestra	NBC Symphony Orchestra
4:45				
5pm	The Moylan Sisters, songs	The Prudential Family Hour	The Star of the Week	
5:15	Horror, Incorporated		Upton Close, news	
5:30	The Musical Steelmakers		The Shadow	
5:45		William L. Shirer, news		

DAYTIME — WINTER, 1943

Monday-Friday

BLUE	CBS	MBS	NBC	
Music	Young Dr. Malone	Martha Deane, talk	The Light of the World	2pm
The Mystery Chef	Joyce Jordan, MD		Lonely Women	2:15
James G. McDonald, news	We Love and Learn	Prescott Robinson, news (Monday only) / Mutual Matinee /	The Guiding Light	2:30
Stella Unger, gossip	Pepper Young's Family	Philadelphia Symphony Orchestra	Betty Crocker, cooking / Hymns of All Churches	2:45
Prescott Presents	David Harum		The Story of Mary Marlin	3pm
	The Landt Trio and Curley		Ma Perkins	3:15
Between the Bookends	Music		Pepper Young's Family	3:30
Music / George Hicks, news			The Right to Happiness	3:45
Club Matinee, Garry Moore	Elizabeth Bemis, news		Mary Noble, Backstage Wife	4pm
	Green Valley, USA		Stella Dallas	4:15
	Informational Talk	Dr. Eddy's Food Forum	Lorenzo Jones	4:30
Music			Young Widder Brown	4:45
The Sea Hound	Madeleine Carroll Reads	Sheelah Carter, gossip	When a Girl Marries	5pm
Hop Harrigan	Mother and Dad	Rambling with Gambling	Portia Faces Life	5:15
Jack Armstrong, the All-American Boy	Missus Goes A Shopping	The Adventures of Superman	Just Plain Bill	5:30
Captain Midnight	The Ben Bernie War Workers' Program	Junior Newscaster	Front Page Farrell	5:45

DAYTIME — WINTER, 1943

Saturday

	BLUE	CBS	MBS	NBC
9am	The Breakfast Club	Joe King, news	Dear Imogene	The Show Without a Name, Garry Moore
9:15		Caucasian Melodies	Health Talk	
9:30		The Garden Gate	Troman Harper, news	
9:45			Claire Wilson, news	
10am	Isabel Manning Hewson, food	Youth on Parade	Rainbow House	The NBC String Quartet
10:15	Songs By Mirandy			
10:30	Hank Lawson's Knights	National Hillbilly Champions		Nellie Revell Presents
10:45				Mario Barini, songs
11am	Game Parade	Red Cross Reports	Prescott Robinson, news	The Creightons
11:15		Milton Bacon, stories	Music	
11:30	The Little Blue Playhouse	Let's Pretend	The US Army Band	The Coast Guard Academy Band
11:45				
12pm	Music By Black	The Armstrong Theater of Today	The Man on the Farm	Don Goddard, news
12:15				Consumer Time
12:30	The Farm and Home Hour	Stars Over Hollywood	Alois Havrilla, news	Golden Melodies
12:45			Frank Victor Orchestra	
1pm	Vincent Lopez Orchestra	Columbia's Country Journal		Pan-American Holiday
1:15			The Coast Guard Program	
1:30	Washington Luncheon	Adventures in Science	Treasury Varieties	All Out for Victory
1:45	Fantasy in Melody	Buffalo Presents		Harold Fleming, news

… LISTINGS FOR 1943 …

DAYTIME — WINTER, 1943

Saturday

	BLUE	CBS	MBS	NBC
2pm	The Metropolitan Opera	Of Men and Books	Lani McIntyre Orchestra	NBC Symphony Orchestra
2:15				
2:30		The Spirit of '43	George Duffy Orchestra	
2:45				
3pm		Detroit Musicale	Concert Ensemble	Minstrel Melodies
3:15				
3:30		Hello from Hawaii	Shady Valley Folks	Charles Dant Orchestra
3:45				
4pm		Report from Washington	Baron Elliott Orchestra	Britain Orchestra
4:15		Report from London		
4:30		Calling Pan-America	Bobby Sherwood Orchestra	Music of the Americas
4:45			Horse Racing	
5pm	Joe Rines Orchestra	Cleveland Symphony Orchestra	Glen Gray Orchestra	Doctors at War
5:15				
5:30				Beverly Mohr, songs
5:45	Sol Lewis, news			Alex Dreier, news

EVENING — SPRING, 1943

Sunday

	BLUE	CBS	MBS	NBC
6pm	Here's to Romance, Buddy Clark	Edward R. Murrow, news	The First Nighter Program	The Catholic Hour
6:15		Irene Rich Dramas		
6:30	Free World Theater	Gene Autry's Melody Ranch	Upton Close, news	The Great Gildersleeve
6:45			Troman Harper, Rumor Detective	
7pm	Drew Pearson, news	Chip Davis, Commando	Symphonic Strings	The Grape Nuts Program, Jack Benny
7:15	Songs America Loves			
7:30	The Quiz Kids	We, the People	Frank Singiser, news	The Fitch Bandwagon
7:45			Samuel Grafton, news	
8pm	Roy Porter, news	Meet Corliss Archer	The American Forum of the Air	The Charlie McCarthy Show
8:15	Neighbors			
8:30	Inner Sanctum Mysteries	Crime Doctor		One Man's Family
8:45		Eric Severeid, news (8:55pm)	Gabriel Heatter, news	
9pm	Walter Winchell's Jergens Journal	The Radio Reader's Digest	Murder Clinic	The Manhattan Merry-Go-Round
9:15	The Chamber Music Society of Lower Basin Street			
9:30	Jimmy Fidler, gossip	The Texaco Star Theater, Fred Allen	Remember	The American Album of Familiar Music
9:45	Dorothy Thompson, news			
10pm	The Goodwill Hour	Take It or Leave It	John B. Hughes, news	The Hour of Charm
10:15			The Song Spinners	
10:30		The Man Behind the Gun	John Stanley, news	What's My Name
10:45			Melody Hall	

EVENING — SPRING, 1943

Monday

BLUE	CBS	MBS	NBC	
H. R. Baukhage, news	Quincy Howe, news	Uncle Don	Family Time Music	6pm
Terry and the Pirates	Mary Small, songs		George Putnam, news	6:15
The Singing Bee	Keep Working, America	Frank Singiser, news	Bill Stern, sports	6:30
Lowell Thomas, news	The World Today	Stan Lomax, sports	Music You Want	6:45
The Coast Guard Dance Band	I Love a Mystery	Louis Bromfield, news	Chesterfield Time	7pm
	Ceiling Unlimited	Arthur Hale, news	John W. Vandercook, news	7:15
The Lone Ranger	Blondie	It Pays to Be Ignorant	Allen Roth Orchestra	7:30
			H. V. Kaltenborn, news	7:45
Earl Godwin, news	Vox Pop	Cal Tinney, news	The Cavalcade of America	8pm
Lum and Abner		Singin' Sam, the Barbasol Man		8:15
True or False	The Gay Nineties Revue	The Better Half	The Voice of Firestone	8:30
	Cecil Brown, news (8:55pm)			8:45
Counterspy	The Lux Radio Theater	Gabriel Heatter, news	The Bell Telephone Hour	9pm
		Pay Off News		9:15
Spotlight Bands		A. L. Alexander's Mediation Board	Dr. I. Q., the Mental Banker	9:30
Grace Morgan, songs (9:55pm)				9:45
Raymond Gram Swing, news	The Lady Esther Screen Guild Theater	Paul Sullivan, news	The Carnation Contented Hour	10pm
The Gracie Fields Victory Show		The Wax Museum		10:15
Rhythm Road, Johnny Morgan	Guy Lombardo Orchestra	Paul Schubert, news	Information, Please	10:30
		Music That Endures		10:45

EVENING — SPRING, 1943

Tuesday

	BLUE	CBS	MBS	NBC
6pm	H. R. Baukhage, news	Frazier Hunt, news	Uncle Don	Family Time Music
6:15	Terry and the Pirates	Edwin C. Hill, news		George Putnam, news
6:30	Peter Hayward, stories	John B. Kennedy, news	Frank Singiser, news	Bill Stern, sports
6:45	Lowell Thomas, news	The World Today	Stan Lomax, sports	Music You Want
7pm	Ella Fitzgerald, songs	I Love a Mystery	Louis Bromfield, news	Chesterfield Time
7:15	Men, Machines and Victory	Chesterfield Time	George Hogan, talk	John W. Vandercook, news
7:30	That's a Fact	The American Melody Hour	Arthur Hale, news	Salute to Youth
7:45	Diane Courtney and the Jesters		The Answer Man	
8pm	Earl Godwin, news	Lights Out	The Cisco Kid	The Purple Heart Show, Ginny Simms
8:15	Lum and Abner			
8:30	Duffy's Tavern	The Colgate Program, Al Jolson	Battle of the Burroughs	Tums Treasure Chest
8:45		Cecil Brown, news (8:55pm)		
9pm	Famous Jury Trials	Burns and Allen	Gabriel Heatter, news	Battle of the Sexes
9:15			Pay Off News	
9:30	Spotlight Bands	Suspense	The Return of Nick Carter	Fibber Magee and Molly
9:45	Grace Morgan, songs (9:55pm)			
10pm	Raymond Gram Swing, news	Jazz Laboratory	John B. Hughes, news	The Pepsodent Show, Bob Hope
10:15	The Gracie Fields Victory Show		The Wax Museum	
10:30	This Nation at War	Congress Speaks	Paul Schubert, news	The Raleigh Cigarette Program, Red Skelton
10:45		Mary Small, songs	Duke Ellington Orchestra	

EVENING — SPRING, 1943

Wednesday

BLUE	CBS	MBS	NBC	
H. R. Baukhage, news	John B. Kennedy, news	Uncle Don	Family Time Music	6pm
Terry and the Pirates	Mary Small, songs		George Putnam, news	6:15
The Singing Bee	Keep Working, America	Frank Singiser, news	Bill Stern, sports	6:30
Lowell Thomas, news	The World Today	Stan Lomax, sports	Music You Want	6:45
What's Your War Job	I Love a Mystery	Louis Bromfield, news	Chesterfield Time	7pm
	Chesterfield Time	Arthur Hale, news	John W. Vandercook, news	7:15
The Lone Ranger	Easy Aces	Can You Top This	Allen Roth Orchestra	7:30
	Mr. Keen, Tracer of Lost Persons		H. V. Kaltenborn, news	7:45
Earl Godwin, news	The New Old Gold Program, Monty Wooley	Cal Tinney, news	Mr. and Mrs. North	8pm
Lum and Abner		Singin' Sam, the Barbasol Man		8:15
Manhattan at Midnight	Dr. Christian	Take a Card	Tommy Dorsey's Variety Show	8:30
	Cecil Brown, news (8:55pm)			8:45
Alias John Freedom	The Mayor of the Town	Gabriel Heatter, news	Time to Smile, Eddie Cantor	9pm
		Pay Off News		9:15
Spotlight Bands	The Milton Berle Show	Soldiers With Wings	Mr. District Attorney	9:30
Grace Morgan, songs (9:55pm)				9:45
Raymond Gram Swing, news	Great Moments in Music	John B. Hughes, news	Kay Kyser's College of Musical Knowledge	10pm
The Gracie Fields Victory Show		The Wax Museum		10:15
The National Radio Forum	The Cresta Blanca Carnival	Paul Schubert, news		10:30
		Duke Ellington Orchestra		10:45

EVENING — SPRING, 1943

Thursday

	BLUE	CBS	MBS	NBC
6pm	H. R. Baukhage, news	Frazier Hunt, news	Uncle Don	Family Music Time
6:15	Terry and the Pirates	The Golden Gate Quartet		George Putnam, news
6:30	Peter Hayward, stories	John B. Kennedy, news	Frank Singiser, news	Bill Stern, sports
6:45	Lowell Thomas, news	The World Today	Stan Lomax, sports	Music You Want
7pm	Those Good Ol' Days	I Love a Mystery	Louis Bromfield, news	Chesterfield Time
7:15		Chesterfield Time	Victory is Our Business	John W. Vandercook, news
7:30	That's a Fact	Easy Aces	Arthur Hale, news	The Bob Burns Show
7:45	Diane Courtney and the Jesters	Mr. Keen, Tracer of Lost Persons	The Answer Man	
8pm	Earl Godwin, news	Grapevine Rancho, Ransom Sherman	This is Our Enemy	Maxwell House Coffee Time, Brice and Morgan
8:15	Lum and Abner			
8:30	America's Town Meeting of the Air	Death Valley Days	The Busy Mr. Bingle	The Aldrich Family
8:45		Cecil Brown, news (8:55pm)		
9pm		Major Bowes' Original Amateur Hour	Gabriel Heatter, news	The Kraft Music Hall, Bing Crosby
9:15			Pay Off News	
9:30	Spotlight Bands	Stage Door Canteen	The Treasure Hour of Song	Vallee Varieties
9:45	Grace Morgan, songs (9:55pm)			
10pm	Raymond Gram Swing, news	The First Line of Defense	Paul Sullivan, news	The Durante - Moore Show
10:15	The Gracie Fields Victory Show		The Wax Museum	
10:30	The Hollywood Radio Theater	Public Affairs	Paul Schubert, news	The March of Time
10:45		Mary Small, songs	Duke Ellington Orchestra	

EVENING — SPRING, 1943

Friday

BLUE	CBS	MBS	NBC	
H. R. Baukhage, news	Quincy Howe, news	Uncle Don	Family Music Time	6pm
Terry and the Pirates	Today at the Duncans		George Putnam, news	6:15
The Singing Bee	Keep Working, America	Frank Singiser, news	Bill Stern, sports	6:30
Lowell Thomas, news	The World Today	Stan Lomax, sports	Music You Want	6:45
Nothing Serious	I Love a Mystery	Louis Bromfield, news	Chesterfield Time	7pm
	Our Secret Weapon	Arthur Hale, news	John W. Vandercook, news	7:15
The Lone Ranger	Easy Aces	Variety Musicale	Allen Roth Orchestra	7:30
	Mr. Keen, Tracer of Lost Persons		H. V. Kaltenborn, news	7:45
Earl Godwin, news	The Kate Smith Hour	Cal Tinney, news	The Cities Service Concerts	8pm
The Parker Family		Public Affairs		8:15
Meet Your Navy	The Adventures of the Thin Man	Sherlock Holmes	Your All-Time Hit Parade	8:30
	Cecil Brown, news (8:55pm)			8:45
Gangbusters	The Phillip Morris Playhouse	Gabriel Heatter, news	Waltz Time	9pm
		Pay Off News		9:15
Spotlight Bands	That Brewster Boy	Double or Nothing	People Are Funny	9:30
Grace Morgan, songs (9:55pm)				9:45
John Gunther, news	The Camel Comedy Caravan, Jack Carson	John B. Hughes, news	Tommy Riggs and Betty Lou	10pm
The Gracie Fields Victory Show		The Wax Museum		10:15
The Korn Kobblers		Paul Schubert, news	Public Affairs	10:30
Elmer Davis, news	Elmer Davis, news	Elmer Davis, news	Elmer Davis, news	10:45

EVENING — SPRING, 1943

Saturday

	BLUE	CBS	MBS	NBC
6pm	H. R. Baukhage, news	Frazier Hunt, news	Uncle Don	Joseph Gallichio Orchestra
6:15	The Korn Kobblers	The People's Platform		George Putnam, news
6:30	Message of Israel		Frank Singiser, news	Religion in the News
6:45		The Three Sisters, songs	Stan Lomax, sports	Paul La Valle Orchestra
7pm	The Falcon	Report to the Nation	The Lenox Avenue Record Man	Day of Reckoning
7:15			Pan-American Music	
7:30	The Danny Thomas Show	Thanks to the Yanks	Arthur Hale, news	The Adventures of Ellery Queen
7:45			The Answer Man	
8pm	Roy Porter, news	The Crumit and Sanderson Quiz	The Fleets In	Abie's Irish Rose
8:15	Boston Symphony Orchestra			
8:30		Hobby Lobby	Upton Close, news	Truth or Consequences
8:45		Eric Sevareid, news (8:55pm)	The Song Spinners	
9pm		Your Hit Parade	The Chicago Theater of the Air	The National Barn Dance
9:15	Edward Tomlinson, news			
9:30	Spotlight Bands			Can You Top This
9:45	Hear America (9:55PM)	Saturday Night Serenade		
10pm	John W. Vandercook, news		John B. Hughes, news	The Colgate Sports Newsreel, Bill Stern
10:15	Public Affairs	Pabst Blue Ribbon Town, Groucho Marx	Saturday Night Bandwagon	Freddy Martin Orchestra
10:30				Let's Play Reporter
10:45	Betty Rann, songs	Eileen Farrell, songs	Lani McIntyre Orchestra	

DAYTIME — SPRING, 1943

Sunday

	BLUE	CBS	MBS	NBC
9am	News	News	News	News
9:15	Coast-to-Coast on a Bus	The Bach Cantata Series	Pauline Alpert, piano	Ernesta Barlow, talk
9:30			The Navy Goes to Church	Marsha Nell, songs
9:45		English Melodies		
10am	Fantasy in Melody	The CBS Church of the Air	Arthur Van Horn, news	The National Radio Pulpit
10:15			Frank Kingdon, news	
10:30	The Southernaires Quartet	Wings Over Jordan	Mystery Hall	The Horn and Hardart Children's Hour
10:45				
11am	Will Osborne Orchestra	Warren Sweeney, news	Marines in Review	
11:15		Vera Brodsky, piano		
11:30	African Trek	Invitation to Learning	The Mutual Radio Chapel	George Putnam, news
11:45				Olivio Santora, yodeler
12pm	The Weekly War Journal	Transatlantic Call	Hawaii Calls	Tapestry Musicale
12:15		Woman Power		
12:30	Stars from the Blue	The Salt Lake Tabernacle Choir	Soldiers of the Press	That They May Live
12:45			Troman Harper, news	
1pm	The Sunday Morning Review	The CBS Church of the Air	The Canary Pet Shop	Rupert Hughes, news
1:15			The Sing a Song of Safety Club	Labor for Victory
1:30		Quincy Howe, news	This is Fort Dix	We Believe
1:45	Martin Agronsky, news	Stoopnagle's Schutter		

DAYTIME — SPRING, 1943

Monday-Friday

BLUE	CBS	MBS	NBC	
The Breakfast Club	Jay Sims, news	Linda Marvin / Dear Imogene	Everything Goes, Garry Moore	*9am*
	The American School of the Air	Victor Lindlahr, health		*9:15*
		Troman Harper, news	Mary Hamman, news	*9:30*
	This Life is Mine	Music	March of Mercy / Richard Liebert, organ	*9:45*
Isabel Manning Hewson, food	Valiant Lady	Alfred W. McCann, food	Robert St. John, news	*10am*
Roy Porter, news	Kitty Foyle		The O'Neills	*10:15*
The Baby Institute	Amanda of Honeymoon Hill	Jimmy Fidler gossip / Ted Steele Orchestra	Helpmate	*10:30*
Gene and Glenn	Bachelor's Children		A Woman of America	*10:45*
Breakfast with Breneman	Mary Lee Taylor, cooking / Food News Round-Up	Bessie Beatty, talk	The Road of Life	*11am*
	Second Husband		Vic and Sade	*11:15*
Music	Bright Horizon		Snow Village Sketches	*11:30*
	Aunt Jenny's True Life Stories		David Harum	*11:45*
	Kate Smith Speaks	Boake Carter, news	Don Goddard, news	*12pm*
	Big Sister	Musical Appetizer	The Ben Brady Show	*12:15*
The Farm and Home Hour	The Romance of Helen Trent	Alois Havrilla, news		*12:30*
	Our Gal Sunday	Judy and Jane	W. W. Chaplin, news	*12:45*
H. R. Baukhage, news	Life Can Be Beautiful	David Bush, talk	Mary Margaret McBride, talk	*1pm*
The Gospel Singer	Ma Perkins	Music		*1:15*
Religious Talk	Vic and Sade	Pegeen Presents		*1:30*
Vincent Lopez Orchestra /	The Goldbergs	The Johnson Family	Carey Longmire, news	*1:45*

DAYTIME — SPRING, 1943

Sunday

	BLUE	CBS	MBS	NBC
2pm	Chaplain Jim, USA	Those We Love	Pass in Review	The University of Chicago Round Table
2:15				
2:30	Yesterday and Today	World News Today	Prescott Robinson, news	The Westinghouse Program, John C. Thomas
2:45			Mutual Matinee	
3pm	The Moylan Sisters, songs	New York Philharmonic Orchestra		Report on Rationing
3:15	Wake Up, America			Upton Close, news
3:30				The Army Hour
3:45				
4pm	National Vespers			
4:15				
4:30	The Green Hornet	Mexican Philharmonic Orchestra	The Coast Guard Band	Lands of the Free
4:45				
5pm	Where Do We Stand	The Prudential Family Hour	Henry Jerome Orchestra	NBC Symphony Orchestra
5:15			Melody Lane	
5:30	The Musical Steelmakers		Bulldog Drummond	
5:45		William L. Shirer, news		

DAYTIME — SPRING, 1943

Monday-Friday

BLUE	CBS	MBS	NBC	
Music	Young Dr. Malone	Martha Deane, talk	The Light of the World	2pm
The Mystery Chef	Joyce Jordan, MD		Lonely Women	2:15
James G. McDonald, news	We Love and Learn	Prescott Robinson, news (Monday only) / Mutual Matinee /	The Guiding Light	2:30
Stella Unger, gossip	Pepper Young's Family	Philadelphia Symphony Orchestra	Betty Crocker, cooking / Hymns of All Churches	2:45
The Coke Club, Morton Downey	David Harum		The Story of Mary Marlin	3pm
My True Story	Joe and Ethel Turp		Ma Perkins	3:15
	Music		Pepper Young's Family	3:30
Between the Bookends			The Right to Happiness	3:45
Club Matinee, Garry Moore	Elizabeth Bemis, news		Mary Noble, Backstage Wife	4pm
Quest for Happiness	Green Valley, USA		Stella Dallas	4:15
Music / Joan Harding, talk	Perry Como, songs	Dr. Eddy's Food Forum	Lorenzo Jones	4:30
The Sea Hound	Recorded Music		Young Widder Brown	4:45
Hop Harrigan	Madeleine Carroll Reads	News	When a Girl Marries	5pm
Dick Tracy	Mother and Dad	Rambling with Gambling	Portia Faces Life	5:15
Jack Armstrong, the All-American Boy	Music	Highway Patrol	Just Plain Bill	5:30
Captain Midnight		The Adventures of Superman	Front Page Farrell	5:45

DAYTIME — SPRING, 1943

Saturday

	BLUE	CBS	MBS	NBC
9am	The Breakfast Club	Joe King, news	Dear Imogene	Everything Goes, Garry Moore
9:15		Red Cross Reports	Victor Lindlahr, health	
9:30		The Garden Gate	Troman Harper, news	
9:45			Claire Wilson, news	
10am	Isabel Manning Hewson, food	Youth on Parade	Rainbow House	The NBC String Quartet
10:15	Quest for Happiness			
10:30		The US Navy Band		Nellie Revell Presents
10:45	Betty Moore, talk			Mario Barini, songs
11am	Game Parade	Let's Pretend	Prescott Robinson, news	Dramas
11:15			Music	
11:30	The Little Blue Playhouse	Fashions in Rations, Billie Burke	The US Army Band	The Coast Guard Academy Band
11:45				
12pm	Music By Black	The Armstrong Theater of Today	The Army-Navy House Party	Don Goddard, news
12:15				Consumer Time
12:30	The Farm and Home Hour	Stars Over Hollywood	Alois Havrilla, news	Golden Melodies
12:45			George Duffy Orchestra	
1pm	News	Columbia's Country Journal		Plot for Victory
1:15	Vincent Lopez Orchestra		Curley Clemens' Rangers	Sketches in Melody
1:30		Adventures in Science	Treasury Varieties	All Out for Victory
1:45	Welcome Lewis, songs	Highways to Health		Harold Fleming, news

DAYTIME — SPRING, 1943

Saturday

	BLUE	CBS	MBS	NBC
2pm	The Metropolitan Opera	Buffalo Presents	Lani McIntyre Orchestra	The Roy Shield Revue
2:15				
2:30		The Spirit of '43	George Duffy Orchestra	
2:45				The National PTA Club
3pm		Of Men and Books	Public Affairs	The US Air Force Band
3:15				
3:30		Detroit Musicale	Shady Valley Folks	Lyrics By Liza
3:45				
4pm		Report from Washington	Elmer Davis, news	Matinee in Rhythm
4:15		Report from London	Public Affairs	
4:30		Calling Pan-America		Minstrel Melodies
4:45				
5pm	Joe Rines	Cleveland Orchestra	Glen Gray	Doctors
5:15				
5:30				The Three Suns
5:45	Sol Lewis, news			Alex Dreier, news

EVENING — SUMMER, 1943

Sunday

	BLUE	CBS	MBS	NBC
6pm	Here's to Romance, Dick Haymes	The Silver Theater	Murder Clinic	The Catholic Hour
6:15				
6:30	The Green Hornet	Gene Autry's Melody Ranch	Upton Close, news	Men at Sea
6:45			Troman Harper, Rumor Detective	
7pm	Drew Pearson, news	The Jerry Lester Show	Duke Ellington Orchestra	Those We Love
7:15	Songs America Loves			
7:30	The Quiz Kids	We, the People	Frank Singiser, news	The Fitch Bandwagon
7:45			Samuel Grafton, news	
8pm	Roy Porter, news	Calling America	A. L. Alexander's Mediation Board	Paul Whiteman Presents
8:15	Neighbors			
8:30	Inner Sanctum Mysteries	Crime Doctor		One Man's Family
8:45		Ned Calmer, news (8:55pm)	Gabriel Heatter, news	
9pm	Walter Winchell's Jergens Journal	The Radio Reader's Digest	Music for an Hour	The Manhattan Merry-Go-Round
9:15	The Chamber Music Society of Lower Basin Street			
9:30		The Texaco Summer Theater, James Melton		The American Album of Familiar Music
9:45	Jimmy Fidler, gossip			
10pm	The Goodwill Hour	Take It or Leave It	John B. Hughes, news	The Hour of Charm
10:15			The Song Spinners	
10:30		William L. Shirer, news	John Stanley, news	Bob Crosby Orchestra
10:45		Maria Kurenko, songs	Tiny Hill Orchestra	

EVENING — SUMMER, 1943

Monday

BLUE	CBS	MBS	NBC	
Walter Clausen, news	Quincy Howe, news	Uncle Don	Jack Arthur, songs	6pm
Terry and the Pirates	Jeri Sullavan, songs		George Putnam, news	6:15
The Singing Bee		Frank Singiser, news	Bill Stern, sports	6:30
Lowell Thomas, news	The World Today	Stan Lomax, sports	Music You Want	6:45
Awake at the Switch	I Love a Mystery	Fulton Lewis Jr., news	Chesterfield Time	7pm
	The Three Sisters, songs	Arthur Hale, news	John W. Vandercook, news	7:15
The Lone Ranger	Blondie	It Pays to Be Ignorant	Allen Roth Orchestra	7:30
			H. V. Kaltenborn, news	7:45
Earl Godwin, news	Vox Pop	Sam Balter, news	The Cavalcade of America	8pm
Lum and Abner		Leo Cherne, news		8:15
The Adventures of Nero Wolfe	The Gay Nineties Revue	The Better Half	The Voice of Firestone	8:30
	Cecil Brown, news (8:55pm)			8:45
Counterspy	Romance	Gabriel Heatter, news	The Bell Telephone Hour	9pm
		Pay Off News		9:15
Spotlight Bands	Broadway Bandbox, Frank Sinatra	The Return of Nick Carter	Dr. I. Q., the Mental Banker	9:30
Grace Morgan, songs (9:55pm)				9:45
Raymond Gram Swing, news	The Lady Esther Screen Guild Theater	Paul Sullivan, news	The Carnation Contented Hour	10pm
Lulu and Johnny, songs		Sunny Skylar, songs		10:15
The Johnny Morgan Show	Guy Lombardo Orchestra	Paul Schubert, news	Vacation Serenade	10:30
		The Longines Symphonette		10:45

EVENING — SUMMER, 1943

Tuesday

	BLUE	CBS	MBS	NBC
6pm	Walter Clausen, news	Quincy Howe, news	Uncle Don	Jack Arthur, songs
6:15	Terry and the Pirates	Edwin C. Hill, news		George Putnam, news
6:30	The Singing Bee	Jeri Sullavan, songs	Frank Singiser, news	Bill Stern, sports
6:45	Lowell Thomas, news	The World Today	Stan Lomax, sports	Music You Want
7pm	Cohen, the Detective	I Love a Mystery	Fulton Lewis Jr., news	Chesterfield Time
7:15		Chesterfield Time	Foreign Correspondent	John W. Vandercook, news
7:30	Men, Machines and Victory	The American Melody Hour	Arthur Hale, news	Salute to Youth
7:45	Diane Courtney and the Jesters		The Answer Man	
8pm	Earl Godwin, news	Lights Out	The American Forum of the Air	The Purple Heart Show, Ginny Simms
8:15	Lum and Abner			
8:30	Noah Webster Says	The Judy Canova Show		Tums Treasure Chest
8:45		Cecil Brown, news (8:55pm)		
9pm	Famous Jury Trials	Colonel Stoopnagle	Gabriel Heatter, news	Battle of the Sexes
9:15			Pay Off News	
9:30	Spotlight Bands	Report to the Nation	The Cisco Kid	The Passing Parade
9:45	Grace Morgan, songs (9:55pm)			
10pm	Raymond Gram Swing, news	Suspense / Passport for Adams	John B. Hughes, news	Johnny Mercer's Music Shop
10:15	Lulu and Johnny, songs		Sunny Skylar, songs	
10:30	This Nation at War	Congress Speaks	Paul Schubert, news	Beat the Band
10:45		Ted Husing, sports	The Longines Symphonette	

EVENING — SUMMER, 1943

Wednesday

BLUE	CBS	MBS	NBC	
Walter Clausen, news	Quincy Howe, news	Uncle Don	Jack Arthur, songs	6pm
Terry and the Pirates	Jeri Sullavan, songs		George Putnam, news	6:15
The Singing Bee		Frank Singiser, news	Bill Stern, sports	6:30
Lowell Thomas, news	The World Today	Stan Lomax, sports	Music You Want	6:45
What's Your War Job	I Love a Mystery	Fulton Lewis Jr., news	Chesterfield Time	7pm
	Chesterfield Time	Arthur Hale, news	John W. Vandercook, news	7:15
The Lone Ranger	Easy Aces	Can You Top This	Allen Roth Orchestra	7:30
	Mr. Keen, Tracer of Lost Persons		H. V. Kaltenborn, news	7:45
Earl Godwin, news	The New Old Gold Program, Monty Wooley	Sam Balter, news	Mr. and Mrs. North	8pm
Lum and Abner		Leo Cherne, news		8:15
Manhattan at Midnight	Dr. Christian	Take a Card	Tommy Dorsey's Variety Show	8:30
	Cecil Brown, news (8:55pm)			8:45
Alias John Freedom	The Mayor of the Town	Gabriel Heatter, news	A Date with Judy	9pm
		Pay Off News		9:15
Spotlight Bands	The Jack Carson Show	Guess Where	Mr. District Attorney	9:30
Grace Morgan, songs (9:55pm)				9:45
Raymond Gram Swing, news	Great Moments in Music	John B. Hughes, news	Kay Kyser's College of Musical Knowledge	10pm
Lulu and Johnny, songs		Sunny Skylar, songs		10:15
Men's Store News	The Cresta Blanca Carnival	Paul Schubert, news		10:30
Joe Rines Orchestra		The Longines Symphonette		10:45

EVENING — SUMMER, 1943

Thursday

	BLUE	CBS	MBS	NBC
6pm	Walter Clausen, news	Ned Calmer, news	Uncle Don	Jack Arthur, songs
6:15	Terry and the Pirates	John L. Sullivan, talk		George Putnam, news
6:30	The Singing Bee	Jeri Sullavan, songs	Frank Singiser, news	Bill Stern, sports
6:45	Lowell Thomas, news	The World Today	Stan Lomax, sports	Music You Want
7pm	Wings to Victory	I Love a Mystery	Fulton Lewis Jr., news	Chesterfield Time
7:15		Chesterfield Time	Victory is Our Business	John W. Vandercook, news
7:30	Music	Easy Aces	Arthur Hale, news	That's Life, Fred Brady
7:45	Diane Courtney and the Jesters	Mr. Keen, Tracer of Lost Persons	The Answer Man	
8pm	Earl Godwin, news	The Roma Wine Show, Charlie Ruggles	This is Our Enemy	Blind Date
8:15	Lum and Abner			
8:30	America's Town Meeting of the Air	Death Valley Days	Just Five Lines	Battle Stations
8:45		Cecil Brown, news (8:55pm)		
9pm		Major Bowes' Original Amateur Hour	Gabriel Heatter, news	The Kraft Music Hall, Bing Crosby
9:15			Pay Off News	
9:30	Spotlight Bands	Stage Door Canteen	You Tell 'em Club	The Sealtest Village Store, Davis and Haley
9:45	Grace Morgan, songs (9:55pm)			
10pm	Raymond Gram Swing, news	The First Line of Defense	Raymond Clapper, news	The Durante - Moore Show
10:15	Lulu and Johnny, songs		Sunny Skylar, songs	
10:30	The Hollywood Radio Theater	Public Affairs	Paul Schubert, news	The March of Time
10:45		Eyes of the Air Force	The Longines Symphonette	

EVENING — SUMMER, 1943

Friday

BLUE	CBS	MBS	NBC	
Walter Clausen, news	Quincy Howe, news	Uncle Don	Jack Arthur, songs	6pm
Terry and the Pirates	Jeri Sullavan, songs		George Putnam, news	6:15
The Singing Bee		Frank Singiser, news	Bill Stern, sports	6:30
Lowell Thomas, news	The World Today	Stan Lomax, sports	Music You Want	6:45
Saludas Amigas, Victoria Cordova	I Love a Mystery	Fulton Lewis Jr., news	Chesterfield Time	7pm
	Our Secret Weapon	Arthur Hale, news	John W. Vandercook, news	7:15
The Lone Ranger	Easy Aces	Variety Musicale	Allen Roth Orchestra	7:30
	Mr. Keen, Tracer of Lost Persons		H. V. Kaltenborn, news	7:45
Earl Godwin, news	Meet Corliss Archer	Sam Balter, news	The Cities Service Concerts	8pm
The Parker Family		Don Redman Orchestra		8:15
History is Fun	The Adventures of the Thin Man	Sherlock Holmes	Your All-Time Hit Parade	8:30
	Cecil Brown, news (8:55pm)			8:45
Gangbusters	The Phillip Morris Playhouse	Gabriel Heatter, news	Waltz Time	9pm
		Pay Off News		9:15
Spotlight Bands	That Brewster Boy	Double or Nothing	People Are Funny	9:30
Grace Morgan, songs (9:55pm)				9:45
John W. Vandercook, news	Thanks to the Yanks	Madison Square Garden Boxing	Tommy Riggs and Betty Lou	10pm
Lulu and Johnny, songs				10:15
Men's Store News	The Three Sisters, songs		The Colgate Sports Newsreel, Bill Stern	10:30
J. K. Lasser, economics	Bill Henry, news		Public Affairs	10:45

EVENING — SUMMER, 1943

Saturday

	BLUE	CBS	MBS	NBC
6pm	Walter Clausen, news	Quincy Howe, news	Uncle Don	Family Time Music
6:15	The Korn Kobblers	The People's Platform		George Putnam, news
6:30	Ella Fitzgerald, songs		Frank Singiser, news	The Art of Living
6:45	Leon Henderson, news	The World Today	Stan Lomax, sports	Joseph Gallichio Orchestra
7pm	The Falcon	The Man Behind the Gun	Sydney Moseley, news	For This We Fight
7:15			Pan-American Music	
7:30	Army Service Forces Present	Benny Goodman Orchestra	Arthur Hale, news	The Adventures of Ellery Queen
7:45			The Answer Man	
8pm	Roy Porter, news	The Crumit and Sanderson Quiz	California Melodies	Charles Dant Orchestra
8:15	Gilbert and Sullivan Festival			
8:30		Hobby Lobby	Foreign Assignment	Words at War
8:45		Ned Calmer, news (8:55pm)	The Song Spinners	
9pm		Your Hit Parade	The Chicago Theater of the Air	The National Barn Dance
9:15	Edward Tomlinson, news			
9:30	Spotlight Bands			Can You Top This
9:45	Harry Wismer, sports (9:55PM)	Saturday Night Serenade		
10pm	John W. Vandercook, news		John B. Hughes, news	The Million Dollar Band, Barry Wood
10:15	Betty Rann, songs	Pabst Blue Ribbon Town, Groucho Marx	Saturday Night Bandwagon	
10:30	The Grant Park Concerts			Who, What, When, Where
10:45		Eileen Farrell, songs	William Ewing, news	

DAYTIME — SUMMER, 1943

Sunday

	BLUE	CBS	MBS	NBC
9am	News	News	Fiesta Time	News
9:15	Coast-to-Coast on a Bus	From the Organ Loft	Pauline Alpert, piano	Ernesta Barlow, talk
9:30			The Navy Goes to Church	Marsha Nell, songs
9:45		English Melodies		
10am	Message of Israel	The CBS Church of the Air	Frank Singiser, news	Highlights of the Bible
10:15			Frank Kingdon, news	
10:30	The Southernaires Quartet	Wings Over Jordan	Pauline Alpert, piano	The Horn and Hardart Children's Hour
10:45			Charles Hodges, news	
11am	Production Story	Warren Sweeney, news	Marines in Review	
11:15		Vera Brodsky, piano		
11:30	African Trek	Invitation to Learning	The Mutual Radio Chapel	George Putnam, news
11:45				Olivio Santora, yodeler
12pm	The Weekly War Journal	The Salt Lake Tabernacle Choir	The Army Air Force Show	The First Piano Quartet
12:15				
12:30	Stars from the Blue	Transatlantic Call	Soldiers of the Press	That They May Live
12:45		Woman Power	Troman Harper, news	
1pm	This is Official	The CBS Church of the Air	Recorded Music	Rupert Hughes, news
1:15			Ginger and Lanny, songs	Labor for Victory
1:30	The Kidoodlers Novelty Quartet	Edward R. Murrow, news	This is Fort Dix	The Dinning Sisters, songs
1:45	Max Hill, news	The Little Show, Robert Q. Lewis		Your Radio Reporter

DAYTIME — SUMMER, 1943

Monday-Friday

BLUE	CBS	MBS	NBC	
The Breakfast Club	Joe King, news	The Quiz Wizard	Everything Goes, Garry Moore	9am
	Music	Music		9:15
	This Life is Mine	Troman Harper, news	Mary Hamman, news	9:30
	The Landt Trio and Curley	Music	Robert St. John, news	9:45
Isabel Manning Hewson, food	Valiant Lady	Alfred W. McCann, food	Lora Lawton	10am
Roy Porter, news	Kitty Foyle		The Open Door	10:15
The Baby Institute	Amanda of Honeymoon Hill	Lyrics By Loretta	Helpmate	10:30
Talk / Quest for Happiness	Bachelor's Children		A Woman of America	10:45
Breakfast with Breneman	Mary Lee Taylor, cooking / Milton Bacon, stories	Bessie Beatty, talk	The Road of Life	11am
	Second Husband		Vic and Sade	11:15
Gilbert Martyn, news	Bright Horizon		Snow Village Sketches	11:30
Living Should Be Fun	Aunt Jenny's True Life Stories		David Harum	11:45
Religious Talk	Kate Smith Speaks	Boake Carter, news	Don Goddard, news	12pm
	Big Sister	Musical Appetizer	Music / That's a Fact	12:15
The Farm and Home Hour	The Romance of Helen Trent	Alois Havrilla, news	Mirth and Madness, Jack Kirkwood	12:30
	Our Gal Sunday	The Handy Man		12:45
H. R. Baukhage, news	Life Can Be Beautiful	Sydney Moseley, news	Mary Margaret McBride, talk	1pm
The Women's Exchange	Ma Perkins	Lanny and Ginger, songs		1:15
	Vic and Sade	Vincent Lopez Orchestra		1:30
Music	The Goldbergs		Robert McCormick, news	1:45

DAYTIME — SUMMER, 1943

Sunday

	BLUE	CBS	MBS	NBC
2pm	Chaplain Jim, USA	Ceiling Unlimited	The Show Shop	The University of Chicago Round Table
2:15				
2:30	Yesterday and Today	World News Today	Prescott Robertson, news	The Westinghouse Program, John C. Thomas
2:45			Mutual Matinee	
3pm	Those Good Old Days	New York Philharmonic Orchestra		Report on Rationing
3:15	Hanson W. Baldwin, news			Upton Close, news
3:30	Hot Copy			The Army Hour
3:45				
4pm	National Vespers			
4:15				
4:30	Chautauqua Symphony Orchestra	The Pause That Refreshes	Spear Orchestra	The Editors Speak
4:45				
5pm	Where Do We Stand	The Prudential Family Hour	Will Osborne Orchestra	NBC Symphony Orchestra
5:15				
5:30	Sneak Previews		Bulldog Drummond	
5:45		Irene Rich Dramas		

DAYTIME — SUMMER, 1943

Monday-Friday

BLUE	CBS	MBS	NBC	
	Young Dr. Malone	Martha Deane, talk	The Guiding Light	2pm
The Mystery Chef	Joyce Jordan, MD		Lonely Women	2:15
Ed East and Polly, songs	We Love and Learn	Maxine Keith, talk	The Light of the World	2:30
	Pepper Young's Family		Hymns of All Churches	2:45
The Coke Club, Morton Downey	Elizabeth Bemis, news	Mary Foster	The Story of Mary Marlin	3pm
My True Story	Joe and Ethel Turp	Linda's First Love	Ma Perkins	3:15
	The John Gart Trio	Dr. Eddy's Food Forum	Pepper Young's Family	3:30
Between the Bookends	Green Valley, USA		The Right to Happiness	3:45
Blue Frolics	Your Home Front Reporter	Personality Parade	Mary Noble, Backstage Wife	4pm
			Stella Dallas	4:15
Westbrook Van Voorhis, news	Perry Como, songs	Full Speed Ahead	Lorenzo Jones	4:30
The Sea Hound	Recorded Music		Young Widder Brown	4:45
Hop Harrigan	Madeleine Carroll Reads	Rambling with Gambling	When a Girl Marries	5pm
Dick Tracy	Mother and Dad	The Black Hood	Portia Faces Life	5:15
Jack Armstrong, the All-American Boy	Are You a Genius	Chick Carter, Boy Detective	Just Plain Bill	5:30
Archie Andrews	American Women	The Adventures of Superman	Front Page Farrell	5:45

DAYTIME — SUMMER, 1943

Saturday

	BLUE	CBS	MBS	NBC
9am	The Breakfast Club	Joe King, news	Dear Imogene	Everything Goes, Garry Moore
9:15		Red Cross Reports	Victor Lindlahr, health	
9:30		The Garden Gate	Troman Harper, news	
9:45			Claire Wilson, comment	
10am	Isabel Manning Hewson, food	Youth on Parade	Rainbow House	The NBC String Quartet
10:15	Quest for Happiness			
10:30		The US Navy Band		Nellie Revell Presents
10:45	The Andrini Continentals			Shorty and Sue
11am	Game Parade	Let's Pretend	Prescott Robinson, news	Dramas
11:15			Music	
11:30	The Little Blue Playhouse	Fashions in Rations, Billie Burke	Hello, Mom	The Coast Guard Academy Band
11:45				
12pm	Swing Shift Frolics	The Armstrong Theater of Today	The Army-Navy House Party	Don Goddard, news
12:15				Consumer Time
12:30	The Farm and Home Hour	Stars Over Hollywood	Alois Havrilla, news	Golden Melodies
12:45			George Duffy Orchestra	
1pm	News	Columbia's Country Journal		Plot for Victory
1:15	The Adrian Rollini Trio		Curley Clemens' Rangers	Sketches in Melody
1:30	Sylvia Marlowe, harpsichord	Adventures in Science	Vincent Lopez Orchestra	All Out for Victory
1:45	Welcome Lewis, songs	Highways to Health		Elmer Peterson, news

DAYTIME — SUMMER, 1943

Saturday

	BLUE	CBS	MBS	NBC
2pm	Musette's Music Box	I Sustain the Wings	Lani McIntyre Orchestra	The Roy Shield Revue
2:15				
2:30	Tommy Tucker Topics	The Spirit of '43	George Duffy Orchestra	
2:45				Harold Fleming, news
3pm	Van Alexander Orchestra	Of Men and Books	The Black Castle	The US Air Force Band
3:15			The Norton Sisters, songs	
3:30	George Hicks, news	Detroit Musicale	Shep Fields Orchestra	Lyrics By Liza
3:45	The Marshalls Mixed Quartet			
4pm	Concert Ensemble	Report from Washington	Paul Martell Orchestra	Matinee in Rhythm
4:15		Report from London	Horse Racing	
4:30		Calling Pan-America	The Brazilian Parade	Minstrel Melodies
4:45	News			
5pm	Horace Heidt Orchestra	It's Maritime	Glen Gray Orchestra	Not for Glory
5:15				
5:30		Chip Davis, Commando		Bonnie Lou Smith, songs
5:45				W. W. Chaplin, news

EVENING — FALL, 1943

Sunday

	ABC	CBS	MBS	NBC
6pm	Saludas Amigas, Victoria Cordova	The Silver Theater	The First Nighter Program	The Catholic Hour
6:15				
6:30	Dunninger, the Mentalist	America in the Air	Upton Close, news	The Great Gildersleeve
6:45			Troman Harper, Rumor Detective	
7pm	Drew Pearson, news	The Jerry Lester Show	Jan Garber Orchestra	The Grape Nuts Program, Jack Benny
7:15	Dorothy Thompson, news			
7:30	The Quiz Kids	We, the People	Frank Singiser, news	The Fitch Bandwagon
7:45			Samuel Grafton, news	
8pm	Roy Porter, news	Broadway Bandbox, Frank Sinatra	A. L. Alexander's Mediation Board	The Charlie McCarthy Show
8:15	That's a Good One			
8:30	Keepsakes, Dorothy Kirsten	Crime Doctor		One Man's Family
8:45		Ned Calmer, news (8:55pm)	Gabriel Heatter, news	
9pm	Walter Winchell's Jergens Journal	The Radio Reader's Digest	Cleveland Symphony Orchestra	The Manhattan Merry-Go-Round
9:15	The Chamber Music Society of Lower Basin Street			
9:30		The Texaco Star Theater, James Melton		The American Album of Familiar Music
9:45	Jimmy Fidler, gossip			
10pm	The Gertrude Lawrence Theater	Take It or Leave It	John B. Hughes, news	The Hour of Charm
10:15			Sonny Skylar, songs	
10:30	The Goodwill Hour	The Adventures of the Thin Man	John Stanley, news	Bob Crosby Orchestra
10:45			Don Redman Orchestra	

EVENING — FALL, 1943

Monday

ABC	CBS	MBS	NBC	
John B. Kennedy, news	Quincy Howe, news	Sydney Moseley, news	Jack Arthur, songs	6pm
Terry and the Pirates	The Squibb Show	Lanny and Ginger, songs	George Putnam, news	6:15
The Singing Bee	Jeri Sullavan, songs	Frank Singiser, news	Bill Stern, sports	6:30
Lowell Thomas, news	The World Today	Stan Lomax, sports	Music You Want	6:45
Mary Small's Revue	I Love a Mystery	Fulton Lewis Jr., news	Chesterfield Time	7pm
	Ed Sullivan Entertains	Arthur Hale, news	John W. Vandercook, news	7:15
The Lone Ranger	Blondie	It Pays to Be Ignorant	Allen Roth Orchestra	7:30
			H. V. Kaltenborn, news	7:45
Earl Godwin, news	Vox Pop	Sam Balter, news	The Cavalcade of America	8pm
Lum and Abner		Leo Cherne, news		8:15
The Johnny Morgan Show	The Gay Nineties Revue	Sherlock Holmes	The Voice of Firestone	8:30
	Bill Henry, news (8:55pm)			8:45
Counterspy	The Lux Radio Theater	Gabriel Heatter, news	The Bell Telephone Hour	9pm
		The Gracie Fields Victory Show		9:15
Spotlight Bands		The Return of Nick Carter	Dr. I. Q., the Mental Banker	9:30
Grace Morgan, songs (8:55pm)				9:45
Raymond Gram Swing, news	The Lady Esther Screen Guild Theater	John B. Hughes, news	The Carnation Contented Hour	10pm
Men, Machines and Victory		Sunny Skylar, songs		10:15
The Hollywood Radio Theater	Guy Lombardo Orchestra	Paul Schubert, news	Information, Please	10:30
		The Longines Symphonette		10:45

EVENING — FALL, 1943

Tuesday

	ABC	CBS	MBS	NBC
6pm	John B. Kennedy, news	Quincy Howe, news	Sydney Moseley, news	Jack Arthur, songs
6:15	Terry and the Pirates	Edwin C. Hill, news	Lanny and Ginger, songs	George Putnam, news
6:30	Welcome Lewis, songs	Jeri Sullavan, songs	Frank Singiser, news	Bill Stern, sports
6:45	Lowell Thomas, news	The World Today	Stan Lomax, sports	Music You Want
7pm	Awake at the Switch	I Love a Mystery	Fulton Lewis Jr., news	Chesterfield Time
7:15		Chesterfield Time	Foreign Correspondent	John W. Vandercook, news
7:30	Redd Evans Club Time	The American Melody Hour	Arthur Hale, news	Salute to Youth
7:45	Diane Courtney and the Jesters		The Answer Man	
8pm	Earl Godwin, news	Big Town	Sinfonettia	The Purple Heart Show, Ginny Simms
8:15	Lum and Abner			
8:30	Duffy's Tavern	The Judy Canova Show	Battle of the Burroughs	Tums Treasure Chest
8:45		Bill Henry, news (8:55pm)		
9pm	Famous Jury Trials	Burns and Allen	Gabriel Heatter, news	The Molle' Mystery Theater
9:15			The Gracie Fields Victory Show	
9:30	Spotlight Bands	Report to the Nation	The American Forum of the Air	Fibber Magee and Molly
9:45	Grace Morgan, songs (9:55pm)			
10pm	Raymond Gram Swing, news	Suspense		The Pepsodent Show, Bob Hope
10:15	Listen to Lulu		John B. Hughes, news	
10:30	This Nation at War	Congress Speaks	Paul Schubert, news	The Raleigh Cigarette Program, Red Skelton
10:45		Guy Lombardo Orchestra	The Longines Symphonette	

EVENING — FALL, 1943

Wednesday

ABC	CBS	MBS	NBC	
John B. Kennedy, news	Quincy Howe, news	Sydney Moseley, news	Jack Arthur, songs	6pm
Terry and the Pirates	The Squibb Show	Lanny and Ginger, songs	George Putnam, news	6:15
The Singing Bee	Jeri Sullavan, songs	Frank Singiser, news	Bill Stern, sports	6:30
Lowell Thomas, news	The World Today	Stan Lomax, sports	Music You Want	6:45
The Falcon	I Love a Mystery	Fulton Lewis Jr., news	Chesterfield Time	7pm
	Chesterfield Time	Arthur Hale, news	John W. Vandercook, news	7:15
The Lone Ranger	Easy Aces	Can You Top This	Allen Roth Orchestra	7:30
	Mr. Keen, Tracer of Lost Persons		H. V. Kaltenborn, news	7:45
Earl Godwin, news	The New Old Gold Program, Monty Wooley	Sam Balter, news	Mr. and Mrs. North	8pm
Lum and Abner		Leo Cherne, news		8:15
Battle of the Sexes	Dr. Christian	Take a Card	Beat the Band	8:30
	Bill Henry, news (8:55pm)			8:45
The Fitch Bandwagon	The Mayor of the Town	Gabriel Heatter, news	Time to Smile, Eddie Cantor	9pm
		The Gracie Fields Victory Show		9:15
Spotlight Bands	The Jack Carson Show	Guess Who	Mr. District Attorney	9:30
Grace Morgan, songs (9:55pm)				9:45
Raymond Gram Swing, news	Great Moments in Music	John B. Hughes, news	Kay Kyser's College of Musical Knowledge	10pm
Public Affairs		Sunny Skylar, songs		10:15
Men's Store News	The Cresta Blanca Carnival	Paul Schubert, news		10:30
Letter to Your Service Man		The Longines Symphonette		10:45

EVENING — FALL, 1943

Thursday

	ABC	CBS	MBS	NBC
6pm	John B. Kennedy, news	Ned Calmer, news	Sydney Moseley, news	Jack Arthur, songs
6:15	Terry and the Pirates	Bob Becker's Dog Talks	Lanny and Ginger, songs	George Putnam, news
6:30	Welcome Lewis, songs	Jeri Sullavan, songs	Frank Singiser, news	Bill Stern, sports
6:45	Lowell Thomas, news	The World Today	Stan Lomax, sports	Music You Want
7pm	Wings to Victory	I Love a Mystery	Fulton Lewis Jr., news	Chesterfield Time
7:15		Chesterfield Time	Victory is Our Business	John W. Vandercook, news
7:30	Redd Evans Club Time	Easy Aces	Arthur Hale, news	The Bob Burns Show
7:45	Diane Courtney and the Jesters	Mr. Keen, Tracer of Lost Persons	The Answer Man	
8pm	Earl Godwin, news	The Roma Wine Show, Charlie Ruggles	The Better Half	Maxwell House Coffee Time, Brice and Morgan
8:15	Lum and Abner			
8:30	America's Town Meeting of the Air	Death Valley Days	The Human Adventure	The Aldrich Family
8:45		Bill Henry, news (8:55pm)		
9pm		Major Bowes' Original Amateur Hour	Gabriel Heatter, news	The Kraft Music Hall, Bing Crosby
9:15			The Gracie Fields Victory Show	
9:30	Spotlight Bands	The Birdseye Open House, Dinah Shore	You Tell 'em Club	The Sealtest Village Store, Davis and Haley
9:45	Grace Morgan, songs (9:55pm)			
10pm	Raymond Gram Swing, news	The First Line of Defense	Raymond Clapper, news	Abbott and Costello
10:15	Listen to Lulu		Dale Carnegie, inspirational	
10:30	Public Affairs	Here's to Romance, Dick Haymes	Paul Schubert, news	The March of Time
10:45			The Longines Symphonette	

EVENING — FALL, 1943

Friday

ABC	CBS	MBS	NBC	
John B. Kennedy, news	Quincy Howe, news	Sydney Moseley, news	Jack Arthur, songs	6pm
Terry and the Pirates	The Squibb Show	Lanny and Ginger, songs	George Putnam, news	6:15
The Singing Bee	Jeri Sullavan, songs	Frank Singiser, news	Bill Stern, sports	6:30
Lowell Thomas, news	The World Today	Stan Lomax, sports	Music You Want	6:45
Archie Andrews	I Love a Mystery	Fulton Lewis Jr., news	Chesterfield Time	7pm
	Dateline	Arthur Hale, news	John W. Vandercook, news	7:15
The Lone Ranger	Easy Aces	Variety Musicale	Allen Roth Orchestra	7:30
	Mr. Keen, Tracer of Lost Persons		H. V. Kaltenborn, news	7:45
Earl Godwin, news	The Kate Smith Hour	Sam Balter, news	The Cities Service Concerts	8pm
The Parker Family		Jimmy Walker, comment		8:15
Meet Your Navy		The Cisco Kid	Your All-Time Hit Parade	8:30
	Bill Henry, news (8:55pm)			8:45
Gangbusters	The Phillip Morris Playhouse	Gabriel Heatter, news	Waltz Time	9pm
		The Gracie Fields Victory Show		9:15
Spotlight Bands	That Brewster Boy	Double or Nothing	People Are Funny	9:30
Grace Morgan, songs (9:55pm)				9:45
John Gunther, news	The Durante - Moore Show	Cedric Foster, news	Amos 'n' Andy	10pm
Public Affairs		Sunny Skylar, songs		10:15
Men's Store News	Stage Door Canteen	Paul Schubert, news	The Colgate Sports Newsreel, Bill Stern	10:30
Letter to Your Service Man		The Longines Symphonette	The Missions of War	10:45

EVENING — FALL, 1943

Saturday

	ABC	CBS	MBS	NBC
6pm	John B. Kennedy, news	Quincy Howe, news	Sydney Moseley, news	Family Music Time
6:15	The Korn Kobblers	The People's Platform	Lanny and Ginger, songs	George Putnam, news
6:30			Frank Singiser, news	Religion in the News
6:45	Leon Henderson, news	The World Today	Stan Lomax, sports	Rupert Hughes, news
7pm	What's New	The Man Behind the Gun	Troman Harper, news	For This We Fight
7:15			The Black Castle	
7:30		Thanks to the Yanks	Arthur Hale, news	The Adventures of Ellery Queen
7:45			The Answer Man	
8pm	Roy Porter, news	Pabst Blue Ribbon Town, Groucho Marx	California Melodies	Abie's Irish Rose
8:15	Boston Symphony Orchestra			
8:30		Inner Sanctum Mysteries	Foreign Assignment	Truth or Consequences
8:45		Ned Calmer, news (8:55pm)		
9pm		Your Hit Parade	The Chicago Theater of the Air	The National Barn Dance
9:15	Edward Tomlinson, news			
9:30	Spotlight Bands			Can You Top This
9:45	Harry Wismer, sports (9:55PM)	Saturday Night Serenade		
10pm	John Gunther, news		John B. Hughes, news	The Million Dollar Band, Barry Woods
10:15	Army Service Forces Presents	Correction, Please	Saturday Night Bandwagon	
10:30				Grand Ole Opry
10:45	Betty Rann, songs	Public Affairs	Al Donahue Orchestra	

DAYTIME — FALL, 1943

Sunday

	ABC	CBS	MBS	NBC
9am	News	News	Fiesta Time	News
9:15	Coast-to-Coast on a Bus	From the Organ Loft		Ernesta Harlow, talk
9:30			The Navy Goes to Church	Marcia Nell, songs
9:45		God's Country		
10am	Message of Israel	The CBS Church of the Air	Henry Gladstone, news	The National Radio Pulpit
10:15			Frank Kingdon, news	
10:30	The Southernaires Quartet	Wings Over Jordan	Pauline Alpert, piano	The Horn and Hardart Children's Hour
10:45			Charles Hodges, news	
11am	Production Story	The Blue Jacket Choir	Marines in Review	
11:15				
11:30	The Hour of Faith	Invitation to Learning	The Mutual Radio Chapel	George Putnam, news
11:45				The Little Betsy Ross Girl Variety Program
12pm	Moments of Memory	The Salt Lake Tabernacle Choir	Soldiers With Wings	Tapestry Musicale
12:15	The Weekly War Journal			
12:30	Sammy Kaye's Sunday Serenade	Transatlantic Call	Soldiers of the Press	Stradivari Orchestra
12:45			Troman Harper, news	
1pm	Wake Up, America	The CBS Church of the Air	The Canary Pet Shop	Your Radio Reporter
1:15			Lorraine Sherwood, talk	Labor for Victory
1:30		Edward R. Murrow, news	Music for an Hour	The University of Chicago Round Table
1:45	Francis Drake, news	Curt Massey, songs		

DAYTIME — FALL, 1943

Monday-Friday

ABC	CBS	MBS	NBC	
The Breakfast Club	Joe King, news	Victor Lindlahr, health	Everything Goes, Garry Moore	9am
	The American School of the Air	Talk and Music		9:15
		Alfred W. McCann, food	Music	9:30
	This Life is Mine		Robert St. John, news	9:45
Isabel Manning Hewson, food	Valiant Lady	Henry Gladstone, news	Lora Lawton	10am
Roy Porter, news	Kitty Foyle	Bessy Beatty, talk	The Open Door	10:15
The Baby Institute	Amanda of Honeymoon Hill		Helpmate	10:30
Sweet River	Bachelor's Children		Music	10:45
Breakfast with Breneman	Mother and Dad / Mary Lee Taylor, cooking	Troman Harper, news	The Road of Life	11am
	Second Husband	Talk and Music	Vic and Sade	11:15
Gilbert Martyn, news	Bright Horizon	Music / The Quiz Wizard	Brave Tomorrow	11:30
Living Should Be Fun	Aunt Jenny's True Life Stories	Tobe's Topics / What's Your Idea	David Harum	11:45
Religious Talk	Kate Smith Speaks	Boake Carter, news	Don Goddard, news	12pm
Talk and Music / That's a Fact	Big Sister	Music / Jimmy Fidler, gossip	Recorded Music	12:15
The Farm and Home Hour	The Romance of Helen Trent	Alois Havrilla, news	Mirth and Madness, Jack Kirkwood	12:30
	Our Gal Sunday	The Handy Man		12:45
H. R. Baukhage, news	Life Can Be Beautiful	Ray Dady, news	Mary Margaret McBride, talk	1pm
The Women's Exchange	Ma Perkins	The Jack Berch Show		1:15
	Bernadine Flynn, news	Vincent Lopez Orchestra		1:30
Music	The Goldbergs		Carey Longmire, news	1:45

DAYTIME — FALL, 1943

Sunday

	ABC	CBS	MBS	NBC
2pm	Chaplain Jim, USA	Ceiling Unlimited		Those We Love
2:15				
2:30	National Vespers	World News Today	Troman Harper, news	The Westinghouse Program, John C. Thomas
2:45		Songs of America (2:55pm)	Melody Lane	
3pm	Those Good Old Days	New York Philharmonic Orchestra	This is Fort Dix	Report on Rationing
3:15	Hanson W. Baldwin, news			Upton Close, news
3:30	Hot Copy		Bulldog Drummond	The Army Hour
3:45				
4pm	The Metropolitan Opera Auditions		Here's Mexico	
4:15				
4:30	This is Official	The Pause That Refreshes	Murder Clinic	Lands of the Free
4:45				
5pm	Where Do We Stand	The Prudential Family Hour	Fireside Party	NBC Symphony Orchestra
5:15				
5:30	The Musical Steelmakers		The Shadow	
5:45		Irene Rich Dramas		

DAYTIME — FALL, 1943

Monday-Friday

ABC	CBS	MBS	NBC	
Rodriguez and Sutherland, news	Young Dr. Malone	Martha Deane, talk	The Guiding Light	2pm
The Mystery Chef	Joyce Jordan, MD		Lonely World	2:15
Ed East and Polly, songs	We Love and Learn	Maxine Keith, talk	The Light of the World	2:30
	Perry Mason		Betty Crocker, cooking /	2:45
The Coke Club, Morton Downey	The Story of Mary Marlin	Mary Foster	A Woman of America	3pm
My True Story	Elizabeth Bemis, news	Linda's First Love	Ma Perkins	3:15
	Now and Forever	Dr. Eddy's Food Forum	Pepper Young's Family	3:30
Between the Bookends	Green Valley, USA		The Right to Happiness	3:45
Blue Frolics	Your Home Front Reporter	Rambling with Gambling	Mary Noble, Backstage Wife	4pm
			Stella Dallas	4:15
Westbrook Van Voorhis, news	Something to Talk About	Full Speed Ahead	Lorenzo Jones	4:30
The Sea Hound	Perry Como, songs		Young Widder Brown	4:45
Hop Harrigan	The Eddie Dunn Show	Uncle Don	When a Girl Marries	5pm
Dick Tracy		The Black Hood	Portia Faces Life	5:15
Jack Armstrong, the All-American Boy	The Landt Trio and Curley	Chick Carter, Boy Detective	Just Plain Bill	5:30
Captain Midnight	American Women	The Adventures of Superman	Front Page Farrell	5:45

DAYTIME — FALL, 1943

Saturday

	ABC	CBS	MBS	NBC
9am	The Breakfast Club	Joe King, news	Songs for Saturday	Everything Goes, Garry Moore
9:15		Red Cross Reports	Victor Lindlahr, health	
9:30		The Garden Gate	Red River Dave	
9:45		Of Men and Books	Claire Wilson, news	
10am	Isabel Manning Hewison, food	Youth on Parade	Rainbow House	Nellie Revell Presents
10:15	The Greenfield Chapel Choir			Music
10:30	Alias John Freedom	Columbia's Country Journal		Baseball Quiz
10:45				Bob Becker's Dog Talks
11am	Xavier Cugat Orchestra	Let's Pretend	Prescott Robinson, news	The Hook and Ladder Follies
11:15			Music	
11:30	The Land of the Lost	Fashions in Rations, Billie Burke	Hello, Mom	The Coast Guard Academy Band
11:45				
12pm	Game Parade	The Armstrong Theater of Today	The Man on the Farm	Don Goddard, news
12:15				Consumer Time
12:30	The Farm and Home Hour	Stars Over Hollywood	Alois Havrilla, news	Mirth and Madness, Jack Kirkwood
12:45			Your OPA	
1pm	Swing Shift Frolics	Campana Serenade, Dick Powell	Ted Astor Orchestra	That They May Live
1:15				
1:30	Tommy Tucker Topics	Chip Davis, Commando	Vincent Lopez Orchestra	David Grupp Orchestra
1:45				Elmer W. Peterson, news

DAYTIME — FALL, 1943

Saturday

	ABC	CBS	MBS	NBC
2pm	Joe Rines Orchestra	Detroit Musicale	Lani McIntyre Orchestra	The Roy Shield Revue
2:15				
2:30		Sports	Sports	
2:45	Sports			Sports
3pm				
3:15				
3:30				
3:45				
4pm				
4:15				
4:30				
4:45				
5pm		It's Maritime	Uncle Don	
5:15			Bob Stanley Orchestra	
5:30	Tommy Tucker's Topics	Mother and Dad		The Three Suns
5:45			Eleanor King, news	W. W. Chaplin, news

LISTINGS FOR 1944

EVENING — WINTER, 1944

Sunday

	ABC	CBS	MBS	NBC
6pm	The Radio Hall of Fame	The Silver Theater	The First Nighter Program	The Catholic Hour
6:15				
6:30		America in the Air	Upton Close, news	The Great Gildersleeve
6:45			The Little Show, Robert Q. Lewis	
7pm	Drew Pearson, news	William L. Shirer, news	The Mysterious Traveler	The Grape Nuts Program, Jack Benny
7:15	Dorothy Thompson, news	Columbia Presents Perry Como		
7:30	The Quiz Kids	We, the People	Frank Singiser, news	The Fitch Bandwagon
7:45			Samuel Grafton, news	
8pm	The Greenfield Chapel Choir	The Jerry Lester Show	A. L. Alexander's Mediation Board	The Charlie McCarthy Show
8:15	The Ink Spots			
8:30	Keepsakes, Dorothy Kirsten	Crime Doctor		One Man's Family
8:45		Ned Calmer, news (8:55pm)	Gabriel Heatter, news	
9pm	Walter Winchell's Jergens Journal	The Radio Reader's Digest	Cleveland Symphony Orchestra	The Manhattan Merry-Go-Round
9:15	The Chamber Music Society of Lower Basin Street			
9:30		The Texaco Star Theater, Fred Allen		The American Album of Familiar Music
9:45	Jimmy Fidler, gossip			
10pm	The Gertrude Lawrence Theater	Take It or Leave It	Cedric Foster, news	The Hour of Charm
10:15			The Goodwill Hour	
10:30	America Tomorrow	Congress Speaks	Paul Schubert, news	The Raleigh Cigarette Program, Red Skelton
10:45		Report on Radio	The Longines Symphonette	

EVENING — WINTER, 1944

Monday

ABC	CBS	MBS	NBC	
John B. Kennedy, news	Quincy Howe, news	Sydney Moseley, news	George Putnam, news	6pm
Terry and the Pirates	The Squibb Show	Lanny and Ginger, songs	Serenade to America	6:15
Whose War is This	Jeri Sullavan, songs	Frank Singiser, news		6:30
Henry J. Taylor, news	The World Today	Stan Lomax, sports	Lowell Thomas, news	6:45
Horace Heidt Orchestra	I Love a Mystery	Fulton Lewis Jr., news	Chesterfield Time	7pm
	Ed Sullivan Entertains	Arthur Hale, news	John W. Vandercook, news	7:15
The Lone Ranger	Blondie	It Pays to Be Ignorant	Allen Roth Orchestra	7:30
			H. V. Kaltenborn, news	7:45
Earl Godwin, news	Vox Pop	Sam Balter, news	The Cavalcade of America	8pm
Lum and Abner		Fulton Oursler, news		8:15
Blind Date	The Gay Nineties Revue	Sherlock Holmes	The Voice of Firestone	8:30
	Bill Henry, news (8:55pm)			8:45
Counterspy	The Lux Radio Theater	Gabriel Heatter, news	The Bell Telephone Hour	9pm
		Believe It or Not		9:15
Spotlight Bands		The Paul Winchell - Jerry Mahoney Show	Dr. I. Q., The Mental Banker	9:30
Short Story (9:55pm)				9:45
Raymond Gram Swing, news	The Lady Esther Screen Guild Theater	Henry Gladstone, news	The Carnation Contented Hour	10pm
Out of the Shadows		A New Birth of Freedom		10:15
Star for a Night	The Cresta Blanca Carnival	Paul Schubert, news		10:30
		The Longines Symphonette		10:45

EVENING — WINTER, 1944

Tuesday

	ABC	CBS	MBS	NBC
6pm	John B. Kennedy, news	Quincy Howe, news	Sydney Moseley, news	George Putnam, news
6:15	Terry and the Pirates	Edwin C. Hill, news	Lanny and Ginger, songs	Serenade to America
6:30	Whose War is This	Jack Smith, songs	Frank Singiser, news	
6:45	Henry J. Taylor news	The World Today	Stan Lomax, sports	Lowell Thomas, news
7pm	Awake at the Switch	I Love a Mystery	Fulton Lewis Jr., news	Chesterfield Time
7:15		Chesterfield Time	Foreign Correspondent	John W. Vandercook, news
7:30	The Girl Back Home	The American Melody Hour	Arthur Hale, news	Everything for the Boys
7:45	Diane Courtney and the Jesters		The Answer Man	
8pm	Earl Godwin, news	Big Town	The Black Castle	The Purple Heart Show, Ginny Simms
8:15	Lum and Abner		Fulton Oursler, news	
8:30	Duffy's Tavern	The Judy Canova Show	Battle of the Burroughs	A Date with Judy
8:45		Bill Henry, news (8:55pm)		
9pm	Famous Jury Trials	Burns and Allen	Gabriel Heatter, news	The Molle' Mystery Theater
9:15			Believe It or Not	
9:30	Spotlight Bands	Report to the Nation	The American Forum of the Air	Fibber Magee and Molly
9:45	Short Story (9:55pm)			
10pm	Raymond Gram Swing, news	Theater Guild Dramas		The Pepsodent Show, Bob Hope
10:15	Chester Bowles, news		Jimmy Walker, comment	
10:30	America Tomorrow	Congress Speaks	Paul Schubert, news	The Raleigh Cigarette Program, Red Skelton
10:45		Report on Radio	The Longines Symphonette	

EVENING — WINTER, 1944

Wednesday

ABC	CBS	MBS	NBC	
John B. Kennedy, news	Quincy Howe, news	Sydney Moseley, news	George Putnam, news	6pm
Terry and the Pirates	The Squibb Show	Lanny and Ginger, songs	Serenade to America	6:15
Whose War is This	Ely Culbertson, talk	Frank Singiser, news		6:30
Henry J. Taylor, news	The World Today	Stan Lomax, sports	Lowell Thomas, news	6:45
The Connee Boswell Show	I Love a Mystery	Fulton Lewis Jr., news	Chesterfield Time	7pm
	Chesterfield Time	Arthur Hale, news	John W. Vandercook, news	7:15
The Lone Ranger	Easy Aces	Can You Top This	Allen Roth Orchestra	7:30
			H. V. Kaltenborn, news	7:45
Earl Godwin, news	The New Old Gold Program, Monty Wooley	Sam Balter, news	Mr. and Mrs. North	8pm
Lum and Abner		Fulton Oursler, news		8:15
Battle of the Sexes	Dr. Christian	Xavier Cugat Orchestra	Beat the Band	8:30
	Bill Henry, news (8:55pm)			8:45
Dunninger, the Mentalist	Songs By Sinatra	Gabriel Heatter, news	Time to Smile, Eddie Cantor	9pm
		Believe It or Not		9:15
Spotlight Bands	The Jack Carson Show	Guess Who	Mr. District Attorney	9:30
Short Story (9:55pm)				9:45
Raymond Gram Swing, news	Great Moments in Music	Royal Arch Gunnison, news	Kay Kyser's College of Musical Knowledge	10pm
Kay Armen Sings		Arch Ward, sports		10:15
Star for a Night	The Cresta Blanca Carnival	Paul Schubert, news		10:30
		The Longines Symphonette		10:45

EVENING — WINTER, 1944

Thursday

	ABC	CBS	MBS	NBC
6pm	John B. Kennedy, news	Ned Calmer, news	Sydney Moseley, news	George Putnam, news
6:15	Terry and the Pirates	Bob Becker's Dog Talks	Lanny and Ginger, songs	Serenade to America
6:30	Whose War is This	Jeri Sullavan, songs	Frank Singiser, news	
6:45	Henry J. Taylor, news	The World Today	Stan Lomax, sports	Lowell Thomas, news
7pm	The House on Q Street	I Love a Mystery	Fulton Lewis Jr., news	Chesterfield Time
7:15		Chesterfield Time	Victory is Our Business	John W. Vandercook, news
7:30	The Air Lane Trio	Mr. Keen, Tracer of Lost Persons	Arthur Hale, news	The Bob Burns Show
7:45	Diane Courtney and the Jesters		The Answer Man	
8pm	Earl Godwin, news	Suspense	The Black Castle	Maxwell House Coffee Time, Brice and Morgan
8:15	Lum and Abner		Fulton Oursler, news	
8:30	America's Town Meeting of the Air	Death Valley Days	The Human Adventure	The Aldrich Family
8:45		Bill Henry, news (8:55pm)		
9pm		Major Bowes' Original Amateur Hour	Gabriel Heatter, news	The Kraft Music Hall, Bing Crosby
9:15			Believe It or Not	
9:30	Spotlight Bands	The Birdseye Open House, Dinah Shore	The Treasure Hour of Song	The Sealtest Village Store, Davis and Haley
9:45	Short Story (9:55pm)			
10pm	Raymond Gram Swing, news	The First Line of Defense	Henry Gladstone, news	Abbott and Costello
10:15	Kay Armen Sings		Dale Carnegie, inspirational	
10:30	Wings to Victory	Here's to Romance, Dick Haymes	Paul Schubert, news	The March of Time
10:45			The Longines Symphonette	

EVENING — WINTER, 1944

Friday

ABC	CBS	MBS	NBC	
John B. Kennedy, news	Quincy Howe, news	Sydney Moseley, news	George Putnam, news	6pm
Terry and the Pirates	The Squibb Show	Lanny and Ginger, songs	Serenade to America	6:15
Whose War is This	Jeri Sullavan, songs	Frank Singiser, news		6:30
Henry J. Taylor, news	The World Today	Stan Lomax, sports	Lowell Thomas, news	6:45
The Adventures of Nero Wolfe	I Love a Mystery	Fulton Lewis Jr., news	Chesterfield Time	7pm
	Dateline	Arthur Hale, news	John W. Vandercook, news	7:15
The Lone Ranger	Friday on Broadway	Variety Musicale	Allen Roth Orchestra	7:30
			H. V. Kaltenborn, news	7:45
Earl Godwin, news	The Kate Smith Hour	Sam Balter, news	The Cities Service Concerts	8pm
The Parker Family		Fulton Oursler, news		8:15
Meet Your Navy		Freedom of Opportunity	Your All-Time Hit Parade	8:30
	Bill Henry, news (8:55pm)			8:45
Gangbusters	The Phillip Morris Playhouse	Gabriel Heatter, news	Waltz Time	9pm
		Believe It or Not		9:15
Spotlight Bands	That Brewster Boy	Double or Nothing	People Are Funny	9:30
Short Story (9:55pm)				9:45
John W. Vandercook, news	The Durante - Moore Show	Cedric Foster, news	Amos 'n' Andy	10pm
Listen to Lulu		Sunny Skylar, songs		10:15
Letter to Your Service Man	Stage Door Canteen	Paul Schubert, news	The Colgate Sports Newsreel, Bill Stern	10:30
The Girl Back Home		The Longines Symphonette	The Missions of War	10:45

EVENING — WINTER, 1944

Saturday

	ABC	CBS	MBS	NBC
6pm	John B. Kennedy, news	Quincy Howe, news	Sydney Moseley, news	George Putnam, news
6:15	Storyland Theater	The People's Platform	Lanny and Ginger, songs	Recorded Music
6:30	Andy Russell, songs		Frank Singiser, news	The Three Suns
6:45	Leon Henderson, news	The World Today	Stan Lomax, sports	Religion in the News
7pm	What's New	The Man Behind the Gun	The Return of Nick Carter	The American Story Teller
7:15				
7:30		Thanks to the Yanks	Arthur Hale, news	The Adventures of Ellery Queen
7:45			The Answer Man	
8pm	Early American Dance Music	Pabst Blue Ribbon Town, Groucho Marx	The Black Castle	Abie's Irish Rose
8:15	Edward Tomlinson, news		Stan Lomax, sports	
8:30	Boston Symphony Orchestra	Inner Sanctum Mysteries	The Cisco Kid	Truth or Consequences
8:45		Ned Calmer, news (8:55pm)		
9pm		Your Hit Parade	The Chicago Theater of the Air	The National Barn Dance
9:15				
9:30	Spotlight Bands			Can You Top This
9:45	Quick Quiz (9:55pm)	Saturday Night Serenade		
10pm	John W. Vandercook, news		Royal Arch Gunnison, news	The Million Dollar Band, Barry Woods
10:15	Army Service Forces Presents	Correction, Please	Saturday Night Bandwagon	
10:30				Grand Ole Opry
10:45	Betty Rann, songs	Public Affairs	Leo Cherne, news	

DAYTIME — WINTER, 1944

Sunday

	ABC	CBS	MBS	NBC
9am	News	News	California Melodies	News
9:15	Coast-to-Coast on a Bus	From the Organ Loft		Ernesta Harlow, talk
9:30			The Navy Goes to Church	June Winters, songs
9:45		New Voices in Song		Music
10am	Message of Israel	The CBS Church of the Air	Henry Gladstone, news	The National Radio Pulpit
10:15			Frank Kingdon, news	
10:30	The Southernaires Quartet	Wings Over Jordan	The Mutual Radio Chapel	The Horn and Hardart Children's Hour
10:45				
11am	What's Your War Job	The Blue Jacket Choir	Marines in Revue	
11:15				
11:30	The Hour of Faith	Invitation to Learning	Pauline Alpert, piano	George Putnam, news
11:45			John Stanley, news	The Little Betsy Ross Girl Variety Program
12pm	The Weekly War Journal	The Salt Lake Tabernacle Choir	Soldiers With Wings	Tapestry Musicale
12:15				
12:30	Moments of Memory	Transatlantic Call	Soldiers of the Press	Stradivari Orchestra
12:45	The Moylan Sisters, songs		Troman Harper, news	
1pm	John B. Kennedy, news	The CBS Church of the Air	The Canary Pet Shop	Your Radio Reporter
1:15	Music By Marias		Lorraine Sherwood, talk	Labor for Victory
1:30	Sammy Kaye's Sunday Serenade	Edward R. Murrow, news	Music for an Hour	The University of Chicago Round Table
1:45		Public Affairs		

DAYTIME — WINTER, 1944

Monday-Friday

ABC	CBS	MBS	NBC	
The Breakfast Club	Joe King, news	Victor Lindlahr, health	Mirth and Madness, Jack Kirkwood	*9am*
	The American School of the Air	Talk and Music		*9:15*
		Alfred W. McCann, food	Adelaide Hawley, talk	*9:30*
	Isabel Manning Hewson, food		Riohard Harkness, news	*9:45*
Sweet River	Valiant Lady	Henry Gladstone, news	Lora Lawton	*10am*
Paul Neilson, news	Kitty Foyle	Bessy Beatty, talk	The World's Greatest Stories	*10:15*
The Baby Institute	The Open Door		Helpmate	*10:30*
The Humbard Family, songs	Bachelor's Children		Tommy Taylor, songs	*10:45*
Breakfast with Breneman	Amanda of Honeymoon Hill	Troman Harper, news	The Road of Life	*11am*
	Second Husband	Talk and Music	Vic and Sade	*11:15*
Gilbert Martyn, news	Bright Horizon	The Quiz Wizard / Pegeen Presents	Brave Tomorrow	*11:30*
Living Should Be Fun	Aunt Jenny's True Life Stories	Tobe's Topics / What's Your Idea	David Harum	*11:45*
Religious Talk	Kate Smith Speaks	Boake Carter, news	Don Goddard, news	*12pm*
Talk and Music / That's a Fact	Big Sister	Mealtime Melodies	Music	*12:15*
The Farm and Home Hour	The Romance of Helen Trent	Alois Havrilla, news		*12:30*
	Our Gal Sunday	The Handy Man		*12:45*
H. R. Baukhage, news	Life Can Be Beautiful	Ray Dady, news	Mary Margaret McBride, talk	*1pm*
The Women's Exchange	Ma Perkins	The Jack Berch Show		*1:15*
	Bernadine Flynn, news	Vincent Lopez Orchestra		*1:30*
Music / Songs	The Goldbergs		Carey Longmire, news	*1:45*

DAYTIME — WINTER, 1944

Sunday

	ABC	CBS	MBS	NBC
2pm	Chaplain Jim, USA	Ceiling Unlimited		Those We Love
2:15				
2:30	National Vespers	World News Today	Troman Harper, news	The Westinghouse Program, John C. Thomas
2:45		Songs of America (2:55pm)	Melody Lane	
3pm	The Life of Riley	New York Philharmonic Orchestra	This is Fort Dix	Report on Rationing
3:15				Upton Close, news
3:30	Hot Copy		Bulldog Drummond	The Army Hour
3:45				
4pm	Fun Valley, Al Pearce		The Show of the Week	
4:15				
4:30	The Metropolitan Opera Auditions	The Pause That Refreshes	The Abe Lincoln Story	Lands of the Free
4:45				
5pm	Where Do We Stand	The Prudential Family Hour	Fireside Party	NBC Symphony Orchestra
5:15				
5:30	The Musical Steelmakers		The Shadow	
5:45		Irene Rich Dramas		

DAYTIME — WINTER, 1944

Monday-Friday

ABC	CBS	MBS	NBC	
Rodriguez and Sutherland, news	Young Dr. Malone	Martha Deane, talk	The Guiding Light	2pm
The Mystery Chef	Joyce Jordan, MD		Today's Children	2:15
Ed East and Polly, songs	We Love and Learn	Maxine Keith, talk	The Light of the World	2:30
	Perry Mason		Betty Crocker, cooking /	2:45
The Coke Club, Morton Downey	The Story of Mary Marlin	Mary Foster	A Woman of America	3pm
My True Story	Elizabeth Bemis, news	Linda's First Love	Ma Perkins	3:15
	Now and Forever	Dr. Eddy's Food Forum	Pepper Young's Family	3:30
Little Jack Little Orchestra	This Life is Mine		The Right to Happiness	3:45
Blue Frolics /	Broadway Matinee	Rambling with Gambling	Mary Noble, Backstage Wife	4pm
The Ozark Ramblers			Stella Dallas	4:15
Westbrook Van Voorhis, news	Music	Talk and Music	Lorenzo Jones	4:30
The Sea Hound	Raymond Scott Orchestra		Young Widder Brown	4:45
Hop Harrigan	The Eddie Dunn Show	Uncle Don	When a Girl Marries	5pm
Dick Tracy		Archie Andrews	Portia Faces Life	5:15
Jack Armstrong, the All-American Boy	The Landt Trio and Curley	Chick Carter, Boy Detective	Just Plain Bill	5:30
Captain Midnight	American Women	The Adventures of Superman	Front Page Farrell	5:45

DAYTIME — WINTER, 1944

Saturday

	ABC	CBS	MBS	NBC
9am	The Breakfast Club	Joe King, news	Songs for Saturday	The First Piano Quartet
9:15		The Garden Gate	Lorraine Sherwood, talk	
9:30			Red River Dave	Adelaide Hawley, talk
9:45		Isabel Manning Hewson, food	Claire Wilson, news	Paranov Orchestra
10am	The Yankee Doodle Quiz	Youth on Parade	Rainbow House	The Road to Danger
10:15				
10:30	The Green Hornet	Mary Lee Taylor, cooking		Saturday Showdown
10:45				Bob Becker's Dog Talks
11am	On Stage America	Let's Pretend	Prescott Robinson, news	The Hook and Laddie Follies
11:15			Music	
11:30	The Land of the Lost	Fashions in Rations, Billie Burke	Hollywood Melodies	Lighted Windows
11:45				
12pm	The Little Blue Playhouse	The Armstrong Theater of Today	The Man on the Farm	Don Goddard, news
12:15				Consumer Time
12:30	The Farm and Home Hour	Stars Over Hollywood	Alois Havrilla, news	Atlantic Spotlight
12:45			Your OPA	
1pm	Horace Heidt Orchestra	Campana Serenade, Dick Powell	Treasury Varieties	Here's to Youth
1:15				
1:30		Aunt Jemima	Vincent Lopez Orchestra	The Baxters
1:45		The Burl Ives Show		Elmer W. Peterson, news

DAYTIME — WINTER, 1944

Saturday

	ABC	CBS	MBS	NBC
2pm	The Metropolitan Opera	Of Men and Books	Lani McIntyre Orchestra	The Roy Shield Revue
2:15				
2:30		Calling Pan-America	George Duffy Orchestra	The Grantland Rice Story
2:45				
3pm		Columbia's Country Journal	This is Halloran	Orchestras of the Nation
3:15				
3:30		Philadelphia Symphony Orchestra	The Army-Navy House Party	
3:45				
4pm			Shep Fields Orchestra	Rupert Hughes, news
4:15				Harold Fleming, news
4:30		Colonel Stoopnagle	For Parents Only	Doctors at War
4:45				
5pm		Meet Corliss Archer	Uncle Don	Your America
5:15			Jan Garber Orchestra	
5:30	Ted Fio Rito Orchestra	Mother and Dad		Cesar Saerchinger, news
5:45	Hello Sweetheart, Nancy Martin		Eleanor King, news	Curt Massey, songs

EVENING — SPRING, 1944

Sunday

	ABC	CBS	MBS	NBC
6pm	The Radio Hall of Fame	The Silver Theater	Roosty of the AAF	The Catholic Hour
6:15				
6:30		America in the Air	Upton Close, news	The Great Gildersleeve
6:45			Stanley Maxted, talk	
7pm	Drew Pearson, news	William L. Shirer, news	The Mysterious Traveler	The Grape Nuts Program, Jack Benny
7:15	Dorothy Thompson, news	Columbia Presents Perry Como		
7:30	The Quiz Kids	We, the People	Frank Singiser, news	The Fitch Bandwagon
7:45			Samuel Grafton, news	
8pm	The Greenfield Chapel Choir	The Star and the Story	A. L. Alexander's Mediation Board	The Charlie McCarthy Show
8:15	Andy Russell, songs			
8:30	Keepsakes, Dorothy Kirsten	Crime Doctor		One Man's Family
8:45		Ned Calmer, news (8:55pm)	Gabriel Heatter, news	
9pm	Walter Winchell's Jergens Journal	The Radio Reader's Digest	Cleveland Symphony Orchestra	The Manhattan Merry-Go-Round
9:15	The Chamber Music Society of Lower Basin Street			
9:30		The Texaco Star Theater, Fred Allen		The American Album of Familiar Music
9:45	Jimmy Fidler, gossip			
10pm	Listen, the Women	Take It or Leave It	Cedric Foster, news	The Hour of Charm
10:15			The Goodwill Hour	
10:30	Guy Lombardo Orchestra	The Adventures of the Thin Man		Bob Crosby Orchestra
10:45				

EVENING — SPRING, 1944

Monday

ABC	CBS	MBS	NBC	
John B. Kennedy, news	Harry Marble, news	Sydney Moseley, news	George Putnam, news	6pm
Terry and the Pirates	The Squibb Show	Imogene Carpenter, songs	Serenade to America	6:15
Whose War is This	Arthur Godfrey, songs	Frank Singiser, news		6:30
Henry J. Taylor, news	The World Today	Stan Lomax, sports	Lowell Thomas, news	6:45
Horace Heidt Orchestra	I Love a Mystery	Fulton Lewis Jr., news	Chesterfield Time	7pm
	Ed Sullivan Entertains	The Answer Man	John W. Vandercook,	7:15
The Lone Ranger	Blondie	The Bright Lights of New York, Louis Sobel	Allen Roth Orchestra	7:30
			H. V. Kaltenborn, news	7:45
Earl Godwin, news	Vox Pop	Cecil Brown, news	The Cavalcade of America	8pm
Lum and Abner		Fulton Oursler, news		8:15
Blind Date	The Gay Nineties Revue	Sherlock Holmes	The Voice of Firestone	8:30
	Bill Henry, news (8:55pm)			8:45
Counterspy	The Lux Radio Theater	Gabriel Heatter, news	The Bell Telephone Hour	9pm
		The Return of Nick Carter		9:15
Spotlight Bands		The Paul Winchell - Jerry Mahoney Show	Information, Please	9:30
Short Story (9:55pm)				9:45
Raymond Gram Swing, news	The Lady Esther Screen Guild Theater	Henry Gladstone, news	The Carnation Contented Hour	10pm
Top of the Evening		The Insider		10:15
The Hollywood Radio Theater	Broadway Showtime, William Gaxton	The Longines Symphonette	Dr. I. Q., The Mental Banker	10:30
				10:45

EVENING — SPRING, 1944

Tuesday

	ABC	CBS	MBS	NBC
6pm	John B. Kennedy, news	Harry Marble, news	Sydney Moseley, news	George Putnam, news
6:15	Terry and the Pirates	Edwin C. Hill, news	Imogene Carpenter, songs	Serenade to America
6:30	Whose War is This	Jack Smith, songs	Frank Singiser, news	
6:45	Henry J. Taylor news	The World Today	Stan Lomax, sports	Lowell Thomas, news
7pm	Let Yourself Go, Milton Berle	I Love a Mystery	Fulton Lewis Jr., news	Chesterfield Time
7:15		The Passing Parade	Ted Steele Records	John W. Vandercook, news
7:30	Diane Courtney and the Jesters	The American Melody Hour	Arthur Hale, news	Everything for the Boys
7:45	Josef Stopek Orchestra		The Answer Man	
8pm	Earl Godwin, news	Big Town	Paul Schubert, news	The Purple Heart Show, Ginny Simms
8:15	Lum and Abner		Fulton Oursler, news	
8:30	Duffy's Tavern	The Judy Canova Show	Pick and Pat Time	A Date with Judy
8:45		Bill Henry, news (8:55pm)		
9pm	Famous Jury Trials	Burns and Allen	Gabriel Heatter, news	The Molle' Mystery Theater
9:15			The Return of Nick Carter	
9:30	Spotlight Bands	Report to the Nation	The American Forum of the Air	Fibber Magee and Molly
9:45	Short Story (9:55pm)			
10pm	Raymond Gram Swing, news	Columbia Presents Corwin		The Pepsodent Show, Bob Hope
10:15	Ilene Woods, songs		The Insider	
10:30	Creeps By Night	Congress Speaks	The Longines Symphonette	The Raleigh Cigarette Program, Red Skelton
10:45		Guy Lombardo Orchestra		

EVENING — SPRING, 1944

Wednesday

ABC	CBS	MBS	NBC	
John B. Kennedy, news	Harry Marble, news	Sydney Moseley, news	George Putnam, news	6pm
Terry and the Pirates	The Squibb Show	Imogene Carpenter, songs	Serenade to America	6:15
Whose War is This	Arthur Godfrey, songs	Frank Singiser, news		6:30
Henry J. Taylor, news	The World Today	Stan Lomax, sports	Lowell Thomas, news	6:45
The Connee Boswell Show	I Love a Mystery	Fulton Lewis Jr., news	Chesterfield Time	7pm
	The Passing Parade	The Answer Man	John W. Vandercook, news	7:15
The Lone Ranger	Easy Aces	Can You Top This	Allen Roth Orchestra	7:30
			H. V. Kaltenborn, news	7:45
Earl Godwin, news	The New Old Gold Program, Allan Jones	Cecil Brown, news	Mr. and Mrs. North	8pm
Lum and Abner		Fulton Oursler, news		8:15
My Best Girls	Dr. Christian	Xavier Cugat Orchestra	Beat the Band	8:30
	Bill Henry, news (8:55pm)			8:45
Dunninger, the Mentalist	Songs By Sinatra	Gabriel Heatter, news	Time to Smile, Eddie Cantor	9pm
		The Return of Nick Carter		9:15
Spotlight Bands	The Jack Carson Show	The First Nighter Program	Mr. District Attorney	9:30
Short Story (9:55pm)				9:45
Raymond Gram Swing, news	Great Moments in Music	Royal Arch Gunnison, news	Kay Kyser's College of Musical Knowledge	10pm
Top of the Evening		Arch Ward, sports		10:15
Soldiers With Wings	The Cresta Blanca Carnival	The Longines Symphonette		10:30
				10:45

EVENING — SPRING, 1944

Thursday

	ABC	CBS	MBS	NBC
6pm	John B. Kennedy, news	Ned Calmer, news	Sydney Moseley, news	George Putnam, news
6:15	Terry and the Pirates	Bob Becker's Dog Talks	Imogene Carpenter, songs	Serenade to America
6:30	Whose War is This	Jeri Sullavan, songs	Frank Singiser, news	
6:45	Henry J. Taylor, news	The World Today	Stan Lomax, sports	Lowell Thomas, news
7pm	Kelly's Courthouse	I Love a Mystery	Fulton Lewis, Jr., news	Chesterfield Time
7:15		The Passing Parade	Victory is Our Business	John W. Vandercook, news
7:30	Diane Courtney and the Jesters	Mr. Keen, Tracer of Lost Persons	Arthur Hale, news	The Bob Burns Show
7:45	Josef Stopek Orchestra		The Answer Man	
8pm	Earl Godwin, news	Suspense	Paul Schubert, news	Maxwell House Coffee Time, Brice and Morgan
8:15	Lum and Abner		Fulton Oursler, news	
8:30	America's Town Meeting of the Air	Death Valley Days	The Human Adventure	The Aldrich Family
8:45		Bill Henry, news (8:55pm)		
9pm		Major Bowes' Original Amateur Hour	Gabriel Heatter, news	The Kraft Music Hall, Bing Crosby
9:15			The Return of Nick Carter	
9:30	Spotlight Bands	The Birdseye Open House, Dinah Shore	The Treasure Hour of Song	The Sealtest Village Store, Davis and Haley
9:45	Short Story (9:55pm)			
10pm	Raymond Gram Swing, news	The First Line of Defense	Henry Gladstone, news	Abbott and Costello
10:15	Ilene Woods, songs		Dale Carnegie, inspirational	
10:30	Stop and Go	Here's to Romance, Dick Haymes	The Longines Symphonette	The March of Time
10:45				

EVENING — SPRING, 1944

Friday

ABC	CBS	MBS	NBC	
John B. Kennedy, news	Quincy Howe, news	Sydney Moseley, news	George Putnam, news	6pm
Terry and the Pirates	The Squibb Show	Imogene Carpenter, songs	Serenade to America	6:15
Whose War is This	Arthur Godfrey, songs	Frank Singiser, news		6:30
Henry J. Taylor, news	The World Today	Stan Lomax, sports	Lowell Thomas, news	6:45
The Adventures of Nero Wolfe	I Love a Mystery	Fulton Lewis, Jr., news	Chesterfield Time	7pm
	We, Who Dream	Arthur Hale, news	John W. Vandercook, news	7:15
The Lone Ranger	Friday on Broadway	Variety Musicale	Allen Roth Orchestra	7:30
			H. V. Kaltenborn, news	7:45
Earl Godwin, news	The Kate Smith Hour	Cecil Brown, news	The Cities Service Concerts	8pm
The Parker Family		Fulton Oursler, news		8:15
Meet Your Navy		Freedom of Opportunity	Your All-Time Hit Parade	8:30
	Bill Henry, news (8:55pm)			8:45
Gangbusters	It Pays to Be Ignorant	Gabriel Heatter, news	Waltz Time	9pm
		The Return of Nick Carter		9:15
Spotlight Bands	That Brewster Boy	Double or Nothing	People Are Funny	9:30
Short Story (9:55pm)				9:45
Leland Stowe, news	The Durante - Moore Show	Cedric Foster, news	Amos 'n' Andy	10pm
Top of the Evening		The Insider		10:15
Letter to Your Service Man	Stage Door Canteen	The Longines Symphonette	The Colgate Sports Newsreel, Bill Stern	10:30
Concert Ensemble			Public Affairs	10:45

EVENING — SPRING, 1944

Saturday

	ABC	CBS	MBS	NBC
6pm	John B. Kennedy, news	Quincy Howe, news	Sydney Moseley, news	George Putnam, news
6:15	Storyland Theater	The People's Platform	Public Affairs	The Hollywood Theater
6:30	The Ink Spots		Frank Singiser, news	The Three Suns
6:45	Leon Henderson, news	The World Today	Stan Lomax, sports	Religion in the News
7pm	Those Good Ol' Days	The Mayor of the Town	Guess Who	The American Story Teller
7:15				
7:30	Music America Loves	Thanks to the Yanks	Arthur Hale, news	The Adventures of Ellery Queen
7:45			The Answer Man	
8pm	Early American Dance Music	Pabst Blue Ribbon Town, Groucho Marx	Bob Stanley Orchestra	Abie's Irish Rose
8:15	Edward Tomlinson, news			
8:30	Boston Symphony Orchestra	Inner Sanctum Mysteries	The Cisco Kid	Truth or Consequences
8:45		Ned Calmer, news (8:55pm)		
9pm		Your Hit Parade	The Chicago Theater of the Air	The National Barn Dance
9:15				
9:30	Spotlight Bands			Can You Top This
9:45	Quick Quiz (9:55pm)	Saturday Night Serenade		
10pm	Leland Stowe, news		Royal Arch Gunnison, news	Palmolive Party, Barry Woods and Patsy Kelly
10:15	Army Service Forces Presents	Correction, Please	True Detective Mysteries	
10:30				Grand Ole Opry
10:45	Harry Wismer, sports	Public Affairs	Leo Cherne, news	

DAYTIME — SPRING, 1944

Sunday

	ABC	CBS	MBS	NBC
9am	News	News	The Silver Strings	News
9:15	Coast-to-Coast on a Bus	From the Organ Loft		Ernesta Barlow, talk
9:30			The Navy Goes to Church	Alice Cornell, songs
9:45		New Voices in Song		Music
10am	Message of Israel	The CBS Church of the Air	Henry Gladstone, news	The National Radio Pulpit
10:15			Frank Kingdon, news	
10:30	The Southernaires Quartet	Wings Over Jordan	The Mutual Radio Chapel	The Horn and Hardart Children's Hour
10:45				
11am	What's Your War Job	The Blue Jacket Choir	Marines in Review	
11:15				
11:30	The Hour of Faith	Invitation to Learning	California Melodies	Don Hollenbeck, news
11:45				The Little Betsy Ross Girl Variety Program
12pm	The Weekly War Journal	The Salt Lake Tabernacle Choir	The Show Shop	Tapestry Musicale
12:15				
12:30	Moments of Memory	Transatlantic Call	Soldiers of the Press	Stradivari Orchestra
12:45	The Moylan Sisters, songs		Troman Harper, news	
1pm	John B. Kennedy, news	The CBS Church of the Air	The Canary Pet Shop	Your Radio Reporter
1:15	Music By Marias		Lorraine Sherwood, talk	Labor for Victory
1:30	Sammy Kaye's Sunday Serenade	Edward R. Murrow, news	Music for an Hour	The University of Chicago Round Table
1:45		Health Talk		

DAYTIME — SPRING, 1944

Monday-Friday

ABC	CBS	MBS	NBC	
The Breakfast Club	Joe King, news	Victor Lindlahr, health	Mirth and Madness, Jack Kirkwood	9am
	The American School of the Air	Talk and Music		9:15
		Alfred W. McCann, food	Adelaide Hawley, talk	9:30
	Isabel Manning Hewson, food		Alice Cornell, songs	9:45
Sweet River	Valiant Lady	Henry Gladstone, news	Lora Lawton	10am
My True Story	Kitty Foyle	Bessy Beatty, talk	Robert St. John, news	10:15
	The Open Door		Helpmate	10:30
Songs / Listening Post	Bachelor's Children		Tommy Taylor, songs	10:45
Breakfast with Breneman	Amanda of Honeymoon Hill	Troman Harper, news	The Road of Life	11am
	Second Husband	Talk and Music	Vic and Sade	11:15
Gilbert Martyn, news	Bright Horizon	The Quiz Wizard / Pegeen Presents	Brave Tomorrow	11:30
The Baby Institute	Aunt Jenny's True Life Stories	Tobe's Topics / What's Your Idea	David Harum	11:45
Religious Talk	Kate Smith Speaks	Boake Carter, news	Don Goddard, news	12pm
Music	Big Sister	Mealtime Melodies	Music	12:15
The Farm and Home Hour	The Romance of Helen Trent	Henry Gladstone, news		12:30
	Our Gal Sunday	The Juke Box		12:45
H. R. Baukhage, news	Life Can Be Beautiful	Ray Dady, news	Mary Margaret McBride, talk	1pm
The Women's Exchange	Ma Perkins	The Jack Berch Show		1:15
	Bernadine Flynn, news	Vincent Lopez Orchestra		1:30
Music / Songs	The Goldbergs		Carey Longmire, news	1:45

DAYTIME — SPRING, 1944

Sunday

	ABC	CBS	MBS	NBC
2pm	Chaplain Jim, USA	Ceiling Unlimited		Those We Love
2:15				
2:30	National Vespers	World News Today	Troman Harper, news	The Westinghouse Program, John C. Thomas
2:45		Songs of America (2:55pm)	Art Kassel Records	
3pm	The Life of Riley	New York Philharmonic Orchestra	This is Fort Dix	The Sheaffer Parade
3:15				Upton Close, news
3:30	Hot Copy		Bulldog Drummond	The Army Hour
3:45				
4pm	Fun Valley, Al Pearce		Wide Horizons	
4:15				
4:30	The World of Song	The Pause That Refreshes	The Abe Lincoln Story	Lands of the Free
4:45				
5pm	Mary Small's Revue	The Prudential Family Hour	Green Valley, USA	NBC Symphony Orchestra
5:15				
5:30	The Musical Steelmakers		The Shadow	
5:45		Irene Rich Dramas		

DAYTIME — SPRING, 1944

Monday-Friday

ABC	CBS	MBS	NBC	
Walter Kiernan, news	Portia Faces Life	Martha Deane, talk	The Guiding Light	2pm
The Mystery Chef	Joyce Jordan, MD		Today's Children	2:15
Ed East and Polly, songs	Young Dr. Malone	Prescott Robinson, news	The Light of the World	2:30
	Perry Mason	The Consumers' Quiz	Betty Crocker, cooking / Hymns of All Churches	2:45
The Coke Club, Morton Downey	The Story of Mary Marlin	The Black Castle	A Woman of America	3pm
Appointment with Life	Bob Trout, news	Sunny Skylar, songs	Ma Perkins	3:15
	Now and Forever	Dr. Eddy's Food Forum	Pepper Young's Family	3:30
Ethel and Albert	This Life is Mine		The Right to Happiness	3:45
Blue Frolics /	Broadway Matinee	Rambling with Gambling	Mary Noble, Backstage Wife	4pm
The Ozark Ramblers			Stella Dallas	4:15
Westbrook Van Voorhis, news	Music	Full Speed Ahead	Lorenzo Jones	4:30
The Sea Hound	Raymond Scott Orchestra		Young Widder Brown	4:45
Hop Harrigan	The Eddie Dunn Show	Uncle Don	When a Girl Marries	5pm
Dick Tracy		Archie Andrews	We Love and Learn	5:15
Jack Armstrong, the All-American Boy	The Landt Trio and Curley	Chick Carter, Boy Detective	Just Plain Bill	5:30
Captain Midnight	American Women	The Adventures of Superman	Front Page Farrell	5:45

DAYTIME — SPRING, 1944

Saturday

	ABC	CBS	MBS	NBC
9am	The Breakfast Club	Joe King, news	Songs for Saturday	The First Piano Quartet
9:15		The Garden Gate	Lorraine Sherwood, talk	
9:30			Red River Dave	Adelaide Hawley, talk
9:45		Isabel Manning Hewson, food	Claire Wilson, news	Encores Orchestra
10am	The Yankee Doodle Quiz	Youth on Parade	Rainbow House	Mirth and Madness, Jack Kirkwood
10:15				
10:30	The Ozark Ramblers	Mary Lee Taylor, cooking		Betty Moore, home talk
10:45				Bob Becker's Dog Talks
11am	On Stage America	Let's Pretend	Prescott Robinson, news	The Hook and Ladder Follies
11:15			Music	
11:30	The Land of the Lost	Fashions in Rations, Billie Burke	Hollywood Melodies	Lighted Windows
11:45				
12pm	The Little Blue Playhouse	The Armstrong Theater of Today	The Man on the Farm	Don Goddard, news
12:15				Consumer Time
12:30	The Farm and Home Hour	Stars Over Hollywood	Henry Gladstone, news	Atlantic Spotlight
12:45			The Juke Box	
1pm	The Andrini Continentals	Grand Central Station	Lee Castle Orchestra	Here's to Youth
1:15	Transatlantic Quiz			
1:30	The Vagabonds Quartet	Columbia's Country Journal	Vincent Lopez Orchestra	The Baxters
1:45	Salon Ensemble			John McVane, news

DAYTIME — SPRING, 1944

Saturday

	ABC	CBS	MBS	NBC
2pm	The Metropolitan Opera	Of Men and Books	Lani McIntyre Orchestra	The Roy Shield Revue
2:15		Adventures in Science		
2:30		Calling Pan-America	George Duffy Orchestra	The Grantland Rice Story
2:45				
3pm		Detroit Musicale	This is Halloran	Orchestras of the Nation
3:15				
3:30		Philadelphia Symphony Orchestra	Jack Bundy's Carnival	
3:45				
4pm			Justin Stone Orchestra	Rupert Hughes, news
4:15			Horse Racing	Harold Fleming, news
4:30		Colonel Stoopnagle	The Show Shop	Doctors at War
4:45				
5pm		Meet Corliss Archer	Uncle Don	Your America
5:15			Tommy Dorsey Orchestra	
5:30	Tea Dance Music	Mother and Dad		Cesar Saerchinger, news
5:45	Hello Sweetheart, Nancy Martin		Eleanor King, news	Curt Massey, songs

EVENING — SUMMER, 1944

Sunday

	ABC	CBS	MBS	NBC
6pm	The Philco Summer Hour	The Silver Theater	Quick as a Flash	The Catholic Hour
6:15				
6:30		America in the Air	Upton Close, news	Men at Sea
6:45			Dick Brown, songs	
7pm	Drew Pearson, news	Report to the Nation	Stan Lomax, sports	Your All-Time Hit Parade
7:15	Don Gardiner, news		Leo Cherne, news	
7:30	The Quiz Kids	The Eddie Garr Revue	Frank Singiser, news	The Fitch Bandwagon
7:45			Max Lerner, news	
8pm	The Greenfield Chapel Choir	Blondie	A. L. Alexander's Mediation Board	The Gracie Fields Show
8:15	Andy Russell, songs			
8:30	Keepsakes, Dorothy Kirsten	Crime Doctor		One Man's Family
8:45		Ned Calmer, news (8:55pm)	Gabriel Heatter, news	
9pm	Walter Winchell's Jergens Journal	The Radio Reader's Digest	Leonidas Witherall	The Manhattan Merry-Go-Round
9:15	The Chamber Music Society of Lower Basin Street			
9:30		The Texaco Star Theater, James Melton	Music Quiz	The American Album of Familiar Music
9:45	Jimmy Fidler, gossip			
10pm	The Life of Riley	Take It or Leave It	Cedric Foster, news	The Hour of Charm
10:15			The Goodwill Hour	
10:30	Keeping Up with the World	We, the People		The Jackie Gleason - Les Tremayne Show
10:45				

EVENING — SUMMER, 1944

Monday

ABC	CBS	MBS	NBC	
Bruno Shaw, news	Quincy Howe, news	Sydney Moseley, news	George Putnam, news	6pm
Ethel and Albert	The Squibb Show	The Mutual Newsreel	Serenade to America	6:15
Whose War is This	Jeri Sullavan, songs	Frank Singiser, news		6:30
Henry J. Taylor, news	The World Today	Stan Lomax, sports	Lowell Thomas, news	6:45
Horace Heidt Orchestra	I Love a Mystery	Fulton Lewis Jr., news	Johnny Mercer's Music Shop	7pm
	Dateline	The Answer Man	John W. Vandercook, news	7:15
The Lone Ranger	The Bob Hawk Show	The Bright Lights of New York, Louis Sobel	Allen Roth Orchestra	7:30
			H. V. Kaltenborn, news	7:45
News	Vox Pop	Cecil Brown, news	The Cavalcade of America	8pm
Lum and Abner		The Return of Nick Carter		8:15
Blind Date	The Gay Nineties Revue	Sherlock Holmes	The Voice of Firestone	8:30
	Bill Henry, news (8:55pm)			8:45
Counterspy	The Mayor of the Town	Gabriel Heatter, news	The Bell Telephone Hour	9pm
		Screen Test		9:15
Spotlight Bands	The Man Called X	Music of Worship	Vacation Serenade	9:30
Short Story (9:55pm)				9:45
Raymond Gram Swing, news	The Lady Esther Screen Guild Theater	Henry Gladstone, news	The Carnation Contented Hour	10pm
Ted Malone from England		Paul Schubert, news		10:15
The Hollywood Radio Theater	The Johnny Morgan Show	The Longines Symphonette	Dr. I. Q., The Mental Banker	10:30
				10:45

EVENING — SUMMER, 1944

Tuesday

	ABC	CBS	MBS	NBC
6pm	John B. Kennedy, news	Quincy Howe, news	Sydney Moseley, news	George Putnam, news
6:15	Ethel and Albert	Edwin C. Hill, news	The Mutual Newsreel	Serenade to America
6:30	Whose War is This	Jeri Sullavan, songs	Frank Singiser, news	
6:45	Henry J. Taylor news	The World Today	Stan Lomax, sports	Lowell Thomas, news
7pm	The Land of the Lost	I Love a Mystery	Fulton Lewis Jr., news	Johnny Mercer's Music Shop
7:15		The Passing Parade	Ted Steele Records	John W. Vandercook, news
7:30	Diane Courtney and the Jesters	The American Melody Hour	Arthur Hale, news	Everything for the Boys, Dick Haymes
7:45	Don't You Believe It		The Answer Man	
8pm	News	Big Town	Frank Singiser, news	The Purple Heart Show, Ginny Simms
8:15	Lum and Abner		The Return of Nick Carter	
8:30	Nitwit Court	Theater of Romance	Sinfonietta	A Date with Judy
8:45		Bill Henry, news (8:55pm)		
9pm	Famous Jury Trials	The Jack Pepper Show	Gabriel Heatter, news	The Molle' Mystery Theater
9:15			Screen Test	
9:30	Spotlight Bands	The Doctor Fights	The American Forum of the Air	Words at War
9:45	Short Story (9:55pm)			
10pm	Raymond Gram Swing, news	Columbia Presents Corwin		The Charlotte Greenwood Show
10:15	George Hicks, news		Paul Schubert, news	
10:30	Let Yourself Go, Milton Berle	Congress Speaks	The Longines Symphonette	The Raleigh Room, Hildegarde
10:45		Public Affairs		

EVENING — SUMMER, 1944

Wednesday

ABC	CBS	MBS	NBC	
John B. Kennedy, news	Quincy Howe, news	Sydney Moseley, news	George Putnam, news	6pm
Ethel and Albert	The Squibb Show	The Mutual Newsreel	Serenade to America	6:15
Whose War is This	Jeri Sullavan, songs	Frank Singiser, news		6:30
Henry J. Taylor, news	The World Today	Stan Lomax, sports	Lowell Thomas, news	6:45
Scramby Andy	I Love a Mystery	Fulton Lewis Jr., news	Johnny Mercer's Music Shop	7pm
	The Passing Parade	The Answer Man	John W. Vandercook, news	7:15
The Lone Ranger	Easy Aces	Can You Top This	Allen Roth Orchestra	7:30
			H. V. Kaltenborn, news	7:45
News	The New Old Gold Program, Allan Jones	Cecil Brown, news	Mr. and Mrs. North	8pm
Lum and Abner		The Return of Nick Carter		8:15
My Best Girls	Dr. Christian	Guy Lombardo Orchestra	Beat the Band	8:30
	Bill Henry, news (8:55pm)			8:45
Dunninger, the Mentalist	Songs By Sinatra	Gabriel Heatter, news	The Alan Young Show	9pm
		Screen Test		9:15
Spotlight Bands	The Mildred Bailey Show	The First Nighter Program	Mr. District Attorney	9:30
Short Story (9:55pm)				9:45
Raymond Gram Swing, news	Great Moments in Music	Royal Arch Gunnison, news	Kay Kyser's College of Musical Knowledge	10pm
Ted Malone from England		Paul Schubert, news		10:15
Pages of Melody	Colonel Stoopnagle	The Longines Symphonette		10:30
				10:45

EVENING — SUMMER, 1944

Thursday

	ABC	CBS	MBS	NBC
6pm	John B. Kennedy, news	Ned Calmer, news	Sydney Moseley, news	George Putnam, news
6:15	Ethel and Albert	Ted Husing, sports	The Mutual Newsreel	Serenade to America
6:30	Whose War is This	Jeri Sullavan, songs	Frank Singiser, news	
6:45	Henry J. Taylor, news	The World Today	Stan Lomax, sports	Lowell Thomas, news
7pm	Musical Mysteries	I Love a Mystery	Fulton Lewis Jr., news	Johnny Mercer's Music Shop
7:15		The Passing Parade	Victory is Our Business	John W. Vandercook, news
7:30	Diane Courtney and the Jesters	Mr. Keen, Tracer of Lost Persons	Arthur Hale, news	Charlie Chan
7:45	Chester Bowles, talk		The Answer Man	
8pm	News	Suspense	Frank Singiser, news	Those We Love
8:15	Lum and Abner		The Return of Nick Carter	
8:30	America's Town Meeting of the Air	Death Valley Sheriff	The Better Half	Music of the Evening
8:45		Bill Henry, news (8:55pm)		
9pm		Major Bowes' Original Amateur Hour	Gabriel Heatter, news	The Kraft Music Hall, Bing Crosby
9:15			Screen Test	
9:30	Spotlight Bands	Meet Corliss Archer	Starlight Serenade	The Sealtest Village Store, Davis and Haley
9:45	Short Story (9:55pm)			
10pm	Raymond Gram Swing, news	The First Line of Defense	Henry Gladstone, news	Harry Savoy Orchestra
10:15	George Hicks, news		Dale Carnegie, inspirational	
10:30	Stop and Go	Here's to Romance, Dick Haymes	The Longines Symphonette	The March of Time
10:45				

EVENING — SUMMER, 1944

Friday

ABC	CBS	MBS	NBC	
John B. Kennedy, news	Quincy Howe, news	Sydney Moseley, news	George Putnam, news	6pm
Ethel and Albert	The Squibb Show	The Mutual Newsreel	Serenade to America	6:15
Whose War is This	Jeri Sullavan, songs	Frank Singiser, news		6:30
Henry J. Taylor, news	The World Today	Stan Lomax, sports	Lowell Thomas, news	6:45
Blondie	I Love a Mystery	Fulton Lewis Jr., news	Johnny Mercer's Music Shop	7pm
	We, Who Dream	The Answer Man	John W. Vandercook, news	7:15
The Lone Ranger	Friday on Broadway	Variety Musicale	Allen Roth Orchestra	7:30
			H. V. Kaltenborn, news	7:45
News	Maxwell House Coffee Time, Charlie Ruggles	Cecil Brown, news	The Cities Service Concerts	8pm
The Parker Family		The Return of Nick Carter		8:15
Meet Your Navy	Service to the Front	Freedom of Opportunity	The Adventures of the Thin Man	8:30
	Bill Henry, news (8:55pm)			8:45
Gangbusters	It Pays to Be Ignorant	Gabriel Heatter, news	Waltz Time	9pm
		Screen Test		9:15
Spotlight Bands	That Brewster Boy	Double or Nothing	People Are Funny	9:30
Short Story (9:55pm)				9:45
Earl Godwin, news	The Durante - Moore Show	Cedric Foster, news	Boston Blackie	10pm
Ted Malone from England		Paul Schubert, news		10:15
Letter to Your Service Man	Stage Door Canteen	The Longines Symphonette	The Colgate Sports Newsreel, Bill Stern	10:30
The Andrini Continentals			Public Affairs	10:45

EVENING — SUMMER, 1944

Saturday

	ABC	CBS	MBS	NBC
6pm	Bruno Shaw, news	Quincy Howe, news	Sydney Moseley, news	George Putnam, news
6:15	Harry Wismer, sports	The People's Platform	The Mutual Newsreel	The Hollywood Theater
6:30	The Green Hornet		Frank Singiser, news	The Three Suns
6:45		The World Today	Stan Lomax, sports	The Art of Living
7pm	Correspondents Abroad	It's Maritime	Guess Who	They Call Me GI Joe
7:15	Leland Stowe, news			
7:30	Music America Loves	Mrs. Miniver	Arthur Hale, news	The Adventures of Ellery Queen
7:45			The Answer Man	
8pm	Early American Dance Music	The Kenny Baker Program	Frank Singiser, news	Abie's Irish Rose
8:15			Music	
8:30	Boston Symphony Orchestra	Inner Sanctum Mysteries	The Cisco Kid	Men at Sea
8:45		Ned Calmer, news (8:55pm)		
9pm		Your Hit Parade	The Chicago Theater of the Air	The National Barn Dance
9:15				
9:30	Spotlight Bands			Can You Top This
9:45	Quick Quiz (9:55pm)	Saturday Night Serenade		
10pm	Guy Lombardo Orchestra		Royal Arch Gunnison, news	Palmolive Party, Barry Woods and Patsy Kelly
10:15		Correction, Please	Victory Auction	
10:30	The Ozark Ramblers			Grand Ole Opry
10:45		Public Affairs	Bob Strong Orchestra	

DAYTIME — SUMMER, 1944

Sunday

	ABC	CBS	MBS	NBC
9am	News	News	Marines in Review	News
9:15	Coast-to-Coast on a Bus	From the Organ Loft		Ernesta Barlow, talk
9:30			The Navy Goes to Church	Songs for Strings
9:45		New Voices in Song		Music
10am	Message of Israel	The CBS Church of the Air	Leo Egan, news	Highlights of the Bible
10:15			Frank Kingdon, news	
10:30	The Southernaires Quartet	Wings Over Jordan	The Mutual Radio Chapel	The Horn and Hardart Children's Hour
10:45				
11am	AAF Symphonic Flight	The Blue Jacket Choir	Paul Manning, talk	
11:15			The Insider	
11:30	The Hour of Faith	Invitation to Learning	California Melodies	Clyde Kittell, news
11:45			High School at Home	The Little Betsy Ross Girl Variety Program
12pm	The Weekly War Journal	The Salt Lake Tabernacle Choir	The Show Shop	Tapestry Musicale
12:15				
12:30	Moments of Memory	Transatlantic Call	Soldiers of the Press	Stradivari Orchestra
12:45	The Moylan Sisters, songs		Prescott Robinson, news	
1pm	John B. Kennedy, news	The CBS Church of the Air	Pauline Alpert, piano	Your Radio Reporter
1:15	Music By Marias		Lorraine Sherwood, talk	Labor for Victory
1:30	Sammy Kaye's Sunday Serenade	Edward R. Murrow, news	Music for an Hour	The University of Chicago Round Table
1:45		Health Talk		

DAYTIME — SUMMER, 1944

Monday-Friday

ABC	CBS	MBS	NBC	
The Breakfast Club	Joe King, news	Xavier Cugat Records	Mirth and Madness, Jack Kirkwood	9am
	The Sing Along Club	Bing Crosby Records		9:15
		Alfred W. McCann, food	Adelaide Hawley, talk	9:30
	This Life is Mine		Alice Cornell, songs	9:45
My True Story	Valiant Lady	Henry Gladstone, news	Lora Lawton	10am
	The Light of the World	Bessy Beatty, talk	Robert St. John, news	10:15
Kay Armen Sings	This Changing World		Finders Keepers	10:30
Songs / Listening Post	Bachelor's Children			10:45
Breakfast with Breneman	Amanda of Honeymoon Hill	Troman Harper, news	The Road of Life	11am
	Second Husband	Talk and Music	Vic and Sade	11:15
Gilbert Martyn, news	Bright Horizon	Music / The Quiz Wizard	The Hollywood Theater of the Air	11:30
Cliff Edwards, songs	Aunt Jenny's True Life Stories	Tobe's Topics / What's Your Idea	David Harum	11:45
Glamour Manor, Cliff Arquette	Kate Smith Speaks	Boake Carter, news	Don Goddard, news	12pm
	Big Sister	Mealtime Melodies	Maggie McNellis, talk	12:15
The Farm and Home Hour	The Romance of Helen Trent	Henry Gladstone, news	Music	12:30
	Our Gal Sunday	The Juke Box		12:45
H. R. Baukhage, news	Life Can Be Beautiful	Ray Dady, news	Mary Margaret McBride, talk	1pm
The Women's Exchange	Ma Perkins	The Jack Berch Show		1:15
	Bernadine Flynn, news	Vincent Lopez Orchestra		1:30
Galen Drake, talk	The Goldbergs	The American Women's Jury	Morgan Beatty, news	1:45

DAYTIME — SUMMER, 1944

Sunday

	ABC	CBS	MBS	NBC
2pm	Chaplain Jim, USA	Dangerously Yours		The Church in Action
2:15				
2:30	National Vespers	World News Today	Prescott Robinson, news	The Lee Sweetland Show
2:45		Songs of America (2:55pm)	Stanley Maxted, talk	
3pm	Listen, the Women	New York Philharmonic Orchestra	This is Fort Dix	The Sheaffer Parade
3:15				Upton Close, news
3:30	Rex Maupin Orchestra		The Mysterious Traveler	The Army Hour
3:45				
4pm	Fish Pond		The Human Adventure	
4:15				
4:30	The World of Song	The Pause That Refreshes	Roosty of the AAF	Pursuit of Learning
4:45				
5pm	Mary Small's Revue	The Prudential Family Hour	Green Valley, USA	NBC Symphony Orchestra
5:15				
5:30	Hot Copy		Bulldog Drummond	
5:45		William L. Shirer, news		

DAYTIME — SUMMER, 1944

Monday-Friday

ABC	CBS	MBS	NBC	
Walter Kiernan, news	Portia Faces Life	Martha Deane, talk	The Guiding Light	*2pm*
The Mystery Chef	Joyce Jordan, MD		Today's Children	*2:15*
Ed East and Polly, songs /	Young Dr. Malone	Prescott Robinson, news	The Woman in White	*2:30*
Ladies Be Seated	Perry Mason	Jane Cowl, talk	Betty Crocker, cooking / Hymns of All Churches	*2:45*
The Coke Club, Morton Downey	The Story of Mary Marlin	Real Stories from Real Life	A Woman of America	*3pm*
Hollywood Star Time	Tena and Tim	Success Stories	Ma Perkins	*3:15*
Appointment with Life	Bob Trout, news	Dr. Eddy's Food Forum	Pepper Young's Family	*3:30*
	The High Places		The Right to Happiness	*3:45*
Correspondents Abroad	Service Time	Rambling with Gambling	Mary Noble, Backstage Wife	*4pm*
The Don Norman Show			Stella Dallas	*4:15*
Westbrook Van Voorhis, news	Music	Full Speed Ahead	Lorenzo Jones	*4:30*
Hop Harrigan	Raymond Scott Orchestra		Young Widder Brown	*4:45*
Terry and the Pirates	The Eddie Dunn Show	Uncle Don	When a Girl Marries	*5pm*
Dick Tracy		Chick Carter, Boy Detective	We Love and Learn	*5:15*
Jack Armstrong, the All-American Boy	Terry Allen and the Three Sisters	The Tom Mix Ralston Straightshooters	Just Plain Bill	*5:30*
The Sea Hound	Wilderness Road	The Adventures of Superman	Front Page Farrell	*5:45*

DAYTIME — SUMMER, 1944

Saturday

	ABC	CBS	MBS	NBC
9am	The Breakfast Club	Joe King, news	Something for the Girls	Rhythms for Saturday
9:15		The Garden Gate	Lorraine Sherwood, talk	
9:30			Your OPA	Adelaide Hawley, talk
9:45		David Shoop Orchestra	Claire Wilson, news	Encores Orchestra
10am	Fannie Hurst Presents	Youth on Parade	Rainbow House	Adventure Ahead
10:15				
10:30	What's Cooking	Mary Lee Taylor, cooking		Baseball Quiz
10:45				Alex Dreier, news
11am	On Stage America	Let's Pretend	Troman Harper, news	The First Piano Quartet
11:15			Music	
11:30	The Land of the Lost	Fashions in Rations, Billie Burke	Hookey Hall	Melody Round-Up
11:45				
12pm	The Little Blue Playhouse	The Armstrong Theater of Today	Hello, Moon	Don Goddard, news
12:15				Consumer Time
12:30	The Farm and Home Hour	Stars Over Hollywood	Henry Gladstone, news	Atlantic Spotlight
12:45			The Juke Box	
1pm	News	Grand Central Station	The Business Men's Forum	Here's to Youth
1:15	Transatlantic Quiz		Buddy Rogers Orchestra	
1:30	Swing Shift Frolics	Columbia's Country Journal	Vincent Lopez Orchestra	Indiana Indigo
1:45				John McVane, news

DAYTIME — SUMMER, 1944

Saturday

	ABC	CBS	MBS	NBC
2pm	Women in Blue	Of Men and Books	Lani McIntyre Orchestra	Joseph Gallichio Orchestra
2:15		Adventures in Science		
2:30	Slanguage Quiz	Calling Pan-America	George Duffy Orchestra	The Grantland Rice Story
2:45				
3pm	Twenty-One Stars	Detroit Musicale	This is Halloran	Minstrel Melodies
3:15				
3:30	Eddie Condon's Jazz Concert	The Visiting Hour	Bob Strong Orchestra	Burt Berhman Orchestra
3:45				
4pm	Horace Heidt Orchestra	Boot Camp Parade	The Adrian Rollini Trio	Rupert Hughes, news
4:15				Barbara and the Boys
4:30		Horse Racing	The Show Shop	Doctors at War
4:45				
5pm	The Saturday Concert	Casey, Crime Photographer	Uncle Don	Your America
5:15			Glen Gray Orchestra	
5:30		Mother and Dad	Lee Castle Orchestra	The Phil D'Arcy Quartet
5:45	Hello Sweetheart, Nancy Martin			Curt Massey, songs

EVENING — FALL, 1944

Sunday

	ABC	CBS	MBS	NBC
6pm	The Radio Hall of Fame	The Adventures of Ozzie and Harriet	Quick as a Flash	The Catholic Hour
6:15				
6:30		The Baby Snooks Show	Upton Close, news	The Great Gildersleeve
6:45			Dick Brown, songs	
7pm	Drew Pearson, news	The Kate Smith Hour	Leonidas Witherall	The Lucky Strike Program, Jack Benny
7:15	Don Gardiner, news			
7:30	The Quiz Kids		Frank Singiser, news	The Fitch Bandwagon
7:45			Max Lerner, news	
8pm	The Greenfield Chapel Choir	Blondie	A. L. Alexander's Mediation Board	The Charlie McCarthy Show
8:15	Dorothy Thompson, news			
8:30	Stop and Go	Crime Doctor		One Man's Family
8:45		Bob Trout, news (8:55pm)	Gabriel Heatter, news	
9pm	Walter Winchell's Jergens Journal	The Radio Reader's Digest	Steel Horizons	The Manhattan Merry-Go-Round
9:15	Hollywood Mystery Time			
9:30		The Texaco Star Theater, James Melton	Cedric Foster, news	The American Album of Familiar Music
9:45	Jimmy Fidler, gossip		The Columbus Boy's Choir	
10pm	The Life of Riley	Take It or Leave It	The Goodwill Hour	The Hour of Charm
10:15				
10:30	Keeping Up with the World	We, the People		The Old Gold Comedy Theater of the Air
10:45			Norman Carey, songs	

EVENING — FALL, 1944

Monday

ABC	CBS	MBS	NBC	
John B. Kennedy, news	Quincy Howe, news	Sydney Moseley, news	Don Hollenbeck, news	6pm
Ethel and Albert	The Squibb Show	Ramona, songs	Serenade to America	6:15
Whose War is This	Paul E. Fitzpatrick, news	Frank Singiser, news		6:30
Henry J. Taylor, news	The World Today	Stan Lomax, sports	Lowell Thomas, news	6:45
Horace Heidt Orchestra	I Love a Mystery	Fulton Lewis Jr., news	Johnny Mercer's Music Shop	7pm
	Hedda Hopper, gossip	Claude Hopkins Orchestra	John W. Vandercook, news	7:15
The Lone Ranger	The Bob Hawk Show	Bulldog Drummond	Allen Roth Orchestra	7:30
			H. V. Kaltenborn, news	7:45
Leon Decker, news	Vox Pop	Cecil Brown, news	The Cavalcade of America	8pm
Lum and Abner		Sunny Skylar, songs		8:15
Blind Date	The Gay Nineties Revue	Sherlock Holmes	The Voice of Firestone	8:30
	Bill Henry, news (8:55pm)			8:45
Counterspy	The Lux Radio Theater	Gabriel Heatter, news	The Bell Telephone Hour	9pm
		Screen Test		9:15
Spotlight Bands		Music of Worship	Information, Please	9:30
Short Story (9:55pm)				9:45
Raymond Gram Swing, news	The Lady Esther Screen Guild Theater	Henry Gladstone, news	The Carnation Contented Hour	10pm
Ted Malone from England		Paul Shubert, news		10:15
Hollywood Show Time	The Johnny Morgan Show	The Longines Symphonette	Dr. I. Q., the Mental Banker	10:30
				10:45

EVENING — FALL, 1944

Tuesday

	ABC	CBS	MBS	NBC
6pm	John B. Kennedy, news	Quincy Howe, news	Sydney Moseley, news	Don Hollenbeck, news
6:15	Ethel and Albert	Edwin C. Hill, news	The Mutual Newsreel	Serenade to America
6:30	Whose War is This	Ted Husing, sports	Frank Singiser, news	
6:45	Henry J. Taylor, news	The World Today	Stan Lomax, sports	Lowell Thomas, news
7pm	The American Side Show	I Love a Mystery	Fulton Lewis Jr., news	Johnny Mercer's Music Shop
7:15		Music That Satisfies	Claude Hopkins Orchestra	John W. Vandercook, news
7:30	Public Affairs	The American Melody Hour	Arthur Hale, news	Everything for the Boys, Dick Haymes
7:45			The Answer Man	
8pm	Leon Decker, news	Big Town	Frank Singiser, news	The Purple Heart Show, Ginny Simms
8:15	Lum and Abner		Sunny Skylar, songs	
8:30	The Alan Young Show	Theater of Romance	The Better Half	A Date with Judy
8:45		Bill Henry, news (8:55pm)		
9pm	Famous Jury Trials	Burns and Allen	Gabriel Heatter, news	The Molle' Mystery Theater
9:15			Screen Test	
9:30	Spotlight Bands	This is My Best	The American Forum of the Air	Fibber Magee and Molly
9:45	Short Story (9:55pm)			
10pm	Raymond Gram Swing, news	Service to the Front		The Pepsodent Show, Bob Hope
10:15	George Hicks, news		Paul Schubert, news	
10:30	Let Yourself Go, Milton Berle	Congress Speaks	The Longines Symphonette	The Raleigh Room, Hildegarde
10:45		Ferdinand Eberstadt, news		

EVENING — FALL, 1944

Wednesday

ABC	CBS	MBS	NBC	
John B. Kennedy, news	Quincy Howe, news	Sydney Moseley, news	Don Hollenbeck, news	6pm
Ethel and Albert	The Squibb Show	Ramona, songs	Serenade to America	6:15
Whose War is This	Jeri Sullavan, songs	Frank Singiser, news		6:30
Henry J. Taylor, news	The World Today	Stan Lomax, sports	Lowell Thomas, news	6:45
On Stage Everybody	I Love a Mystery	Fulton Lewis Jr., news	Johnny Mercer's Music Shop	7pm
	Music That Satisfies	The Answer Man	John W. Vandercook, news	7:15
The Lone Ranger	Easy Aces	Can You Top This	Allen Roth Orchestra	7:30
			H. V. Kaltenborn, news	7:45
Leon Decker, news	The Jack Carson Show	Cecil Brown, news	Mr. and Mrs. North	8pm
Lum and Abner		Sunny Skylar, songs		8:15
My Best Girl	Dr. Christian	Stop That Villain	Carton of Cheer, Henny Youngman	8:30
	Bill Henry, news (8:55pm)			8:45
Dunninger, the Mentalist	Songs By Sinatra	Gabriel Heatter, news	Time to Smile, Eddie Cantor	9pm
		Screen Test		9:15
Spotlight Bands	Which is Which	The First Nighter Program	Mr. District Attorney	9:30
Short Story (9:55pm)				9:45
Raymond Gram Swing, news	Great Moments in Music	Sumner Welles, news	Kay Kyser's College of Musical Knowledge	10pm
Ted Malone from England		Paul Shubert, news		10:15
Scramby Amby	The Electric Hour, Nelson Eddy	The Longines Symphonette		10:30
				10:45

EVENING — FALL, 1944

Thursday

	ABC	CBS	MBS	NBC
6pm	John B. Kennedy, news	Warren Sweeney, news	Sydney Moseley, news	Don Hollenbeck, news
6:15	Ethel and Albert	Calling Pan-America	The Mutual Newsreel	Serenade to America
6:30	Whose War is This		Frank Singiser, news	
6:45	Henry J. Taylor, news	The World Today	Stan Lomax, sports	Lowell Thomas, news
7pm	Fred Waring Orchestra	I Love a Mystery	Fulton Lewis Jr., news	Johnny Mercer's Music Shop
7:15		Music That Satisfies	Victory is Our Business	John W. Vandercook, news
7:30	Charlie Chan	Mr. Keen, Tracer of Lost Persons	Arthur Hale, news	The Bob Burns Show
7:45			The Answer Man	
8pm	Earl Godwin, news	Suspense	Frank Singiser, news	Maxwell House Coffee Time, Frank Morgan
8:15	Lum and Abner		Sunny Skylar, songs	
8:30	America's Town Meeting of the Air	Death Valley Sheriff	Sammy Kaye Orchestra	The Birdseye Open House, Dinah Shore
8:45		Bill Henry, news (8:55pm)		
9pm		Major Bowes' Original Amateur Hour	Gabriel Heatter, news	The Kraft Music Hall, Bing Crosby
9:15			Screen Test	
9:30	Spotlight Bands	Meet Corliss Archer	Starlight Serenade	The Sealtest Village Store, Davis and Haley
9:45	Short Story (9:55pm)			
10pm	Raymond Gram Swing, news	The First Line of Defense	Henry Gladstone, news	Abbott and Costello
10:15	George Hicks, news		Dale Carnegie, inspirational	
10:30	The Side Show, Dave Elman	Here's to Romance, Martha Tilton	The Longines Symphonette	The March of Time
10:45				

EVENING — FALL, 1944

Friday

ABC	CBS	MBS	NBC	
John B. Kennedy, news	Quincy Howe, news	Sydney Moseley, news	Don Hollenbeck, news	6pm
Ethel and Albert	The Squibb Show	Ramona, songs	Serenade to America	6:15
Whose War is This	Jeri Sullavan, news	Frank Singiser, news		6:30
Henry J. Taylor, news	The World Today	Stan Lomax, sports	Lowell Thomas, news	6:45
Happy Island	I Love a Mystery	Fulton Lewis Jr., news	Johnny Mercer's Music Shop	7pm
	Raymond Scott Orchestra	The Answer Man	John W. Vandercook, news	7:15
The Lone Ranger	Friday on Broadway	Variety Musicale	Allen Roth Orchestra	7:30
			H. V. Kaltenborn, news	7:45
Leon Decker, news	The Aldrich Family	Cecil Brown, news	Highways in Melody	8pm
The Parker Family		Sunny Skylar, songs		8:15
Public Affairs	The Adventures of the Thin Man	Freedom of Opportunity	Duffy's Tavern	8:30
	Bill Henry, news (8:55pm)			8:45
Gangbusters	It Pays to Be Ignorant	Gabriel Heatter, news	Waltz Time	9pm
		Screen Test		9:15
Spotlight Bands	That Brewster Boy	Double or Nothing	People Are Funny	9:30
Short Story (9:55pm)				9:45
Earl Godwin, news	The Durante - Moore Show	Madison Square Garden Boxing	Amos 'n' Andy	10pm
Ted Malone from England				10:15
The Doctors Talk It Over	Stage Door Canteen		The Colgate Sports Newsreel, Bill Stern	10:30
Letter to Your Service Man			Public Affairs	10:45

EVENING — FALL, 1944

Saturday

	ABC	CBS	MBS	NBC
6pm	Bruno Shaw, news	Quincy Howe, news	Shirley Eder, news	Don Hollenbeck, news
6:15	Harry Wismer, sports	The People's Platform	The Mutual Newsreel	Music
6:30	Edward Tomlinson, news		Frank Singiser, news	
6:45	Lucille Delval, songs	The World Today	Stan Lomax, sports	Religion in the News
7pm	Correspondents Abroad	The Mayor of the Town	Guess Who	The World's Great Novels
7:15	Leland Stowe, news			
7:30	Meet Your Navy	America in the Air	Arthur Hale, news	The Adventures of Ellery Queen
7:45			The Answer Man	
8pm	Early American Dance Music	The Kenny Baker Program	Frank Singiser, news	The Rudy Vallee Show
8:15			Bob Stanley Orchestra	
8:30	Boston Symphony Orchestra	Inner Sanctum Mysteries	Detroit Symphony Orchestra	Truth or Consequences
8:45		Bob Trout, news (8:55pm)		
9pm		Your Hit Parade		The National Barn Dance
9:15	Edward Tomlinson, news			
9:30	Spotlight Bands		The Chicago Theater of the Air	Can You Top This
9:45	Quick Quiz (9:55pm)	Saturday Night Serenade		
10pm	Guy Lombardo Orchestra			Palmolive Party, Barry Wood and Patsy Kelly
10:15		Correction, Please		
10:30	The Man Called X		The Mysterious Traveler	Grand Ole Opry
10:45		Public Affairs		

DAYTIME — FALL, 1944

Sunday

	ABC	CBS	MBS	NBC
9am	News	News	Hollywood Melodies	News
9:15	Coast-to-Coast on a Bus	From the Organ Loft		Ernesta Barlow, talk
9:30			The Navy Goes to Church	Songs for Strings
9:45		New Voices in Song		Music
10am	Message of Israel	The CBS Church of the Air	Leo Egan, news	The National Radio Pulpit
10:15			Frank Kingdon, news	
10:30	The Southernaires Quartet	Wings Over Jordan	The Mutual Radio Chapel	The Horn and Hardart Children's Hour
10:45				
11am	AAF Symphonic Flight	The Blue Jacket Choir	Paul Manning, news	
11:15			High School at Home at Home	
11:30	The Hour of Faith	Invitation to Learning	Brunch with the Fitzgeralds	Clyde Kitell, news
11:45				The Little Betsy Ross Girl Variety Program
12pm	The Weekly War Journal	The Salt Lake Tabernacle Choir	The Show Shop	The Eternal Light
12:15				
12:30	Moments of Memory	Transatlantic Call	Soldiers of the Press	Stradivari Orchestra
12:45	Josephine Houston, songs			
1pm	John B. Kennedy, news	The CBS Church of the Air	The Canary Pet Shop	Your Radio Reporter
1:15	Gordon Frazier, news		Cy Walter, piano	The Robert Merrill Show
1:30	Sammy Kaye's Sunday Serenade	Public Affairs	True Detective Mysteries	The University of Chicago Round Table
1:45		Edward R. Murrow, news		

DAYTIME — FALL, 1944

Monday-Friday

ABC	CBS	MBS	NBC	
The Breakfast Club	Joe King, news	Victor Lindhahr, health	Mirth and Madness, Jack Kirkwood	9am
	The American School of the Air	Bing Crosby Records		9:15
		Alfred W. McCann, food	Adelaide Hawley, talk	9:30
	This Life is Mine		Alice Cornell, songs	9:45
My True Story	Valiant Lady	Henry Gladstone, news	Lora Lawton	10am
	The Light of the World	Bessy Beatty, talk	Robert St. John, news	10:15
Cliff Edwards, songs	This Changing World		Finders Keepers	10:30
Music / Listening Post	Bachelor's Children			10:45
Breakfast with Breneman	Amanda of Honeymoon Hill	Arthur Gaeth, news	The Road of Life	11am
	Second Husband Husband	Music / Jimmy Fidler, gossip	Rosemary	11:15
Gilbert Martyn, news	Bright Horizon	Music / The Quiz Wizard	The Dreft Star Playhouse	11:30
The Jack Berch Show	Aunt Jenny's True Life Stories	Tobe's Topics / What's Your Idea	David Harum	11:45
Glamour Manor, Cliff Arquette	Kate Smith Speaks	Boake Carter, news	Don Goddard, news	12pm
	Big Sister	Music	Maggie McNellis, talk	12:15
The Farm and Home Hour	The Romance of Helen Trent	Henry Gladstone, news	Music	12:30
	Our Gal Sunday	The Juke Box		12:45
H. R. Baukhage, news	Life Can Be Beautiful	The Consumers' Quiz	Mary Margaret McBride, talk	1pm
The Women's Exchange	Ma Perkins	Terry's House Party		1:15
	Bernadine Flynn, news	Vincent Lopez Orchestra		1:30
Galen Drake, talk	The Goldbergs	The American Women's Jury	Morgan Beatty, news	1:45

DAYTIME — FALL, 1944

Sunday

	ABC	CBS	MBS	NBC
2pm	Chaplain Jim, USA	Matinee Theater	The Hollywood Theater	Those We Love
2:15				
2:30	National Vespers	World News Today	Prescott Robinson, news	The Westinghouse Program, John C. Thomas
2:45			The Voice of Broadway	
3pm	The Charlotte Greenwood Show	New York Philharmonic Orchestra	The Quiz of Two Cities	The Sheaffer Parade
3:15				
3:30	Miss Hattie		The Return of Nick Carter	The Army Hour
3:45				
4pm	Listen, the Women		Your America	
4:15				
4:30	The World of Song	The Pause That Refreshes	What's the Name of That Song	Music America Loves Best
4:45				
5pm	Mary Small's Revue	The Prudential Family Hour	You Can't Take It With You	NBC Symphony Orchestra
5:15				
5:30	Hot Copy		The Shadow	
5:45		William L. Shirer, news		

DAYTIME — FALL, 1944

Monday-Friday

ABC	CBS	MBS	NBC	
	Joyce Jordan, MD	Cedric Foster, news	The Guiding Light	2pm
	Two on a Clue	Jane Cowl, talk	Today's Children	2:15
Ed East and Polly, songs / Ladies Be Seated	Young Dr. Malone	Prescott Robinson, news	The Woman in White	2:30
	Perry Mason	Real Stories from Real Life	Betty Crocker, cooking / Hymns of All Churches	2:45
The Coke Club, Morton Downey	The Story of Mary Marlin	Martha Deane, talk	A Woman of America	3pm
Hollywood Star Time	Tena and Tim	Linda's First Love	Ma Perkins	3:15
Appointment with Life /	The High Places	Rambling with Gambling	Pepper Young's Family	3:30
Music	Bob Trout, news		The Right to Happiness	3:45
Correspondents Abroad	Service Time	John Gambling, news	Mary Noble, Backstage Wife	4pm
Music		Sunny Skylar, songs	Stella Dallas	4:15
Westbrook Van Voorhis, news	Music	Dr. Eddy's Food Forum	Lorenzo Jones	4:30
Hop Harrigan	Raymond Scott Orchestra		Young Widder Brown	4:45
Terry and the Pirates	The Eddie Dunn Show / The Sing Along Club	Uncle Don	When a Girl Marries	5pm
Dick Tracy		Chick Carter, Boy Detective	Portia Faces Life	5:15
Jack Armstrong, the All-American Boy	Terry Allen and the Three Sisters	The Adventures of Superman	Just Plain Bill	5:30
Captain Midnight	Wilderness Road	The Tom Mix Ralston Straight Shooters	Front Page Farrell	5:45

DAYTIME — FALL, 1944

Saturday

	ABC	CBS	MBS	NBC
9am	The Breakfast Club	Joe King, news	Cleveland Symphony Orchestra	Rhythms for Saturday
9:15		The Garden Gate		
9:30		Columbia's Country Journal		Adelaide Hawley, talk
9:45				Encores Orchestra
10am	Fannie Hurst Presents	Youth on Parade	Rainbow House	Smilin' Ed's Buster Brown Gang
10:15				
10:30	What's Cooking	Mary Lee Taylor, cooking		Baseball Quiz
10:45				Alex Dreier, news
11am	Lois Long, shopping	Let's Pretend	Prescott Robinson, news	The First Piano Quartet
11:15	Transatlantic Quiz		Lorraine Sherwood, talk	
11:30	The Land of the Lost	The Billie Burke Show	Hookey Hall	Melody Roundup
11:45				
12pm	Swing Shift Frolics	The Armstrong Theater of Today	Hello, Mom	Don Goddard, news
12:15				Consumer Time
12:30	The Farm and Home Hour	Stars Over Hollywood	The Juke Box	Atlantic Spotlight
12:45				
1pm	Slanguage Quiz	Grand Central Station	This is Halloran	Adventure Ahead
1:15				
1:30	Eddie Condons' Jazz Concert	Report to the Nation	Vincent Lopez Orchestra	The Baxters
1:45				John McVane, news

DAYTIME — FALL, 1944

Saturday

	ABC	CBS	MBS	NBC
2pm	Sports	Detroit Musicale	Lani McIntyre Orchestra	Musiciana
2:15				
2:30		Sports	Sports	Sports
2:45				
3pm				
3:15				
3:30				
3:45				
4pm				
4:15				
4:30				
4:45				
5pm	The Saturday Concert	Philadelphia Symphony Orchestra	Uncle Don	Grand Hotel
5:15			Leo Egan, news	
5:30			Lee Castle Orchestra	Rupert Hughes, news
5:45	Hello Sweetheart, Nancy Martin		Shirley Eder, talk	Curt Massey, songs

LISTINGS FOR 1945

EVENING — WINTER, 1945

Sunday

	ABC	CBS	MBS	NBC
6pm	The Radio Hall of Fame	The Adventures of Ozzie and Harriet	Quick as a Flash	The Catholic Hour
6:15				
6:30		The Baby Snooks Show	Upton Close, news	The Great Gildersleeve
6:45			Dick Brown, songs	
7pm	Drew Pearson, news	The Kate Smith Hour	Leonidas Witherall	The Lucky Strike Program, Jack Benny
7:15	Don Gardiner, news			
7:30	The Quiz Kids		Frank Singiser, news	The Fitch Bandwagon
7:45			Paul Schubert, news	
8pm	The Greenfield Chapel Choir	Blondie	A. L. Alexander's Mediation Board	The Charlie McCarthy Show
8:15	Dorothy Thompson, news			
8:30	Stop and Go	Crime Doctor		The Eddie Bracken Show
8:45		Bob Trout, news (8:55pm)	Gabriel Heatter, news	
9pm	Walter Winchell's Jergens Journal	The Radio Reader's Digest	Steel Horizons	The Manhattan Merry-Go-Round
9:15	Hollywood Mystery Time			
9:30		The Texaco Star Theater, James Melton	Cedric Foster, news	The American Album of Familiar Music
9:45	Jimmy Fidler, gossip		The Jerry Cooper Show	
10pm	The Life of Riley	Take It or Leave It	Earl Wilson's Broadway Column	The Hour of Charm
10:15			Ramona and Her Mighty Minstrels	
10:30	One Foot in Heaven	We, the People	The Columbus Boy's Choir	The Old Gold Comedy Theater of the Air
10:45			Jay Johnson, songs	

EVENING — WINTER, 1945

Monday

ABC	CBS	MBS	NBC	
Walter Kiernan, news	Quincy Howe, news	Sydney Moseley, news	Don Hollenbeck, news	6pm
Ethel and Albert	The Squibb Show	Ramona, songs	Serenade to America	6:15
Whose War is This	Sally Moore, songs	Fred Vandeventer, news		6:30
Peggy Mann, songs	The World Today	Stan Lomax, sports	Lowell Thomas, news	6:45
Correspondents Abroad	The Jack Kirkwood Show	Fulton Lewis Jr., news	The Chesterfield Supper Club	7pm
Raymond Gram Swing, news	Hedda Hopper, gossip	The Answer Man	John W. Vandercook, news	7:15
The Lone Ranger	The Bob Hawk Show	Bulldog Drummond	Allen Roth Orchestra	7:30
			H. V. Kaltenborn, news	7:45
Ted Malone from England	Vox Pop	Cecil Brown, news	The Cavalcade of America	8pm
Lum and Abner		Curt Massey, songs		8:15
Blind Date	Burns and Allen	Sherlock Holmes	The Voice of Firestone	8:30
	Bill Henry, news (8:55pm)			8:45
Happy Island	The Lux Radio Theater	Gabriel Heatter, news	The Bell Telephone Hour	9pm
		Real Stories from Real Life		9:15
Spotlight Bands		Music of Worship	Information, Please	9:30
Short Story (9:55pm)				9:45
Guy Lombardo Orchestra	The Lady Esther Screen Guild Theater	Henry Gladstone, news	The Carnation Contented Hour	10pm
		Paul Shubert, news		10:15
Hollywood Show Time	The Johnny Morgan Show	The Longines Symphonette	Dr. I. Q., The Mental Banker	10:30
				10:45

EVENING — WINTER, 1945

Tuesday

	ABC	CBS	MBS	NBC
6pm	Walter Kiernan, news	Quincy Howe, news	Sydney Moseley, news	Don Hollenbeck, news
6:15	Ethel and Albert	Edwin C. Hill, news	The Mutual Newsreel	Serenade to America
6:30	Whose War is This	Ted Husing, sports	Fred Vandeventer, news	
6:45	Peggy Mann, songs	The World Today	Stan Lomax, sports	Lowell Thomas, news
7pm	Correspondents Abroad	The Jack Kirkwood Show	Fulton Lewis Jr., news	The Chesterfield Supper Club
7:15	Raymond Gram Swing, news	Music That Satisfies	The Strange Dr. Weird	John W. Vandercook, news
7:30	One Man's Family	The American Melody Hour	Arthur Hale, news	Everything for the Boys, Dick Haymes
7:45			The Answer Man	
8pm	Ted Malone from England	Big Town	Frank Singiser, news	The Purple Heart Show, Ginny Simms
8:15	Lum and Abner		Curt Massey, songs	
8:30	The Alan Young Show	Theater of Romance	The Roy Rogers Show	A Date with Judy
8:45		Bill Henry, news (8:55pm)		
9pm	The Gracie Fields Show	Inner Sanctum Mysteries	Gabriel Heatter, news	The Molle' Mystery Theater
9:15			Real Stories from Real Life	
9:30	Spotlight Bands	This is My Best	The American Forum of the Air	Fibber Magee and Molly
9:45	Short Stories (9:55pm)			
10pm	Listen, the Women	Service to the Front		The Pepsodent Show, Bob Hope
10:15			Paul Schubert, news	
10:30	Hal McIntyre Orchestra	Congress Speaks	The Longines Symphonette	The Raleigh Room, Hildegarde
10:45		Behind the Scenes at CBS		

EVENING — WINTER, 1945

Wednesday

ABC	CBS	MBS	NBC	
Walter Kiernan, news	Quincy Howe, news	Sydney Moseley, news	Don Hollenbeck, news	6pm
Ethel and Albert	The Squibb Show	Ramona, songs	Serenade to America	6:15
Whose War is This	Encore Appearance	Fred Vandeventer, news		6:30
Peggy Mann, songs	The World Today	Stan Lomax, sports	Lowell Thomas, news	6:45
Correspondents Abroad	The Jack Kirkwood Show	Fulton Lewis Jr., news	The Chesterfield Supper Club	7pm
Raymond Gram Swing, news	Music That Satisfies	The Answer Man	John W. Vandercook, news	7:15
The Lone Ranger	The Adventures of Ellery Queen	Can You Top This	Allen Roth Orchestra	7:30
			H. V. Kaltenborn, news	7:45
Ted Malone from England	The Jack Carson Show	Cecil Brown, news	Mr. and Mrs. North	8pm
Lum and Abner		Curt Massey, songs		8:15
Counterspy	Dr. Christian	The Better Half	Carton of Cheer, Henny Youngman	8:30
	Bill Henry, news (8:55pm)			8:45
Keeping Up with the World	Songs By Sinatra	Gabriel Heatter, news	Time to Smile, Eddie Cantor	9pm
		Real Stories from Real Life		9:15
Spotlight Bands	Which is Which	The Cisco Kid	Mr. District Attorney	9:30
Short Story (9:55pm)				9:45
The Ice Box Follies, Niles and Prindle	Great Moments in Music	Sumner Welles, news	Kay Kyser's College of Musical Knowledge	10pm
		Paul Shubert, news		10:15
Scramby Amby	Let Yourself Go, Milton Berle	The Longines Symphonette		10:30
				10:45

EVENING — WINTER, 1945

Thursday

	ABC	CBS	MBS	NBC
6pm	Walter Kiernan, news	Warren Sweeney, news	Sydney Moseley, news	Don Hollenbeck, news
6:15	Ethel and Albert	Calling Pan-America	The Mutual Newsreel	Serenade to America
6:30	Whose War is This		Fred Vandeventer, news	
6:45	Peggy Mann, songs	The World Today	Stan Lomax, sports	Lowell Thomas, news
7pm	Correspondents Abroad	The Jack Kirkwood Show	Fulton Lewis Jr., news	The Chesterfield Supper Club
7:15	Raymond Gram Swing, news	Music That Satisfies	Victory is Our Business	John W. Vandercook, news
7:30	Charlie Chan	Mr. Keen, Tracer of Lost Persons	Arthur Hale, news	The Bob Burns Show
7:45			The Answer Man	
8pm	Earl Godwin, news	Suspense	Frank Singiser, news	Maxwell House Coffee Time, Frank Morgan
8:15	Lum and Abner		Curt Massey, songs	
8:30	America's Town Meeting of the Air	Death Valley Sheriff	Sammy Kaye Orchestra	The Birdseye Open House, Dinah Shore
8:45		Bill Henry, news (8:55pm)		
9pm		Major Bowes' Original Amateur Hour	Gabriel Heatter, news	The Kraft Music Hall, Bing Crosby
9:15			Real Stories from Real Life	
9:30	Spotlight Bands	Meet Corliss Archer	The Treasure Hour of Song	The Sealtest Village Store, Davis and Haley
9:45	Short Story (9:55pm)			
10pm	Fred Waring Orchestra	The First Line of Defense	Henry Gladstone, news	Abbott and Costello
10:15			Dale Carnegie, inspirational	
10:30	The March of Time	Here's to Romance, Martha Tilton	The Longines Symphonette	The Rudy Vallee Show
10:45				

EVENING — WINTER, 1945

Friday

ABC	CBS	MBS	NBC	
Walter Kiernan, news	Quincy Howe, news	Sydney Moseley, news	Don Hollenbeck, news	6pm
Ethel and Albert	The Squibb Show	Ramona, songs	Serenade to America	6:15
Whose War is This	Sally Moore, songs	Fred Vandeventer, news		6:30
Peggy Mann, songs	The World Today	Stan Lomax, sports	Lowell Thomas, news	6:45
Correspondents Abroad	The Jack Kirkwood Show	Fulton Lewis Jr., news	The Chesterfield Supper Club	7pm
Raymond Gram Swing, news	Tommy Dorsey Orchestra	The Answer Man	John W. Vandercook, news	7:15
The Lone Ranger	Friday on Broadway	Variety Musicale	Allen Roth Orchestra	7:30
			H. V. Kaltenborn, news	7:45
Stars of the Future	The Aldrich Family	Cecil Brown, news	Highways in Melody	8pm
		Curt Massey, songs		8:15
Army Nurse	The Adventures of the Thin Man	Freedom of Opportunity	Duffy's Tavern	8:30
	Bill Henry, news (8:55pm)			8:45
Famous Jury Trials	It Pays to Be Ignorant	Gabriel Heatter, news	Waltz Time	9pm
		Real Stories from Real Life		9:15
Spotlight Bands	That Brewster Boy	Double or Nothing	People Are Funny	9:30
Short Story (9:55pm)				9:45
The Norman Cordon Show	The Durante - Moore Show	Madison Square Garden Boxing	Amos 'n' Andy	10pm
				10:15
The Doctors Talk It Over	Stage Door Canteen		The Colgate Sports Newsreel, Bill Stern	10:30
Letter to Your Service Man			Public Affairs	10:45

EVENING — WINTER, 1945

Saturday

	ABC	CBS	MBS	NBC
6pm	Bruno Shaw, news	Quincy Howe, news	Sydney Moseley, news	Don Hollenbeck, news
6:15	Harry Wismer, sports	The People's Platform	Strictly Personal	Friendship Ranch
6:30	Edward Tomlinson, news		Fred Vandeventer, news	
6:45	Labor USA	The World Today	Stan Lomax, sports	Religion in the News
7pm	Correspondents Abroad	The Mayor of the Town	Guess Who	The World's Great Novels
7:15	Leland Stowe, news			
7:30	Meet Your Navy	America in the Air	Arthur Hale, news	The Saint
7:45			The Answer Man	
8pm	Early American Dance Music	Pabst Blue Ribbon Town, Danny Kaye	Frank Singiser, news	Gaslight Gaieties
8:15			Music for Remembrance	
8:30	Boston Symphony Orchestra	The FBI in Peace and War	Detroit Symphony Orchestra	Truth or Consequences
8:45		Bob Trout, news (8:55pm)		
9pm		Your Hit Parade		The National Barn Dance
9:15	Edward Tomlinson, news			
9:30	Spotlight Bands		The Mysterious Traveler	Can You Top This
9:45	Quick Quiz (9:55pm)	Saturday Night Serenade		
10pm	The Andy Russell Show		The Chicago Theater of the Air	The Judy Canova Show
10:15		Here Comes Elmer, Al Pearce		
10:30	The Man Called X			Grand Ole Opry
10:45		Public Affairs		

DAYTIME — WINTER, 1945

Sunday

	ABC	CBS	MBS	NBC
9am	News	News	Uncle Don Reads the Comics	News
9:15	Coast-to-Coast on a Bus	From the Organ Loft		Ernesta Harlow, talk
9:30			The Navy Goes to Church	Songs for Strings
9:45		New Voices in Song		Music
10am	Message of Israel	The CBS Church of the Air	Leo Egan, news	The National Radio Pulpit
10:15			Frank Kingdon, news	
10:30	The Southernaires Quartet	Wings Over Jordan	The Mutual Radio Chapel	The Horn and Hardart
10:45				
11am	AAF Symphonic Flight	The Blue Jacket Choir	Paul Manning, news	
11:15			High School at Home	
11:30	The Hour of Faith	Invitation to Learning	Brunch with the Fitzgeralds	Clyde Kitell, news
11:45				The Little Betsy Ross Girl Variety Program The Eternal Light
12pm	The Weekly War Journal	The Salt Lake Tabernacle Choir	The Show Shop	
12:15				
12:30	Moments of Memory	Transatlantic Call	Soldiers of the Press	Stradivari Orchestra
12:45	Josephine Houston, songs		Prescott Robinson, news	
1pm	John B. Kennedy, news	The CBS Church of the Air	The Canary Pet Shop	Your Radio Reporter
1:15	Gordon Frazier, news		Cy Walter, piano	America United
1:30	Sammy Kaye's Sunday Serenade	Public Affairs	True Detective Mysteries	The University of Chicago Round Table
1:45		Edward R. Murrow, news		

DAYTIME — WINTER, 1945

Monday-Friday

ABC	CBS	MBS	NBC	
The Breakfast Club	Joe King, news	Victor Lindhahr, health	Mirth and Madness, Jack Kirkwood	9am
	The American School of the Air	Bing Crosby Records		9:15
		Alfred W. McCann, food	Adelaide Hawley, talk	9:30
	This Life is Mine		Daytime Classics	9:45
My True Story	Valiant Lady	Henry Gladstone, news	Lora Lawton	10am
	The Light of the World	Bessy Beatty, talk	Robert St. John, news	10:15
Tommy Taylor and Ilene Woods, songs	The Strange Romance of Evelyn Winters		Finders Keepers	10:30
Listening Post / Lisa Sergio, talk	Bachelor's Children			10:45
Breakfast with Breneman	Amanda of Honeymoon Hill	Arthur Gaeth, news	The Road of Life	11am
	Second Husband	Music / Jimmy Fidler, gossip	Rosemary	11:15
Gilbert Martyn, news	Bright Horizon	The Quiz Wizard / Take It Easy Time	The Dreft Star Playhouse	11:30
The Jack Berch Show	Aunt Jenny's True Life Stories	Tobe's Topics / What's Your Idea	David Harum	11:45
Glamour Manor, Cliff Arquette	Kate Smith Speaks	Gabriel Heatter, news	Don Goddard, news	12pm
	Big Sister	The Coke Club, Morton Downey	Maggie McNellis, talk	12:15
The Farm and Home Hour	The Romance of Helen Trent	Henry Gladstone, news	Music	12:30
	Our Gal Sunday	The Answer Man		12:45
H. R. Baukhage, news	Life Can Be Beautiful	Jack Bundy's Album	Mary Margaret McBride, talk	1pm
The Women's Exchange	Ma Perkins	Vincent Lopez Orchestra		1:15
	Bernadine Flynn, news	Stone and Brite, songs		1:30
Galen Drake, talk	The Goldbergs	The American Women's Jury	Morgan Beatty, news	1:45

DAYTIME — WINTER, 1945

Sunday

	ABC	CBS	MBS	NBC
2pm	Chaplain Jim, USA	Matinee Theater	The Hollywood Theater	Those We Love
2:15				
2:30	National Vespers	World News Today	Prescott Robinson, news	The Westinghouse Program, John C. Thomas
2:45			Bob Stanley Orchestra	
3pm	The Charlotte Greenwood Show	New York Philharmonic Orchestra	The Quiz of Two Cities	The Sheaffer Parade
3:15				
3:30	Miss Hattie		The Return of Nick Carter	The Army Hour
3:45				
4pm	Musical Bouquet		Your America	
4:15				
4:30	The Eight to the Bar Ranch, Andrew Sisters	The Electric Hour, Nelson Eddy	What's the Name of That Song	Music America Loves Best
4:45				
5pm	Mary Small's Revue	The Prudential Family Hour	Let's Face the Issue	NBC Symphony Orchestra
5:15				
5:30	The Metropolitan Opera Auditions		The Shadow	
5:45		William L. Shirer, news		

DAYTIME — WINTER, 1945

Monday-Friday

ABC	CBS	MBS	NBC	
John B. Kennedy, news	Joyce Jordan, MD	Cedric Foster, news	The Guiding Light	2pm
Galen Drake, talk	Two on a Clue	Jane Cowl, talk	Today's Children	2:15
Ladies Be Seated	Perry Mason	Leo Egan, news	The Woman in White	2:30
	Tena and Tim	True Detective Mysteries	Betty Crocker, cooking / Hymns of All Churches	2:45
Frank Knight, songs	The Story of Mary Marlin	Martha Deane, talk	A Woman of America	3pm
Appointment with Life /	High Places	Linda's First Love	Ma Perkins	3:15
Music	The Sing Along Club	Rambling with Gambling	Pepper Young's Family	3:30
Songs			The Right to Happiness	3:45
Westbrook Van Voorhis, news	House Party	John Gambling, news	Mary Noble, Backstage Wife	4pm
Correspondents Abroad		Jay Johnson, songs	Stella Dallas	4:15
Music	Feature Story	Dr. Eddy's Food Forum	Lorenzo Jones	4:30
Hop Harrigan	Music		Young Widder Brown	4:45
Terry and the Pirates	Service Talk	Uncle Don	When a Girl Marries	5pm
Dick Tracy		The Adventures of Superman	Portia Faces Life	5:15
Jack Armstrong, the All-American Boy	Terry Allen and the Three Sisters	The House of Mystery	Just Plain Bill	5:30
Captain Midnight	Wilderness Road	The Tom Mix Ralston Straight Shooters	Front Page Farrell	5:45

DAYTIME — WINTER, 1945

Saturday

	ABC	CBS	MBS	NBC
9am	The Breakfast Club	Joe King, news	Cleveland Symphony Orchestra	Home is What You Make It
9:15		The Garden Gate		
9:30		Columbia's Country Journal		Adelaide Hawley, talk
9:45				Encores Orchestra
10am	What's Cooking	Youth on Parade	Rainbow House	The Grantland Rice Story
10:15				
10:30	The Land of the Lost	Mary Lee Taylor, cooking		Julie Conway, songs
10:45				Alex Dreier, news
11am	Kay Armen Sings	Let's Pretend	Prescott Robinson, news	The First Piano Quartet
11:15			Lorraine Sherwood, talk	
11:30	Transatlantic Quiz	The Billie Burke Show	Hookey Hall	Smilin' Ed's Buster Brown Gang
11:45	Lois Long, shopping			
12pm	Jean Tighe, songs	The Armstrong Theater of Today	Hello, Mom	Don Goddard, news
12:15	Radie Harris, gossip			Consumer Time
12:30	The Farm and Home Hour	Stars Over Hollywood	Henry Gladstone, news	Atlantic Spotlight
12:45			The Answer Man	
1pm	Eddie Condon's Jazz Concert	Grand Central Station	Vincent Lopez Orchestra	Adventure Ahead
1.15				
1:30	Soldiers With Wings	Report to the Nation	Symphonies for Youth	The Baxters
1:45				John McVane, news

DAYTIME — WINTER, 1945

Saturday

	ABC	CBS	MBS	NBC
2pm	The Metropolitan Opera	Of Men and Books		These Are Our Men
2:15		Adventures in Science		
2:30		Carolina Hayride	Leo Egan, news	Musiciana
2:45			Stanley Maxted, talk	
3pm		The Land is Bright	This is Halloran	Orchestras of the Nation
3:15				
3:30		Syncopation Piece	Where Are They Now	
3:45		Jobs for Tomorrow		
4pm		Report from Washington	Leo Egan, news	Doctors Look Ahead
4:15		Report from Overseas	Johnny Richards Orchestra	
4:30		Assignment Home	Bob Stanley Orchestra	The NBC Comedy Theater
4:45				
5pm		Philadelphia Symphony Orchestra	Uncle Don	Grand Hotel
5:15			The Milt Herth Trio	
5:30			Louis Prima Orchestra	John W. Vandercook, news
5:45	Hello Sweetheart, Marion Mann		Shirley Eder, talk	Tin Pan Alley of the Air

EVENING — SPRING, 1945

Sunday

	ABC	CBS	MBS	NBC
6pm	The Radio Hall of Fame	The Adventures of Ozzie and Harriet	Quick as a Flash	The Catholic Hour
6:15				
6:30		The Baby Snooks Show	Upton Close, news	The Great Gildersleeve
6:45			Dick Brown, songs	
7pm	Drew Pearson, news	The Kate Smith Hour	Leonidas Witherall	The Lucky Strike Program, Jack Benny
7:15	Don Gardiner, news			
7:30	The Quiz Kids		Melvin Elliott, news	The Fitch Bandwagon
7:45			Max Lerner, news	
8pm	The Greenfield Chapel Choir	Blondie	A. L. Alexander's Mediation Board	The Charlie McCarthy Show
8:15	Raymond Moley, news			
8:30	The Jerry Wayne Show	Crime Doctor		The Eddie Bracken Show
8:45		Ned Calmer, news (8:55pm)	Gabriel Heatter, news	
9pm	Walter Winchell's Jergens Journal	The Radio Reader's Digest	Steel Horizons	The Manhattan Merry-Go-Round
9:15	Hollywood Mystery Time			
9:30		The Texaco Star Theater, James Melton	Cedric Foster, news	The American Album of Familiar Music
9:45	Jimmy Fidler, gossip		Dorothy Thompson, news	
10pm	The Life of Riley	Take It or Leave It	Earl Wilson's Broadway Column	The Hour of Charm
10:15			This is Helen Hayes	
10:30	One Foot in Heaven	We, the People	The Sealed Book	The Old Gold Comedy Theater of the Air
10:45				

EVENING — SPRING, 1945

Monday

ABC	CBS	MBS	NBC	
Walter Kiernan, news	Harry Marble, news	Paul Schubert, news	Don Hollenbeck, news	6pm
What Are the Facts	James Carroll, songs	George Paxton Orchestra	Serenade to America	6:15
Whose War is This	Sally Moore, songs	Fred Vandeventer, news		6:30
Peggy Mann, songs	The World Today	Stan Lomax, sports	Lowell Thomas, news	6:45
Taylor Grant, news	The Jack Kirkwood Show	Fulton Lewis Jr., news	The Chesterfield Supper Club	7pm
Raymond Gram Swing, news	Hedda Hopper, gossip	The Answer Man	John W. Vandercook, news	7:15
The Lone Ranger	The Bob Hawk Show	Bulldog Drummond	Allen Roth Orchestra	7:30
			H. V. Kaltenborn, news	7:45
Ted Malone from England	Vox Pop	Cecil Brown, news	The Cavalcade of America	8pm
Lum and Abner		Curt Massey, songs		8:15
Blind Date	Burns and Allen	Sherlock Holmes	The Voice of Firestone	8:30
	Bill Henry, news (8:55pm)			8:45
Melody in the Night	The Lux Radio Theater	Gabriel Heatter, news	The Bell Telephone Hour	9pm
		Real Stories from Real Life		9:15
Spotlight Bands		The Better Half	Information, Please	9:30
Short Story (9:55pm)				9:45
Guy Lombardo Orchestra	The Lady Esther Screen Guild Theater	Dr. A. L. Sachar, health	The Carnation Contented Hour	10pm
		Paul Schubert, news		10:15
Hollywood Show Time	The Cameron Andrews Show	The Longines Symphonette	Dr. I. Q., The Mental Banker	10:30
				10:45

EVENING — SPRING, 1945

Tuesday

	ABC	CBS	MBS	NBC
6pm	Walter Kiernan, news	Harry Marble, news	Paul Schubert, news	Don Hollenbeck, news
6:15	What Are the Facts	Edwin C. Hill, news	The Mutual Newsreel	Serenade to America
6:30	Whose War is This	Ted Husing, sports	Fred Vandeventer, news	
6:45	Peggy Mann, songs	The World Today	Stan Lomax, sports	Lowell Thomas, news
7pm	Taylor Grant, news	The Jack Kirkwood Show	Fulton Lewis Jr., news	The Chesterfield Supper Club
7:15	Raymond Gram Swing, news	Music That Satisfies	The Strange Dr. Weird	John W. Vandercook, news
7:30	One Man's Family	The American Melody Hour	Arthur Hale, news	Everything for the Boys, Dick Haymes
7:45			The Answer Man	
8pm	Ted Malone from England	Big Town	Frank Singiser, news	The Purple Heart Show, Ginny Simms
8:15	Lum and Abner		Curt Massey, songs	
8:30	The Alan Young Show	Theater of Romance	The Roy Rogers Show	A Date with Judy
8:45		Bill Henry, news (8:55pm)		
9pm	Donald Dame, songs	Inner Sanctum Mysteries	Gabriel Heatter, news	The Molle' Mystery Theater
9:15	Hedda Hopper, gossip		Real Stories from Real Life	
9:30	Spotlight Bands	This is My Best	The American Forum of the Air	Fibber Magee and Molly
9:45	Short Story (9:55pm)			
10pm	Transatlantic Quiz	Service to the Front		The Pepsodent Show, Bob Hope
10:15			It Happened in 1955	
10:30	Glen Gray Orchestra	Congress Speaks	The Longines Symphonette	The Raleigh Room, Hildegarde
10:45		Behind the Scenes at CBS		

EVENING — SPRING, 1945

Wednesday

ABC	CBS	MBS	NBC	
Walter Kiernan, news	Harry Marble, news	Paul Schubert, news	Don Hollenbeck, news	6pm
What Are the Facts	Lyn Murray Orchestra	Duke Ellington Orchestra	Serenade to America	6:15
Whose War is This	Eileen Farrell, songs	Fred Vandeventer, news		6:30
Peggy Mann, songs	The World Today	Stan Lomax, sports	Lowell Thomas, news	6:45
Taylor Grant, news	The Jack Kirkwood Show	Fulton Lewis Jr., news	The Chesterfield Supper Club	7pm
Raymond Gram Swing, news	Music That Satisfies	The Answer Man	John W. Vandercook, news	7:15
The Lone Ranger	The Adventures of Ellery Queen	Can You Top This	Allen Roth Orchestra	7:30
			H. V. Kaltenborn, news	7:45
Ted Malone from England	The Jack Carson Show	Cecil Brown, news	Mr. and Mrs. North	8pm
Lum and Abner		Curt Massey, songs		8:15
Counterspy	Dr. Christian	Barney Grant	The Gay Mrs. Featherstone	8:30
	Bill Henry, news (8:55pm)			8:45
Watch Tower for Tomorrow	Songs By Sinatra	Gabriel Heatter, news	Time to Smile, Eddie Cantor	9pm
		Real Stories from Real Life		9:15
Spotlight Bands	Which is Which	The Brownstone Theater	Mr. District Attorney	9:30
Short Story (9:55pm)				9:45
The Ice Box Follies, Niles and Prindle	Great Moments in Music	Dale Carnegie, inspirational	Kay Kyser's College of Musical Knowledge	10pm
		Sidney Moseley, news		10:15
Rex Maupin Orchestra	Let Yourself Go, Milton Berle	The Longines Symphonette		10:30
				10:45

EVENING — SPRING, 1945

Thursday

	ABC	CBS	MBS	NBC
6pm	Walter Kiernan, news	Ned Calmer, news	Paul Schubert, news	Don Hollenbeck, news
6:15	What Are the Facts	Calling Pan-America	Lani McIntyre Orchestra	Serenade to America
6:30	Whose War is This		Fred Vandeventer, news	
6:45	Peggy Mann, songs	The World Today	Stan Lomax, sports	Lowell Thomas, news
7pm	Taylor Grant, news	The Jack Kirkwood Show	Fulton Lewis Jr., news	The Chesterfield Supper Club
7:15	Raymond Gram Swing, news	Music That Satisfies	Victory is Our Business	John W. Vandercook, news
7:30	The Man from G-2	Mr. Keen, Tracer of Lost Persons	Arthur Hale, news	The Bob Burns Show
7:45			The Answer Man	
8pm	Earl Godwin, news	Suspense	Frank Singiser, news	Maxwell House Coffee Time, Frank Morgan
8:15	Lum and Abner		Curt Massey, songs	
8:30	America's Town Meeting of the Air	Death Valley Sheriff	Hercule Poirot	The Birdseye Open House, Dinah Shore
8:45		Bill Henry, news (8:55pm)		
9pm		Shower of Stars	Gabriel Heatter, news	The Kraft Music Hall, Bing Crosby
9:15			Real Stories from Real Life	
9:30	Spotlight Bands	Meet Corliss Archer	The Treasure Hour of Song	The Sealtest Village Store, Davis and Haley
9:45	Short Story (9:55pm)			
10pm	Fred Waring Orchestra	The First Line of Defense	Arch Oboler's Plays	Abbott and Costello
10:15				
10:30	The March of Time	Romance, Rhythm and Ripley	The Longines Symphonette	The Rudy Vallee Show
10:45				

EVENING — SPRING, 1945

Friday

ABC	CBS	MBS	NBC	
Walter Kiernan, news	Harry Marble, news	Paul Schubert, news	Don Hollenbeck, news	6pm
What Are the Facts	James Carroll, songs	Duke Ellington Orchestra	Serenade to America	6:15
Whose War is This	Sally Moore, songs	Fred Vandeventer, news		6:30
Peggy Mann, songs	The World Today	Stan Lomax, sports	Lowell Thomas, news	6:45
Taylor Grant, news	The Jack Kirkwood Show	Fulton Lewis Jr., news	The Chesterfield Supper Club	7pm
Raymond Gram Swing, news	Report to the People	The Answer Man	John W. Vandercook, news	7:15
The Lone Ranger	Friday on Broadway	Variety Musicale	Allen Roth Orchestra	7:30
			H. V. Kaltenborn, news	7:45
Stars of the Future	The Aldrich Family	Cecil Brown, news	Highways in Melody	8pm
		Curt Massey, songs		8:15
This is Your FBI	The Adventures of the Thin Man	Freedom of Opportunity	Duffy's Tavern	8:30
	Bill Henry, news (8:55pm)			8:45
Famous Jury Trials	It Pays to Be Ignorant	Gabriel Heatter, news	Waltz Time	9pm
		Real Stories from Real Life		9:15
Spotlight Bands	Those Websters	Double or Nothing	People Are Funny	9:30
Short Story (9:55pm)				9:45
Sammy Kaye Orchestra	The Durante - Moore Show	Madison Square Garden Boxing	Amos 'n' Andy	10pm
				10:15
The Doctors Talk It Over	Stage Door Canteen		The Colgate Sports Newsreel, Bill Stern	10:30
Letter to Your Service Man			Public Affairs	10:45

EVENING — SPRING, 1945

Saturday

	ABC	CBS	MBS	NBC
6pm	Bruno Shaw, news	Harry Marble, news	Paul Schubert, news	Don Hollenbeck, news
6:15	Harry Wismer, sports	The People's Platform	Strictly Personal	Friendship Ranch
6:30	Edward Tomlinson, news		Fred Vandeventer, news	
6:45	Labor USA	The World Today	Stan Lomax, sports	Religion in the News
7pm	Correspondents Abroad	The Mayor of the Town	Guess Who	Our Foreign Policy
7:15	Leland Stowe, news			
7:30	Meet Your Navy	America in the Air	Arthur Hale, news	The Robert Q. Lewis Show
7:45			The Answer Man	
8pm	Early American Dance Music	Pabst Blue Ribbon Town, Danny Kaye	Frank Singiser, news	Gaslight Gaieties
8:15			Dr. A. L. Sachar, health	
8:30	Boston Symphony Orchestra	The FBI in Peace and War	Symphony of the Americas	Truth or Consequences
8:45		Ned Calmer, news (8:55pm)		
9pm		Your Hit Parade	Hawaii Calls	The National Barn Dance
9:15	Edward Tomlinson, news			
9:30	Spotlight Bands		Calling All Detectives	Can You Top This
9:45	Quick Quiz (9:55pm)	Saturday Night Serenade		
10pm	The Andy Russell Show		The Chicago Theater of the Air	The Judy Canova Show
10:15		Here Comes Elmer, Al Pearce		
10:30	Glen Gray Orchestra			Grand Ole Opry
10:45		Public Affairs		

DAYTIME — SPRING, 1945

Sunday

	ABC	CBS	MBS	NBC
9am	News	News	Uncle Don Reads the Comics	News
9:15	Coast-to-Coast on a Bus	From the Organ Loft		Story to Order
9:30			The Navy Goes to Church	Songs for Strings
9:45		New Voices in Song		Music
10am	Message of Israel	The CBS Church of the Air	Leo Egan, news	The National Radio Pulpit
10:15			Frank Kingdon, news	
10:30	The Southernaires Quartet	Wings Over Jordan	The Mutual Radio Chapel	The Horn and Hardart Children's Hour
10:45				
11am	AAF Symphonic Flight	The Blue Jacket Choir	Paul Manning, news	
11:15			High School at Home	
11:30	The Hour of Faith	Invitation to Learning	Brunch with Dorothy and Dick	Clyde Kitell, news
11:45				The Little Betsy Ross Girl Variety Program
12pm	The Weekly War Journal	The Salt Lake Tabernacle Choir	The Show Shop	The Eternal Light
12:15				
12:30	Notes from a Diary	Transatlantic Call	Soldiers of the Press	NBC Concert Orchestra
12:45	The Piano Playhouse		Prescott Robinson, news	
1pm	John B. Kennedy, news	The CBS Church of the Air	The Canary Pet Shop	Your Radio Reporter
1:15	George Hicks, news		Cy Walter, piano	America United
1:30	Sammy Kaye's Sunday Serenade	Problems of Peace	Sweetheart Time	The University of Chicago Round Table
1:45		Edward R. Murrow, news		

LISTINGS FOR 1945

DAYTIME — SPRING, 1945

Monday-Friday

ABC	CBS	MBS	NBC	
The Breakfast Club	Joe King, news	Victor Lindhahr, health	Ed East and Polly, songs	9am
	The American School of the Air	Bing Crosby Records		9:15
		Alfred W. McCann, food	Adelaide Hawley, talk	9:30
	This Life is Mine		Betty Crocker, rations	9:45
My True Story	Valiant Lady	Henry Gladstone, news	Robert St. John, news	10am
	The Light of the World	Bessy Beatty, talk	Lora Lawton	10:15
The Don Milton Show	The Strange Romance of Evelyn Winters		The Road of Life	10:30
Listening Post / Lisa Sergio, talk	Bachelor's Children		Joyce Jordan, MD	10:45
Breakfast with Breneman	Amanda of Honeymoon Hill	Prescott Robinson, news	The Happy Felton Show	11am
	Second Husband	Music / Jimmy Fidler, gossip		11:15
Gilbert Martyn, news	Bright Horizon	The Quiz Wizard / Take It Easy Time	The Dreft Star Playhouse	11:30
The Jack Berch Show	Aunt Jenny's True Life Stories	Tobe's Topics / What's Your Idea	David Harum	11:45
Glamour Manor, Cliff Arquette	Kate Smith Speaks	William Lang, news	Don Goddard, news	12pm
	Big Sister	The Coke Club, Morton Downey	Maggie McNellis, talk	12:15
The Women's Exchange	The Romance of Helen Trent	Henry Gladstone, news	Music	12:30
	Our Gal Sunday	The Answer Man		12:45
H. R. Baukhage, news	Life Can Be Beautiful	Jack Bundy's Album	Mary Margaret McBride, talk	1pm
Rosa Rio, organ	Ma Perkins	Tello-Test Quiz		1:15
Galen Drake, talk	Bernadine Flynn, news	Vincent Lopez Orchestra		1:30
	Young Dr. Malone	The John J. Anthony Program	Morgan Beatty, news	1:45

DAYTIME — SPRING, 1945

Sunday

	ABC	CBS	MBS	NBC
2pm	Chaplain Jim, USA	Stradivari Orchestra	The Longines Symphonette	Jo Stafford and Lawrence Brooks, songs
2:15				
2:30	National Vespers	World News Today	Prescott Robinson, news	The Westinghouse Program, John C. Thomas
2:45			Dale Carnegie, inspirational	
3pm	Kay's Canteen	New York Philharmonic Orchestra	The Quiz of Two Cities	The Sheaffer Parade
3:15				
3:30	Miss Hattie		The Hollywood Theater	The Army Hour
3:45				
4pm	Musical Bouquet		Your America	
4:15				
4:30	The Eight to the Bar Ranch, Andrew Sisters	The Electric Hour, Nelson Eddy	What's the Name of That Song	Music America Loves Best
4:45				
5pm	Mary Small's Revue	The Prudential Family Hour	Let's Face the Issue	NBC Symphony Orchestra
5:15				
5:30	The Charlotte Greenwood Show		The Return of Nick Carter	
5:45		William L. Shirer, news		

DAYTIME — SPRING, 1945

Monday-Friday

ABC	CBS	MBS	NBC	
John B. Kennedy, news	Two on a Clue	Cedric Foster, news	The Guiding Light	2pm
Ethel and Albert	Rosemary	Jane Cowl, talk	Today's Children	2:15
Music	Perry Mason	Leo Egan, news	The Woman in White	2:30
Correspondents Abroad	Tena and Tim	Never Too Old	Betty Crocker, cooking / Hymns of All Churches	2:45
Appointment with Life	Time to Remember	Martha Deane, talk	A Woman of America	3pm
	Off the Record		Ma Perkins	3:15
Ladies Be Seated		Rambling with Gambling	Pepper Young's Family	3:30
	The Landt Trio and Curley		The Right to Happiness	3:45
Westbrook Van Voorhis, news	House Party	John Gambling, news	Mary Noble, Backstage Wife	4pm
Music		Jay Johnson, songs	Stella Dallas	4:15
Janet Flanner, news	Feature Story	Dr. Eddy's Food Forum	Lorenzo Jones	4:30
Hop Harrigan	The Danny O'Neil Show		Young Widder Brown	4:45
Terry and the Pirates	Service Talk	Uncle Don	When a Girl Marries	5pm
Dick Tracy		The Adventures of Superman	Portia Faces Life	5:15
Jack Armstrong, the All-American Boy	Cimarron Tavern	The House of Mystery	Just Plain Bill	5:30
Captain Midnight	Wilderness Road	The Tom Mix Ralston Straight Shooters	Front Page Farrell	5:45

DAYTIME — SPRING, 1945

Saturday

	ABC	CBS	MBS	NBC
9am	The Breakfast Club	Joe King, news	Wings for Tomorrow	Home is What You Make It
9:15		The Garden Gate		
9:30		Columbia's Country Journal	Sewing Course	Adelaide Hawley, talk
9:45				Encores Orchestra
10am	What's Cooking	Youth on Parade	Rainbow House	Your Host is Buffalo
10:15				
10:30	The Land of the Lost	Mary Lee Taylor, cooking		Bern Klassen, songs
10:45				Alex Dreier, news
11am	Harry Kogen Orchestra	Let's Pretend	Prescott Robinson, news	The First Piano Quartet
11:15			Lorraine Sherwood, talk	
11:30	Betty Moore, home talk	The Billie Burke Show	Hookey Hall	Smilin' Ed's Buster Brown Gang
11:45	Lois Long, shopping			
12pm	Herman and Banta, xylophone	The Armstrong Theater of Today	Hello, Mom	Don Goddard, news
12:15	Radie Harris, gossip			Consumer Time
12:30	The Farm and Home Hour	Stars Over Hollywood	Henry Gladstone, news	Atlantic Spotlight
12:45			The Answer Man	
1pm	Fun Canteen	Grand Central Station	Jack Bundy's Album	The Veterans Advisor
1:15			Vincent Lopez Orchestra	The NBC Comedy Theater
1:30	Soldiers With Wings	Report to the Nation	The Human Adventure	The Baxters
1:45				John McVane, news

DAYTIME — SPRING, 1945

Saturday

	ABC	CBS	MBS	NBC
2pm	John B. Kennedy, news	Of Men and Books	Wings for Tomorrow	Joseph Gallichio Orchestra
2:15	Theodora Lynch, songs	Adventures in Science		
2:30	It's a Hit	Carolina Hayride	Leo Egan, news	The Grantland Rice Story
2:45			Stanley Maxted, talk	
3pm	Saturday Senior Swing	The Land is Bright	This is Halloran	Orchestras of the Nation
3:15				
3:30	The Fitzgeralds, talk	Public Affairs	Where Are They Now	
3:45		The Builders of Victory		
4pm	NBC Symphony Orchestra	Report from Washington	Leo Egan, news	Doctors Look Ahead
4:15		Report from Overseas	Jay Johnson, songs	
4:30		Assignment Home	Bob Stanley Orchestra	Music on Display
4:45				
5pm	A Date with the Duke	Philadelphia Symphony Orchestra	Uncle Don	Grand Hotel
5:15			Leo Egan, news	
5:30			Sonny Dunham Orchestra	John W. Vandercook, news
5:45	Jean Tighe, songs		Shirley Eder, talk	Tin Pan Alley of the Air

EVENING — SUMMER, 1945

Sunday

	ABC	CBS	MBS	NBC
6pm	The Philco Summer Hour	The Silver Theater	The Abbott Mysteries	The Catholic Hour
6:15				
6:30	Donald Dame and Louise Carlyle, songs	Report to the Nation	Cedric Foster, news	Men at Sea
6:45			Postcard Serenade, Judy Lang	
7pm	Drew Pearson, news	Men of Vision	Opinion Requested	Wayne King Orchestra
7:15	Don Gardiner, news			
7:30	The Quiz Kids	That's My Pop	Melvin Elliott, news	Rogue's Gallery
7:45			Max Lerner, news	
8pm	String Ensemble	Blondie	A. L. Alexander's Mediation Board	The Spike Jones Show
8:15	Raymond Moley, news			
8:30	The Fighting AAF	Crime Doctor		Tommy Dorsey Orchestra
8:45		Ned Calmer, news (8:55pm)	Gabriel Heatter, news	
9pm	Ray Henle, news	The Radio Reader's Digest	Steel Horizons	The Manhattan Merry-Go-Round
9:15	Hollywood Mystery Time			
9:30		The Texaco Star Theater, James Melton	Double or Nothing	The American Album of Familiar Music
9:45	Jimmy Fidler, gossip			
10pm	Transatlantic Quiz	Take It or Leave It	The Brownstone Theater	The Hour of Charm
10:15				
10:30	Freddy Martin Orchestra	We, the People	The Sealed Book	Meet Me at Parky's
10:45				

EVENING — SUMMER, 1945

Monday

ABC	CBS	MBS	NBC	
Walter Kiernan, news	Quincy Howe, news	Paul Schubert, news	Lyle Van, news	6pm
What Are the Facts	James Carroll, songs	The Man on the Street	Serenade to America	6:15
Whose War is This	Sally Moore, songs	Fred Vandeventer, news		6:30
Charlie Chan	The World Today	Stan Lomax, sports	Lowell Thomas, news	6:45
Taylor Grant, news	Ted Husing, sports	Fred Morrison, news	The Chesterfield Supper Club	7pm
Raymond Gram Swing, news	Hedda Hopper, gossip	The Answer Man	John W. Vandercook, news	7:15
The Lone Ranger	The Bob Hawk Show	Bulldog Drummond	Allen Roth Orchestra	7:30
			H. V. Kaltenborn, news	7:45
Pick and Pat	Vox Pop	Cecil Brown, news	C. M. H. Drama	8pm
The News of Tomorrow		Now It Can Be Told		8:15
Meet Your Navy	The Merry Life of Mary Christmas	Boston Blackie	The Voice of Firestone	8:30
	Bill Henry, news (8:55pm)			8:45
Guy Lombardo Orchestra	The Marlin Hurt and Beulah Show	Gabriel Heatter, news	The Bell Telephone Hour	9pm
		Real Stories from Real Life		9:15
Rex Maupin Orchestra	The Sea Has a Story	Spotlight Bands	The Rise' Stevens Show	9:30
Short Story (9:55pm)				9:45
Tokyo Calling	The Lady Esther Screen Guild Theater	Victory Auction	The Carnation Contented Hour	10pm
				10:15
Reunion, USA	The Stu Erwin Show	The Longines Symphonette	Dr. I. Q., The Mental Banker	10:30
				10:45

EVENING — SUMMER, 1945

Tuesday

	ABC	CBS	MBS	NBC
6pm	Walter Kiernan, news	Quincy Howe, news	Paul Schubert, news	Lyle Van, news
6:15	What Are the Facts	Edwin C. Hill, news	The Man on the Street	Serenade to America
6:30	Whose War is This	The Voice of Eileen Farrell	Fred Vandeventer, news	
6:45	Charlie Chan	The World Today	Stan Lomax, sports	Lowell Thomas, news
7pm	Taylor Grant, news	Ted Husing, sports	Fred Morrison, news	The Chesterfield Supper Club
7:15	Raymond Gram Swing, news	The Danny O'Neil Show	Xavier Cugat Records	John W. Vandercook, news
7:30	County Fair	The American Melody Hour	Arthur Hale, news	Everything for the Boys, Dick Haymes
7:45			The Answer Man	
8pm	Pick and Pat	Big Town	Frank Singiser, news	Talent Theater, Ginny Simms
8:15	The News of Tomorrow		Now It Can Be Told	
8:30	The Alan Young Show	Theater of Romance	The Falcon	A Date with Judy
8:45		Bill Henry, news (8:55pm)		
9pm	Guy Lombardo Orchestra	Columbia Presents Corwin	Gabriel Heatter, news	The Navy Hour
9:15			Real Stories from Real Life	
9:30	Radie Harris, gossip	The Doctor Fights	The American Forum of the Air	The Victor Borge Show
9:45	Short Story (9:55pm)			
10pm	George Olsen Orchestra	Just Entertainment		The Man Called X
10:15			Paul Schubert, news	
10:30	Suit Yourself	Congress Speaks	The Longines Symphonette	An Evening with Romberg
10:45		Behind the Scenes at CBS		

EVENING — SUMMER, 1945

Wednesday

ABC	CBS	MBS	NBC	
Walter Kiernan, news	Quincy Howe, news	Paul Schubert, news	Lyle Van, news	*6pm*
What Are the Facts	James Carroll, songs	The Man on the Street	Serenade to America	*6:15*
Whose War is This	Sally Moore, songs	Fred Vandeventer, news		*6:30*
Charlie Chan	The World Today	Stan Lomax, sports	Lowell Thomas, news	*6:45*
Taylor Grant, news	Ted Husing, sports	Fred Morrison, news	The Chesterfield Supper Club	*7pm*
Raymond Gram Swing, news	The Danny O'Neil Show	The Answer Man	John W. Vandercook, news	*7:15*
The Lone Ranger	The Adventures of Ellery Queen	Can You Top This	Allen Roth Orchestra	*7:30*
			H. V. Kaltenborn, news	*7:45*
Pick and Pat	The Saint	Cecil Brown, news	Mr. and Mrs. North	*8pm*
The News of Tomorrow		Now It Can Be Told		*8:15*
The Fishing and Hunting Club	Dr. Christian	Barney Grant	The Gay Mrs. Featherstone	*8:30*
	Bill Henry, news (8:55pm)			*8:45*
Curtain Time	Crime Photographer	Gabriel Heatter, news	Wednesday with You	*9pm*
		Real Stories from Real Life		*9:15*
Jones and I	Detect and Collect	Spotlight Bands	Mr. District Attorney	*9:30*
Short Story (9:55pm)				*9:45*
Counterspy	Great Moments in Music	The Human Adventure	Kay Kyser's College of Musical Knowledge	*10pm*
				10:15
Lee Mortimer, news	GI Laffs	The Longines Symphonette		*10:30*
Janet Flanner, news				*10:45*

EVENING — SUMMER, 1945

Thursday

	ABC	CBS	MBS	NBC
6pm	Walter Kiernan, news	Ned Calmer, news	Paul Schubert, news	Lyle Van, news
6:15	What Are the Facts	Calling Pan-America	The Man on the Street	Serenade to America
6:30	Whose War is This		Fred Vandeventer, news	
6:45	Charlie Chan	The World Today	Stan Lomax, sports	Lowell Thomas, news
7pm	Taylor Grant, news	Ted Husing, sports	Fred Morrison, news	The Chesterfield Supper Club
7:15	Raymond Gram Swing, news	The Danny O'Neil Show	Victory is Our Business	John W. Vandercook, news
7:30	George Olsen Orchestra	Mr. Keen, Tracer of Lost Persons	Arthur Hale, news	Philo Vance
7:45			The Answer Man	
8pm	Pick and Pat	Suspense	Frank Singiser, news	Roy Shield Orchestra
8:15	Earl Godwin, news		Now It Can Be Told	
8:30	America's Town Meeting of the Air	Maisie	Hercule Poirot	The Adventures of Topper
8:45		Bill Henry, news (8:55pm)		
9pm		Shower of Stars	Gabriel Heatter, news	The Kraft Music Hall, Bing Crosby
9:15			Real Stories from Real Life	
9:30	Van Cleave Orchestra	Meet Corliss Archer	Starlight Serenade	The Sealtest Village Store, Jack Haley
9:45	Short Story (9:55pm)			
10pm	One Foot in Heaven	The First Line of Defense	Arch Oboler's Plays	Mystery in the Air
10:15				
10:30	The March of Time	Romance, Rhythm and Ripley	The Longines Symphonette	We Came This Way
10:45				

EVENING — SUMMER, 1945

Friday

ABC	CBS	MBS	NBC	
Walter Kiernan, news	Quincy Howe, news	Paul Schubert, news	Lyle Van, news	*6pm*
What Are the Facts	James Carroll, songs	The Man on the Street	Serenade to America	*6:15*
Whose War is This	The Voice of Eileen Farrell	Fred Vandeventer, news		*6:30*
Charlie Chan	The World Today	Stan Lomax, sports	Lowell Thomas, news	*6:45*
Taylor Grant, news	Ted Husing, sports	Fred Morrison, news	The Chesterfield Supper Club	*7pm*
Raymond Gram Swing, news	The Danny O'Neil Show	The Answer Man	John W. Vandercook, news	*7:15*
The Lone Ranger	The Jerry Wayne Show	Variety Musicale	Allen Roth Orchestra	*7:30*
			Richard Harkness, news	*7:45*
Blind Date	The Aldrich Family	Cecil Brown, news	Highways in Melody	*8pm*
		Now It Can Be Told		*8:15*
Pages of Melody	The Adventures of the Thin Man	Freedom of Opportunity	Correction, Please	*8:30*
	Bill Henry, news (8:55pm)			*8:45*
Famous Jury Trials	It Pays to Be Ignorant	Gabriel Heatter, news	Waltz Time	*9pm*
		Real Stories from Real Life		*9:15*
The Sheriff	Those Websters	Spotlight Bands	People Are Funny	*9:30*
Short Story (9:55pm)				*9:45*
The Man from G-2	The Ray Bolger Show	Madison Square Garden Boxing	Dunninger, the Mentalist	*10pm*
				10:15
The Doctors Talk It Over	Harry James Orchestra		The Colgate Sports Newsreel, Bill Stern	*10:30*
The Andrini Continentals			Public Affairs	*10:45*

EVENING — SUMMER, 1945

Saturday

	ABC	CBS	MBS	NBC
6pm	Wilfred Fleisher, news	Quincy Howe, news	Paul Schubert, news	Lyle Van, news
6:15	Harry Wismer, sports	The People's Platform	Strictly Personal	Music of Manhattan
6:30	Hank D'Amico Orchestra		Fred Vandeventer, news	
6:45	Labor USA	The World Today	Stan Lomax, sports	The Art of Living
7pm	Jobs After Victory	St. Louis Municipal Opera	Guess Who	Our Foreign Policy
7:15	Correspondents Abroad			
7:30	Edgar Hayes Orchestra	America in the Air	Arthur Hale, news	Noah Webster Says
7:45			The Answer Man	
8pm	Summer Serenade	The Land is Bright	Frank Singiser, news	Milton Katims Orchestra
8:15			Music for Remembrance	
8:30	Gilbert and Sullivan Music	Viva America	Detroit Symphony Orchestra	Fantasies from Lights Out
8:45		Ned Calmer, news (8:55pm)		
9pm		Your Hit Parade		The National Barn Dance
9:15				
9:30	Flight to the Pacific		Calling All Detectives	Can You Top This
9:45	Quick Quiz (9:55pm)	Saturday Night Serenade		
10pm	Hoosier Hop		The Chicago Theater of the Air	I Sustain the Wings
10:15		Assignment Home		
10:30	Hayloft Hoedown			Grand Ole Opry
10:45		Public Affairs		

DAYTIME — SUMMER, 1945

Sunday

	ABC	CBS	MBS	NBC
9am	News	News	Uncle Don Reads the Comics	News
9:15	Coast-to-Coast on a Bus	From the Organ Loft		Story to Order
9:30			The Navy Goes to Church	Songs for Strings
9:45		New Voices in Song		Music
10am	Message of Israel	The CBS Church of the Air	Leo Egan, news	Highlights of the Bible
10:15			Frank Kingdon, news	
10:30	The Southernaires Quartet	The Camp Meetin' Choir	The Mutual Radio Chapel	The Horn and Hardart Children's Hour
10:45				
11am	Brunch with the Fitzgeralds	The Blue Jacket Choir	Paul Manning, news	
11:15			The Musical Beauty Box	
11:30	The Hour of Faith	Invitation to Learning	Brunch with Dorothy and Dick	Charles F. McCarthy, news
11:45				The Little Betsy Ross Girl Variety Program
12pm	The Weekly War Journal	The Salt Lake Tabernacle Choir	The Show Shop	The Eternal Light
12:15				
12:30	Friendship Ranch	Transatlantic Call	One Man's Destiny	NBC Concert Orchestra
12:45			Melvin Elliott, news	
1pm	John B. Kennedy, news	The CBS Church of the Air	Commentators' Round Table	Ed Herlihy, news
1:15	Arthur Feldman, news		Pauline Alpert, piano	America United
1:30	Sammy Kaye's Sunday Serenade	Problems of Peace	Sweetheart Time	The University of Chicago Round Table
1:45		Edward R. Murrow, news		

DAYTIME — SUMMER, 1945

Monday-Friday

ABC	CBS	MBS	NBC	
The Breakfast Club	Joe King, news	The Jack Berch Show	Ed East and Polly, songs	9am
	Arthur Godfrey Time	Bing Crosby Records		9:15
		Alfred W. McCann, food	Adelaide Hawley, talk	9:30
	This Life is Mine		Daytime Classics	
My True Story	Valiant Lady	Henry Gladstone, news	Robert St. John, news	10am
	The Light of the World	Bessy Beatty, talk	Lora Lawton	10:15
Betty Crocker, cooking / Hymns of All Churches	The Strange Romance of Evelyn Winters		The Road of Life	10:30
Listening Post / Lisa Sergio, talk	Bachelor's Children		Joyce Jordan, MD	10:45
Breakfast with Breneman	Amanda of Honeymoon Hill	Prescott Robinson, news	Fred Waring Orchestra	11am
	Second Husband	Tello-Test Quiz		11:15
Gilbert Martyn, news	A Woman's Life	Success Magazine / Take It Easy Time	Barry Cameron	11:30
Between the Bookends	Aunt Jenny's True Life Stories	Tobe's Topics / What's Your Idea	David Harum	11:45
Glamour Manor, Cliff Arquette	Kate Smith Speaks	William Lang, news	Don Goddard, news	12pm
	Big Sister	The Coke Club, Morton Downey	Maggie McNellis, talk	12:15
The Women's Exchange	The Romance of Helen Trent	Henry Gladstone, news	Talk / The Jack Smith Show	12:30
	Our Gal Sunday	The Answer Man	Henry Jerome Orchestra	12:45
H. R. Baukhage, news	Life Can Be Beautiful	Jack Bundy's Album	Mary Margaret McBride, talk	1pm
Constance Bennett, talk	Ma Perkins	Vincent Lopez Orchestra		1:15
Galen Drake, talk	Meet Margaret MacDonald	Phil Brito, songs		1:30
	Young Dr. Malone	The John J. Anthony Program	W. W. Chaplin, news	1:45

DAYTIME — SUMMER, 1945

Sunday

	ABC	CBS	MBS	NBC
2pm	Kay Armen Sings	Stradivari Orchestra	Chaplain Jim, USA	Jo Stafford and Lawrence Brooks, songs
2:15				
2:30	National Vespers	World News Today	Melvin Elliott, news	The Westinghouse Program, John C. Thomas
2:45			Mysteries of Crooked Square	
3pm	Melodies to Remember	Columbia Symphony Orchestra	The Quiz of Two Cities	The Sheaffer Parade
3:15				
3:30	The Washington Story		Return to Duty	One Man's Family
3:45				
4pm	Musical Bouquet		Your America	The Army Hour
4:15				
4:30	Sunday at N-K Ranch, Curt Massey	The Electric Summer Hour	Time for Crime	Tommy Dorsey Orchestra
4:45			Harvey Harding, songs	
5pm	Mary Small's Revue	The Prudential Family Hour	Leave It to Mike	NBC Symphony Orchestra
5:15				
5:30	The Charlotte Greenwood Show		The Return of Nick Carter	
5:45		William L. Shirer, news		

DAYTIME — SUMMER, 1945

Monday-Friday

ABC	CBS	MBS	NBC	
John B. Kennedy, news	Two on a Clue	Cedric Foster, news	The Guiding Light	2pm
Ethel and Albert	Rosemary	Jane Cowl, talk	Today's Children	2:15
The Fitzgeralds, talk	Perry Mason	Queen for a Day	The Woman in White	2:30
	Tena and Tim		Betty Crocker, cooking / Hymns of All Churches	2:45
Best Sellers	Time to Remember	Martha Deane, talk	A Woman of America	3pm
	Off the Record		Ma Perkins	3:15
Ladies Be Seated		Rambling with Gambling	Pepper Young's Family	3:30
	The Landt Trio and Curley		The Right to Happiness	3:45
The Jack Berch Show	House Party	John Gambling, news	Mary Noble, Backstage Wife	4pm
Westbrook Van Voorhis, news		Jay Johnson, songs	Stella Dallas	4:15
David Wills, news	Feature Story	Dr. Eddy's Food Forum	Lorenzo Jones	4:30
Tennessee Jed	The Danny O'Neil Show		Young Widder Brown	4:45
Terry and the Pirates	Service Talk	Uncle Don	When a Girl Marries	5pm
Dick Tracy		The Adventures of Superman	Portia Faces Life	5:15
Jack Armstrong, the All-American Boy	Cimarron Tavern	The House of Mystery	Just Plain Bill	5:30
The Singing Story Lady	The Sparrow and the Hawk	The Tom Mix Ralston Straight Shooters	Front Page Farrell	5:45

DAYTIME — SUMMER, 1945

Saturday

	ABC	CBS	MBS	NBC
9am	The Breakfast Club	Joe King, news	Wings for Tomorrow	Home is What You Make It
9:15		The Garden Gate		
9:30		Columbia's Country Journal	The Feeling is Mutual	Archie Andrews
9:45				
10am	What's Cooking	Youth on Parade	Rainbow House	Teentimer's Canteen
10:15				
10:30	The Land of the Lost	Mary Lee Taylor, cooking		Doc, Duke and the Colonel
10:45				Alex Dreier, news
11am	Harry Kogen Orchestra	Let's Pretend	Prescott Robinson, news	The First Piano Quartet
11:15			Lorraine Sherwood, talk	
11:30	The Vagabonds Quartet	The Billie Burke Show	Hookey Hall	Smilin' Ed's Buster Brown Gang
11:45	Chet Gaylord, songs			
12pm	The Piano Playhouse	The Armstrong Theater of Today	It's Up to Youth	Don Goddard, news
12:15	The Andrini Continentals			Consumer Time
12:30	The Farm and Home Hour	Stars Over Hollywood	Henry Gladstone, news	Atlantic Spotlight
12:45			The Answer Man	
1pm	Mess Call	Grand Central Station	Jack Bundy's Album	The Veterans Advisor
1:15			Vincent Lopez Orchestra	Russ David Orchestra
1:30	Round-Up Time	Elliot Lawrence Orchestra	Hello, Mom	The Baxters
1:45				Edward Tomlinson, news

DAYTIME — SUMMER, 1945

Saturday

	ABC	CBS	MBS	NBC
2pm	John B. Kennedy, news	Of Men and Books	What's the Name of That Song	The Sky-High Revue
2:15	Ilene Woods, songs	Adventures in Science		
2:30	It's a Hit	Barnyard Follies	Leo Egan, news	
2:45			Stanley Maxted, talk	
3pm	Saturday Senior Swing	Your Marine Corps	This is Halloran	The Radio Institute Play
3:15				
3:30	Randy Brooks Orchestra	Public Affairs	Where Are They Now	Music on Display
3:45		Ten from Tokyo		
4pm	NBC Symphony Orchestra	Report from Washington	Leo Egan, news	Jerry Freeman Orchestra
4:15		Report from Overseas	Jay Johnson, songs	
4:30		Jack Kerr, songs	Bob Stanley Orchestra	World of Melody
4:45		Horse Racing		Your Radio Reporter
5pm	A Date with the Duke	We Deliver the Goods	Uncle Don	Grand Hotel
5:15			The Ken Carson Show	
5:30		Treasury Bandstand		John W. Vandercook, news
5:45			Lanny and Ginger, songs	Tin Pan Alley of the Air

EVENING — FALL, 1945

Sunday

	ABC	CBS	MBS	NBC
6pm	The Radio Hall of Fame	The Adventures and Ozzie and Harriet	Quick as a Flash	The Catholic Hour
6:15				
6:30	Phil Davis' Sunday Party	The Baby Snooks Show	Cedric Foster, news	The Great Gildersleeve
6:45			Forest Lewis Jr., news	
7pm	Drew Pearson, news	The Adventures of the Thin Man	Opinion Requested	The Lucky Strike Program, Jack Benny
7:15	Don Gardiner, news			
7:30	The Quiz Kids	Blondie	Melvin Elliott, news	The Fitch Bandwagon
7:45			Max Lerner, news	
8pm	The Ford Sunday Evening Hour	The Marlin Hurt and Beulah Show	A. L. Alexander's Mediation Board	The Charlie McCarthy Show
8:15				
8:30		Crime Doctor		The Fred Allen Show
8:45		Ned Calmer, news (8:55pm)	Gabriel Heatter, news	
9pm	Walter Winchell's Jergens Journal	Request Performance	Hercule Poirot	The Manhattan Merry-Go-Round
9:15	Hollywood Mystery Time			
9:30		The Texaco Star Theater, James Melton	Double or Nothing	The American Album of Familiar Music
9:45	Jimmy Fidler, gossip			
10pm	The Theater Guild on the Air	Take It or Leave It	The Operatic Revue	The Hour of Charm
10:15				
10:30		We, the People	The Hollywood Theater	Meet Me at Parky's
10:45				

EVENING — FALL, 1945

Monday

ABC	CBS	MBS	NBC	
Walter Kiernan, news	Quincy Howe, news	Paul Schubert, news	Lyle Van, news	6pm
Here's Morgan	James Carroll, songs	The Man on the Street	Serenade to America	6:15
Harry Wismer, sports	The Voice of Eileen Farrell	Fred Vandeventer, news		6:30
Charlie Chan	The World Today	Stan Lomax, sports	Lowell Thomas, news	6:45
Taylor Grant, news	The Jack Kirkwood Show	Fulton Lewis Jr., news	The Chesterfield Supper Club	7pm
Raymond Gram Swing, news	The Jack Smith Show	The Answer Man	John W. Vandercook, news	7:15
The Lone Ranger	The Bob Hawk Show	Cecil Brown, news	Red Barber's Star Review	7:30
		Bill Brandt, sports	H. V. Kaltenborn, news	7:45
Lum and Abner	Vox Pop	Bulldog Drummond	The Cavalcade of America	8pm
Hedda Hopper, gossip				8:15
Movie Quiz	Joanie's Tea Room	Sherlock Holmes	The Voice of Firestone	8:30
	Bill Henry, news (8:55pm)			8:45
Memo to America	The Lux Radio Theater	Gabriel Heatter, news	The Bell Telephone Hour	9pm
		Real Stories from Real Life		9:15
Pacific Serenade		Spotlight Bands	Information, Please	9:30
Short Story (9:55pm)				9:45
Public Affairs	The Lady Esther Screen Guild Theater	Radio Auction	The Carnation Contented Hour	10pm
				10:15
	Public Affairs	The Better Half	Dr. I. Q., the Mental Banker	10:30
				10:45

EVENING — FALL, 1945

Tuesday

	ABC	CBS	MBS	NBC
6pm	John B. Kennedy, news	Quincy Howe, news	Paul Schubert, news	Lyle Van, news
6:15	Here's Morgan	Edwin C. Hill, news	The Man on the Street	Serenade to America
6:30	Harry Wismer, sports	Evelyn Pasen, songs	Fred Vandeventer, news	
6:45	Charlie Chan	The World Today	Stan Lomax, sports	Lowell Thomas, news
7pm	Taylor Grant, news	The Jack Kirkwood Show	Fulton Lewis Jr., news	The Chesterfield Supper Club
7:15	Raymond Gram Swing, news	The Jack Smith Show	The Answer Man	John W. Vandercook, news
7:30	County Fair	The American Melody Hour	Arthur Hale, news	His Honor, the Barber
7:45			Bill Brandt, sports	
8pm	Lum and Abner	Big Town	Frank Singiser, news	Johnny Presents
8:15	Radie Harris, gossip		The Kenny Baker Program	
8:30	The Alan Young Show	Theater of Romance	The Falcon	A Date with Judy
8:45		Bill Henry, news (8:55pm)		
9pm	Guy Lombardo Orchestra	Inner Sanctum Mysteries	Gabriel Heatter, news	Amos 'n' Andy
9:15			Real Stories from Real Life	
9:30	The Doctors Talk It Over	This is My Best	The American Forum of the Air	Fibber Magee and Molly
9:45	Short Story (9:55pm)			
10pm	Concert Time	Bob Crosby Orchestra		The Pepsodent Show, Bob Hope
10:15			Paul Schubert, news	
10:30	The Choice of the Week	Congress Speaks	The Longines Symphonette	The Raleigh Room, Hildegarde
10:45	Gay Claridge Orchestra	Behind the Scenes at CBS		

EVENING — FALL, 1945

Wednesday

ABC	CBS	MBS	NBC	
Walter Kiernan, news	Warren Sweeney, news	Paul Schubert, news	Lyle Van, news	6pm
Here's Morgan	James Carroll, songs	The Man on the Street	Serenade to America	6:15
Harry Wismer, sports	The Voice of Eileen Farrell	Fred Vandeventer, news		6:30
Charlie Chan	The World Today	Stan Lomax, sports	Lowell Thomas, news	6:45
Taylor Grant, news	The Jack Kirkwood Show	Fulton Lewis Jr., news	The Chesterfield Supper Club	7pm
Raymond Gram Swing, news	The Jack Smith Show	The Answer Man	John W. Vandercook, news	7:15
The Lone Ranger	The Adventures of Ellery Queen	Cecil Brown, news	Red Barber's Star Review	7:30
		Bill Brandt, sports	H. V. Kaltenborn, news	7:45
Lum and Abner	The Jack Carson Show	Can You Top This	Mr. and Mrs. North	8pm
George Hick, news				8:15
The Fishing and Hunting Club	Dr. Christian	The Fresh Up Show, Bert Wheeler	An Evening with Romberg	8:30
	Bill Henry, news (8:55pm)			8:45
One Foot in Heaven	Songs By Sinatra	Gabriel Heatter, news	Time to Smile, Eddie Cantor	9pm
		Real Stories from Real Life		9:15
Pages of Melody	Maisie	Spotlight Bands	Mr. District Attorney	9:30
Short Story (9:55pm)				9:45
Counterspy	Great Moments in Music	The Ralph Slater Show	Kay Kyser's College of Musical Knowledge	10pm
				10:15
Lee Mortimer, news	The N-K Musical Showroom, Andrews Sisters	The Longines Symphonette		10:30
Janet Flanner, news				10:45

EVENING — FALL, 1945

Thursday

	ABC	CBS	MBS	NBC
6pm	Walter Kiernan, news	Ned Calmer, news	Paul Schubert, news	Lyle Van, news
6:15	Here's Morgan	Patti Clayton, songs	The Man on the Street	Serenade to America
6:30	Harry Wismer, sports	Encore Appearance	Fred Vandeventer, news	
6:45	Charlie Chan	The World Today	Stan Lomax, sports	Lowell Thomas, news
7pm	Taylor Grant, news	The Jack Kirkwood Show	Fulton Lewis Jr., news	The Chesterfield Supper Club
7:15	Raymond Gram Swing, news	The Jack Smith Show	The Answer Man	John W. Vandercook, news
7:30	Boston Blackie	Mr. Keen, Tracer of Lost Persons	Arthur Hale, news	The Bob Burns Show
7:45			Bill Brandt, sports	
8pm	Lum and Abner	Suspense	Frank Singiser, news	Maxwell House Coffee Time, Burns and Allen
8:15	Earl Godwin, news		The Kenny Baker Program	
8:30	America's Town Meeting of the Air	The FBI in Peace and War	Rogue's Gallery	The Birdseye Open House, Dinah Shore
8:45		Bill Henry, news (8:55pm)		
9pm		Music Millions Love	Gabriel Heatter, news	The Kraft Music Hall, Bing Crosby
9:15			Real Stories from Real Life	
9:30	Detect and Collect	Hobby Lobby	Starlight Serenade	The Sealtest Village Store, Arden and Haley
9:45	Short Story (9:55pm)			
10pm	Curtain Time	The First Line of Defense	Arch Oboler's Plays	Abbott and Costello
10:15				
10:30	The Fighting AAF	The Powder Box Theater	The Longines Symphonette	The Rudy Vallee Show
10:45				

EVENING — FALL, 1945

Friday

ABC	CBS	MBS	NBC	
Walter Kiernan, news	Quincy Howe, news	Paul Schubert, news	Lyle Van, news	6pm
Here's Morgan	James Carroll, songs	The Man on the Street	Serenade to America	6:15
Harry Wismer, sports	The Voice of Eileen Farrell	Fred Vandeventer, news		6:30
Charlie Chan	The World Today	Stan Lomax, sports	Lowell Thomas, news	6:45
Taylor Grant, news	The Jack Kirkwood Show	Fulton Lewis Jr., news	The Chesterfield Supper Club	7pm
Raymond Gram Swing, news	The Jack Smith Show	The Answer Man	John W. Vandercook, news	7:15
The Lone Ranger	The Ginny Simms Show	Frank Singiser, news	Red Barber's Star Review	7:30
		Bill Brandt, sports	H. V. Kaltenborn, news	7:45
Blind Date	The Aldrich Family	Variety Musicale	Highways in Melody	8pm
				8:15
This is Your FBI	Kate Smith Sings	Freedom of Opportunity	Duffy's Tavern	8:30
	Bill Henry, news (8:55pm)			8:45
Famous Jury Trials	It Pays to Be Ignorant	Gabriel Heatter, news	People Are Funny	9pm
		Real Stories from Real Life		9:15
The Sheriff	Those Websters	Spotlight Bands	Waltz Time	9:30
Short Story (9:55pm)				9:45
Madison Square Garden Boxing	The Jimmy Durante Show	Leave It to Mike	The Molle' Mystery Theater	10pm
				10:15
	Pabst Blue Ribbon Town, Danny Kaye	The Longines Symphonette	The Colgate Sports Newsreel, Bill Stern	10:30
			Public Affairs	10:45

EVENING — FALL, 1945

Saturday

	ABC	CBS	MBS	NBC
6pm	William Fleisher, news	Quincy Howe, news	Paul Schubert, news	Lyle Van, news
6:15	Harry Wismer, sports	The People's Platform	Strictly Personal	Music of Manhattan
6:30			Fred Vandeventer, news	
6:45	Labor USA	The World Today	Stan Lomax, sports	Religion in the News
7pm	Jobs After Victory	The Textron Theater	Guess Who	Our Foreign Policy
7:15	Correspondents Abroad			
7:30	Dick Tracy	America in the Air	Arthur Hale, news	Noah Webster Says
7:45			Tom Harmon, sports	
8pm	Woody Herman Orchestra	The Dick Haymes Show	Frank Singiser, news	The Life of Riley
8:15			The Kenny Baker Program	
8:30	The Man from G-2	The Mayor of the Town	Cosmo Tune Time	Truth or Consequences
8:45		Ned Calmer, news (8:55pm)		
9pm	Gangbusters	Your Hit Parade	Leave It to the Girls	The National Barn Dance
9:15				
9:30	Boston Symphony Orchestra		Break the Bank	Can You Top This
9:45		Saturday Night Serenade		
10pm			The Chicago Theater of the Air	The Judy Canova Show
10:15		Report to the Nation		
10:30	Hayloft Hoedown			Grand Ole Opry
10:45		Public Affairs		

DAYTIME — FALL, 1945

Sunday

	ABC	CBS	MBS	NBC
9am	News	News	Uncle Don Reads The Comics	News
9:15	Coast-to-Coast on a Bus	From the Organ Loft		Story to Order
9:30			The Mutual Radio Chapel	Songs for Strings
9:45		New Voices in Song		Music
10am	Message of Israel	The CBS Church of the Air	Leo Egan, news	The National Radio Pulpit
10:15			Frank Kingdon, news	
10:30	The Southernaires Quartet	The Legend Singers	The Land of the Lost	The Horn and Hardart Children's Hour
10:45				
11am	Brunch with the Fitzgeralds	The Blue Jacket Choir	Judy Lang, songs	
11:15			The Musical Beauty Box	
11:30	The Hour of Faith	Invitation to Learning	Brunch with Dorothy and Dick	Charles F. McCarthy, news
11:45				The Little Betsy Ross Girl Variety Program
12pm	This Week Around the World	The Salt Lake Tabernacle Choir	The Show Shop	The Eternal Light
12:15				
12:30	Friendship Ranch	Transatlantic Call	One Man's Destiny	NBC Concert Orchestra
12:45				
1pm	John B. Kennedy, news	The CBS Church of the Air	The Canary Pet Shop	Ed Herlihy, news
1:15	Orson Welles, talk		Ilka Chase, talk	America United
1:30	Sammy Kaye's Sunday Serenade	Problems of Peace	Sports	The University of Chicago Round Table
1:45		Edward R. Murrow, news		

DAYTIME — FALL, 1945

Monday-Friday

ABC	CBS	MBS	NBC	
The Breakfast Club	Joe King, news	Frazier Hunt, news	Ed East and Polly, songs	*9am*
	Arthur Godfrey Time	Bing Crosby Records		*9:15*
		Alfred W. McCann, food	Adelaide Hawley, talk	*9:30*
			Daytime Classics	*9:45*
My True Story	Valiant Lady	Henry Gladstone, news	Robert St. John, news	*10am*
	The Light of the World	Bessy Beatty, talk	Lora Lawton	*10:15*
Hymns of All Churches	The Strange Romance of Evelyn Winters		The Road of Life	*10:30*
Listening Post / Lisa Sergio, talk	Bachelor's Children		Joyce Jordan, MD	*10:45*
Breakfast with Breneman	Amanda of Honeymoon Hill	Prescott Robinson, news	Fred Waring Orchestra	*11am*
	Second Husband	Tello-Test Quiz		*11:15*
Gilbert Martyn, news	A Woman's Life	Success Story / Take It Easy Time	Barry Cameron	*11:30*
Between the Bookends	Aunt Jenny's True Life Stories	Victor Lindlahr, health	David Harum	*11:45*
Glamour Manor, Cliff Arquette	Kate Smith Speaks	William Lang, news	Don Goddard, news	*12pm*
	Big Sister	Hymns You Love, Richard Maxwell	Maggie McNellis, talk	*12:15*
The Women's Exchange	The Romance of Helen Trent	Henry Gladstone, news	The Jack Smith Show	*12:30*
	Our Gal Sunday	The Answer Man	The Art Van Damme Quartet	*12:45*
H. R. Baukhage, news	Life Can Be Beautiful	Musical Appetizer	Mary Margaret McBride, talk	*1pm*
Constance Bennett, talk	Ma Perkins	Jack Bundy's Album		*1:15*
Galen Drake, talk	Meet Margaret MacDonald	Vincent Lopez Orchestra		*1:30*
	Young Dr. Malone	The John J. Anthony Program	Morgan Beatty, news	*1:45*

DAYTIME — FALL, 1945

Sunday

	ABC	CBS	MBS	NBC
2pm	Arthur Feldman, news	Stradivari Orchestra		Harvest of Stars
2:15	Dorothy Claire, songs			
2:30	National Vespers	The Weekly News Review		The Westinghouse Program, John C. Thomas
2:45				
3pm	Melodies to Remember	New York Philharmonic Orchestra		The Sheaffer Parade
3:15				
3:30	Jean Tighe and Bob Johnson, songs			One Man's Family
3:45				
4pm	Musical Bouquet		Your America	The Army Hour
4:15				
4:30	Jones and I	The Electric Hour, Nelson Eddy	The Nebbs	Music America Loves Best
4:45				
5pm	Mary Small's Revue	The Prudential Family Hour	The Shadow	NBC Symphony Orchestra
5:15				
5:30	The Charlotte Greenwood Show	Gene Autry's Melody Ranch	The Return of Nick Carter	
5:45		William L. Shirer, news		

DAYTIME — FALL, 1945

Monday-Friday

ABC	CBS	MBS	NBC	
John B. Kennedy, news	Two on a Clue	Cedric Foster, news	The Guiding Light	2pm
Ethel and Albert	Perry Mason	Jane Cowl, talk	Today's Children	2:15
The Fitzgeralds, talk	Rosemary	Queen for a Day	The Woman in White	2:30
	Tena and Tim		Betty Crocker, cooking / Hymns of All Churches	2:45
Best Sellers	Time to Remember	Martha Deane, talk	A Woman of America	3pm
	Off the Record		Ma Perkins	3:15
Ladies Be Seated		Rambling with Gambling	Pepper Young's Family	3:30
	The Landt Trio and Curley		The Right to Happiness	3:45
The Jack Berch Show	House Party	John Gambling, news	Mary Noble, Backstage Wife	4pm
Westbrook Van Voorhis, news		Jay Johnson, songs	Stella Dallas	4:15
David Wills, news	Hal Winters, songs	Dr. Eddy's Food Forum	Lorenzo Jones	4:30
Hop Harrigan	Feature Story		Young Widder Brown	4:45
Terry and the Pirates	The American School of the Air	Uncle Don	When a Girl Marries	5pm
Dick Tracy		The Adventures of Superman	Portia Faces Life	5:15
Jack Armstrong, the All-American Boy	Cimarron Tavern	Captain Midnight	Just Plain Bill	5:30
Tennessee Jed	Sparrow and the Hawk	The Tom Mix Ralston Straight Shooters	Front Page Farrell	5:45

DAYTIME — FALL, 1945

Saturday

	ABC	CBS	MBS	NBC
9am	The Breakfast Club	Joe King, news	Where Are They Now	Home is What You Make It
9:15		The Garden Gate		
9:30		Columbia's Country Journal	It's Up to Youth	Adelaide Hawley, talk
9:45				Doc, Duke and the Colonel
10am	Galen Drake, talk	Give and Take	Henry Gladstone, news	Teentimer's Canteen
10:15	Club Time		Uncle Don	
10:30	Johnny Thompson and Ilene Woods, songs	Mary Lee Taylor, cooking	Rainbow House	Archie Andrews
10:45				
11am	Harry Kogen Orchestra	Let's Pretend	Prescott Robinson, news	The First Piano Quartet
11:15			Lorraine Sherwood, talk	
11:30	The Vagabonds Quartet	The Billie Burke Show	Hookey Hall	Smilin' Ed's Buster Brown Gang
11:45	Chet Gaylord, songs			
12pm	The Piano Playhouse	The Armstrong Theater of Today	The House of Mystery	John McVane, news
12:15	Elizabeth Woodward, songs			Consumer Time
12:30	Home and Garden	Stars Over Hollywood	Henry Gladstone, news	Atlantic Spotlight
12:45			The Answer Man	
1pm	Saturday Senior Swing	Grand Central Station	The Man on the Farm	The National Farm and Home Hour
1:15			Vincent Lopez Orchestra	
1:30	Round-Up Time	Crime Photographer	Jack Bundy's Album	The Veterans Advisor
1:45	Sports		Sports	Edward Tomlinson, news

DAYTIME — FALL, 1945

Saturday

	ABC	CBS	MBS	NBC
2pm		Of Men and Books		Your Host is Buffalo
2:15		Adventures in Science		Sports
2:30		Chuck Foster Orchestra		
2:45		Sports		
3pm				
3:15				
3:30				
3:45				
4pm				
4:15			Sports Comments	
4:30			Win, Lose or Draw	
4:45				
5pm	A Date with the Duke		Don Pastor Orchestra	
5:15				
5:30		Treasury Bandstand	Louis Jordan Orchestra	John W. Vandercook, news
5:45	Pleasure Parade, Paula Kelly		Lanny and Ginger, songs	Tin Pan Alley of the Air

www.ingramcontent.com/pod-product-compliance
Lightning Source LLC
Chambersburg PA
CBHW050425240426
43661CB00055B/2269

Ben Maynor Media

Let's Pretend AND THE GOLDEN AGE OF RADIO
by Arthur Anderson

THE BLACK GARBO
NINA MAE MCKINNEY

STOOGE HEAVY
SECOND BANANA TO THE THREE STOOGES AND OTHER FILM COMEDY GREATS
VERNON DENT

Comic Strips & Comic Books of Radio's Golden Age
A Biography of All Radio Shows Based on Comics
by Ron Lackmann

Classic Cinema. Timeless TV. Retro Radio.

WWW.BEARMANORMEDIA.COM

Dangerous Curves atop Hollywood Heels
The Lives, Careers, and Misfortunes of 14 Hard-Luck Girls of the Silent Screen
BY MICHAEL G. ANKERICH

JUDY CANOVA is SINGIN' IN THE CORN
by Ben Ohmart

The Real Joyce Compton
BEHIND THE BUBBLES BLONDE MOVIE IMAGES
BY JOYCE COMPTON AND MICHAEL G. ANKERICH

THE BICKERSONS SCRIPTS
By: PHILIP RAPP
VOLUME ONE
EDITED BY BEN OHMART